P9-AFY-841

Fodor's 94 Washington, D.C.

Fodor's Travel Publications, Inc.
New York • Toronto • London • Sydney • Auckland

Fodor's Washington, D.C.

Editor: Larry Peterson
Contributors: Jeanne Cooper, John F. Kelly, Marcy Pritchard
Creative Director: Fabrizio La Rocca
Cartographer: David Lindroth
Illustrator: Karl Tanner
Cover Photograph: Peter Guttman

Design: Vignelli Associates

Special Sales

Contents

Foreword

While every care has been taken to assure the accuracy of the information in this guide, the passage of time will always bring change, and consequently, the publisher cannot accept responsibility for errors that may occur.

All prices and opening times quoted here are based on information supplied to us at press time. Hours and admission fees may change, however, and the prudent traveler will avoid inconvenience by calling ahead.

Fodor's wants to hear about your travel experiences, both pleasant and unpleasant. When a hotel or restaurant fails to live up to its billing, let us know and we will investigate the complaint and revise our entries where the facts warrant it.

Send your letters to the editors of Fodor's Travel Publications, 201 East 50th Street, New York, NY 10022.

Highlights'94 and Fodor's Choice

Highlights '94

Washington kicked off last year with its favorite kind of party: a presidential inauguration. Bill Clinton started his term with a bang, complete with a generous helping of Hollywood celebrities and a two-day party on the Mall. In addition to a new president, the city is now also host to the largest crop of congressional freshman since 1948. Still, how much of the city's atmosphere will change after 12 years of Republican administrations remains to be seen. One thing is for certain: With a southerner in the White House, Washington is reasserting its own southerness. New "southern" restaurants have opened and existing restaurants have changed their menus, all in an attempt to capitalize on the man from Hope, Arkansas (nevermind his fondness for fast food).

Like the Democrats, tourist Washington is coming off a good year. This is the first full year for the new **United States Holocaust Memorial Museum,** the **National Postal Museum,** and the beautifully renovated **Freer Gallery of Art.**

The National Zoological Park mourned last year's death of giant panda Ling-Ling but has been getting rave reviews for **Amazonia,** a complete rain-forest ecosystem under a glass roof. Creatures of a different kind can be found at the National Museum of Natural History's revamped insect zoo, now called the **O. Orkin Insect Zoo,** in honor of the company that donated funds for its renovation. And the National Air and Space Museum has a neat new permanent exhibit called **"Where Next, Columbus?,"** which looks at the feasibility of space travel.

Return visitors to the Smithsonian museums will see something new: a **collection box.** Pummeled by the recession, the Smithsonian last year decided to seek suggested donations at five of its museums: Air and Space, Natural History, American Art, the National Portrait Gallery, and the National Zoo. Administrators insist it isn't the first step on the slippery slope toward paid admission.

The historic **Octagon House,** where the treaty ending the War of 1812 was signed, is nearing the end of a $4 million restoration that will return it to its 1815 appearance. It greets the new year with an exhibit on America's great avenues, including New York's Fifth and Washington's own Pennsylvania. This year should also see the end of the long restoration of the Library of Congress's grand **Jefferson Building.** Other Washington fixtures getting a sprucing up include the **Hirshhorn Museum's** exterior plaza, which received a new landscape treatment, and **Freedom,** the patched-up and painted statue atop the U.S. Capitol building.

Washington's Metro system keeps getting bigger. **Five new stations** on the Green Line, which leads northeast into Prince George's County, Maryland, are due for completion by December 1993.

The capital's arts community is also strong. Last year saw the first full season of the beautifully restored **Warner Theatre,** its chandeliered space the setting for all manner of road shows. Not content to rest on its laurels, the acclaimed **Arena Stage,** one of the country's most respected regional repertory theaters, has launched a program to develop new American plays. The **Shakespeare Theatre** has settled comfortably into new space it acquired in 1992. The **Center for the Arts** at George Mason University in Fairfax, Virginia, has earned a reputation for a broad range of offerings, from dance to theater. Also out in the 'burbs, Maryland's **Olney Theater** last year completed a renovation of its charming space, a former barn that now has all the amenities of a modern theater. And Washington's plucky smaller theater companies—most operating downtown, some toiling in the suburbs—continue to impress audiences and critics with their eclectic mix.

Capital Centre, in Landover, Maryland, home field of the Bullets of basketball and the Capitals of hockey, has been renamed **USAir Arena** as part of a 10-year deal between the arena, the teams, and the airline.

Washington's well-publicized murder rate has dipped a little, though not nearly as much as the citizens of the district hope. And after more than 200 years, Congress is still undecided about exactly how to treat DC: should it stay a political no man's land with no real representation, or become a state?

Fodor's Choice

No two people will agree on what makes a perfect vacation, but it's fun and helpful to know what others think. We hope you'll have a chance to experience some of Fodor's Choices yourself while visiting Washington. For detailed information about each entry, refer to the appropriate sections (given in parentheses) within this guidebook.

Sights

The view of Washington from Arlington House in Arlington National Cemetery

The view of the Mall from the foot of Capitol Hill

The Washington skyline from the roof of the Kennedy Center for the Performing Arts

Buildings and Monuments

The White House (Tour 3: The White House Area)

The East building of the National Gallery of Art (Tour 1: The Mall)

The Jefferson Memorial (Tour 2: The Monuments)

Union Station (Tour 4: Capitol Hill)

The Vietnam Veterans Memorial (Tour 2: The Monuments)

Washington Cathedral (Churches, Temples, and Mosques)

Activities

Strolling the streets of Georgetown on a weekend morning before 10 (Tour 6: Georgetown)

Bicycling along the C & O Canal (Chapter 10, Excursions)

Visiting the Aviary at the National Zoo (Tour 9: Cleveland Park and the National Zoo)

Taking a boat ride to Mount Vernon (Chapter 10, Excursions)

Exploring the city with Scandal Tours (Chapter 1, Essential Information)

Seeing a movie at the Air and Space Museum (Tour 1: The Mall)

Museums

The Phillips Collection (Tour 7: Dupont Circle)

The National Air and Space Museum (Tour 1: The Mall)

The Corcoran Gallery of Art (Tour 3: The White House)

The National Museum of African Art (Tour 1: The Mall)

The National Museum of American History (Tour 1: The Mall)

The United States Holocaust Memorial Museum (Tour 1: The Mall)

Capital Children's Museum (Museums and Galleries)

Parks and Gardens

Rock Creek Park

Dumbarton Oaks Garden

Lafayette Square

The National Arboretum

Restaurants

Jean-Louis at the Watergate (French, *Very Expensive*)

Obelisk (Italian, *Expensive*)

Red Sage (Southwestern/Tex-Mex, *Expensive*)

The Bombay Club (Indian, *Moderate*)

Sarinah Satay House (Indonesian, *Moderate*)

Meskerem (Ethiopian, *Inexpensive*)

Hotels

Hay-Adams Hotel (*Very Expensive*)

The Willard Inter-Continental (*Very Expensive*)

Hotel Washington (*Moderate*)

Morrison-Clark Inn Hotel (*Moderate*)

Kalorama Guest House (*Inexpensive*)

Nightlife

Blues Alley

Comedy Cafe

Gross National Product

The Dubliner

Washington, D.C. Area

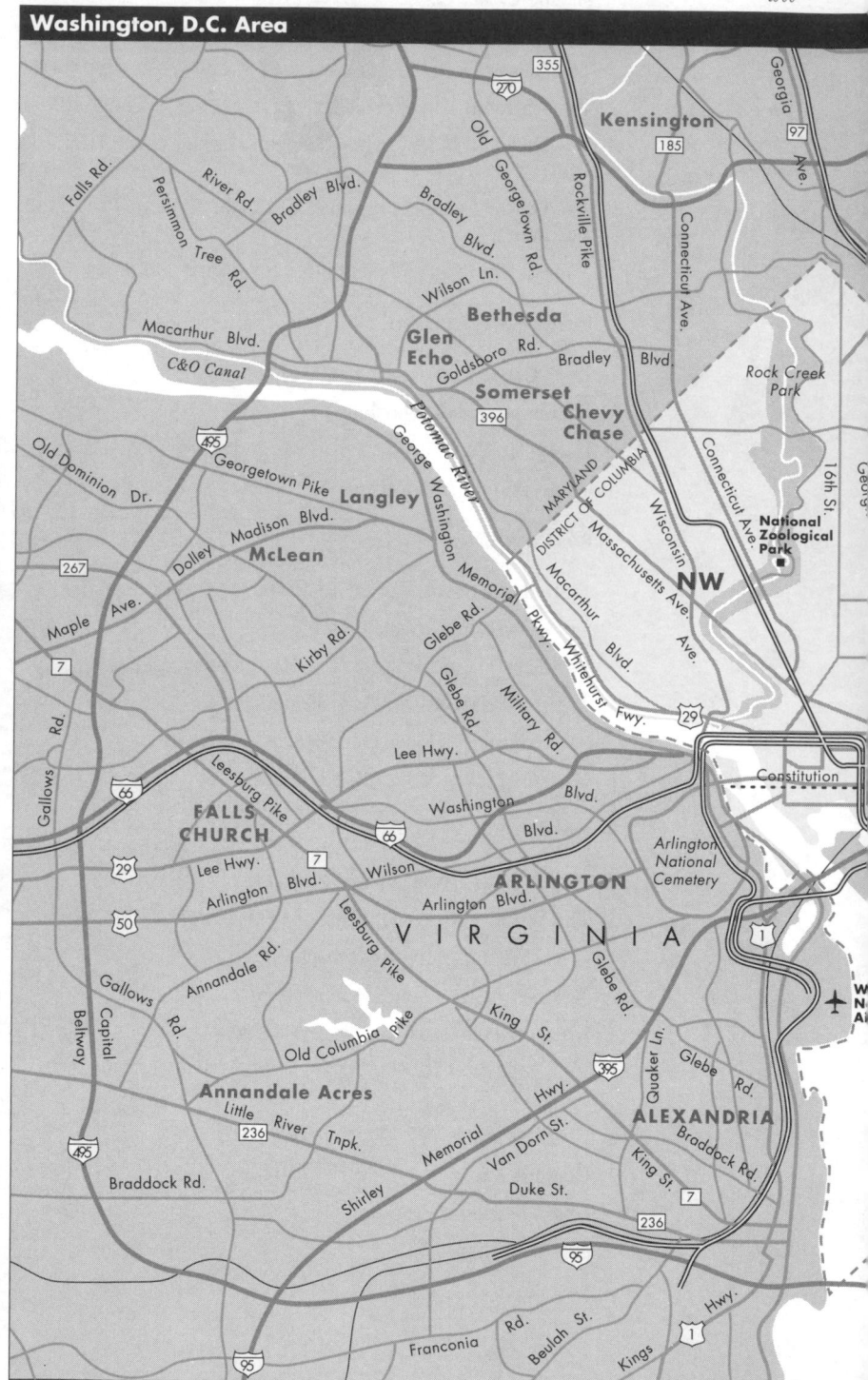

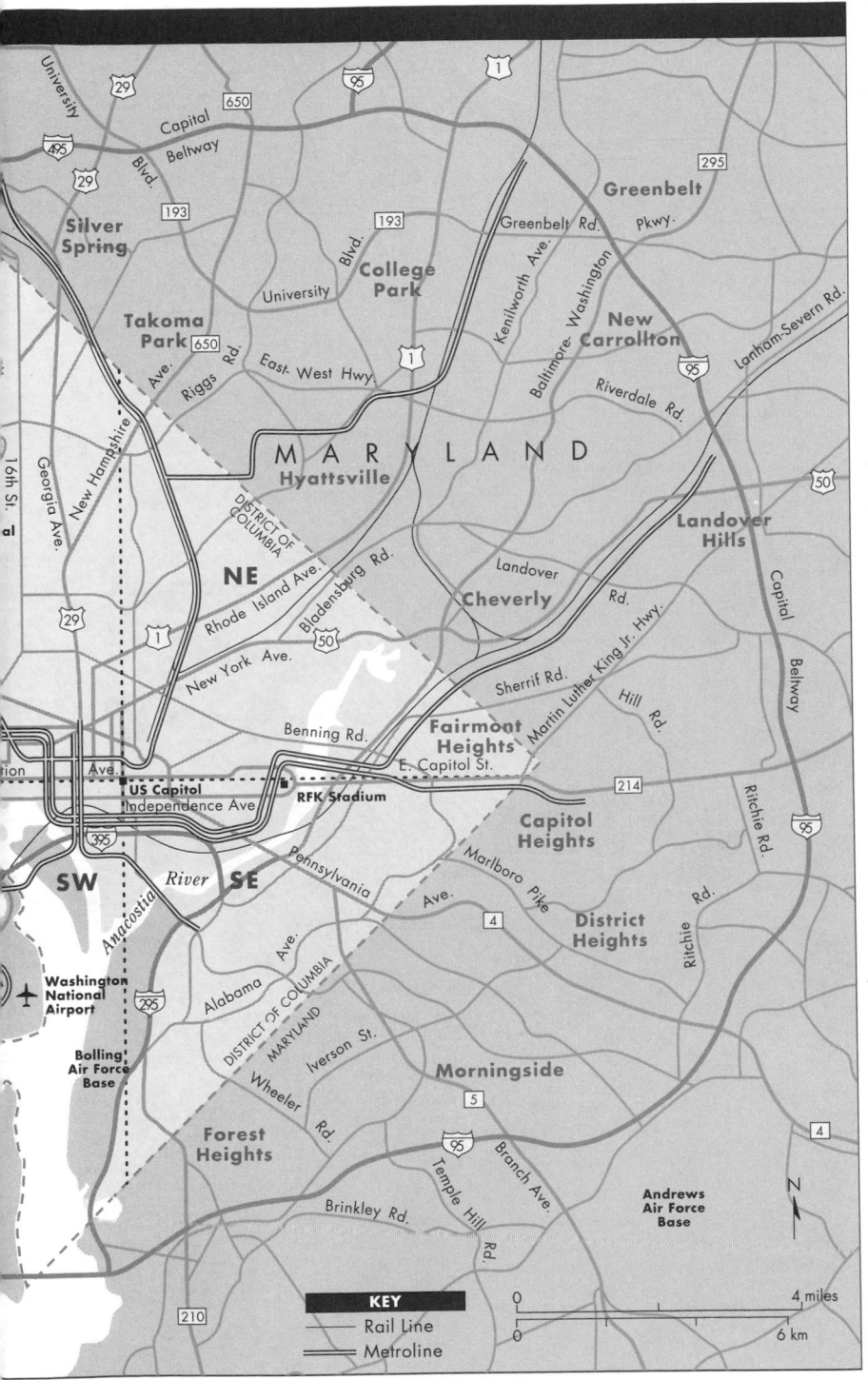

KEY
— Rail Line
═ Metroline

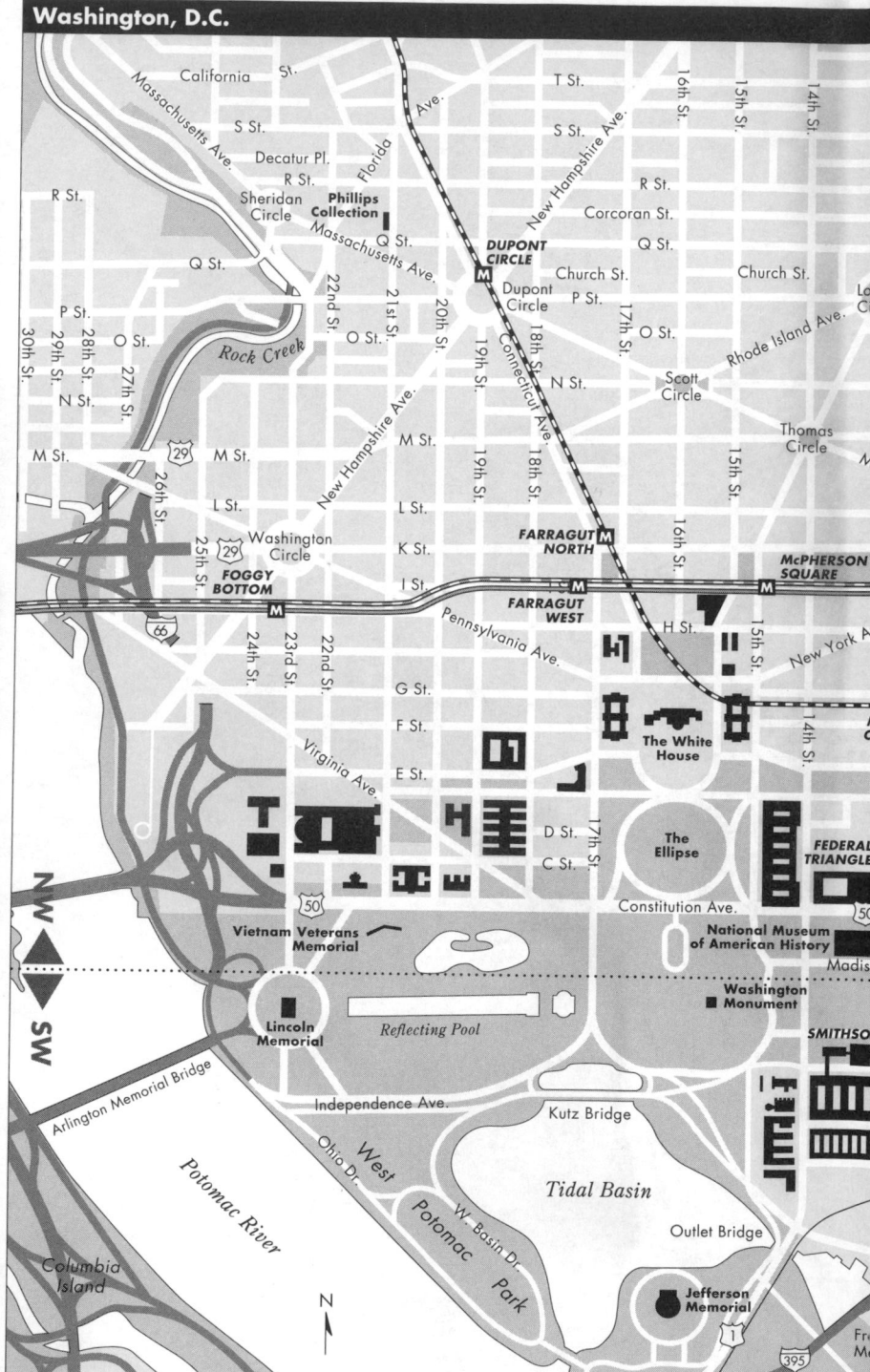

California St.

Massachusetts Ave.

S St.

Decatur Pl.

R St.

Sheridan Circle

Phillips Collection

T St.

S St.

New Hampshire Ave.

R St.

Corcoran St.

16th St.

15th St.

14th St.

Florida Ave.

Q St.

Massachusetts Ave.

Q St.

Church St.

Q St.

Church St.

R St.

Q St.

30th St.

29th St.

28th St.

27th St.

P St.

O St.

N St.

22nd St.

21st St.

20th St.

O St.

DUPONT CIRCLE

Dupont Circle

18th St.

P St.

17th St.

O St.

Scott Circle

Rhode Island Ave.

Lo Ci

Rock Creek

19th St.

Connecticut Ave.

N St.

Thomas Circle

26th St.

29

M St.

M St.

M St.

19th St.

18th St.

15th St.

N

25th St.

29

Washington Circle

L St.

K St.

L St.

16th St.

McPHERSON SQUARE

FOGGY BOTTOM

24th St.

23rd St.

22nd St.

I St.

FARRAGUT NORTH

FARRAGUT WEST

66

Pennsylvania Ave.

H St.

15th St.

New York A

G St.

F St.

14th St.

C

Virginia Ave.

E St.

The White House

50

D St.

C St.

17th St.

The Ellipse

FEDERAL TRIANGLE

50

Constitution Ave.

Vietnam Veterans Memorial

National Museum of American History

Madis

NW

Lincoln Memorial

Reflecting Pool

Washington Monument

SMITHSO

SW

Arlington Memorial Bridge

Independence Ave.

Kutz Bridge

Ohio Dr.

West

Potomac

Potomac River

W. Basin Dr.

Park

Tidal Basin

Outlet Bridge

Columbia Island

N

Jefferson Memorial

1

Fre Me

395

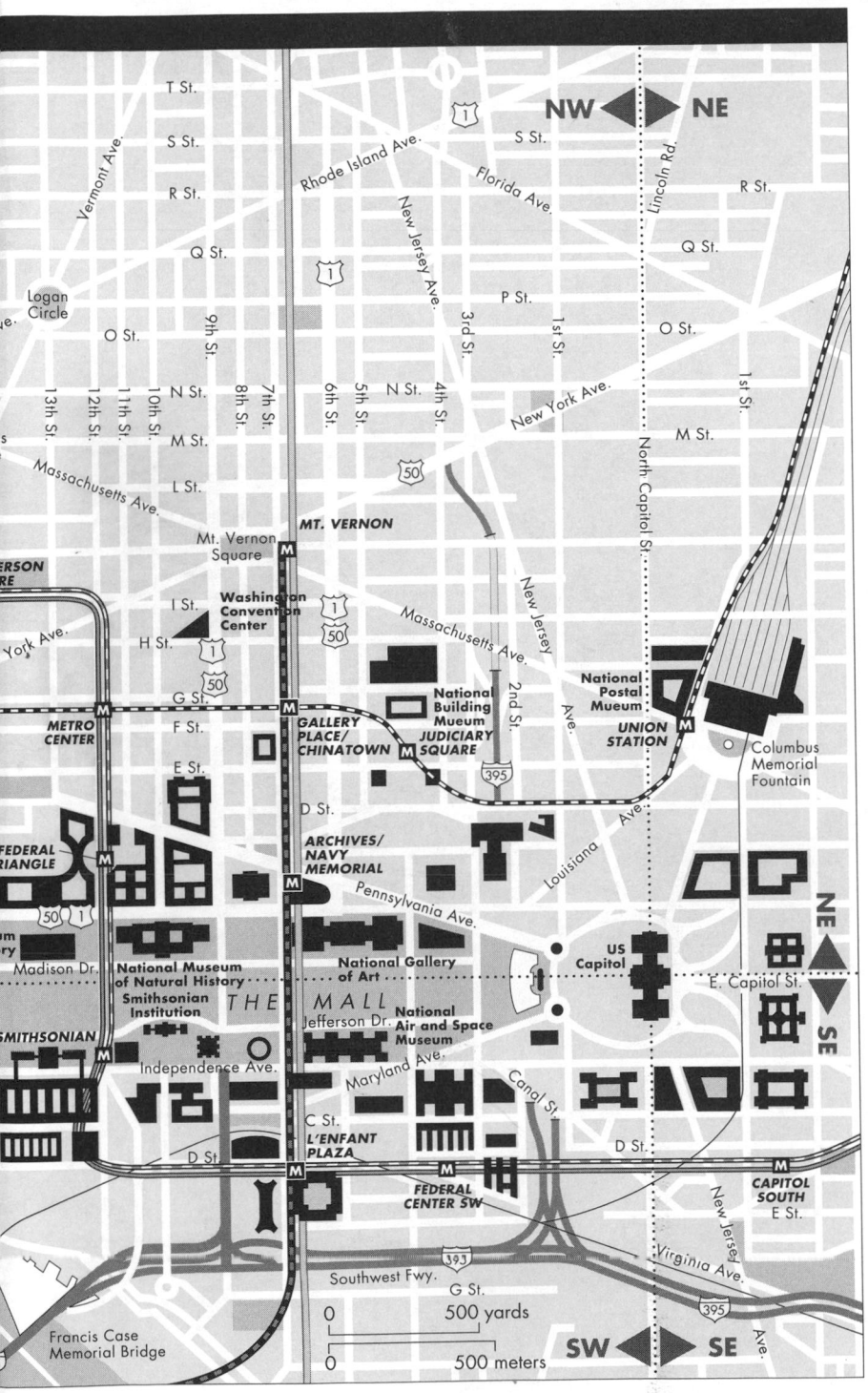

Washington, D.C. Metro System

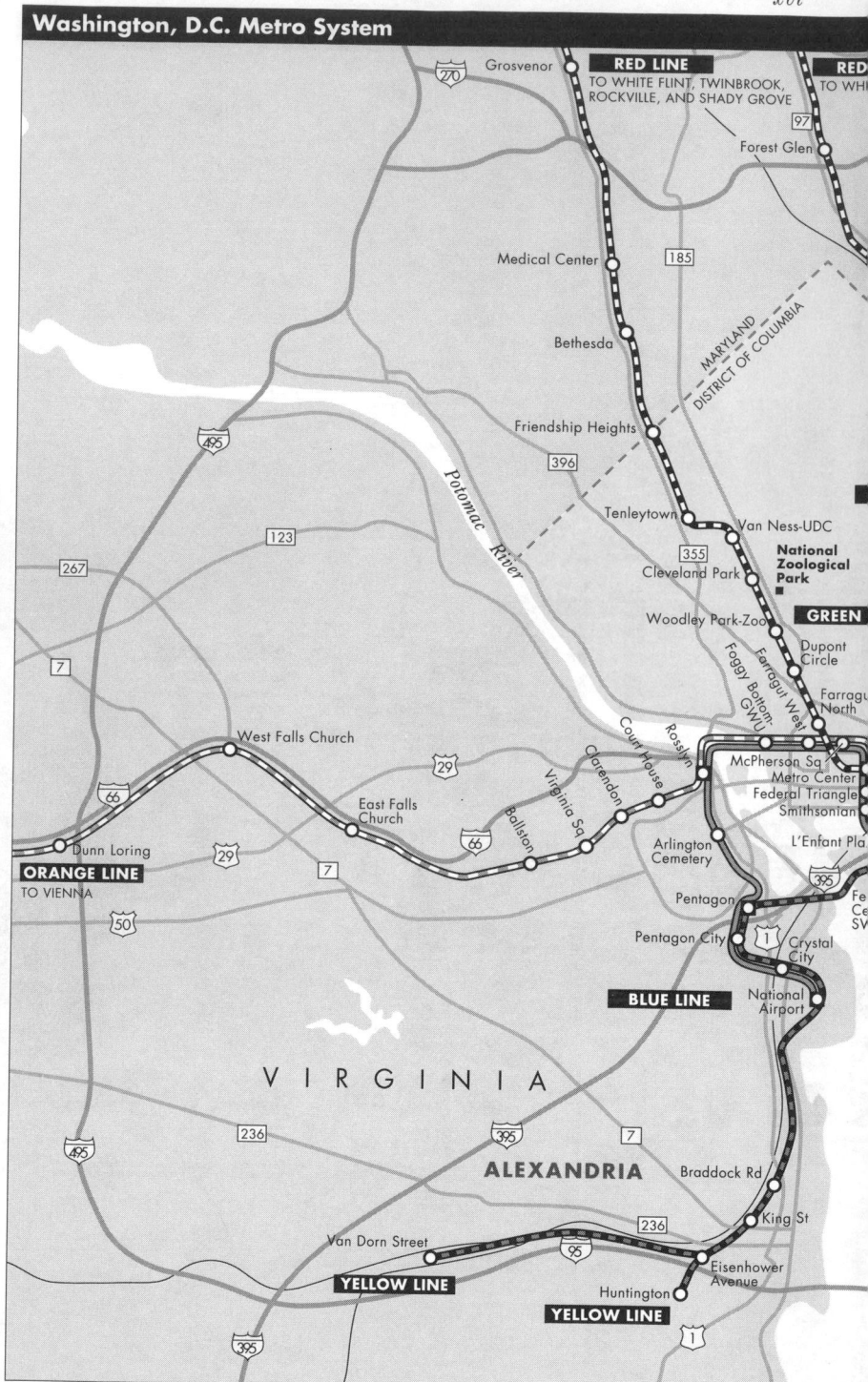

Grosvenor

RED LINE
TO WHITE FLINT, TWINBROOK, ROCKVILLE, AND SHADY GROVE

RED
TO WH

Forest Glen

Medical Center

Bethesda

MARYLAND
DISTRICT OF COLUMBIA

Friendship Heights

Tenleytown

Van Ness-UDC

National Zoological Park

Cleveland Park

Woodley Park-Zoo

GREEN

Dupont Circle

Farragut North

Potomac River

Foggy Bottom; GWU

Farragut West

West Falls Church

Court House

Rosslyn

East Falls Church

Clarendon

Virginia Sq

Ballston

McPherson Sq
Metro Center
Federal Triangle
Smithsonian

L'Enfant Pla

Dunn Loring

ORANGE LINE
TO VIENNA

Arlington Cemetery

Pentagon

Fe
Ce
SV

395

Pentagon City

Crystal City

BLUE LINE

National Airport

V I R G I N I A

ALEXANDRIA

Braddock Rd

King St

Van Dorn Street

YELLOW LINE

Huntington

Eisenhower Avenue

YELLOW LINE

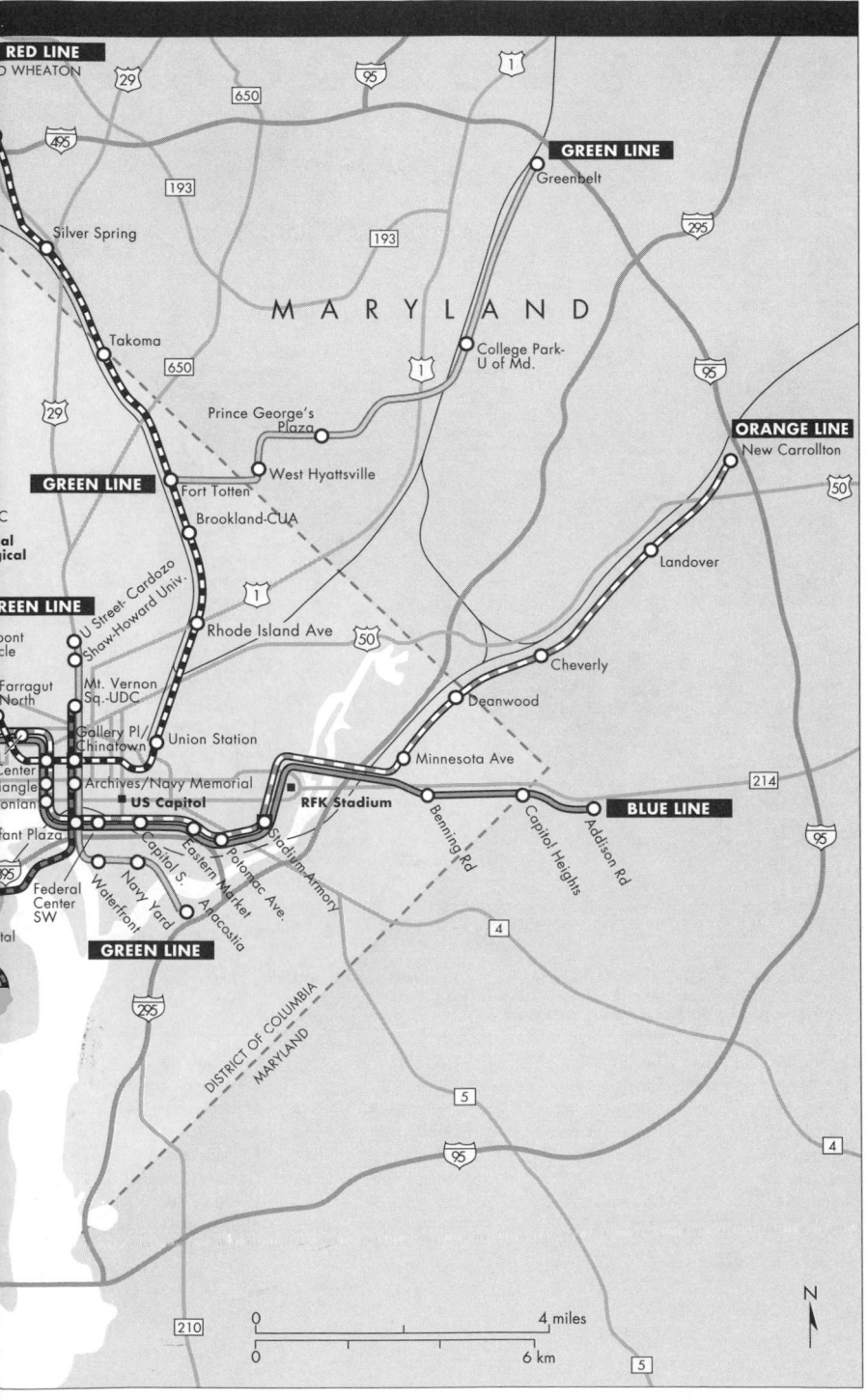

RED LINE
O WHEATON

GREEN LINE
Greenbelt

MARYLAND

Silver Spring

Takoma

College Park-
U of Md.

Prince George's
Plaza

GREEN LINE

West Hyattsville

Fort Totten
Brookland-CUA

ORANGE LINE
New Carrollton

Landover

GREEN LINE

U Street-Cardozo
Show-Howard Univ.

Rhode Island Ave

Cheverly

pont
cle

Farragut
North

Mt. Vernon
Sq.-UDC

Gallery Pl/
Chinatown

Deanwood

Union Station

Minnesota Ave

Center
iangle
sonian

Archives/Navy Memorial

US Capitol

RFK Stadium

BLUE LINE

fant Plaza

Federal
Center
SW

Capitol S.

Navy Yard

Waterfront

Eastern
Market

Potomac Ave.

Stadium Armory

Anacostia

Benning Rd

Capitol Heights

Addison Rd

GREEN LINE

DISTRICT OF COLUMBIA
MARYLAND

0   4 miles

0   6 km

N

World Time Zones

Numbers below vertical bands relate each zone to Greenwich Mean Time (0 hrs.).
Local times frequently differ from these general indications,
as indicated by light-face numbers on map.

Algiers, **29**	Berlin, **34**	Delhi, **48**	Istanbul, **40**
Anchorage, **3**	Bogotá, **19**	Denver, **8**	Jerusalem, **42**
Athens, **41**	Budapest, **37**	Djakarta, **53**	Johannesburg, **44**
Auckland, **1**	Buenos Aires, **24**	Dublin, **26**	Lima, **20**
Baghdad, **46**	Caracas, **22**	Edmonton, **7**	Lisbon, **28**
Bangkok, **50**	Chicago, **9**	Hong Kong, **56**	London (Greenwich), **27**
Beijing, **54**	Copenhagen, **33**	Honolulu, **2**	Los Angeles, **6**
	Dallas, **10**		Madrid, **38**
			Manila, **57**

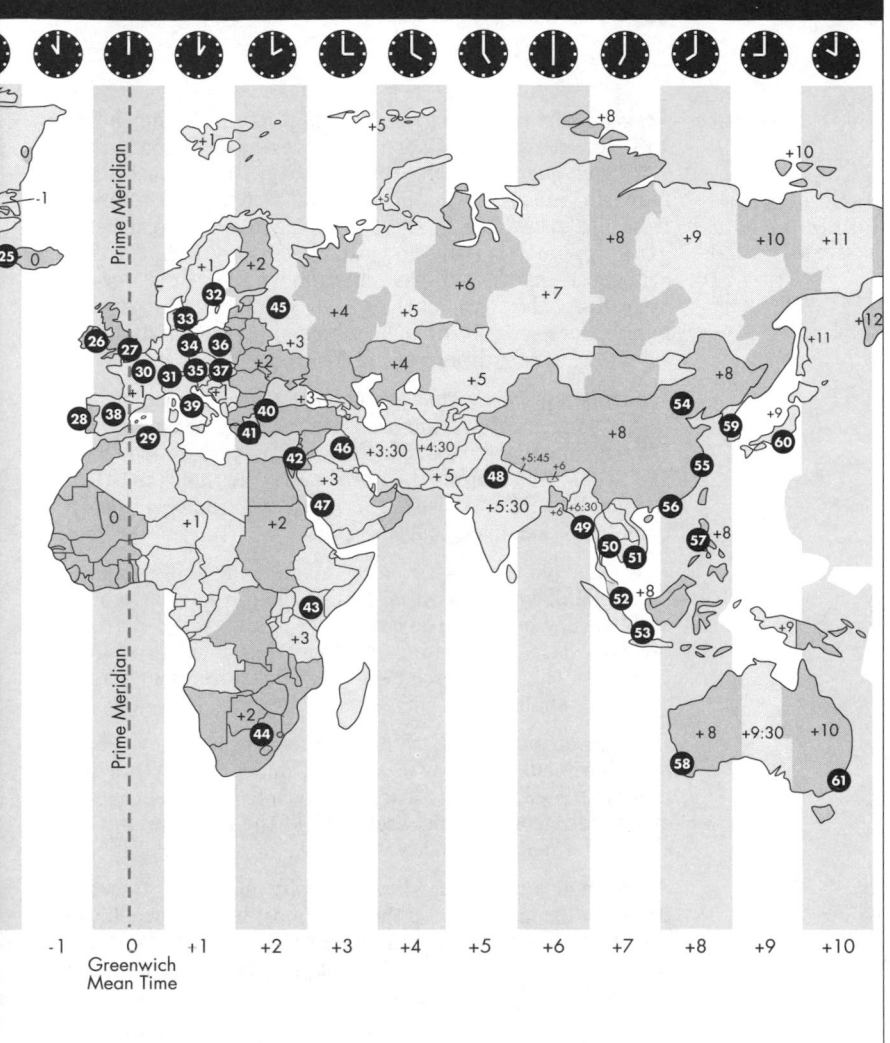

Mecca, **47**
Mexico City, **12**
Miami, **18**
Montréal, **15**
Moscow, **45**
Nairobi, **43**
New Orleans, **11**
New York City, **16**

Ottawa, **14**
Paris, **30**
Perth, **58**
Reykjavík, **25**
Rio de Janeiro, **23**
Rome, **39**
Saigon (Ho Chi Minh City), **51**

San Francisco, **5**
Santiago, **21**
Seoul, **59**
Shanghai, **55**
Singapore, **52**
Stockholm, **32**
Sydney, **61**
Tokyo, **60**

Toronto, **13**
Vancouver, **4**
Vienna, **35**
Warsaw, **36**
Washington, D.C., **17**
Yangon, **49**
Zürich, **31**

Introduction

By Deborah Papier

A native Washingtonian, Deborah Papier has worked as an editor and writer for numerous local newspapers and magazines.

To a surprising degree, Washington is a city much like any other. True, it does not have a baseball team, that sine qua non of an urban identity. But in most other respects, life in the nation's capital is not that different from life elsewhere in the nation. People are born here, grow up, get jobs—by no means invariably with the federal government—and have children who repeat the cycle. Very often, they live out their lives without ever testifying before Congress, being indicted for influence peddling, or attending a state dinner at the White House.

Which is not to say that the federal government does not cast a long shadow over the city. Among Washington's 630,000 inhabitants are an awful lot of lawyers, journalists, and people who include the word "policy" in their job titles. It's just that DC—to use the vernacular—is much more of a hometown than most tourists realize.

Just a few blocks away from the monuments and museums on the Mall are residential and business districts whose scale is very human. The houses are a crazy quilt of architectural styles, kept in linear formation by rows of lush trees. On the commercial streets, bookstores and ethnic groceries abound.

It is often said that Washington does not have any "real" neighborhoods, the way nearby Baltimore does. While it's true that Washingtonians are not given to huddling together on their front stoops, each area of the city does have a clearly defined personality.

Sometimes, this personality is a split one. Take Georgetown, for example. One of the city's most in-bred, exclusive communities—its residents successfully fought to keep out the subway—Georgetown is a magnet for the young and the restless from miles around.

On any day of the week the streets are full of teenagers with dripping ice cream cones. Friday and Saturday nights it's almost impossible to make your way through the crowds of tourists and natives. Halloween in Georgetown is as close as Washington gets to Mardi Gras, though things aren't quite as weird and wild as they were a few years ago.

Another distinctive neighborhood is Dupont Circle. Insofar as there is a bohemian Washington, it can be found here. This is where the artists and activists used to live, before the rents got too high, and where the hippies hung out, back at the dawning of the New Age. Now Dupont Circle is home to the most visible segment of Washington's gay community.

Adjacent to Dupont Circle is Adams-Morgan, long the city's most intensely ethnic neighborhood. In recent years Adams-Morgan has begun to lose some of its Hispanic flavor, as New American restaurants have begun to crowd out the Latin places. But you're still likely to hear more Spanish than English on the streets here.

As different as Georgetown, Dupont Circle, and Adams-Morgan are, they have one thing in common. They are all on the same side of the line that divides white from black Washington. With the exception of Capitol Hill, whites live west of 16th Street, while blacks—who make up the majority of the population—live to the east of it.

That's a long-standing demographic pattern, unchanged despite the supposed advent of integration. Whites and blacks now work together in the downtown offices, but they go off in different directions when they head home, and rarely encounter one another when they go out for the evening. At the Kennedy Center, for example, there are few black faces to be found.

Meanwhile, there is no comparable center for black culture. The riots of 1968 wiped out most of the black clubs and businesses, and while the area around 14th and U streets where they once flourished is finally being rebuilt, its vitality is unlikely to be re-created.

Further down on 14th Street, another aspect of Washington life is breathing its last: The 14th Street red-light district is almost gone. The city was determined to clean up the strip, and to everyone's surprise it succeeded.

Nor is much left of the tacky commercial district around 9th and F streets. This was Washington's original downtown, which deteriorated when the city's center shifted to the west, to the "new" downtown of Connecticut Avenue and K Street. But the "old" downtown is being rejuvenated. The department stores that once drew crowds with their window displays have been renovated; there are new hotels and office buildings; and as the construction dust clears, the area is looking pretty good.

But the success or failure of an urban renewal project is probably not a matter of the utmost concern to the visitor. What many people who come here are worried about is crime. Crime is certainly a major problem here, as it is in other big cities, but Washington is not nearly as dangerous as its well-publicized homicide rate might lead you to believe. Most visitors have relatively little to fear. The drug-related shootings that have made Washington the murder capital generally take place in remote sections of the city. Unless you go seeking out the drug markets, there isn't much chance you'll get caught in the crossfire of rival drug gangs. Crimes against property are more widespread, but still far from ubiquitous. Unlike New York, Washington is not full of expert pickpockets; nor is it plagued by gold-chain snatchers.

The city's Metro is generally safe, even at night. However, if you're going to have to walk from your stop in a neighborhood that isn't well lit and trafficked, you probably should invest in a taxi. Of course, even exercising normal prudence, it is still possible that you will have an encounter with someone who believes that what's yours ought to be his. If that happens, don't argue.

Your attachment to the contents of your wallet is certain to be tested in another way, however. Panhandlers are now a fixture of the cityscape, and there is no avoiding their importunities. How you respond to them is a matter only your conscience can advise you on. Wealth and poverty have always coexisted here, but until recently poverty kept its distance. It's now omnipresent, wearing a very human face.

1 Essential Information

Before You Go

Visitor Information

Contact the **Washington, D.C., Convention and Visitors Association** (1212 New York Ave. NW, 6th floor, Washington, DC 20005, tel. 202/789–7000) and the **National Park Service** (Office of Public Affairs, National Capital Region, 1100 Ohio Dr. SW, Washington, DC 20242, tel. 202/619–7222).

If you're planning to visit sites in the surrounding areas, contact the **Maryland Department of Economic and Employment/Tourism Development** (Office of Tourist Development, 217 E. Redwood St., 9th floor, Baltimore, MD 21202, tel. 410/333–6611) and the **Virginia Division of Tourism** (1021 E. Cary St., 14th floor, Richmond, VA 23219, tel. 804/786–4484).

Tours and Packages

Should you buy your travel arrangements to Washington, DC, packaged or do it yourself? There are advantages either way. Buying packaged arrangements saves you money, particularly if can find a program that includes exactly the features you want. You also get a pretty good idea of what your trip will cost from the outset. Generally, you have two options: fully escorted tours and independent packages. Escorted tours are one option if you don't mind having limited free time and traveling with strangers. Escorted tours are most often via motorcoach, with a tour director in charge. Your baggage is handled, your time rigorously scheduled, and most meals planned. Escorted tours are therefore the most hassle-free way to see a destination, as well as generally the least expensive. Independent packages allow plenty of flexibility. They generally include airline travel and hotels, with certain options available, such as sightseeing, car rental, and excursions. Independent packages are usually more expensive than escorted tours, but your time is your own.

Travel agents are your best source of recommendations for both tours and packages. They will have the largest selection, and the cost to you is the same as buying direct. Whatever program you ultimately choose, be sure to find out exactly what is included: taxes, tips, transfers, meals, baggage handling, ground transportation, entertainment, excursions, sports or recreation (and rental equipment if necessary). Ask about the level of hotel used, its location, the size of its rooms, the kind of beds, and its amenities, such as pool, room service, or programs for children, if they're important to you. Find out the operator's cancellation penalties. Nearly everyone charges them, and the only way to avoid them is to buy trip-cancellation insurance (*see* Insurance, *below*). Also ask about the single supplement, a surcharge assessed to solo travelers. Some operators do not make you pay it if you agree to be matched up with a roommate of the same sex, even if one is not found by departure time. Remember that a program that has features you won't use, whether for rental sporting equipment or discounted museum admissions, may not be the most cost-wise choice for you. Don't buy a Rolls-Royce, even at a reduced price, if all you want is a Chevy!

Fully Escorted Tours Escorted tours are usually sold in three categories: deluxe, first-class, and tourist or budget class. The most important differences are the price, of course, and the level of accommodations. Some operators specialize in one category, while others offer a range.

Top operators include **Maupintour** (Box 807, Lawrence, KS 66044, tel. 913/843–1211 or 800/255–4266) and **Tauck Tours** (11 Wilton Rd., Westport, CT 06881, tel. 203/226–6911 or 800/468–2825) in the deluxe category; **Amtrak** (tel. 800/321–8684), **Domenico Tours** (751 Broadway, Bayonne, NJ 07002, tel. 201/823–8687 or 800/554–8687), and **Globus-Gateway** (95-25 Queens Blvd., Rego Park, NY 11374, tel. 718/268–7000 or 800/221–0090) in the first-class range; and Globus's sister operator, **Cosmos** (at the same address), in the budget category.

Most itineraries are jam-packed with sightseeing, so you see a lot in a short amount of time (usually one place per day). To judge just how fast-paced the tour is, review the itinerary carefully. If you are in a different hotel each night, you will be getting up early each day to head out, travel to your next destination, do some sightseeing, have dinner, and go to bed, then you'll start all over again. If you want some free time, make sure it's mentioned in the tour brochure; if you want to be escorted to every meal, confirm that any tour you consider does that. Also, when comparing programs, be sure to find out if the motorcoach is air-conditioned and has a rest room on board. Make your selection based on price and stops on the itinerary.

Independent Packages Independent packages are offered by airlines, tour operators who may also do escorted programs, and any number of other companies from large, established firms to small, new entrepreneurs. Washington packages are available from **American Airlines Fly AAway Vacations** (tel. 800/321–2121), **Delta Dream Vacations** (tel. 800/872–7786), and **United Airlines' Vacation Planning Center** (tel. 800/328–6877). If you prefer to travel by train, **Amtrak** (*see* Fully Escorted Tours, *above*) offers a number of packages that combine rail travel to Washington with lodging and other area attractions. **Supercities** (7855 Haskell Ave., Van Nuys, CA 91406, tel. 818/988–7844 or 800/333–1234) specializes in packages to European and U.S. cities.

Their programs come in a wide range of prices based on levels of luxury and options—in addition to hotel and airfare, sightseeing, car rental, transfers, admission to local attractions, and other extras. Note that when pricing different packages, it sometimes pays to purchase the same arrangements separately, as when a rock-bottom promotional airfare is being offered, for example. Again, base your choice what's available at your budget for the destinations you want to visit.

Special-Interest Travel Special-interest programs may be fully escorted or independent. Some require a certain amount of expertise, but most are for the average traveler with an interest and are usually hosted by experts in the subject matter. When the program is escorted, it enjoys the advantages and disadvantages of all escorted programs; because your fellow travelers are apt to be passionate or knowledgeable about the subject, they can prove as enjoyable a part of your travel experience as the destination itself. The price range is wide, but the cost is usually higher—sometimes a lot higher—than for ordinary escorted tours and packages, because of the expert guiding and special activities. (*See also* Traveling with Children and Hints for Older Travelers, *below.*)

Music **Dailey-Thorp Travel** (330 W. 58th St., New York, NY 10019, tel. 212/307–1555) offers performing-arts packages that include the city's ballet, opera, and symphony.

Art/Architecture **The National Fine Arts Association** (5301 Wisconsin Ave. NW, Suite 400, Washington, DC 20015, tel. 202/966–3800) designs tours to museums and historic homes.

Tips for British Travelers

Tourist Information Contact the **United States Travel and Tourism Administration** (Box 1EN, London W1A 1EN, tel. 071/495–4466).

Passports and Visas British citizens need a valid 10-year passport. A visa is not necessary unless (1) you are planning to stay more than 90 days; (2) your trip is for purposes other than vacation; (3) you have at some time been refused a visa, or refused admission to, the United States, or have been required to leave by the U.S. Immigration and Naturalization Service; or (4) you do not have a return or onward ticket. You will need to fill out the Visa Waiver Form I–94W supplied by the airline.

To apply for a visa or for more information, call the U.S. Embassy's Visa Information Line (tel. 0891/200–290; calls cost 48p per minute or 36p per minute cheap rate). If you qualify for visa-free travel but want a visa anyway, you must apply in writing, enclosing a self-addressed envelope, to the U.S. Embassy's Visa Branch (5 Upper Grosvenor St., London W1A 2JB) or, for residents of Northern Ireland, to the U.S. Consulate General (Queen's House, Queen St., Belfast BT1 6EO). Submit a completed Nonimmigrant Visa Application (Form 156), a valid passport, a photograph, and evidence of your intended departure from the United States after a temporary visit. If you require a visa, call 0891/234–224 to schedule an interview.

Customs British visitors age 21 or over may import the following into the United States: 200 cigarettes or 50 cigars or 2 kilograms of tobacco; one U.S. liter of alcohol; gifts to the value of $100. Restricted items include meat products, seeds, plants, and fruits. Never carry illegal drugs.

Returning to the United Kingdom, you may import duty-free 200 cigarettes, 100 cigarillos, 50 cigars, or 250 grams of tobacco; 1 liter of spirits or 2 liters of fortified or sparkling wine; 2 liters of still table wine; 60 milliliters of perfume; 250 milliliters of toilet water; plus £36 worth of other goods, including gifts and souvenirs.

Insurance Most tour operators, travel agents, and insurance agents sell specialized policies covering accident, medical expenses, personal liability, trip cancellation, and loss or theft of personal property. Some policies include coverage for delayed departure and legal expenses, winter sports, accidents, or motoring abroad. You can also purchase an annual travel-insurance policy valid for every trip you make during the year in which it's purchased (usually only trips of less than 90 days). Before you leave, make sure you will be covered if you have a preexisting medical condition or are pregnant; your insurers may not pay for routine or continuing treatment or may require a note from your doctor certifying your fitness to travel.

The **Association of British Insurers,** a trade association representing 450 insurance companies, advises extra medical coverage for visitors to the United States.

For advice by phone or a free booklet, "Holiday Insurance," that sets out what to expect from a holiday-insurance policy and gives price guidelines, contact the Association of British Insurers (51 Gresham St., London EC2V 7HQ, tel. 071/600–3333; 30 Gordon St., Glasgow G1 3PU, tel. 041/226–3905; Scottish Provincial Bldg., Donegall Sq. W, Belfast BT1 6JE, tel. 0232/249176; call for other locations).

Tour Operators Tour operators offering packages to Washington, DC, include **British Airways Holidays** (Atlantic House, Hazelwick Ave., Three Bridges, Crawley, West Sussex RH10 1NP, tel. 0293/611611); **Key to America** (15 Feltham Rd., Ashford, Middlesex TW15 1DQ, tel. 0784/248777); **Kuoni Travel** (Kuoni House, Dorking, Surrey RH5 4AZ, tel. 0306/742222); **North American Vacations** (Acorn House, 172/174 Albert Rd., Jarrow, Tyne & Wear NE32 5JA, tel. 091/483–6226); **Premier Holidays** (Premier Travel Center, Westbrook, Milton Rd., Cambridge CB4 1YQ, tel. 0223/355977).

Airfares Fares vary enormously. Fares from consolidators are usually the cheapest, followed by promotional fares such as

APEX (advance purchase excursion). A few phone calls should reveal the current picture. When comparing fares, don't forget to figure airport taxes and weekend supplements. Once you know which airline is going your way at the right time for the least money, book immediately, since seats at the lowest prices often sell out quickly. Travel agents will generally hold a reservation for up to five days, especially if you give a credit card number.

Airlines flying direct from Heathrow to Washington include **British Airways** (tel. 081/897–4000), **USAir** (tel. 0800/ 777333), and **United Airlines** (tel. 081/990-9900). Flight time is approximately seven hours on all routes.

Travelers with Disabilities Main information sources include the **Royal Association for Disability and Rehabilitation** (RADAR, 25 Mortimer St., London W1N 8AB, tel. 071/637–5400), which publishes travel information for the disabled in Britain, and **Mobility International** (228 Borough High St., London SE1 1JX, tel. 071/403–5688), the headquarters of an international membership organization that serves as a clearinghouse of travel information for people with disabilities.

When to Go

Washington has two delightful seasons: spring and autumn. In spring, the city's ornamental fruit trees are budding, and its many gardens are in bloom. By autumn, most of the summer crowds have left and visitors can enjoy the museums, galleries, and timeless monuments in peace. Summers can be uncomfortably hot and humid (local legend has it that Washington was considered a "tropical hardship post" by some European diplomats). Winter witnesses the lighting of the National Christmas Tree and countless historic-house tours, but the weather is often bitter, with a handful of modest snowstorms that somehow bring this "southern" city to a standstill. If you're interested in government, visit when Congress is in session. When lawmakers break for recess (for Christmas, Easter, July 4, and other holiday periods), the city seems a little less vibrant.

What follows are the average daily maximum and minimum temperatures for Washington.

Climate	**Jan.**	47F	8C	**May**	76F	24C	**Sept.**	79F	26C
		34	−1		58	14		61	16
	Feb.	47F	8C	**June**	85F	29C	**Oct.**	70F	21C
		31	−1		65	18		52	11
	Mar.	56F	13C	**July**	88F	31C	**Nov.**	56F	13C
		38	3		70	21		41	5
	Apr.	67F	19C	**Aug.**	86F	30C	**Dec.**	47F	8C
		47	8		68	20		32	0

Information Sources For current weather conditions for cities in the United States and abroad, plus the local time and helpful travel tips, call the **Weather Channel Connection** (tel. 900/ WEATHER; 95¢ per minute) from a touch-tone phone.

Festivals and Seasonal Events

Washington has a lively calendar of special events; listed below are some of the most important or unusual.

Jan. 5–9: Washington Antiques Show at the Omni Shoreham Hotel is an established, high-quality presentation for buyers and browsers. (Tel. 202/234–0700.)

Jan. 17: Martin Luther King Jr.'s Birthday is celebrated with speeches, dance, choral performances, and special readings. For more information, contact the Martin Luther King, Jr. Memorial Library (tel. 202/727–1186); the National Park Service (tel. 202/619–7222); the Smithsonian (tel. 202/357–2700); Arlington, Virginia, celebrations (tel. 703/358–5920).

Jan. 19: Robert E. Lee's Birthday is marked with 19th-century music and period food at Arlington House, the Custis-Lee mansion in Arlington Cemetery. (Tel. 703/557–0613.)

Feb.: African-American History Month features special events, museum exhibits, and cultural programs. (Tel. 202/ 357–2700 or 202/727–1186.)

Feb. 12: Lincoln's Birthday celebrations include a wreath-laying ceremony and a reading of the Gettysburg Address at the Lincoln Memorial. (Tel. 202/619–7222.)

Feb. 14: Frederick Douglass's Birthday is celebrated with a wreath-laying ceremony at the Frederick Douglass National Historic Site in Anacostia. (Tel. 202/619-7222 or 202/ 426–5961.)

Mid-Feb.: The Chinese New Year's Festival explodes in Chinatown, amid hails of firecrackers and a dragon-led parade. (Tel. 202/638–1041 or 202/724–4091.)

Feb. 21: George Washington's Birthday is celebrated with a parade down Washington Street in Old Town Alexandria, a historic-homes tour, and Revolutionary War reenactments. (Tel. 703/838–4200 or 703/838–5005.)

Mar. 4–6: The Spring Antiques Show hosts more than 185 dealers from 20 states, Canada, and Europe, at the Armory. (Tel. 301/738–1966 or 202/547–9215 during show.)

Mid-Mar.: St. Patrick's Day and Festival begins with a parade down Constitution Avenue at 1 PM on March 13 (tel. 703/208–3548). The following days feature theater, folk music, and dance concerts (tel. 202/347–1450). For information on Old Town Alexandria's March 12 parade festivities, call 703/838–4200. Arlington House in Arlington National Cemetery goes green as well (tel. 703/557–0613).

Mar. 20. Annual Bach Marathon honors Johann Sebastian's birthday. Ten organists each play the massive pipe organ at Chevy Chase Presbyterian Church (1 Chevy Chase Circle NW, tel. 202/363–2202) from 1 to 6.

Mar. 26: Smithsonian Kite Festival, for kite makers and kite flyers of all ages, is held at the Washington Monument grounds. (Tel. 202/357–3030.)

Apr.: Imagination Celebration, an annual month-long festival for young people at the John F. Kennedy Center for the Performing Arts, draws some of the nation's best children's theater companies. (Tel. 202/467–4600.)

Apr. 3–10: The National Cherry Blossom Festival opens with the traditional Japanese Lantern Lighting ceremony on the 3rd. (Tel. 202/728–1137 for the parade, 202/646–0366, or 202/619–7222.)

Apr. 4: The White House Easter Egg Roll brings children ages 8 and under, with an accompanying adult, to the White House lawn. (Tel. 202/456–7041.)

Apr. 13: The anniversary of **Thomas Jefferson's Birthday** is marked by military drills and a wreath-laying at his memorial. (Tel. 202/619–7222.)

Mid-Apr.: White House Spring Garden Tours are walks around the Jacqueline Kennedy Rose Garden and the West Lawn; public rooms within the White House can also be visited. (Tel. 202/456–7041.)

Mid-Apr.: Smithsonian's Washington Craft Show exhibits one-of-a-kind, handcrafted objects of original design by 100 of the country's best artisans. (Tel. 202/357–2700.)

Apr. 23: The Alexandria Garden Tour finds six private gardens and another half-dozen historical sites open to the public, with afternoon tea at the historic Athaeneum. (Tel. 703/838–4200.)

Apr. 23–24: "Wings & Things" is the annual open house at the Paul E. Garber Facility, the National Air and Space Museum's storage and restoration annex in suburban Maryland. (Tel. 202/357–2700.)

Late Apr.–early May: The D.C. International Film Festival is where dozens of foreign and American films premiere. Tickets are required. (Tel. 202/727–2396.)

Late Apr.–early May: Georgetown House Tour, now in its 67th year, offers the opportunity to view private homes. Admission includes high tea at historic St. John's Georgetown Parish Church. (Tel. 202/338–1796.)

Early May: Georgetown Garden Tour shows off more than a dozen private gardens in one of the city's loveliest and most historic neighborhoods. (Tel. 202/333–6896.)

May 6–7: Washington National Cathedral Flower Mart salutes a different country each year, with flower booths, crafts, and demonstrations. (Tel. 202/537–6200.)

Mid-May: The Armed Forces Open House at Andrews Air Force Base in suburban Maryland features two days' worth of static aircraft and weapons displays, precision parachute jumps, and either the Navy's Blue Angels or Air Force Thunderbirds aerobatic team. (Tel. 301/568–5995.)

Mid-May: Malcolm X Day pays tribute to the slain civil-rights leader. A week of workshops and films culminates in a commemoration on May 15, when concerts and speeches are held in Anacostia Park. (Tel. 202/543–8365.)

May 29: The Memorial Day Weekend Concert, performed by

the National Symphony Orchestra at 8 PM on the West Lawn of the U.S. Capitol, officially welcomes the summer to Washington. (Tel. 202/619–7222.)

May 30: Memorial Day Jazz Festival marks the 16th annual jazz festival in Old Town Alexandria and features big-band music performed by local artists. (Tel. 703/883–4686.)

May 30: Memorial Day is recognized with a wreath-laying ceremony at the Vietnam Veterans Memorial and a concert by the National Symphony. (Tel. 202/619–7222.)

Late May–early Sept.: The **Military Band Summer Concert Series,** featuring the bands of the different branches of the Armed Forces, runs from Memorial Day to Labor Day. Every August the Army Band performs the *1812 Overture,* complete with real cannons. (Tel. 202/433–2525, 703/696–3718, 202/433–4011, 202/767–5658.)

June: Shakespeare Free for All is a series of free, nightly performances at the open-air Carter Barron Amphitheater by the Washington Shakespeare Theatre (Tel. 202/393–2700 or 202/619–7222.)

Early June: The family-oriented **Alexandria Waterfront Festival** promotes the American Red Cross and recognizes Alexandria's rich maritime heritage. Tall ships are open for visits, and there are arts and crafts displays, a 10K run, and a blessing of the fleet. (Tel. 703/549–8300.)

Mid-June–Aug.: The **Big Band Concert Series** offers performances at the Sylvan Theater on the Washington Monument grounds every Wednesday evening. (Tel. 202/619–7222.)

July: Washington National Cathedral's Summer Festival of Music features everything from Renaissance choral music to contemporary instrumental fare. (Tel. 202/537–6200.)

July 1–4: D.C. Free Jazz Festival showcases the city's and the world's most accomplished and innovative musicians in free concerts—many of them held outdoors.

July 1–4 and **July 7–10: The Festival of American Folklife,** sponsored by the Smithsonian and held on the Mall, celebrates the music, arts, crafts, and foods of various nations' cultures. (Tel. 202/357–2700.)

July 4: The Independence Day Celebration includes a grand parade that follows a route past many of the capital's historic monuments. In the evening, the National Symphony Orchestra performs for free on the steps of the Capitol building; this is followed by a fireworks display over the Washington Monument. (Tel. 202/619–7222.)

July 13–Aug. 31: The Twilight Tattoo Series features the 3rd U.S. Infantry, the U.S. Army Band, the Drill Team, and the Old Guard Fife and Drum Corps on the Ellipse grounds, between the White House and the Washington Monument, every Wednesday evening at 7. (Tel. 703/696–3718.)

July 23–24: The Virginia Scottish Games, one of the largest Scottish festivals in the United States, features traditional Highland dance, bagpipes, a national professional heptathlon, animal events, and fiddling competitions on the

Episcopal High School grounds (3901 W. Braddock Rd., Alexandria, tel. 703/838–4200).

Late July: Latin American Festival spotlights Washington's large Latino community, with activities on the Mall and in the Adams–Morgan and Mount Pleasant neighborhoods. (Tel. 202/724–4091.)

Early Sept.: The National Frisbee Festival is the nation's largest noncompetitive assembly of Frisbee lovers. The disc-catching canines almost steal the show from the two-legged pros. (National Mall near the Smithsonian's National Air and Space Museum, tel. 301/645–5043.)

Sept. 4: The Labor Day Weekend Concert features the National Symphony Orchestra on the West Lawn of the U.S. Capitol. (Tel. 202/416–8100.)

Sept. 11: Adams–Morgan Day celebrates with live music, crafts, and cuisine the African and Hispanic character of this unique neighborhood. (Tel. 202/332–3292.)

Sept. 12: The **John F. Kennedy Center's Open House** throws open its doors to jugglers, musicians, dancers, and other performers on all five stages. Thousands throng to this free event every year. (Tel. 202/467–4600.)

Sept. 17: The Constitution Day Commemoration observes the anniversary of the signing of the United States Constitution. Events include a naturalization ceremony, speakers, and band concerts. (National Archives, tel. 202/501–5000.)

Late Sept.: The Washington National Cathedral Open House is a chance to share in cathedral-related crafts, music, and activities, including a climb up the central tower. (Tel. 202/537–6200.)

Sept. 24: Rock Creek Park Day celebrates the park's 104th birthday, with international and national music, children's activities, foods, and arts and crafts. The party runs from noon to dusk. (Tel. 202/426–6832.)

Late Sept.: Blacksmithing Days at the National Building Museum feature films, workshops, and hands-on demonstrations of the smithy's art. (Tel. 202/272–2448.)

Mid-Oct.: White House Fall Garden Tours provide an opportunity to see the splendid gardens of the White House, including the famous Rose Gardens and the South Lawn. (Tel. 202/456–7041.)

Oct. 24: Theodore Roosevelt's Birthday is celebrated on Roosevelt Island in the Potomac with tours of the island, exhibits, and family activities. (Tel. 202/619–7222.)

Oct. 23–30: The Washington International Horse Show is DC's major equestrian event. (Tel. 301/840–0281.)

Late Oct.: The Marine Corps Marathon attracts thousands of world-class runners. It begins at the Iwo Jima Marine Corps Memorial in Arlington, Virginia. (Tel. 703/690–3431.)

Nov. 11: Veteran's Day activities include a service at Arlington National Cemetery and an 11 AM wreath-laying ceremony at the Tomb of the Unknown Soldier, led by the president or other ranking official. (Tel. 202/475–0843.)

Mid-Nov.–late Dec.: *A Christmas Carol* returns year after year to historic Ford's Theatre. (Tel. 202/347–4833.)

Dec.: Christmas celebrations start early in the month. Major events include carol singing with the U.S. Marine Band, the National Museum of American History's annual display of Christmas trees, the People's Christmas Tree Lighting at the Capitol, and the Pageant of Peace and lighting of the National Christmas Tree on the Ellipse grounds.

Early Dec.: The Washington National Cathedral's Open House celebrates the season's holidays with bagpipers, choral sing-alongs, and seasonal decorations in the Gothic-style cathedral. (Tel. 202/537–6200.)

Dec. 3: The 24th Annual Scottish Christmas Walk salutes Alexandria's Scottish heritage with a parade, bagpipers, house tours, crafts, and children's events. (Tel. 703/838–4200.)

Dec. 10–11: Old Town Christmas Candlelight Tours visit historic Ramsay House, Gadsby's Tavern Museum, the Lee-Fendall House, and the Carlyle House in Old Town Alexandria. Included in the tour are music, colonial dancing, and light refreshments. (Tel. 703/838–4200.)

Mid-Dec.: The People's Christmas Tree Lighting on the west side of the U.S. Capitol celebrates its 31st anniversary this year. Military bands perform. (Tel. 202/224–3069.)

Mid-Dec.–Jan. 1: The National Christmas Tree Lighting/Pageant of Peace is accompanied by seasonal music and caroling. In mid-December (usually the second Thursday) the president lights the National Christmas Tree (on the Ellipse just south of the White House) at dusk. For the next few weeks the Ellipse grounds are the site of nightly choral performances, a Nativity scene, a burning Yule log, and a display of lighted Christmas trees representing each state and territory in the United States. (Tel. 202/619–7222.)

Dec. 10–Jan. 9, 1995: U.S. Botanic Gardens' Poinsettia Show bursts forth with more than 1,000 of the traditional holiday red, white, and pink flowers as well as a display of Christmas wreaths and trees. (Tel. 202/225–8333 or 202/225–7099.)

Mid–late Dec.: *Nutcracker Suite* is performed by the Washington Ballet at Lisner Auditorium. (Tel. 202/362–3606.)

Dec. 23–25: The Washington National Cathedral Christmas Celebration and Services include Christmas carols, pageants, and seasonal choral performances. (Tel. 202/537–6200.)

What to Pack

Clothing Washington is basically informal, although many restaurants require a jacket and tie. Area theaters and nightclubs range from the slightly dressy (John F. Kennedy Center) to extremely casual (Wolf Trap Farm Park). For sightseeing and casual dining, jeans and sneakers are acceptable just about anywhere. In summer, you'll want shorts and light shirts. Even in August, though, you might still want to have a shawl or light jacket for air-conditioned restaurants. Good walking shoes are a must. In January and February, you'll need a heavy coat and snow boots.

Miscellaneous If you have a health problem that may require you to purchase a prescription drug, take enough to last the duration of the trip. And don't forget to pack a list of the addresses of offices that supply refunds for lost or stolen traveler's checks.

Luggage Free baggage allowances on an airline depend on the air-
Regulations line, the route, and the class of your ticket. In general, on domestic flights and on international flights between the United States and foreign destinations, you are entitled to check two bags—neither exceeding 62 inches, or 158 centimeters (length + width + height), or weighing more than 70 pounds (32 kilograms). A third piece may be brought aboard as a carryon; its total dimensions are generally limited to less than 45 inches (114 centimeters), so it will fit easily under the seat in front of you or in the overhead compartment. There are variations, so ask in advance. The only rule, a Federal Aviation Administration safety regulation that pertains to carry-on baggage on U.S. airlines, requires only that carryons be properly stowed and allows the airline to limit allowances and tailor them to different aircraft and operational conditions. Charges for excess, oversize, or overweight pieces vary, so inquire before you pack.

Safeguarding Your Before leaving home, itemize your bags' contents and their
Luggage worth; this list will help you estimate the extent of your loss if your bags go astray. To minimize that risk, tag them inside and out with your name, address, and phone number. (If you use your home address, cover it so that potential thieves can't see it.) At check-in, make sure that the tag attached by baggage handlers bears the correct three-letter code for your destination. If your bags do not arrive with you, or if you detect damage, do not leave the airport until you've filed a written report with the airline.

Insurance In the event of loss, damage, or theft on domestic flights, airlines limit their liability to $1,250 per passenger. Excess-valuation insurance can be bought directly from the airline at check-in but leaves your bags vulnerable on the ground. Your own homeowner's policy may fill the gap; or you may want special luggage insurance. Sources include **The Travelers Companies** (1 Tower Sq., Hartford, CT 06183, tel. 203/277–0111 or 800/243–3174) and **Wallach and Company, Inc.** (107 W. Federal St., Box 480, Middleburg, VA 22117, tel. 703/687–3166 or 800/237–6615), underwritten by Lloyds, London.

Cash Machines

Automated-teller machines (ATMs) are proliferating; many are tied to international networks such as **Cirrus** and **Plus**. You can use your bank card at ATMs away from home to withdraw money from your checking account and get cash advances on a credit-card account (providing your card has been programmed with a personal identification number, or PIN). Check in advance on limits on withdrawals and cash advances within specified periods. Remember that you are charged interest on credit-card cash advances from ATMs as well as on those from tellers. And note that transaction fees for ATM withdrawals outside your home turf will probably be higher than for withdrawals at home. For specific Cirrus locations in the United States and Canada, call 800/424-7787 (for U.S. Plus locations, 800/843-7587), and press the area code and first three digits of the number you're calling from (or the calling area where you want an ATM).

Traveling with Cameras, Camcorders, and Laptops

About Film and Cameras If your camera is new or if you haven't used it for a while, shoot and develop a few rolls of film before leaving home. Pack some lens tissue and an extra battery for your built-in light meter, and invest in an inexpensive skylight filter to both protect your lens and provide some definition in hazy shots. Store film in a cool, dry place—never in the car's glove compartment or on the shelf under the rear window. Films above ISO 400 are more sensitive to damage from airport security X-rays than others; very high speed films, ISO 1,000 and above, are exceedingly vulnerable. To protect your film, don't put it in checked luggage; carry it with you in a plastic bag and ask for a hand inspection. Such requests are honored at American airports. Don't depend on a lead-lined bag to protect film in checked luggage—the airline may very well turn up the dosage of radiation to see what you've got in there. Airport metal detectors do not harm film, although you'll set off the alarm if you walk through one with a roll in your pocket. Call the Kodak Information Center (tel. 800/242-2424) for details.

About Camcorders Before your trip, put new or long-unused camcorders through their paces, and practice panning and zooming. Invest in a skylight filter to protect the lens, and check the lithium battery that lights up the LCD (liquid crystal display) modes. As for the rechargeable nickel-cadmium batteries that are the camera's power source, take along an extra pair, so while you're using your camcorder you'll have one battery ready and another recharging.

About Videotape Unlike still-camera film, videotape is not damaged by X-rays. However, it may well be harmed by the magnetic field of a walk-through metal detector. Airport security personnel may want you to turn the camcorder on to prove that that's what it is, so make sure the battery is charged when you get to the airport.

About Laptops Security X-rays do not harm hard-disk or floppy-disk storage. Most airlines allow you to use your laptop aloft but request that you turn it off during takeoff and landing so as not to interfere with navigation equipment. Make sure the battery is charged when you arrive at the airport, because you may be asked to turn on the computer at security checkpoints to prove that it is what it appears to be. If you're a heavy computer user, consider traveling with a backup battery.

Traveling with Children

Washington is a natural destination for families. For more on what to see and do and where to stay and eat, *see* Chapter 4, Washington for Children.

Publications *A Kid's Guide to Washington, D.C.* (Gulliver Books/
Local Guides Harcourt Brace Jovanovich, 111 5th Ave., New York, NY 10003; $6.95) includes games, photographs, maps, and a travel diary. *Kidding Around Washington, D.C., A Young Person's Guide to the City,* by Anne Pedersen (John Muir Publications, Box 613, Santa Fe, NM 87504, tel. 505/982–4078; $9.95), highlights the sites in each neighborhood that are of most interest to children; it includes maps of each major sector of the city.

Newsletter **Family Travel Times,** published 10 times a year by **Travel With Your Children** (TWYCH, 45 W. 18th St., 7th Floor Tower, New York, NY 10011, tel. 212/206–0688; annual subscription $55), covers destinations, types of vacations, and modes of travel.

Books *Great Vacations with Your Kids*, by Dorothy Jordan and Marjorie Cohen (Penguin USA, 120 Woodbine St., Bergenfield, NJ 07621, tel. 800/253–6476; $13), and *Traveling with Children—And Enjoying It*, by Arlene K. Butler (Globe Pequot Press, Box 833, Old Saybrook, CT 06475, tel. 800/243–0495 or 800/962–0973 in CT; $11.95 plus $3 shipping per book), both help you plan your trip with children from toddlers to teens.

Tour Operators **GrandTravel** (6900 Wisconsin Ave., Suite 706, Chevy Chase, MD 20815, tel. 301/986–0790 or 800/247–7651) offers international and domestic tours for grandparents traveling with their grandchildren. The catalogue, as charmingly written and illustrated as a children's book, positively invites armchair traveling with lap-sitters aboard. **Rascals in Paradise** (650 5th St., Suite 505, San Francisco, CA 94107, tel. 415/978–9800 or 800/872–7225) specializes in programs for families.

Getting There On domestic flights, children under 2 not occupying a seat
Airfares travel free, and older children currently travel on the "lowest applicable" adult fare.

Baggage In general, infants paying 10% of the adult fare are allowed one carry-on bag, not to exceed 70 pounds or 45 inches (length + width + height). The adult baggage allowance applies for children paying half or more of the adult fare. Check with the airline for particulars.

Safety Seats The FAA recommends the use of safety seats aloft and details approved models in the free leaflet **"Child/Infant Safety Seats Recommended for Use in Aircraft"** (available from the Federal Aviation Administration, APA–200, 800 Independence Ave. SW, Washington, DC 20591, tel. 202/267–3479). Airline policy varies. U.S. carriers must allow FAA-approved models, but because these seats are strapped into a regular passenger seat, they may require that parents buy a ticket even for an infant under 2 who would otherwise ride free.

Facilities Aloft Airlines do provide other facilities and services for children, such as children's meals and freestanding bassinets (to those sitting in seats on the bulkhead, where there's enough legroom to accommodate them). Make your request when reserving. The annual February/March issue of *Family Travel Times* gives details of the children's services of dozens of airlines (*see above*). "Kids and Teens in Flight" (free from the U.S. Department of Transportation, tel. 202/366–2220) offers tips for children flying alone.

Lodgings In addition to offering family discounts and special rates for children (for example, some large hotel chains do not charge anything extra for children under 12 if they stay in their parents' room), many hotels and resorts arrange for baby-sitting services and run a variety of special children's programs. If you are going to travel with your children, be sure to check with your travel agent for more information or ask a hotel representative about children's programs when you are making reservations.

Baby-sitting Services Make your child-care arrangements with the hotel concierge or housekeeper.

Hints for Travelers with Disabilities

Organizations Several organizations provide travel information for people with disabilities, usually for a membership fee, and some publish newsletters and bulletins. Among them are the **Information Center for Individuals with Disabilities** (Fort Point Pl., 27–43 Wormwood St., Boston, MA 02210, tel. 617/727–5540 or 800/462–5015 in MA between 11 and 4, or leave message, TDD/TTY tel. 617/345–9743); **Mobility International USA** (Box 3551, Eugene, OR 97403, voice and TDD tel. 503/343–1284), the U.S. branch of an international organization based in Britain (*see above*) and present in 30 countries; **MossRehab Hospital Travel Information Service** (1200 W. Tabor Rd., Philadelphia, PA 19141, tel. 215/456–9603, TDD tel. 215/456–9602); the **Society for the Advancement of Travel for the Handicapped** (SATH, 347 5th Ave., Suite 610, New York, NY 10016, tel. 212/447–7284, fax 212/725–8253); the **Travel Industry and Disabled Exchange** (TIDE, 5435 Donna Ave., Tarzana, CA 91356, tel. 818/368–

5648); and **Travelin' Talk** (Box 3534, Clarksville, TN 37043, tel. 615/552–6670).

Travel Agencies and Tour Operators **Directions Unlimited** (720 N. Bedford Rd., Bedford Hills, NY 10507, tel. 914/241–1700), a travel agency, has expertise in tours and cruises for the disabled. **Evergreen Travel Service** (4114 198th St. SW, Suite 13, Lynnwood, WA 98036, tel. 206/776–1184 or 800/435–2288) operates Wings on Wheels Tours for those in wheelchairs, White Cane Tours for the blind, and tours for the deaf and makes group and independent arrangements for travelers with any disability. **Flying Wheels Travel** (143 W. Bridge St., Box 382, Owatonna, MN 55060, tel. 800/535–6790 or 800/722–9351 in MN), a tour operator and travel agency, arranges international tours, cruises, and independent travel itineraries for people with mobility disabilities. **Nautilus,** at the same address as TIDE (*see above*), packages tours for the disabled internationally.

Publications In addition to the fact sheets, newsletters, and books mentioned above are several free publications available from the Consumer Information Center (Pueblo, CO 81009): "New Horizons for the Air Traveler with a Disability," a U.S. Department of Transportation booklet describing changes resulting from the 1986 Air Carrier Access Act and those still to come from the 1990 Americans with Disabilities Act (include Department 608Y in the address), and the Airport Operators Council's *Access Travel: Airports* (Dept. 5804), which describes facilities and services for the disabled at more than 500 airports worldwide. Twin Peaks Press (Box 129, Vancouver, WA 98666, tel. 206/694–2462 or 800/637–2256) publishes the *Directory of Travel Agencies for the Disabled* ($19.95), listing more than 370 agencies worldwide; *Travel for the Disabled* ($19.95), listing some 500 access guides and accessible places worldwide; the *Directory of Accessible Van Rentals* ($9.95) for campers and RV travelers worldwide; and *Wheelchair Vagabond* ($14.95), a collection of personal travel tips. Add $2 per book for shipping.

Getting There **Greyhound** (tel. 800/752–4841; TDD 800/345–3109) will carry a disabled person and companion for the price of a single fare. **Amtrak** (National Railroad Passenger Corp., 60 Massachusetts Ave. NE, Washington, DC 20002, tel. 800/USA–RAIL) advises that you request Redcap service, special seats, or wheelchair assistance when you make reservations. Also note that not all stations are equipped to provide these services. All passengers with disabilities are entitled to a 15% discount on the lowest fare, and there are special fares for children with disabilities as well. Contact Amtrak for a free brochure outlining services for the elderly and people with disabilities.

Hints for Older Travelers

Organizations The **American Association of Retired Persons** (AARP, 601 E St. NW, Washington, DC 20049, tel. 202/434–2277) provides independent travelers the Purchase Privilege Program, which offers discounts on hotels, car rentals, and sightseeing, and the AARP Motoring Plan, provided by Amoco, which furnishes domestic trip-routing information and emergency road-service aid for an annual fee of $39.95 per person or couple ($59.95 for a premium version). AARP also arranges group tours, cruises, and apartment living through AARP Travel Experience from American Express (400 Pinnacle Way, Suite 450, Norcross, GA 30071, tel. 800/927–0111); these can be booked through travel agents, except for the cruises, which must be booked directly (tel. 800/745–4567). AARP membership is open to those 50 and over; annual dues are $8 per person or couple.

Two other membership organizations offer discounts on lodgings, car rentals, and other travel products, along with such nontravel perks as magazines and newsletters. The **National Council of Senior Citizens** (1331 F St. NW, Washington, DC 20004, tel. 202/347–8800) is a nonprofit advocacy group with some 5,000 local clubs across the United States; membership costs $12 per person or couple annually. **Mature Outlook** (6001 N. Clark St., Chicago, IL 60660, tel. 800/336–6330), a Sears Roebuck & Co. subsidiary with 800,000 members, charges $9.95 for an annual membership. Note: When using any senior-citizen identification card for reduced hotel rates, mention it when booking, not when checking out. At restaurants, show your card before you're seated; discounts may be limited to certain menus, days, or hours. If you are renting a car, ask about promotional rates that might improve on your senior-citizen discount.

Tour Operators **Saga International Holidays** (222 Berkeley St., Boston, MA 02116, tel. 800/343–0273), which specializes in group travel for people over 60, offers a selection of variously priced tours and cruises. If you want to take your grandchildren, look into **GrandTravel** (*see* Traveling with Children, *above*).

Further Reading

Classic Washington novels include *Democracy*, by Henry Adams; *Advise and Consent*, by Allen Drury; and Gore Vidal's *Washington, D.C.* Edward P. Jones's critically acclaimed *Lost in the City* is a collection of short stories about black Washingtonians.

Margaret Leach's *Reveille in Washington* re-creates the city during the Civil War. In *All the President's Men*, Bob Woodward and Carl Bernstein detail the events of Watergate.

E. J. Applewhite comments on the architecture of the city in *Washington Itself*. Louis A. Halle's *Springtime in Wash-*

ington is the definitive look at the flora and fauna of the capital. In *Ear on Washington,* gossip columnist Diana McClellan recounts some of the town's juicier stories. *Literary Washington,* by David Cutler, explores past and contemporary writers who have lived in and written about the city. Sites and stories relating to the capital's African-American history are presented in *The Guide to Black Washington,* by Sandra Fitzpatrick and Maria R. Goodwin.

Characters in Margaret Truman's mysteries have been found murdered everywhere from the Smithsonian to the Supreme Court.

Arriving and Departing

By Plane

Flights are either nonstop, direct, or connecting. A **nonstop** flight requires no change of plane and makes no stops. A **direct** flight stops at least once and can involve a change of plane, although the flight number remains the same; if the first leg is late, the second waits. This is not the case with a **connecting** flight, which involves a different plane and a different flight number.

Airports   Most national and international airlines as well as many regional and commuter carriers serve one or more of Washington's three airports. **National Airport,** in Virginia, 4 miles south of downtown Washington, is popular with politicians and their staffs. It is often cramped and crowded, but it's convenient to downtown (20 minutes by subway to the Metro Center stop). Many transcontinental and international flights arrive at **Dulles International Airport,** a spacious facility 26 miles west of Washington. **Baltimore-Washington International (BWI) Airport** is in Maryland, about 25 miles northeast of Washington. All three airports are served by a variety of bus and limousine companies that make scheduled trips between airports and to downtown Washington.

Airlines   National Airport is served by **America West** (tel. 800/247–5692), **American** (tel. 800/433–7300), **Continental** (tel. 800/525–0280), **Delta** (tel. 800/221–1212), **Midwest Express** (tel. 800/452–2022), **Northwest** (tel. 800/225–2525), **TWA** (tel. 800/221–2000), **United** (tel. 800/241–6522), **USAir** (tel. 800/428–4322), and **USAir Shuttle** (tel. 800/428–4322).

Major air carriers serving Dulles include **Aeroflot** (tel. 202/429–4922), **Air France** (tel. 800/237–2747), **Air Wisconsin** (tel. 800/241–6522), **All Nippon Airways** (tel. 800/235–9262), **American** (tel. 800/433–7300), **British Airways** (tel. 800/247–9297), **Business Express** (tel. 800/345–3400), **Continental** (tel. 800/525–0280), **Delta** (tel. 800/221–1212), **Japan Air Lines** (tel. 800/525–3663), **KLM Royal Dutch** (tel. 800/777–5553), **Lufthansa** (tel. 800/645–3880), **Northwest** (tel. 800/

225–2525), **Saudi Arabian** (tel. 800/472–8342), **Swissair** (tel. 800/221–4750), **Taca International** (tel. 800/535–8780), **Transbrazil** (tel. 800/872–3153), **TWA** (tel. 800/221–2000), **United** (tel. 800/241–6522), and **USAir** (tel. 800/428–4322).

Airlines that serve BWI include **Air Jamaica** (tel. 800/523–5585), **Air Ontario** (tel. 800/776–3000), **America West** (tel. 800/247–5692), **American** (tel. 800/433–7300), **Business Express** (tel. 800/345–3400), **Cayman Airways** (tel. 800/422–9626), **Continental** (tel. 800/525–0280), **Delta** (tel. 800/221–1212), **El Al** (tel. 800/223–6700), **Icelandair** (tel. 800/223–5500), **Key Airlines** (tel. 800/786–2386), **LADECO Chilean** (tel. 800/825–2332), **Northwest** (tel. 800/225–2525), **TWA** (tel. 800/221–2000), **United** (tel. 800/241–6522), and **USAir** (tel. 800/428–4322).

Cutting Flight Costs The Sunday travel section of most newspapers is a good source of deals. When booking, particularly through an unfamiliar company, call the Better Business Bureau to find out whether any complaints have been registered against the company, pay with a credit card if you can, and consider trip-cancellation and default insurance.

Promotional Airfares All the less expensive fares, called promotional or discount fares, are round-trip and involve restrictions. The exact nature of the restrictions depends on the airline, the route, and the season and on whether travel is domestic or international, but you must usually buy the ticket—commonly called an APEX (advance purchase excursion) when it's for international travel—in advance (seven, 14, or 21 days are usual). You must also respect certain minimum- and maximum-stay requirements (for instance, over a Saturday night or at least seven and no more than 30, 45, or 90 days), and you must be willing to pay penalties for changes. Airlines generally allow some changes for a fee. But the cheaper the fare, the more likely the ticket is nonrefundable; it would take a death in the family for the airline to give you any of your money back if you had to cancel. The cheapest fares are also subject to availability; because only a certain percentage of the plane's total seats will be sold at that price, they may go quickly.

Consolidators Consolidators or bulk-fare operators—also known as bucket shops—buy blocks of seats on scheduled flights that airlines anticipate they won't be able to sell. They pay wholesale prices, add a markup, and resell the seats to travel agents or directly to the public at prices that still undercut the airline's promotional or discount fares. You pay more than on a charter but ordinarily less than for an APEX ticket, and, even when there is not much of a price difference, the ticket usually comes without the advance-purchase restriction. Moreover, although tickets are marked nonrefundable so you can't turn them in to the airline for a full-fare refund, some consolidators sometimes give you your money back. Carefully read the fine print detailing penalties for changes and cancellations. If you doubt the reliability of a company, call the airline once you've made your booking and confirm that you do, indeed, have a reservation on the flight.

The biggest U.S. consolidator, C.L. Thomson Express, sells only to travel agents. Well-established consolidators selling to the public include **UniTravel** (Box 12485, St. Louis, MO 63132, tel. 314/569–0900 or 800/325–2222); **Council Charter** (205 E. 42nd St., New York, NY 10017, tel. 212/ 661–0311 or 800/800–8222), a division of the Council on International Educational Exchange and a longtime charter operator now functioning more as a consolidator; and **Travac** (989 6th Ave., New York, NY 10018, tel. 212/563– 3303 or 800/872–8800), also a former charterer.

Charter Flights Charters usually have the lowest fares and the most restrictions. Departures are limited and seldom on time, and you can lose all or most of your money if you cancel. (Generally, the closer to departure you cancel, the more you lose, although sometimes you will be charged only a small fee if you supply a substitute passenger.) The charterer, on the other hand, may legally cancel the flight for any reason up to 10 days before departure; within 10 days of departure, the flight may be canceled only if it becomes physically impossible to operate it. The charterer may also revise the itinerary or increase the price after you have bought the ticket, but if the new arrangement constitutes a "major change," you have the right to a refund. Before buying a charter ticket, read the fine print for the company's refund policy and details on major changes. Money for charter flights is usually paid into a bank escrow account, the name of which should be on the contract. If you don't pay by credit card, make your check payable to the escrow account (unless you're dealing with a travel agent, in which case his or her check should be payable to the escrow account). The Department of Transportation's Consumer Affairs Office (I– 25, Washington, DC 20590, tel. 202/366–2220) can answer questions on charters and send you its "Plane Talk: Public Charter Flights" information sheet.

Charter operators may offer flights alone or with ground arrangements that constitute a charter package. Well-established charter operators include **Council Charter** (205 E. 42nd St., New York, NY 10017, tel. 212/661–0311 or 800/ 800–8222), now largely a consolidator, despite its name, and **Travel Charter** (1120 E. Long Lake Rd., Troy, MI 48098, tel. 313/528–3570 or 800/521–5267), with Midwestern departures. **DER Tours** (Box 1606, Des Plaines, IL 60017, tel. 800/782–2424), a charterer and consolidator, sells through travel agents.

Discount Travel Travel clubs offer their members unsold space on airplanes,
Clubs cruise ships, and package tours at nearly the last minute and at well below the original cost. Suppliers thus receive some revenue for their "leftovers," and members get a bargain. Membership generally includes a regular bulletin or

access to a toll-free telephone hot line giving details of available trips departing anywhere from three or four days to several months in the future. Packages tend to be more common than flights alone, so if airfares are your only interest, read the literature before joining. Reductions on hotels are also available. Clubs include **Discount Travel International** (114 Forrest Ave., Suite 203, Narberth, PA 19072, tel. 215/668–7184; $45 annually, single or family), **Moment's Notice** (425 Madison Ave., New York, NY 10017, tel. 212/486–0503; $45 annually, single or family), **Travelers Advantage** (CUC Travel Service, 49 Music Sq. W, Nashville, TN 37203, tel. 800/548–1116; $49 annually, single or family), and **Worldwide Discount Travel Club** (1674 Meridian Ave., Miami Beach, FL 33139, tel. 305/534–2082; $50 annually for family, $40 single).

Smoking Smoking is banned on all domestic flights of less than six hours' duration; the ban also applies to domestic segments of international flights aboard U.S. and foreign carriers.

Between the Airports and Downtown *By Metro* If you are coming into Washington National Airport, don't have too much to carry, and are staying at a hotel near a subway stop, it makes sense to take the Metro downtown. You can walk to the station or catch the free airport shuttle that stops at each terminal and brings you to the National Airport station on the Blue and Yellow lines. The Metro ride downtown takes about 20 minutes and costs between $1 and $1.25, depending on the time of day.

By Bus National and Dulles airports are served continuously by the buses of **Washington Flyer** (tel. 703/685–1400). The ride from National to downtown takes 20 minutes and costs $8 ($14 round-trip); from Dulles, the half-hour ride costs $16 ($26 round-trip). The bus takes you to 1517 K Street NW, where you can board a free shuttle bus that serves downtown hotels. The shuttle bus will also bring you here from your hotel to catch the main airport bus on your return journey. An interairport express travels between Dulles and National. The 45-minute trip costs $16 ($26 round-trip). Washington Flyer also provides service to Maryland and Virginia suburbs. Fares must be paid in cash; children under age 6 ride free.

Airport Connection buses (tel. 301/441–2345) leave BWI every 90 minutes for 1517 K Street NW. The 65-minute ride costs $14 ($25 round-trip); drivers accept traveler's checks in addition to cash.

Some hotels provide van service to and from the airports; check with your hotel.

By Train Free shuttle buses carry passengers between airline terminals and the train station at BWI airport. **Amtrak** (tel. 800/USA–RAIL) and **MARC** (Maryland Rail Commuter Service, tel. 800/325–RAIL) trains run between BWI and Washington's Union Station from around 6 AM to 11 PM. The cost of the 40-minute ride is $10 on an Amtrak train, $4.25 on a

MARC train (weekdays only). BWI is on the MARC system's Penn Line.

By Taxi If you're traveling alone, expect to pay about $9 to get from National Airport to downtown, $45 from Dulles, and $50 from BWI. Unscrupulous cabbies prey on out-of-towners, so if the fare strikes you as astronomical, get the driver's name and cab number and threaten to call the D.C. Taxicab Commission (tel. 202/767–8380). Whatever the fare, a $1 airport surcharge is added to the total at National.

By Limousine Call at least a day ahead and **Diplomat Limousine** (tel. 703/461–6800) will have a limousine waiting for you at the airport. The ride downtown from National or Dulles is about $60, $90 from BWI. **Limousines Unlimited** (tel. 301/621–9191) has a counter at BWI airport and charges $55 from BWI to downtown; or call ahead to have a car waiting for you at National ($45 to downtown) or Dulles ($99).

By Car

I–95 skirts Washington as part of the Beltway, the six- to eight-lane highway that encircles the city. The eastern half of the Beltway is labeled both I–95 and I–495; the western half is just I–495. If you are coming from the south, take I–95 to I–395 and cross the 14th Street bridge to 14th Street in the District. From the north, stay on I–95 south before heading west on Route 50, the John Hanson Highway, which turns into New York Avenue.

Interstate 66 approaches the city from the southwest, but you may not be able to use it during weekday rush hours, when high-occupancy vehicle (or "HOV") restrictions apply: Cars must carry at least three people from 6:30 to 9 AM traveling eastbound inside the Beltway (I–495), and westbound from 4 to 6:30 PM. If you're traveling at off-peak hours or have enough people in your car to satisfy the rules, you can get downtown by taking I–66 across the Theodore Roosevelt Bridge to Constitution Avenue.

Interstate 270 approaches Washington from the northwest before hitting I–495. To get downtown, take I–495 east to Connecticut Avenue south, toward Chevy Chase.

The traffic lights in Washington sometimes stymie visitors. Most of the lights don't hang down over the middle of the streets but stand at the sides of intersections. Also keep in mind that radar detectors are illegal in Virginia and the District.

Car Rentals

Ample public transportation and shuttle service from the airports to downtown make it relatively easy to get by in Washington without renting a car. Traffic is bad, and traffic rules can be confusing even to natives.

Most major car-rental companies are represented in Washington, DC, with both airport and downtown locations, including **Avis** (tel. 800/331–1212 or 800/879–2847 in Canada); **Budget** (tel. 800/527–0700); **Dollar** (tel. 800/800–4000); **Hertz** (tel. 800/654–3131 or 800/263-0600 in Canada); **National** (tel. 800/227–7368), known internationally as InterRent and Europcar. Unlimited-mileage rates range from $33 per day for an economy car to $47 for a large car; weekly unlimited-mileage rates range from $170 to $230. This does not include tax, which in Washington is 8% on car rentals.

Extra Charges Picking up the car in one city and leaving it in another may entail drop-off charges or one-way service fees, which can be substantial. The cost of a collision or loss-damage waiver (*see below*) can be high, also.

Cutting Costs If you know you will want a car for more than a day or two, you can save by planning ahead. Major international companies have programs that discount their standard rates by 15%–30% if you make the reservation before departure (anywhere from two to 14 days), rent for a minimum number of days (typically three or four), and prepay the rental. Ask about these advance-purchase schemes when you call for information. More economical rentals are those that come as part of fly/drive or other packages, even those as bare-bones as the rental plus an airline ticket (*see* Tours and Packages, *above*).

One last tip: Remember to fill the tank when you turn in the vehicle, to avoid being charged for refueling at what you'll swear is the most expensive pump in town.

Insurance and Collision Damage Waiver The standard rental contract includes liability coverage (for damage to public property, injury to pedestrians, etc.) and coverage for the car against fire, theft (not included in certain countries), and collision damage with a deductible— most commonly $2,000–$3,000, occasionally more. In the case of an accident, you are responsible for the deductible amount unless you've purchased the collision damage waiver (CDW), which costs an average $12 a day, although this varies depending on what you've rented, where, and from whom.

Because this adds up quickly, you may be inclined to say "no thanks"—and that's certainly your option, although the rental agent may not tell you so. Planning ahead will help you make the right decision. By all means, find out if your own insurance covers damage to a rental car while traveling (not simply a car to drive when yours is in for repairs). And check whether charging car rentals to any of your credit cards will get you a CDW at no charge. Note before you decline that deductibles are occasionally high enough that totaling a car would make you responsible for its full value. In many other states, laws mandate that renters be told what the CDW costs, that it's optional, and that their own auto insurance may provide the same protection.

By Train

More than 50 trains a day arrive at Washington's restored **Union Station** on Capitol Hill (50 Massachusetts Ave. NE, tel. 202/484–7540 or 800/USA–RAIL). Washington is the last stop on Amtrak's Northeast Corridor line and is a major stop on most routes from the south and west. Metroliner trains travel between New York and Washington five times every weekday.

By Bus

Washington is a major terminal for **Greyhound Bus Lines** (1005 1st St. NE, tel. 301/565–2662). The company also has stations in nearby Silver Spring and Laurel, Maryland, and in Springfield, Virginia. Check with your local Greyhound ticket office for prices and schedules.

Staying in Washington

Important Addresses and Numbers

Because of the growth in Washington and its suburbs, you must now use the appropriate area code: 202 for Washington, 703 for the Virginia suburbs, 301 for D.C.'s nearest Maryland suburbs, and 410 for eastern Maryland, including Annapolis and Baltimore. (It isn't necessary to dial "1" before the number.)

Tourist Information The **Washington, D.C., Convention and Visitors Association** operates a tourist information center behind the Willard Hotel at 1455 Pennsylvania Ave. NW (tel. 202/789–7000 or 202/737–8866 for recorded announcement of upcoming events; open Mon.–Sat. 9–5). The **International Visitor Information Service** (1623 Belmont St. NW, tel. 202/939–5566) answers foreigners' questions about Washington and has maps and brochures on area attractions in eight languages. Rangers from the National Park Service staff information kiosks on the Mall, near the White House, next to the Vietnam Veterans Memorial, and at several other locations throughout the city. **Dial-A-Park** (tel. 202/619–7275) is a recording of events at Park Service attractions in and around Washington. **Dial-A-Museum** (tel. 202/357–2020) is a recording of exhibits and special offerings at Smithsonian Institution museums. If you're planning on doing any sightseeing in Virginia, stop by the **Virginia Travel Center** (1629 K St. NW, tel. 202/659–5523). If Maryland figures in your travel plans, contact the state's **Office of Tourism Development** (tel. 410/333–6611 or 800/282–6632 for Baltimore information specifically).

Emergencies Dial 911 for assistance. The hospital closest to downtown is **George Washington University Hospital** (901 23rd St. NW, tel. 202/994–3211, emergencies only).

Doctors and **Prologue** (tel. 202/DOCTORS) is a referral service that lo-
Dentists cates doctors, dentists, and urgent-care clinics in the greater Washington area. The **DC Dental Society** (tel. 202/547–
7615) operates a referral line weekdays 8–4.

Late-Night **Peoples Drug** operates two 24-hour pharmacies in the Dis-
Pharmacies trict. One is at 14th Street and Thomas Circle NW (tel. 202/
628–0720), the other at 7 Dupont Circle NW (tel. 202/785–
1466).

Opening and Closing Times

Banks are generally open weekdays 9–3. On Friday many stay open until 5 or close at 2 and open again from 4 to 6. Very few banks in the city have lobby hours on Saturday.

Museums are usually open daily 10–5:30; some have extended hours on Thursday. Many private museums are closed Monday or Tuesday, and some museums in government office buildings are closed weekends. The Smithsonian often sets extended spring and summer hours annually for some of its museums (tel. 202/357–2700 for details).

Stores are generally open Monday–Saturday 10–7 (or 8). Some have extended hours on Thursday and many—especially those in shopping or tourist areas such as Georgetown—are open Sunday, anywhere from 10 to noon, closing at 5 or 6.

Getting Around Washington

The city's streets are arranged, said Pierre L'Enfant, the man who designed them in 1791, "like a chessboard overlaid with a wagon wheel." Streets run north and south and east and west in a grid pattern; avenues—most named after states—run diagonally, connecting the various traffic circles scattered throughout the city. The District is divided into four sections: northwest, northeast, southwest, and southeast; the Capitol Building serves as the center of the north/south and east/west axes. North Capitol and South Capitol streets divide the city into east and west; the Mall and East Capitol Street divide the city into north and south. Streets that run north to south are numbered; those that extend east to west are lettered from A to I and K to W, the letter J having been skipped. (Note that I Street is often written as "Eye Street.") After W, two-syllable alphabetical names are used for east/west streets (Adams, Belmont, Clifton, etc.), then three-syllable names (Albemarle, Brandywine, Chesapeake). After the three-syllable names to the north have been exhausted, the streets are named for trees (Aspen, Butternut, Cedar).

Make sure you have a destination's complete address, including the quadrant designation. There are four 4th and D Street intersections in Washington: one each in NW, NE, SW, and SE. Addresses in Washington are coded to the intersections they're closest to. For example, 1785 Massachusetts Avenue NW is between 17th and 18th streets; 600 5th Street NW is at the corner of 5th and F, the sixth letter of the alphabet.

By Subway The **Washington Metropolitan Area Transit Authority** (WMATA) provides bus and subway service in the District and in the Maryland and Virginia suburbs. The **Metro,** opened in 1976, is one of the country's cleanest and safest subway systems. Trains run weekdays 5:30 AM–midnight, weekends 8 AM–midnight. During the weekday rush hours (5:30–9:30 AM and 3–7 PM), trains come along every six minutes. At other times and on weekends and holidays, trains run about every 12–15 minutes. The base fare is $1; the actual price you pay depends on the time of day and the distance traveled. Children under age 5 ride free when accompanied by a paying passenger, but there is a maximum of two children per paying adult.

The computerized **Farecard machines** in Metro stations can seem complicated. You'll need a pocketful of coins or crisp $1, $5, $10, or $20 bills to feed into the machines. If the machine spits your bill back out at you, try folding and unfolding it before asking a native for help. The paper Farecard you purchase should be inserted into the turnstile to enter the platform. Make sure you hang onto the card—you'll need it to exit at your destination.

Some Washingtonians report that the Farecard's magnetic strip interferes with the strips on automatic teller and credit cards. Keep the cards separated in your pocket or wallet. You'll notice that some Farecards have advertisements on the back; others have a line with the words "Sign here" underneath. It's doubtful anyone in Washington has ever signed the back of a Farecard.

For $5 you can buy a pass that allows unlimited rail trips for one day. It's good all day on weekends, on holidays, and after 9:30 AM on weekdays. Passes are available at Metro Sales Outlets (including the Metro Center station) and at many hotels and banks.

For general travel information, call 202/637–7000 or TDD 202/638–3780 seven days a week 6 AM–11:30 PM; for consumer assistance, call 202/637–1328; for transit police, call 202/962–2121. A helpful brochure—"All About the Metro System"—is available by calling the travel information number or writing to the Office of Marketing (WMATA, 600 5th St. NW, Washington, DC 20001).

By Bus WMATA's red, white, and blue **Metrobuses** crisscross the city and nearby suburbs, with some routes running 24 hours a day. All bus rides within the District are $1. Free transfers, good for two hours, are available on buses and in Metro stations. Bus-to-bus transfers are accepted at designated Metrobus transfer points. Rail-to-bus transfers must be picked up before boarding the train. There may be a transfer charge when boarding the bus. There are no bus-to-rail transfers.

By Car A car can be a drawback in Washington. Traffic is horrendous, especially at rush hours, and driving is often confusing, with many lanes and some entire streets changing direction suddenly at certain times of day. Parking is also an adventure; the police are quick to tow away or immobilize with a "boot" any vehicle parked illegally. Since the city's most popular sights are within a short walk of a Metro station anyway, it's best to leave your car at the hotel. Touring by car is a good idea only if you're considering visiting sites in suburban Maryland or Virginia.

Most of the outlying, suburban Metro stations have parking lots, though these fill quickly with city-bound commuters. If you plan to park in one of these lots, arrive early, armed with lots of quarters. Private parking lots downtown are expensive, charging as much as $4 an hour and up to $13 a day. There is free, three-hour parking around the Mall on Jefferson Drive and Madison Drive, though these spots always seem to be filled. You can park free—in some spots all day—in parking areas south of the Lincoln Memorial on Ohio Drive and West Basin Drive in West Potomac Park.

If you find you've been towed from a city street, call 202/727-5000.

By Taxi Taxis in the District are not metered; they operate instead on a curious zone system. Even longtime Washingtonians will ask the cab driver ahead of time how much the fare will be. The basic single rate for traveling within one zone is $3. There is an extra $1.25 charge for each additional passenger and a $1 surcharge during the 4–6:30 PM rush hour. Bulky suitcases larger than three cubic feet are charged at a higher rate, and a $1.50 surcharge is tacked on when you phone for a cab. Two major companies serving the District are **Capitol Cab** (tel. 202/546–2400) and **Diamond Cab** (tel. 202/387–6200). Maryland and Virginia taxis are metered but are not allowed to take passengers between points in Washington.

Guided Tours

Orientation Tours Taking a narrated bus tour is a good way to get your bearings. Both of the tour companies listed here allow you to get off and on as often as you like with no additional charge. If you want to conserve your energy for walking inside Washington's museums, art galleries, and other touring sights, rather than walking *between* them, a bus tour is the way to go.

Tourmobile buses (tel. 202/554–7950 or 202/554–5100), authorized by the National Park Service, stop at 18 historic sites between the Capitol and Arlington National Cemetery; the route includes the White House and the museums on the Mall. Tickets are $8.50 for adults, $4 for children 3–11.

Old Town Trolley Tours (tel. 301/985–3021), orange-and-green motorized trolleys, take in the main downtown sights and also foray into Georgetown and the upper northwest, stopping at out-of-the-way attractions, such as the Washington Cathedral. Tickets are $15 for adults, $7 for children 5–12, and free for the under-5 set.

Bus Tours **Gray Line Tours** (tel. 301/386–8300) have a four-hour motorcoach tour of Washington, Embassy Row, and Arlington National Cemetery that leaves Union Station at 8:30 AM and 2 PM (at 2 PM only November–March); tours of Mount Vernon and Alexandria depart at 8:30 AM (adults $20, children 3–11, $10). An all-day trip combining both tours leaves at 8:30 AM (adults $36, children $18).

Special-Interest Tours Special tours of government buildings—including the Archives, the Capitol, the FBI Building, the Supreme Court, and the White House—can be arranged through your representative's or senator's office. Limited numbers of these so-called VIP tickets are available, so plan up to six months in advance of your trip. With these special passes, your tour will often take you through rooms not open to the public.

A visit to the **Government Printing Office** (H and North Capitol Sts. NW, tel. 202/512–1995), the world's largest in-plant printing operation, will help you understand why Washington is built on paper. In addition to Federal periodicals, brochures, forms, and stationery, the Congressional Record is printed here each night. Free tours are offered Tuesday–Thursday at 9 AM. Reservations are required.

The **Old Executive Office Building** (Pennsylvania Ave. and 17th St. NW, tel. 202/395–5895), a French Second Empire building erected in 1888, formerly the State, Navy, and War Building, is open for tours Saturday 9–noon. Inside you'll see the restored Victorian-style secretary of the navy's office (now used by the vice president), one of the building's two stained-glass rotundas, and the departmental libraries. Reservations are required.

The **Naval Observatory** (34th St. and Massachusetts Ave. NW, tel. 202/653–1507 or 202/653–0020 for group reservations) offers tours every Monday night, except on Federal holidays, to the first 90 people in line at the observatory's south gate across from the British Embassy. The 90-minute tour starts at 7:30 standard time, 8:30 daylight saving time. The selection of astronomical objects shown on the tour depends on the time of year, time of month, and sky conditions.

The opulent 18th- and early 19th-century-style **State Department Diplomatic Reception Rooms** (23rd and C Sts. NW, tel. 202/647–3241), installed on the top floor of the State Department, are patterned after great halls in Europe and rooms found in Colonial American plantations. Filled with museum-quality furnishings—including a Philadelphia highboy, a Paul Revere bowl, and the desk on which the Treaty of Paris was signed—these rooms are used 15–20 times a week to entertain foreign diplomats and heads of state. Tours are given weekdays at 9:30, 10:30, and 2:45. Reservations are required, and for a summer tour you may have to book up to three months in advance. (It's recommended that children be over 12.)

The global **Voice of America** (330 Independence Ave. SW, tel. 202/619–3919), the radio network of the U.S. Information Agency, broadcasts in 43 languages. This free 45-minute tour takes visitors past broadcast studios and the newsroom and explains VOA's purpose. Tours are weekdays at 8:40, 9:40, and 10:40 AM and 1:40 and 2:40 PM, except federal holidays. Enter on C Street. Reservations are advised.

The **Washington, DC, Post Office** (Brentwood Rd. NE between Rhode Island and New York Aves., tel. 202/636–1208) processes more than 5 million pieces of mail each day, as a veritable avalanche of envelopes and packages are transferred in robot-driven bins and sorted by optical scanners and human eyes. Free tours are offered weekdays between 9 and 4. Reservations are required. Not recommended for children under 10.

The Washington Post (1150 15th St. NW, tel. 202/334–7969) offers free 50-minute guided tours for ages 11 and up on Monday from 10 to 3. You'll take in the newsroom, where the reporters work; the production room, where the paper is put together; the press room, where the paper is printed; and the mail room, where finished papers are stacked and bundled for shipment. The *Post* was one of the last major papers in the country to switch to cold type, and a display contrasts this computerized method of putting the paper together with the hot-type method used until 1980. Make reservations for this tour well in advance of your trip.

Walking Tours The **Black History National Recreation Trail** is not a specific walking route but a group of sites within historic neighborhoods, illustrating aspects of African-American history in Washington, from slavery days to the New Deal. A brochure outlining the trail is available from the National Park Service (1100 Ohio Dr. SW, Washington, DC 20242, tel. 202/619–7222).

The National Building Museum sponsors architecturally oriented **Construction Watch and Site Seeing** (tel. 202/272–2448) each spring and fall. On Construction Watch tours, architects and construction-project managers accompany visitors to buildings in various stages of completion and discuss the design and building process. Site Seeing tours are led by architectural historians and go to various Washington neighborhoods and well-known monuments, public buildings, and houses. Tickets range from $7 for Construction Watch tours to $60 for Site Seeing tours, which include bus transportation and a box lunch.

Smithsonian Resident Associate Program (tel. 202/357–3030) routinely offers guided walks and bus tours of neighborhoods in Washington and communities outside the city. Many tours are themed and include sites that illustrate, for example, art deco influences, African-American architecture, or railroad history.

Personal Guides **Guide Service of Washington** (tel. 202/628–2842) will have a licensed guide accompany you in your car, van, or bus. The cost is $98 for a four-hour tour, $142 for an eight-hour tour.

Other Tours Every second Saturday in May, a half-dozen embassies in Washington open their doors as stops on a self-guided **Goodwill Embassy Tour** (tel. 202/636–4225). The cost per ticket is about $25 and includes refreshments, a tour booklet, and free shuttle bus transportation between embassies. The outrageous **Scandal Tours** (tel. 202/783–7212) concentrate on Washington's seamier side with a 90-minute trip past such scandalous locales as Gary Hart's Capitol Hill town house; the Tidal Basin, where Congressman Wilbur Mills and stripper Fanne Fox took an unintended dip; the Old Executive Office Building, where Fawn Hall and Ollie North shredded documents together; and, of course, the Watergate. Costumed look-alikes from the Gross National Product comedy troupe ride on the bus and dramatize the scandals. Tours leave the Washington Hilton and Towers on Saturday at 1. The cost is $27 per person, and reservations are required. For those who want to wade through the scum at their own pace, there is **Scandal Tour In-A-Box,** a 75-minute cassette tape that promises to "bypass the monuments and take you straight into the gutter" ($12.95 in bookstores or from GNP at 1602 S. Springwood Dr., Silver Spring, MD 20910, tel. 202/783–7212).

Moored on the waterfront in Old Town Alexandria, the enclosed boat *The Dandy* (0 Prince St., Alexandria, VA, tel. 703/683–6076 or 703/683–6090) is small enough to cruise under Washington's bridges, allowing it to venture up the Potomac past the Lincoln Memorial to the Kennedy Center and Georgetown. Lunch cruises board weekdays starting at 10:30 AM and weekends starting at 11:30 AM. Dinner cruises board Monday–Thursday at 6 PM, Friday at 7:30 PM, and Sunday at 7:15 PM. A $19 "midnight cruise" boards at 11:30 PM April–October at Washington Harbour in Georgetown. Prices are $25–$29 for lunch and $45–$55 for dinner.

The *Spirit of Washington* (Pier 4, 6th and Water Sts. SW, tel. 202/554–8000 or 202/554–1542), moored at the heart of

Washington's waterfront, gives visitors a waterborne view of some of the area's attractions, including Old Town Alexandria, Washington National Airport, and Hains Point. Lunch cruises board Tuesday–Saturday at 11:30 AM; a Sunday brunch cruise sails at 1. Evening cruises board at 6:30 PM and include dinner and a floor show. Adult "moonlight party cruises" board Friday and Saturday at 11 PM. Prices range from $19 per person for the moonlight cruise to $48.95 for dinner on a Friday or Saturday night. A sister ship, the ***Potomac Spirit,*** sails to Mount Vernon, George Washington's plantation home. The 4½-hour trip is offered mid-March–mid-October, Tuesday–Sunday. During peak tourist season (mid-June–mid-October), boats embark at 9 AM and 2 PM. From mid-March through mid-June, boats leave at 9 AM only. Prices are $19 adults, $17.25 senior citizens, $11.25 children 6–11, under 5 free.

2 Portraits of Washington

Speaking of Washington

Compiled by John F. Kelly

John F. Kelly is an editor for the Washington Post's Weekend *section.*

Washington, D.C., is a bit like the weather: Everybody likes to talk about it. Unlike the weather though, we can do something about Washington. Every few years Americans are invited to throw the bums out and usher a new crop of bums in. And there's no doubt these politicians will form some opinion of their new home.

Politicians, poets, presidents, First Ladies, humorists, foreign visitors—they've all put pen to paper in expressing their opinion of the city that literally arose from the swamp.

"That Indian swamp in the wilderness."—Thomas Jefferson, c. 1789

"A century hence, if this country keeps united, it will produce a city though not so large as London, yet of magnitude inferior to few others in Europe."—George Washington, 1789

"May the spirit which animated the great founder of this city, descend to future generations."—John Adams, 1800

"I had much rather live in the house at Philadelphia. Not one room or chamber is finished of the whole. It is habitable by fires in every part, 13 of which we are required to keep daily or sleep in wet or damp places."—Abigail Adams, 1800 (after moving into the White House)

"This boasted [Pennsylvania] Avenue is as much a wilderness as Kentucky. Some half-starved cattle browsing among the bushes present a melancholy spectacle to the stranger . . . . So very thinly is the city peopled that quails and other birds are constantly shot within a hundred yards of the Capitol."—Charles W. Jansen, 1806

"This embryo capital, where Fancy sees
Squares in morasses, obelisks in trees;
Which second-sighted seers, ev'n now, adorn
With shrines unbuilt, and heroes yet unborn.
Though nought but woods, and Jefferson they see,
Where streets should run, and sages *ought* to be."
—Thomas Moore, 1806

"Washington has certainly an air of more magnificence than any other American town. It is mean in detail, but the outline has a certain grandeur about it."—James Fenimore Cooper, 1838

"In democratic communities the imagination is compressed when men consider themselves; it expands indefinitely when they think of the state. Hence it is that the same men who live on a small scale in cramped dwellings frequently aspire to gigantic splendor in the erection of their public monuments. The Americans have traced out the circuit of an immense city on the site which they intend to make their capital, but which up to the present time is hardly more densely peopled than Pontoise, though, according to them, it will one day contain a million inhabitants. They have already rooted up trees for 10 miles around lest they should interfere with the future citizens of this imaginary metropolis. They have erected a magnificent palace for Congress in the center of the city and have given it the pompous name of the Capitol."—Alexis de Tocqueville, 1840

"This town looks like a large straggling village reared in a drained swamp."—George Combe, 1842

"It is sometimes called the City of Magnificent Distances but it might with greater propriety be termed the City of Magnificent Intentions . . . . Spacious avenues that begin in nothing and lead nowhere; streets, a mile long, that only want houses, roads, and inhabitants; public meetings that need but a public to be complete; and ornaments of great thoroughfares, which only lack great thoroughfares to ornament—are its leading features. One might fancy the season over and most of the houses gone out of town forever with their masters."—Charles Dickens, 1842

"I . . . found the capital still under the empire of King Mud . . . . Were I to say that it was intended to be typical of the condition of the government, I might be considered cynical."—Anthony Trollope, 1862

"Washington is the paradise of gamblers, and contains many handsome and elegantly-fitted-up establishments. It is said at least one hundred of these 'hells' were in full blast during the war."—Dr. John B. Ellis, 1870

"Why, when I think of those multitudes of clerks and congressmen—whole families of them—down there slaving away and keeping the country together, why then I know in my heart there is something so good and motherly about Washington, that grand old benevolent National Asylum for the Helpless."—Mark Twain, 1873

"One of these days this will be a very great city if nothing happens to it."—Henry Adams, 1877

"Wherever the American citizen may be a stranger, he is at home here."—Frederick Douglass, 1877

"Washington is no place in which to carry out inventions."
— Alexander Graham Bell, 1887

"But taking it all in all and after all, Negro life in Washington is a promise rather than a fulfillment. But it is worthy of note for the really excellent things which are promised."—Paul Laurence Dunbar, 1900

"In Washington there is no life apart from government and politics: it is our daily bread; it is the thread which runs through the woof and warp of our lives; it colors everything."—A. Maurice Low, 1900

"What you want is to have a city which every one who comes from Maine, Texas, Florida, Arkansas, or Oregon can admire as being something finer and more beautiful than he had ever dreamed of before."—James Bryce, 1913

"Things get very lonely in Washington sometimes. The real voice of the great people of America sometimes sounds faint and distant in that strange city. You hear politics until you wish that both parties were smothered in their own gas."—Woodrow Wilson, 1919

"Congress has been writing my material for years and I am not ashamed of what I have had. Why should I pay some famous Author, or even myself, to sit down all day trying to dope out something funny to say on the Stage?. . . No, sir, I have found that there is nothing as funny as things that have happened . . .Nothing is so funny as something done in all seriousness . . .Each state elects the most serious man it has in the District . . .He is impressed with the fact that he is leaving Home with the idea that he is to rescue his District from Certain Destruction, and to see that it receives its just amount of Rivers and Harbors, Postoffices and Pumpkin Seeds. Naturally, you have put a pretty big load on that man . . .It's no joking matter to be grabbed up bodily from the Leading Lawyer's Office of Main Street and have the entire populace tell you what is depending on you when you get to Washington."—Will Rogers, 1924

"Washington. . . is the symbol of America. By its dignity and architectural inspiration. . . we encourage that elevation of thought and character which comes from great architecture."—Herbert Hoover, 1929

"Of my first trip to the top of the Washington Monument, which must have been made soon after it was opened in 1888, I recall only the fact that we descended by walking down the long, dark steps, and it seemed a journey without end. There was in those days a bitter debate as to whether a baseball thrown from the top of the monument could be caught by a catcher on the ground, and my father was much interested and full of mathematical proofs that it couldn't be done. Some time later it was tried, and turned out to be very easy."—H. L. Mencken, 1936

"Living in contemporary Washington, caught literally and physically in L'Enfant's dream, and encountering on every hand the brave mementos of Washington, Jefferson, Jackson, Lincoln and Roosevelt, is to live as close as possible to both the source and the climax of the major sequences of the human story."—George Sessions Perry, 1946

"Washington isn't a city, it's an abstraction."—Dylan Thomas, 1950

"There are a number of things wrong with Washington. One of them is that everyone has been too long away from home."—Dwight D. Eisenhower, 1955

"Whatever we are looking for, we come to Washington in millions to stand in silence and try to find it."—Bruce Catton, 1959

"Washington is a literal cesspool of crime and violence."—Sen. James O. Eastland, 1960

"A city of southern efficiency and northern charm."—John F. Kennedy, 1960

"Every dedicated American could be proud that a dynamic experience of democracy in his nation's capital had been made visible to the world."—Martin Luther King, Jr., 1963

"Washington is several miles square and about as tall, say, as the Washington Monument, give or take a little. It is surrounded on all four sides by reality."—Arthur Hoppe, 1975

"One of my earliest recollections of Washington is of a tragicomic speech by Michigan Congressman Fred Bradley, protesting that all the wining and dining was getting him down. 'Banquet life is a physical and mental strain on us hardly imaginable to the folks back home,' said the distraught Bradley. 'The strain is terrific.' He was dragooned into attending altogether too many parties, he complained; but his appeal for fewer invitations was greeted with guffaws. Three weeks later Representative Bradley, age forty-nine, dropped dead. The official diagnosis was heart failure."—Jack Anderson, 1979

"As we quietly approached our new home, I told Rosalyn with a smile that it was a nice-looking place. She said, 'I believe we're going to be happy in the White House.' We were silent for a moment, and then I replied, 'I just hope that we never disappoint the people who made it possible for us to live here.' Rosalyn's prediction proved to be correct, and I did my utmost for four solid years to make my own hope come true."—Jimmy Carter, 1982, from *Keeping Faith: Memoirs of a President*

"The first thing that struck me about the White House was how cold it was. The country was still suffering from the energy crisis, and President Carter had ordered that the White House thermostats be turned down."—Nancy Reagan, 1989, from *My Turn*

Edifice Treks

By John F. Kelly

Washington probably produces more words than any other city in the world. Politicians orate, pundits speculate, and commentators narrate. But Washington's words have a peculiarly fleeting quality. They're copied into notebooks, transferred to computer screens, then set into type and bound into reports that are filed on shelves and forgotten. They're printed in newspapers that yellow and turn to dust. Words are spat out in sound bytes on the evening news, then released into the ether, lost forever. In the wordy war of politics, a paper trail is something best avoided.

But there is a stone trail in Washington, too: The words someone felt were important enough not just to commit to parchment, paper, or videotape, but to engrave in sandstone, marble, or granite. On the buildings of Washington are noble sentiments and self-serving ones, moving odes and contemplative ones.

A reading tour of Washington's inscriptions amounts to an aerobic classical education. The inscriptions, lofty in position and tone, are taken from the Bible, from the Greeks and Romans, from poets and playwrights, from presidents and statesmen. When viewing Washington's inscriptions, soaking up what is in most cases a perfect union of poesy and architecture, it's easy to see why the words "edifice" and "edify" spring from the same root.

Lesson one starts in Union Station, that great Beaux Arts bathhouse on Capitol Hill. Architect Daniel Burnham's 1908 train station is encrusted with carvings that do everything from romantically outline the development of the railroad to offer lessons in both humility and hospitality.

On the western end of the shining white Vermont granite structure, above the entrance to the Metro, is written (in all capital letters, as most inscriptions are):

He that would bring home the wealth of the Indies must carry the wealth of the Indies with him. So it is in travelling. A man must carry knowledge with him if he would bring home knowledge.

A bit heavy to digest when dashing for the *Metroliner* on a rainy Monday morning, but worth mulling over once a seat is found and you chug toward New York, briefcase at your feet, notes spread out on your lap, the words of the boss echoing in your brain: "Sew up the Snebco account, Johnson, and there could be a vice presidency in it for you."

At the other end of the station is the perfect sentiment for the returning hero:

*Welcome the coming, speed the parting guest. Virtue alone
is sweet society. It keeps the key to all heroic hearts and
opens you a welcome in them all.*

These are just two of the half-dozen inscriptions on
Union Station. Above allegorical statues by Louis
Saint-Gaudens that stand over the main entrance are
inscriptions celebrating the forces that created the railroads, including this set singing the praises of fire and electricity:

*Fire: greatest of discoveries, enabling man to live in vari-
ous climates, use many foods, and compel the forces of nature to do his work. Electricity: carrier of light and power,
devourer of time and space, bearer of human speech over
land and sea, greatest servant of man, itself unknown.
Thou has put all things under his feet.*

So inspirational were these and the other Union Station inscriptions thought to be 80 years ago that the Washington
Terminal Company, operators of the station, distributed a
free pamphlet imprinted with them. They probably saved
more than a few sore necks.

Union Station's inscriptions were selected by Charles William Eliot, who was president of Harvard University. According to John L. Andriot's "Guide to the Inscriptions of
the Nation's Capital," Eliot borrowed from such sources as
the Bible, Shakespeare, Alexander Pope, and Ralph Waldo
Emerson. Eliot also penned his own epigrams, a seemingly
modest skill until you start to wonder what you'd come up
with when confronted with a big blank wall that will bear
your words forever.

Eliot wrote the two inscriptions on the City Post Office
right next to the station. The inscriptions, facing Massachusetts Avenue, describe the humble letter carrier as a:

*Carrier of news and knowledge, instrument of trade and
industry, promoter of mutual acquaintance of peace and of
goodwill among men and nations*

. . . and a . . .

*Messenger of sympathy and love, servant of parted friends,
consoler of the lonely, bond of scattered family, enlarger of
the common life.*

It's said that President Woodrow Wilson edited these inscriptions, unaware that the Ivy League wordsmith Eliot
had written them. Like all good editors, Wilson improved
them.

Three long blocks away (right behind the Supreme Court
and *Equal justice under law*) is the Folger Shakespeare Library, where the student of inscriptions can pause and con-
template Stratford-upon-Avon's favorite son. On the
building's E Street side, above bas-relief panels depicting

scenes from Shakespeare's plays, are three commentaries on the playwright, including this from Ben Jonson:

Thou art a moniment without a tombe and art alive still while thy booke doth live and we have wits to read and praise to give.

Folger architect Paul Cret obviously decided not to bury Shakespeare, but praise him.

Rocks and Hard Places

Behind every inscription in Washington is the person who carved it, the man or woman who put chisel or pneumatic drill to stone and with a sharp eye and a steady hand made the most lasting of impressions.

Ann Hawkins is one such carver. (You can admire her chiselwork throughout the National Gallery of Art. She did the names on the Patrons' Permanent Fund in the east building, a roll call of philanthropists.)

"There are two comments I get from people who watch me carve and they make perfect symmetry," says Hawkins. "Half the people say 'Oh, that looks so tedious. You must have a lot of patience.' But I also get 'That looks *fun.*' And they wish they could do it."

Hawkins studied four years before she could carve well enough to take her first paying commission. She's been carving professionally since 1982, and in that time she's decided that stones are "living, breathing things." And each one is different. Sandstone is soft. Slates can be brittle and hard, with knots in them almost like wood. White Vermont marble feels sugary and crumbles a bit at the first stroke. Tennessee pink marble is chunky and firm.

There are a lot of things a stone carver has to take into account before striking the first blow, Hawkins says. "The nature of the stone, the light the inscription will receive, the weathering of the stone, how large the letters will be, what distance they'll be viewed from."

The most important part of carving, she says, is the layout of the inscription. The letters must be spaced correctly, not bunched too tightly together as if they were typeset, but spread comfortably and handsomely. The inscription must look as if it is *of* the stone, not *on* the stone.

Hawkins draws the letters on paper that—"after being measured from every direction" to make sure it's straight—is taped to the stone over sheets of typewriter carbon paper. She then outlines the inscription, transferring it to the stone. With a tungsten carbide-tipped chisel she starts hammering, sometimes working her way around the edges of the letter, sometimes starting in the center and working out. She turns and shifts the blade, roughing the letter in at first, then finishing it, aiming for the perfect

V-shape indentation that is the mark of a hand-carved inscription. (Inscriptions that are machine sandblasted through a stencil have a round center.) As in everything from squash to Frisbee, it's all in the wrist.

If the inscription is outside, the sun will provide the contrast necessary for the letters to be read. As the rays rake across the inscription, the shadows will lengthen, making the words pop. If the inscription is indoors, Hawkins paints the inside of the letters with a lacquer that's mixed with pigment, deepening the color of the stone.

Triangular Logic

If a walk around Washington's inscriptions is a classical education, a perambulation of Federal Triangle is the civics lesson. The limestone cliffs of the Triangle, stretching from their base at 15th Street down Pennsylvania and Constitution avenues, are inscribed with mottoes that immediately conjure up a nobler time.

The walls fairly sing with inscriptions, enjoining passersby to be eternally vigilant (it's *the price of liberty* says the National Archives), to *Study the past* (an understandable sentiment, appearing as it also does on the Archives), and to heed Thomas Jefferson and *Cultivate peace and commerce with all* (on the Commerce Building and an example of one of the tenets of good epigram selection: Try to work the name of the building into at least one inscription).

The Federal Triangle inscriptions also provide justification for the buildings that they decorate and government departments they praise. The inscription on the Internal Revenue Service headquarters on Constitution Avenue is not Dante's *Abandon all hope ye who enter here,* but Oliver Wendell Holmes's *Taxes are what we pay for a civilized society.* Just in case you were wondering what you were paying for every April 15.

Likewise, on the Justice Department we have:

Justice is the great interest of man on earth. Wherever her temple stands there is a foundation for social security, general happiness and the improvement and progress of our race.

While Justice certainly has its share of letters (including this bit of Latin: *Lege atque ordine omnia fiunt*—"By law and order all is accomplished"), the award for the most verbose structure must go to the Commerce Department building. Stretched out along 14th Street, eight stories up and spread out over hundreds of feet, is this edifying ode:

The inspiration that guided our forefathers led them to secure above all things the unity of our country. We rest upon government by consent of the governed and the political order of the United States is the expression of a patriotic ideal

which welds together all the elements of our national ener-
gy promoting the organization that fosters individual initi-
ative. Within this edifice are established agencies that have
been created to buttress the life of the people, to clarify their
problems and coordinate their resources, seeking to lighten
burdens without lessening the responsibility of the citizen.
In serving one and all they are dedicated to the purpose of
the founders and to the highest hopes of the future with their
local administration given to the integrity and welfare of
the nation.

It's a mouthful. But it's also redolent of a time that seems
almost hopelessly naive now, a time when we could use
words like "national energy" and "purpose of the founders"
without smirking. This passage and two other long ones
were created especially for the building, composed, it is believed, by Royal Cortissoz, for 50 years the influential art
critic of the *New York Tribune* (and author of this much
pithier epigram from the Lincoln Memorial: *In this temple*
as in the hearts of the people for whom he saved the union
the memory of Abraham Lincoln is enshrined forever.)

You can imagine Washingtonians in the 1930s watching as
the inscriptions were going up in Federal Triangle, trying
to guess what would be said, as if a huge game of hangman
were being played. At least one Washingtonian wasn't
thrilled with what he saw. In 1934, when the giant Commerce Department Building was in its final stages of construction, one Thomas Woodward wrote a letter to a friend
in the Department of Justice:

"Dear Charley, in the name of your illustrious progenitor—
not the least of whose gifts was the art of epigraphy—do
what you can to stop the inscriptions which are being
smeared over the new Government buildings. I shiver for
the English of our descendants if they are daily exposed to
some of these atrocious inscriptions. Justification for my in-
temperance in language will be found at one glance of the
inscriptions being placed upon the Department of Commerce Building."

Harrumph. It's quite clear that Mr. Woodward was not
happy with the work of Mr. Cortissoz. What's interesting is
to whom he addressed his complaint. The "Charley" in the
letter is Charles W. Eliot II, son of the Harvard president
who composed the Union Station and City Post Office epigrams. The younger Eliot forwarded the letter of complaint to Charles Moore, chairman of the Commission of
Fine Arts, the body responsible—then as now—for re-
viewing the design of government building projects. Moore
allowed as how his commission hadn't been consulted on the
inscriptions. The younger Eliot followed up with a salvo of
his own to Moore:

"I am very grateful to you for giving this matter your
attention, but still I am regretful that the inscriptions

now being carved were not previously checked by your Commission and improved as to form. They seem to be thoroughly bromidic and uninteresting—a lost opportunity."

Eliot had a point. The Commerce Department inscriptions seem lecturing rather than inspirational, long and sour rather than short and sweet. Moore must have forgotten that he once wrote: "Inscriptions are an art in themselves. They should be monumental and express in few words a great sentiment."

Still, there can be poetry in even the longest of inscriptions. Consider this moving sentiment, carved on the hemicycle of the Post Office Department building, facing 14th Street:

The Post Office Department, in its ceaseless labors, pervades every channel of commerce and every theatre of human enterprise, and while visiting as it does kindly, every fireside, mingles with the throbbings of almost every heart in the land. In the amplitude of its beneficence, it ministers to all climes, and creeds, and pursuits, with the same eager readiness and with equal fullness of fidelity. It is the delicate ear trump through which alike nations and families and isolated individuals whisper their joys and their sorrows, their convictions and their sympathies to all who listen for their coming.

What is it about the Post Office that inspires the most poignant inscriptions? And to whom do we talk about getting "ear trump" back into common usage?

Any classical education should include the Greeks, of course, and Washington is lucky enough to offer a textbook not far from the Triangle. The National Academy of Sciences, on Constitution Avenue between 21st and 22nd streets, has along its parapet an inscription not only from a famous Greek philosopher—Aristotle, from his *Metaphysics*—but written in that ancient tongue as well. Translated, it reads:

The search for Truth is in one way hard and in another easy. For it is evident that no one can master it fully nor miss it wholly. But each adds a little to our knowledge of Nature, and from all the facts assembled there arises a certain grandeur.

Oops . . .

What do you do if you're a stone carver and you make a mistake? After all, the expression "carved in stone" isn't much good if fixing a typo on a chunk of marble is as easy as depressing the backspace key.

Ann Hawkins: "If I got a chip, there are epoxy resins I could apply. . . . It's very rare to make a mistake, unless you do something stupid."

On big projects, boo-boos can be lopped out entirely, the offending block of stone cut out and replaced with a "dutchman," a fresh piece that's inserted like a patch and—hopefully—carved correctly.

There's no dutchman in what is perhaps the most obvious mistake in a Washington inscription. Inscribed in three sections on the north wall of the Lincoln Memorial is Abraham Lincoln's second Inaugural address. Twenty lines down in the first block of words is a phrase that concludes: "WITH HIGH HOPES FOR THE EUTURE." The poor stone carver added an extra stroke to the *F*, transforming it into an *E*. Because the inscription is inside—away from the rays of the sun and the shadows they provide—it would be virtually unreadable if the insides of the letters weren't painted black. And so, the bottom stroke of the *E* was left unpainted, making the best of a bad situation.

Back to the Stone Age

The capital's official buildings, monuments, and memorials urge us in various ways to remember the past or strive toward a more perfect future. None of the blank verse, mottoes, or maxims, though, are as moving as what appears on a *V*-shape set of black granite panels set into the ground near the Lincoln Memorial. The inscription isn't made up of words at all, but it's as moving as any sonnet.

Etched into the stone of the Vietnam Veterans Memorial are the names of the more than 58,000 Americans killed in that war. The names weren't carved high atop a pediment out of reach but were sandblasted delicately into the wall. Washington's other inscriptions might be meant to provide edification from a distance, but this memorial is designed to be touched, its inscriptions traced with unsteady fingers. And behind the names we see ourselves, reflected in the stone as true as any mirror.

Which leads us to the state of stone carving in Washington today. Most newer buildings in Washington aren't graced with inscriptions. While a building named after a famous American might once have warranted an inscribed quotation from that person, today we have the James Forrestal Federal Building and the William McChesney Martin, Jr. Federal Reserve Board Building with nary a peep from either gentleman.

Gone, too, is the specially commissioned aphorism meant to enlighten or fire. Inscriptions like those on the Justice and Commerce department buildings—whether you consider them quaint optimism or naive bluster—are in short supply these days.

A new judicial office building went up next to Union Station in 1992. It's pretty enough to look at—lots of glass and a plant-filled atrium—but compared to its 86-year-old neighbor it's mute: nary an inscription on its gleaming walls. An international trade and cultural center is being built in Federal Triangle, but, alas, there are no plans as yet for any heroic inscriptions there, either.

And there probably won't be. After all, the 1990s aren't like the 1930s, the period of Washington's big inscription boom. This is supposed to be the time of little, quiet government, not big, loud government. Why should government buildings assault the eyes of pedestrians and motorists with jingoistic slogans and propagandist mottoes? Shouldn't the feds just get out of our hair?

Perhaps, but somehow when we were willing to not only stand behind our words but carve them immutably into the living stone, it suggested we believed in them a little more, thought them worth remembering, no matter how self-evident or self-aggrandizing they seemed.

We don't seem to do much of that anymore. Maybe it's time to read the writing on the walls.

The Federal Government: How Our System Works

By Betty Ross

A longtime resident of the nation's capital, Betty Ross is the author of A Museum Guide to Washington, D.C., and How to Beat the High Cost of Travel and has contributed to numerous newspapers and magazines.

New York may be the fashion capital of the United States and Los Angeles the center of entertainment, but government—and power—is the name of the game in Washington.

The federal government is a major employer, an important landlord, and a source of contracts, contacts, or conversation for Washingtonians. It is a patron of the arts and a provider for the needy. To some, pervasive government is what's wrong with Washington. To others—particularly the party in power—it's what's right.

The federal government occupies some of the choicest real estate in town, yet pays no taxes to the District of Columbia. On the other hand, although citizens of the District *do* pay taxes, they could not vote until some 20 years ago. This has changed; now they can help elect the president, but still they have only a nonvoting delegate in Congress.

In Washington, the "separation of powers" doctrine becomes more than just a phrase in the Constitution. A visit here gives you a chance to see the legislative, executive, and judicial branches of government in action, to see how the system of checks and balances works. As Boswell put it, you have an opportunity, "instead of thinking how things may be, to see them as they are."

The Legislative Branch

In Pierre L'Enfant's 18th-century plan for the city of Washington, the U.S. Capitol and the White House were just far enough away from each other on Pennsylvania Avenue to emphasize the separation of powers between the legislative and executive branches. L'Enfant chose Jenkins Hill as the site for the Capitol; it is the focal point of an area now called Capitol Hill.

Guided tours of the Capitol leave from the Rotunda almost continuously from 9 AM to 3:30 PM daily throughout the year. The Senate side of the Capitol faces Constitution Avenue, while the House side can be approached from Independence Avenue.

Drop by the office of your senator or representative to pick up passes to the Visitors Galleries. Without a pass, you are not permitted to watch the proceedings. There are two Senate office buildings at First and Constitution Avenue NE, named, respectively, for former senators Everett Dirksen and Richard Russell. A third, honoring Senator Philip A. Hart, opened in November 1982 at Second and Constitution NE.

The House office buildings, named for former Speakers Joseph Cannon, Nicholas Longworth, and Sam Rayburn, are located in that order along Independence Avenue between First Street SE, and First Street SW. It is generally agreed by residents and visitors alike that the Rayburn Building is the least attractive and, at $75 million, one of the most expensive structures in the city.

According to the Constitution, "the Congress shall assemble at least once in every year, and such meeting shall begin at noon on the 3rd day of January, unless they shall by law appoint a different day." In the years before air-conditioning, Congress usually recessed during the summer and reconvened in the fall. Today, however, with congressional calendars more crowded and air-conditioning commonplace, sessions frequently last much longer. It is not unusual for the House and/or Senate to sit through the summer and well into the fall.

Congressional sessions usually begin at noon; committee meetings are generally held in the morning. Check the *Washington Post*'s "Today in Congress" listings to find out what is going on.

Don't be surprised to see only a handful of senators or members of Congress on the floor during a session. Much congressional business dealing with constituent problems is done in committees or in offices. When a vote is taken during a session, bells are rung to summon absent members to the floor.

To save time, many senators and members of Congress make the brief trip between their offices and the Capitol on the congressional subway. Visitors may ride, too. The Senate restaurant in the Capitol—famed for its bean soup—is open to the public at all times. Cafeterias in the Rayburn, Longworth, and Dirksen office buildings are also open to visitors. Watch the hours, however. From 11:30 AM to 1:15 PM, only members of Congress and their staffs are admitted.

There are two senators from each state, who are elected for six-year terms at an annual salary of $101,900 each. The 435 members of the House serve for two years and receive $125,100 per year.

How a Bill Becomes Law

Legislation is a complicated, time-consuming process. Here, briefly, is the usual legislative procedure in the House of Representatives.

- A bill is introduced by a member, who places it in the "hopper," a box on the clerk's desk. It is numbered (H.R. . . .), sent to the Government Printing Office, and made available the next morning in the House Document Room.

- It is referred to a committee.
- The committee reports on the bill, usually after holding a hearing, either before the full committee or before a subcommittee.
- The bill is placed on the House calendar.
- Any bill that involves the Treasury is considered by the House sitting as a Committee of the Whole. In that case, the Speaker appoints a chairman who presides and there is a period of general debate, followed by a reading for amendment, with speeches limited to five minutes.
- A bill is given a second reading and consideration in the House. (Bills considered in Committee of the Whole, however, receive a second reading in committee.) Amendments may be added after the second reading.
- It is given a third reading, which is by title only. The Speaker puts the question to a vote and it may be defeated at this stage by a negative vote.
- If it passes, however, it is sent to the Senate.
- The Senate considers the bill, usually after it has been referred to a committee and reported favorably by that committee.
- If the Senate rejects the House bill, it notifies the House. Otherwise, the bill is returned to the House from the Senate, with or without amendments.
- The House considers the Senate amendments.
- Differences between House and Senate versions of a bill are resolved by a joint House-Senate conference committee.
- The bill is printed in final form or "enrolled" on parchment paper.
- It is proofread by the enrolling clerk, who certifies its correctness.
- Once certified, the bill is signed, first by the Speaker of the House and then by the president of the Senate.
- It is sent to the president of the United States.
- The president approves or disapproves the bill, usually after referring it to the appropriate department for recommendations.
- If the president vetoes the bill, it is returned to the Congress. If it fails to pass by a two-thirds vote, no further action is taken.
- If the bill has either been approved by the president or passed over a veto, it is filed with the secretary of state and then becomes law.

Such a brief summary cannot possibly convey the intrigue, the drama, and the behind-the-scenes maneuvering by members, their staffs, and lobbyists involved in the legislative process. Often the stakes are high and the battles hard fought. If you are lucky, you may be able to watch an important debate or a newsworthy vote during your visit to Capitol Hill.

The Executive Branch

The White House is at 1600 Pennsylvania Avenue NW, the most prestigious address in the country. However, its first occupant, Abigail Adams, was disappointed in the damp, drafty "President's Palace." She complained that it had "not a single apartment finished" and "not the least fence, yard, or other convenience without." On the other hand, Thomas Jefferson found the house "big enough for two emperors, one Pope, and the grand lama"—and still unfinished.

When Franklin Delano Roosevelt became president in 1932, the entire White House staff consisted of fewer than 50 people. Today, approximately 1,800 people work for the executive office of the president. They are crammed into offices in the east and west wings of the White House and in the ornate Executive Office Building (formerly the State, War and Navy Building), adjacent to the White House to the west on Pennsylvania Avenue.

The president's annual salary is $200,000; the vice president receives $160,600. They are elected for a four-year term. If the president dies or becomes incapacitated, the vice president is next in line of succession. He is followed, in order, by the Speaker of the House of Representatives, the president pro tempore of the Senate, the secretaries of state, treasury, and defense, the attorney general, the postmaster general, and the secretaries of the interior, agriculture, commerce, labor, health and human services, housing and urban development, transportation, energy, education, and veterans affairs.

The Judicial Branch

Traditionally, the opening session of the Supreme Court, on the first Monday in October, marks the beginning of Washington's social season, and the quadrennial inaugural festivities add to the excitement. The inaugural week in January usually includes a star-studded gala, as well as receptions honoring the new president, vice president, and their wives.

The Supreme Court meets from October through June in a Corinthian-columned white-marble building at First Street and Maryland Avenue NE. Until 1935, the justices used various rooms in the Capitol. For a while, in the 19th century, they met in taverns, boardinghouses, and the home of the Clerk of the Court, Elias Boudinot Caldwell, at Second and A streets SE. You can see the Old Supreme Court Chamber on the ground floor of the Capitol.

Approximately 5,000 cases are submitted for appeal each year and the justices choose about 3%—roughly 160 cases in all—those which raise constitutional questions or affect the life or liberty of citizens.

Justice Felix Frankfurter said, "The words of the Constitution are so unrestricted by their intrinsic meaning or by their history or by tradition or by prior decisions that they leave the individual Justice free, if indeed they do not compel him, to gather meaning not from reading the Constitution but from reading life."

In the courtroom, the nine black-robed justices are seated in high-backed black leather chairs in front of heavy red velvet draperies. Lawyers for each side present their oral arguments, with the justices often interjecting questions or comments. Generally, the court sits for two weeks and then recesses for two weeks to do research and write opinions.

They are on the bench Monday, Tuesday, and Wednesday from 10 AM to noon and from 1 to 3 PM from October through April and they usually hear about four cases a day. During this first part of the term, the justices meet privately every Wednesday afternoon and all day Friday to discuss the cases they have heard that week and to take a preliminary vote on decisions.

The chief justice assigns different members to write the opinions. If the chief justice is on the minority side in a particular case, however, the senior justice in the majority assigns the opinion. Any justice may write his or her own opinion, agreeing or disagreeing with the majority. During the remainder of the term, in May and June, the justices usually meet every Thursday to decide on releasing their opinions.

Monday is "Decision Day," probably the most interesting time to visit the Supreme Court. That is when the justices announce their decisions and read their opinions.

Throughout the year, in the courtroom, staff members give a brief lecture about the court Monday through Friday, every half-hour from 9:30 AM to 4:30 PM. Lectures are not given on holidays or when the justices are on the bench hearing cases.

Supreme Court justices are appointed by the president with the advice and consent of the Senate. They serve for life or, as the Constitution says, "during good behavior."

Associate justices receive $153,600 per year; the chief justice's salary is $160,600. After ten years of service, justices may resign or retire with full pay.

Veteran court-watcher Anthony Lewis called the Supreme Court a "symbol of continuity, instrument of change," and added that "no more remarkable institution of government exists than the Supreme Court of the United States."

Lobbyists

Virtually every special-interest group in the country, as well as a sprinkling of foreign governments, is represented by someone who "lobbies" for its cause in Washington. Lobbyists frequently conduct their business over luncheons, cocktails, and dinners, as well as on the golf courses or tennis courts of suburban country clubs. Power is the magnet that draws them to the nation's capital.

Lobbyists' backgrounds are as diverse as the causes they represent. They are usually lawyers, public relations executives, or former congressional staff members. Many were once members of Congress or high government officials from all over the United States who have developed "Potomac fever"; that is, they do not return home but find being a Washington representative the ideal way to continue to influence public policy.

Sometimes, it appears that every group is well represented here except the average citizen. Under those circumstances, if you have a pet project, discuss it with your senator or member of Congress—he or she is your lobbyist. In doing so—like Washington's highly skilled and well-paid lobbyists—you would simply be exercising your First Amendment rights to express your beliefs and influence your government.

3 Exploring Washington

By John F. Kelly   The Byzantine workings of the federal government; the nonsensical, sound-bite-ready oratory of the well-groomed politician; murky foreign policy pronouncements issued from Foggy Bottom; and $600 toilet seats ordered by the Pentagon cause many Americans to cast a skeptical eye on anything that happens "inside the Beltway." Washingtonians take it all in stride, though, reminding themselves that, after all, those responsible for political hijinks don't come *from* Washington, they come *to* Washington. Besides, such ribbing is a small price to pay for living in a city whose charms extend far beyond the bureaucratic. World-class museums and art galleries (nearly all of them free), tree-shaded and flower-filled parks and gardens, bars and restaurants that benefit from a large and creative immigrant community, and nightlife that seems to get better with every passing year are as much a part of Washington as floor debates or filibusters.

The location of the city that calls to mind politicking, back scratching, and delicate diplomacy is itself the result of a compromise. Tired of its nomadic existence after having set up shop in eight different locations, Congress voted in 1785 to establish a permanent "Federal town." Northern lawmakers wanted the capital on the Delaware River, in the north, southerners wanted it on the Potomac, in the south. A deal was struck when Virginia's Thomas Jefferson agreed to support the proposal that the federal government assume the war debts of the colonies if New York's Alexander Hamilton and other northern legislators would agree to locate the capital on the banks of the Potomac. George Washington himself selected the exact site of the capital, a diamond-shaped, 100-square-mile plot that encompassed the confluence of the Potomac and Anacostia rivers, not far from the president's estate at Mount Vernon. To give the young city a bit of a head start, Washington included the already thriving tobacco ports of Alexandria, Virginia, and Georgetown, Maryland, in the District of Columbia.

Pierre-Charles L'Enfant, a young French engineer who had fought in the Revolution, offered his services in creating a capital "magnificent enough to grace a great nation." His 1791 plan owes much to Versailles, with ceremonial circles and squares, a grid pattern of streets, and broad, diagonal avenues. It was these grand streets that sparked the first debates over L'Enfant's design and its execution. The families that owned the estates and tobacco farms that would be transformed into Washington had agreed to sell the sites needed for public buildings at $66.66 an acre, with the understanding that profits could be made by selling the remaining land to those who wanted to be near the federal government. They also agreed to turn over for free the land to be used for streets and highways. When they discovered that L'Enfant's streets were 100 feet wide and that one thoroughfare—the Mall—would be 400 feet across, they

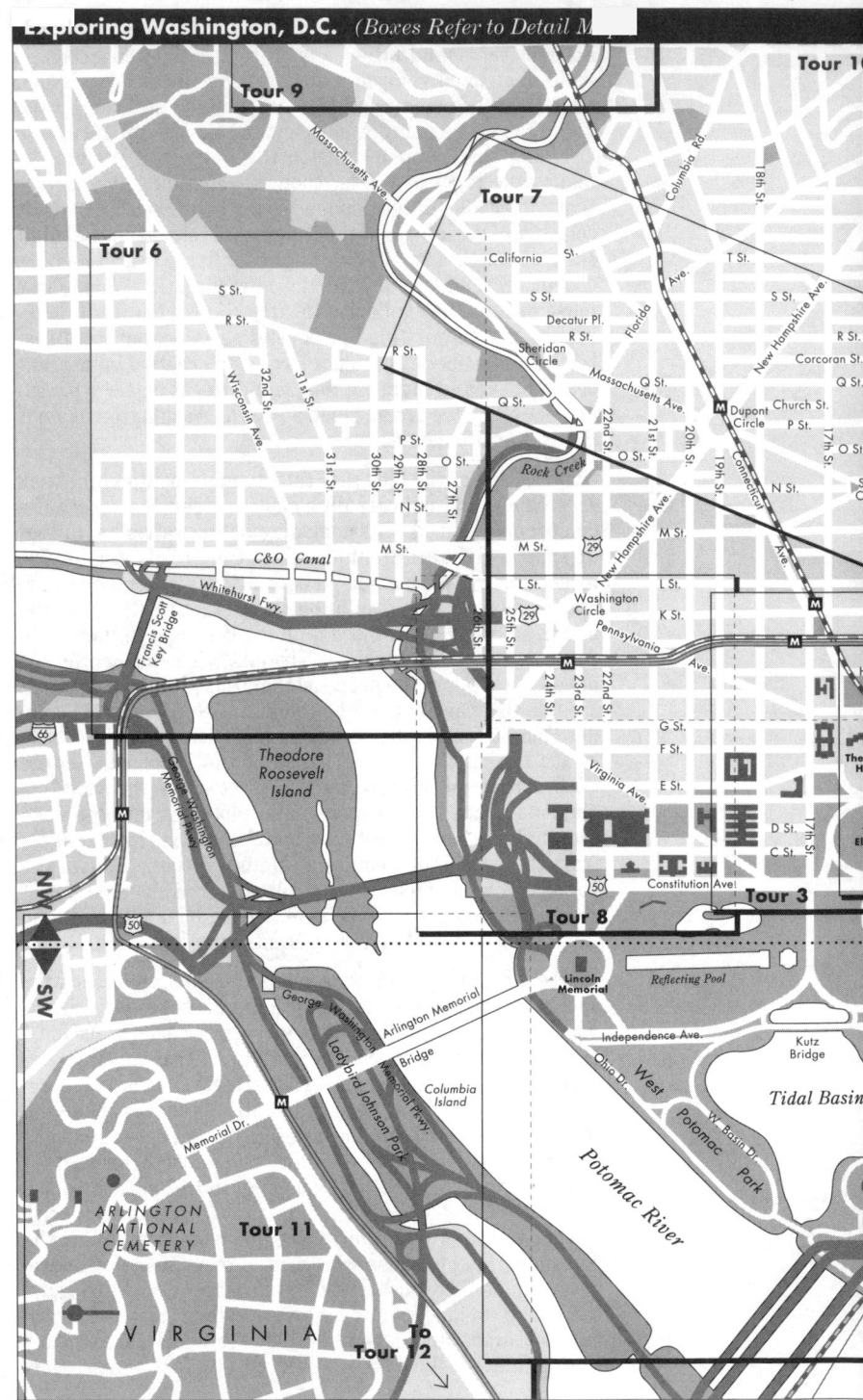

Exploring Washington, D.C. *(Boxes Refer to Detail M*

Tour 9

Tour 1

Tour 7

Tour 6

Massachusetts Ave.

Columbia Rd.

18th St.

California St.

T St.

S St.

S St.

S St.

New Hampshire Ave.

R St.

Decatur Pl.

Florida

R St.

Corcoran St.

32nd St.

Sheridan
Circle

Massachusetts Ave.

Q St.

Q St.

Q St.

Church St.

Wisconsin Ave.

31st St.

31st St.

30th St.

29th St.

28th St.

27th St.

P St.

O St.

N St.

M Dupont
Circle

22nd St.

21st St.

20th St.

19th St.

Connecticut

P St.

17th St.

O St.

N St.

Rock Creek

C&O Canal

M St.

M St.

M St.

29

New Hampshire Ave.

M St.

Whitehurst Fwy.

26th St.

25th St.

L St.

29

Washington
Circle

L St.

Ave.

M

Francis Scott Key Bridge

Pennsylvania

K St.

66

24th St.

23rd St.

22nd St.

Ave.

M

Theodore
Roosevelt
Island

George Washington Memorial Pkwy.

G St.

F St.

Virginia Ave.

E St.

The
He

M

D St.

C St.

17th St.

El

50

Constitution Ave.

Tour 3

Tour 8

NW

50

SW

Lincoln
Memorial

Reflecting Pool

George Washington Memorial Pkwy.

Arlington Memorial

Independence Ave.

Kutz
Bridge

M

Bridge

Columbia
Island

Ladybird Johnson Park

West

Ohio Dr.

W. Basin Dr.

Potomac

Park

Tidal Basin

Memorial Dr.

Potomac River

ARLINGTON
NATIONAL
CEMETERY

Tour 11

V I R G I N I A

To
Tour 12

NW ◀▶ NE

Florida Ave.

U St. Ⓜ

16th St.

15th St.

14th St.

T St.

S St.

R St.

an St.

Q St.

R St.

Q St.

Vermont Ave.

Rhode Island Ave.

Florida Ave.

S St.

P St.

Lincoln Rd.

R St.

Q St.

O St.

Church St.

Logan Circle

O St.

9th St.

🛣1

O St.

Scott Circle

Rhode Island Ave.

13th St.

12th St.

11th St.

10th St.

N St.

8th St.

7th St.

6th St.

5th St.

4th St.

N St.

New York Ave.

1st St.

North Capitol St.

O St.

3rd St.

Thomas Circle

Massachusetts Ave.

M St.

L St.

🛣1

🛣50

New Jersey Ave.

M St.

15th St.

16th St.

Mt. Vernon Square Ⓜ

I St.

Ⓜ

H St.

🛣1

🛣50

H St. 🛣1 🛣50

Massachusetts Ave.

2nd St.

Tour 5

Tour 4

New York Ave.

Ⓜ

G St.

Ⓜ

The White House

15th St.

4th St.

F St.

Ⓜ

I-395

Ⓜ

Union Station

Columbus Memorial Fountain

The Ellipse

E St.

Pennsylvania Ave.

D St.

Louisiana Ave.

Stanton Park

Ⓜ

Ⓜ

Constitution Ave.

NE

Madison Dr.

National Gallery of Art

US Capitol

E. Capitol St.

■ **Washington Monument**

Smithsonian Institution

THE MALL

Jefferson Dr.

National Air and Space Museum

SE

Independence Ave.

Maryland Ave.

Folger Park

C St.

Canal St.

Tour 1

Ⓜ

Ⓜ

Ⓜ

Ⓜ

D St.

E St.

asin

Outlet Bridge

Southwest Fwy.

G St.

New Jersey Ave.

Virginia Ave.

I-395

Jefferson Memorial

I-395

Francis Case Memorial Bridge

I St.

U ⊢——————⊣ **500 yards**

0 ⊢——————⊣ **500 meters**

Washington Canal

N↑

Tour 2

Ⓜ

Ⓜ

SW ◀▶ SE

were horrified. Half the land on the site would be turned over to the government for free for roads.

L'Enfant won the battle of the roads but he couldn't control his obstinate ways and fought often with the three city commissioners Washington had appointed. When the nephew of one of the commissioners started to build a manor house where L'Enfant had planned a street, the Frenchman ordered it torn down. The overzealous L'Enfant was fired and offered $2,500 and a lot near the White House in pay. He refused, thinking it poor compensation for the services he had performed. (A visionary who was a little too headstrong for his own good, L'Enfant spent his later years petitioning Congress with long, rambling missives demanding satisfaction. He died penniless in 1825.)

L'Enfant had written that his plan would "leave room for that aggrandizement and embellishment which the increase in the wealth of the nation will permit it to pursue at any period, however remote." At times it must have seemed remote indeed, for the town grew so slowly that when Charles Dickens visited Washington in 1842 what he saw were "spacious avenues that begin in nothing and lead nowhere; streets a mile long that only want houses, roads, and inhabitants; public buildings that need but a public to be complete and ornaments of great thoroughfares which need only great thoroughfares to ornament."

It took the Civil War—and every war thereafter—to energize the city, by attracting thousands of new residents and spurring building booms that extended the capital in all directions. Streets in the once-backward town were paved in the 1870s and the first streetcars ran in the 1880s. Memorials to famous Americans like Lincoln and Jefferson were built in the first decades of the 20th century, along with the massive Federal Triangle, a monument to thousands of less-famous government workers.

Despite the growth and despite the fact that blacks have always played an important role in the city's history (black mathematician Benjamin Banneker surveyed the land with Pierre L'Enfant in the 18th century), Washington today remains essentially segregated. Whites—who account for about 30% of the population—reside mostly in northwest Washington. Blacks live largely east of Rock Creek Park and south of the Anacostia River.

It's a city of other unfortunate contrasts: Citizens of the capital of the free world couldn't vote in a presidential election until 1964, weren't granted limited home rule until 1974, and are represented in Congress by a single nonvoting delegate (though in 1990 residents elected two "shadow" senators, one of whom is political gadfly Jesse Jackson). Homeless people sleep on steam grates next to multimillion-dollar government buildings, and a flourishing drug trade has earned Washington the dubious distinction of murder capital of the United States. Though it's little consolation to those affected, most crime is restricted to neighborhoods far from the areas visited by tourists.

Still, there's no denying that Washington, the world's first planned capital city, is also one of its most beautiful. And though the federal government dominates the city psychologically as much as the Washington Monument dominates it physically, there are parts of the capital where you can leave politics behind. The tours that follow will take you through the monumental city, the governmental city, and the residential city. As you walk, look for evidence of L'Enfant's hand, still present despite growing pains and frequent deviations from his plan. His Washington was to be a city of vistas—pleasant views that would shift and change from block to block, a marriage of geometry and art. It remains this way today. Like its main industry, politics, Washington's design is a constantly changing kaleidoscope that invites contemplation from all angles.

Tour 1: The Mall

Numbers in the margin correspond to points of interest on the Tour 1: The Mall map.

The Mall is the heart of nearly every visitor's trip to Washington. With nearly a dozen diverse museums ringing the expanse of green, it's the closest thing the capital has to a theme park (unless you count the federal government itself, which has uncharitably been called "Disneyland on the Potomac"). As at a theme park, you may have to stand in an occasional line, but unlike the amusements at Disneyland almost everything you'll see here is free. (You may, however, need free, timed-entry tickets to some of the more popular traveling exhibits. These are usually available at the museum information desk or by phone, for a service charge, from Ticketmaster, tel. 202/432–7328.)

Don't expect to see it all in one day, though. The holdings of the museums and art galleries of the Smithsonian Institution—the largest museum complex in the world—total more than 135 million objects. Only 1% are on public display at any one time, but that's still over a million different objects vying for your attention. If you can, devote at least two days to the Mall. Do the north side one day and the south the next. Or split your sightseeing on the Mall into museums the first day, art galleries the second. Of course, the Mall is more than just a front yard for all these museums. It's a picnicking park and a jogging path, an outdoor stage for festivals and fireworks, and America's town green.

The Mall is bounded on the north and south by Constitution and Independence avenues, and on the east and west by 3rd and 14th streets. Nearly all of the Smithsonian museums lie within these boundaries. (Nearest Metro stops, Smithsonian, Archives/Navy Memorial, or L'Enfant Plaza).

The best place to start an exploration of the museums on the Mall is in front of the first one constructed, the ❶ **Smithsonian Institution Building.** British scientist and founder James Smithson had never visited America. Yet his will stipulated that, should his nephew, Henry James Hungerford, die without an heir, Smithson's entire fortune would go to the United States, "to found at Washington, under the name of the Smithsonian Institution, an establishment for the increase and diffusion of knowledge among men."

Smithson died in 1829, Hungerford in 1835, and in 1838 the United States received $515,169 worth of gold sovereigns. After eight years of congressional debate over the propriety of accepting funds from a private citizen, the Smithsonian Institution was finally established in 1846. The red sandstone, Norman-style headquarters building on Jefferson Drive was completed in 1855 and originally housed all of the Smithsonian's operations, including the science and art collections, research laboratories, and living quarters for the institution's secretary and his family. Known as "the Castle," the building was designed by James Renwick, the architect of St. Patrick's Cathedral in New York City. The statue in front of the Castle's entrance is not of Smithson but of Joseph Henry, the scientist who served as the institution's first secretary. Smithson's body was brought to America in 1904 and is entombed in a small room to the left of the Castle's Mall entrance.

The museums on the Mall are the Smithsonian's most visible presence, but the organization also sponsors traveling exhibitions and maintains research posts in such places as the Chesapeake Bay and the tropics of Panama.

Today the Castle houses Smithsonian administrative offices and is home to the Woodrow Wilson International School for Scholars. To get your bearings or to get help deciding which Mall attractions you want to devote your time to, visit the **Smithsonian Information Center** in the Castle. An orientation film provides an overview of the various Smithsonian museums, and monitors display information on the day's events. The Information Center opens at 9 AM, an hour before the other museums open, so you can plan your day on the Mall without wasting valuable sightseeing time. *1000 Jefferson Dr. SW, tel. 202/357-2700, TDD 202/357-1729. Admission free. Open daily 9–5:30; closed Dec. 25.*

Entry to all Smithsonian museums and federal attractions is free, as are most guided tours of them. Prices for films, special events, etc., are noted.

To the right of the Castle is the pagodalike entrance to the **S. Dillon Ripley Center,** an underground collection of classrooms and offices named after a past Smithsonian secre-

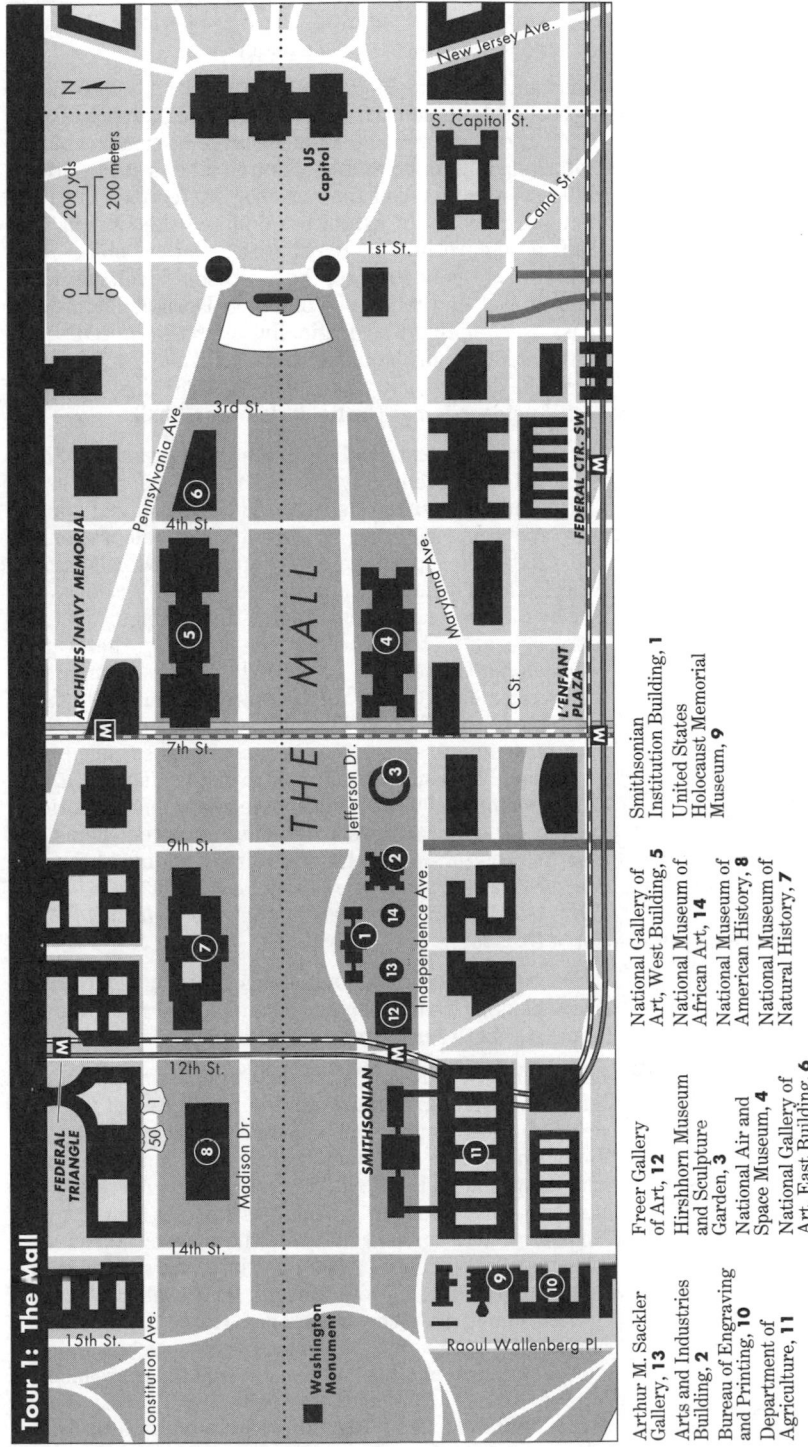

59

Tour 1: The Mall

New Jersey Ave.

S. Capitol St.

US Capitol

Canal St.

1st St.

0 — 200 yds
0 — 200 meters

3rd St.

Pennsylvania Ave.

ARCHIVES/NAVY MEMORIAL

4th St.

5

THE MALL

4

Maryland Ave.

C St.

L'ENFANT PLAZA

M FEDERAL CTR. SW

7th St.

9th St.

Jefferson Dr.

M 3

2

1 14

13

12

Independence Ave.

7

M

12th St.

FEDERAL TRIANGLE

50 11

8

Madison Dr.

SMITHSONIAN

11

14th St.

9

10

15th St.

Constitution Ave.

Washington Monument

Raoul Wallenberg Pl.

Arthur M. Sackler Gallery, **13**

Arts and Industries Building, **2**

Bureau of Engraving and Printing, **10**

Department of Agriculture, **11**

Freer Gallery of Art, **12**

Hirshhorn Museum and Sculpture Garden, **3**

National Air and Space Museum, **4**

National Gallery of Art, East Building, **6**

National Gallery of Art, West Building, **5**

National Museum of African Art, **14**

National Museum of American History, **8**

National Museum of Natural History, **7**

Smithsonian Institution Building, **1**

United States Holocaust Memorial Museum, **9**

tary. Works from around the world are periodically shown in the center's International Gallery.

This tour circles the Mall counterclockwise. Start by walking east on Jefferson Drive to the **Arts and Industries Building,** the second Smithsonian museum to be constructed. In 1876 Philadelphia hosted the United States International Exposition in honor of the nation's Centennial. After the festivities, scores of exhibitors donated their displays to the federal government. In order to house the objects that had suddenly come its way, the Smithsonian commissioned this redbrick and sandstone building. Designed by Adolph Cluss, the building was originally called the United States National Museum, the name that is still engraved in stone above the doorway. It was finished in 1881, just in time to host President James Garfield's inaugural ball.

The Arts and Industries Building housed a variety of artifacts that were eventually moved to other museums as the Smithsonian grew. It was restored to its original appearance and reopened during Bicentennial celebrations in 1976. Today the museum exhibits an extensive collection of American Victoriana; many of the objects on display—which include carriages, tools, furnishings, printing presses, even a steam locomotive—are from the original Philadelphia Centennial. In 1991 the Smithsonian opened the Experimental Gallery in the south quadrant of the Arts and Industries Building. The gallery is a laboratory that allows museum curators to experiment not so much with *what* should be displayed but *how* to display it. To that end, the Experimental Gallery has hosted some unconventional exhibits. One controversial offering exploring homelessness had visitors enter the exhibit by sliding through a morgue drawer. *900 Jefferson Dr. SW, tel. 202/357–2700, TDD 202/357–1729. Admission free. Open daily 10–5:30; closed Dec. 25.*

In front of the Arts and Industries Building is a **carousel** that is popular with young and old alike. In warmer months it operates between 10 and 5:30 ($1 a ride).

The **Hirshhorn Museum** is the next building to the east on Jefferson Drive, and you would be hard-pressed to find a piece of architecture that contrasts more with the gay Victoriana of the Arts and Industries Building. Dubbed "the Doughnut on the Mall," the reinforced-concrete building designed by Gordon Bunshaft is a fitting home for contemporary art. Opened in 1974, the museum manages a collection that includes 4,000 paintings and drawings and 2,000 sculptures donated by Joseph H. Hirshhorn, a Latvian-born immigrant who made his fortune in this country running uranium mines. American artists such as Eakins, Pollock, Rothko, and Stella are represented, as are modern European and Latin masters, including Francis Bacon, Fernando Botero, Magritte, Miró, and Victor Vasarely.

The Hirshhorn's impressive sculpture collection is arranged in the open spaces between the museum's concrete piers and across Jefferson Drive in the sunken **Sculpture Garden**. The display in the Sculpture Garden includes one of the largest public American collections of works by Henry Moore, as well as works by Honoré Daumier, Max Ernst, Alberto Giacometti, Pablo Picasso, and Man Ray. Auguste Rodin's *Burghers of Calais* is a highlight. The severe exterior lines of the museum were softened a bit in 1993 when its plaza was relandscaped by James Urban. Grass and trees provide a counterpoint to the concrete, and a granite walkway rings the museum and its outside sculpture. For those interested in wearable art, there is an assortment of contemporary jewelry and clothing in the museum's gift shop. *Independence Ave. at 7th St. SW, tel. 202/357–2700, TDD 202/357–1729. Admission free. Open daily 10–5:30; closed Dec. 25. Sculpture garden open daily 7:30–dusk.*

❹ Cross 7th Street to get to the **National Air and Space Museum.** Opened in 1976, Air and Space is the most visited museum in the world, attracting 12 million people each year. (It's thought to be the single most-visited building on earth.) Twenty-three galleries tell the story of aviation, from man's earliest attempts at flight. Suspended from the ceiling like plastic models in a child's room are dozens of aircraft, including the actual "Wright Flyer" that Wilbur Wright piloted over the sands of Kitty Hawk, North Carolina; Charles Lindbergh's "Spirit of St. Louis"; the X-1 rocket plane in which Chuck Yeager broke the sound barrier; and the X-15, the fastest plane ever built.

Other highlights include a backup model of the Skylab orbital workshop that visitors can walk through; the Voyager airplane that Dick Rutan and Jeana Yeager flew nonstop around the world; and the USS *Enterprise* model used in the "Star Trek" TV show. Visitors can also touch a piece of the moon: a 4-billion-year-old slice of rock collected by Apollo 17 astronauts. (Moon rock is one of the rarest substances on earth and, soon after the museum opened, a few zealous tourists tried to add the rock to their collections. The display is now wired with a motion alarm and watched by a uniformed guard.)

Don't let long lines deter you from seeing a show in the museum's **Samuel P. Langley Theater.** IMAX films shown on the five-story-high screen—including *The Dream Is Alive, To Fly!* and *The Blue Planet*—usually feature swooping aerial scenes that will convince you you've left the ground. Buy your tickets ($3.25 adults; $2 children, students, and senior citizens; sometimes higher for special films) as soon as you arrive, then look around the museum. (Or, if you prefer, you can buy tickets up to two weeks in advance.) Upstairs, the **Albert Einstein Planetarium** projects images of celestial bodies on a domed ceiling. *Jefferson Dr. at 6th St. SW, tel. 202/357–2700, TDD 202/357–1729. Admission free.*

Open daily 10–5:30; closed Dec. 25. Extended summer hrs determined annually. Double features are often shown in the Langley Theater after the museum has closed. For information, call 202/357–1686.

Time Out Two restaurants are located at the eastern end of the National Air and Space Museum: **The Wright Place** is a table-service restaurant that takes reservations (tel. 202/371–8777); the **Flight Line** is a self-service cafeteria. They each have a large selection of foods, but at peak times lines can be long.

After touring the Air and Space Museum, walk east on Jefferson Drive toward the Capitol. What has been called the last open space left for a museum on the periphery of the Mall is bounded by 3rd and 4th streets and Independence Avenue and Jefferson Drive SW. The Smithsonian's **National Museum of the American Indian** is scheduled to open here in 1998.

To get to the museums on the north side of the Mall, walk north on 4th or 3rd Street. As you walk, look to the left for a good view of the Mall. Notice how the Castle projects slightly into the green rectangle. When it was built, in 1855, Pierre L'Enfant's plan for Washington had been all but forgotten. In this space west of the "Congress House," the Frenchman had envisioned a "Grand Avenue, 400 feet in breadth, and about a mile in length, bordered with gardens, ending in a slope from the houses on each side." In the middle of the 19th century, horticulturalist Andrew Jackson Downing took a stab at converting the Mall into a large, English-style garden, with carriageways curving through groves of trees and bushes. This was far from the "vast esplanade" L'Enfant had in mind, and by the dawn of the 20th century the Mall had become an eyesore. It was dotted with sheds and bisected by railroad tracks. There was even a railroad station at its eastern end.

In 1900 Senator James McMillan, chairman of the Committee on the District of Columbia, asked a distinguished group of architects and artists to study ways of improving Washington's park system. The McMillan Commission, which included architects Daniel Burnham and Charles McKim, landscape architect Frederick Law Olmsted, Jr., and sculptor Augustus Saint-Gaudens, didn't confine its recommendations just to parks; its 1902 report would shape the way the capital looked for decades. The Mall received much of the group's attention and is its most stunning accomplishment. L'Enfant's plan was rediscovered, the sheds, railroad tracks, and carriageways were removed, and Washington finally had the monumental core it had been denied for so long.

Cross Madison Drive to get to the two buildings of the
➎ **National Gallery of Art,** one of the world's foremost collec-

tions of paintings, sculptures, and graphics. If you want to view the museum's holdings in (more or less) chronological order, it's best to start your exploration of this magnificent gallery in the **West Building.** Opened in 1941, the domed building was a gift to the nation from financier Andrew Mellon. (The dome was one of architect John Russell Pope's favorite devices. He designed the domed Jefferson Memorial and, though it's difficult to see from outside, there's a dome on his National Archives, too.)

A wealthy banker and oilman, Andrew Mellon served as secretary of the treasury under three presidents and as ambassador to the United Kingdom. He first came to Washington in 1921, and lived for many years in a luxurious apartment near Dupont Circle, in a building that today houses the National Trust for Historic Preservation (*see* Tour 7: Dupont Circle, *below*). Mellon had long collected great works of art, acquiring them on his frequent trips to Europe. In 1931, when the Soviet government was short on cash and selling off many of its art treasures, Mellon stepped in and bought $6 million worth of Old Masters, including *The Alba Madonna* by Raphael and Botticelli's *Adoration of the Magi.* Mellon promised his collection to America in 1937, the year of his death. He also donated the funds for the construction of the huge gallery and resisted suggestions it be named after him.

The West Building's **Great Rotunda,** with its 16 marble columns surrounding a fountain topped with a statue of Mercury, sets the stage for the masterpieces on display in the more than 100 separate galleries. You'll probably want to wander the rooms at your own pace, taking in the wealth of art. A tape-recorded tour of the building's better-known holdings is available for a $3.50 rental fee ($3 for senior citizens) at the ground floor sales area. If you'd rather explore on your own, get a map at one of the two information desks; one is just inside the Mall entrance (off Madison Drive), the other is near the Constitution Avenue entrance on the ground floor.

The National Gallery's permanent collection includes works from the 13th to the 20th century. A comprehensive survey of Italian paintings and sculpture includes *The Adoration of the Magi* by Fra Angelico and Fra Filippo Lippi and *Ginevra de'Benci*, the only painting by da Vinci in the western hemisphere. Flemish and Dutch works, displayed in a series of attractive paneled rooms, include *Daniel in the Lions' Den*, by Rubens, and a self-portrait by Rembrandt. The Chester Dale Collection comprises works by Impressionist painters such as Degas, Monet, Renoir, and Mary Cassatt.

6 To get to the **National Gallery of Art's East Building** you can take a moving walkway that travels below ground between the two buildings. But to appreciate architect I. M. Pei's impressive, angular East Building, enter it from outside rather than from underground. Exit the West Building through its eastern doors, and cross 4th Street. (As you cross, look to the north: Seeming to float above the Doric columns and pediment of the D.C. Superior Court is the green roof and redbrick pediment of the Pension Building, four blocks away.)

The East Building opened in 1978 in response to the changing needs of the National Gallery. The awkward trapezoidal shape of the building site, which had been taken up by tennis courts and rose bushes planted during Lady Bird Johnson's spruce-up campaign, prompted Pei's dramatic approach: Two interlocking spaces shaped like triangles provide room for galleries, auditoriums, and administrative offices. While the East Building's triangles contrast sharply with the symmetrical classical facade and gentle dome of the West Building, both buildings are constructed of pink marble from the same Tennessee quarries. Despite its severe angularity, Pei's building is inviting. The axeblade-like southwest corner has been darkened and polished smooth by thousands of hands irresistibly drawn to it.

The atrium of the East Building is dominated by two massive works of art: Alexander Calder's mobile *Untitled* (recently refurbished to make it rotate more easily) and *Woman*, a huge wall-hanging by Joan Miró. The galleries here generally display modern art, though the East Building serves as a home for major temporary exhibitions that span years and artistic styles. *Madison Dr. and 4th St. NW, tel. 202/737–4215, TDD 202/842–6176. Admission free. Open Mon.–Sat. 10–5, Sun. 11–6; closed Dec. 25. Extended spring and summer hrs determined annually.*

Time Out Two restaurants on the concourse level between the East and West buildings of the National Gallery offer bleary-eyed and foot-sore museum goers the chance to recharge. The **buffet** serves a wide variety of soups, sandwiches, salads, hot entrees, and desserts. The **Cascade Cafe** has a smaller selection, but customers enjoy the soothing effect of the gentle waterfall that splashes against the glass-covered wall.

Between 7th and 9th streets is the **National Sculpture Garden and Ice Rink** (tel. 202/371–5340). In the winter, skates are rented out for use on the circular rink. Ice cream and other refreshments are available at the green building during the summer.

⑦ The **National Museum of Natural History** houses the majority of the Smithsonian's collection of objects, a total of some 118 million specimens. It was constructed in 1910, and two wings were added in the '60s. It is a museum's museum, filled with bones, fossils, stuffed animals, and other natural delights. Exhibits also explore the exploits of humans, the world's most adaptive inhabitants.

The first-floor hall under the rotunda is dominated by a stuffed, eight-ton, 13-foot African bull elephant, one of the largest specimens ever found. (The tusks are fiberglass; the original ivory ones were apparently far too heavy for the stuffed elephant to support.) Off to the right is the popular **Dinosaur Hall.** Fossilized skeletons on display range from a 90-foot-long diplodocus to a tiny thesalosaurus neglectus (a small dinosaur so named because its disconnected bones sat forgotten for years in a college drawer before being reassembled).

In the west wing are displays on birds, mammals, and sea life. Many of the preserved specimens are from the collection of animals bagged by Teddy Roosevelt on his trips to Africa. Not everything in the museum is dead, though. The sea-life display features a living coral reef, complete with fish, plants, and simulated waves. The halls north of the rotunda contain tools, clothing, and other artifacts from many cultures, including those of Native America and of Asia, the Pacific, and Africa.

The highlight of the second floor is the **mineral and gem collection.** Objects include the largest sapphire on public display in the country (the Logan Sapphire, 423 carats), the largest uncut diamond (the Oppenheimer Diamond, 253.7 carats), and, of course, the Hope Diamond, a blue gem found in India and reputed to carry a curse (though Smithsonian guides are quick to pooh-pooh this notion). The amazing gem collection is second in value only to the crown jewels of Great Britain. (The Hall of Gems is scheduled to close in mid-1994 for an 18-month renovation, but its more spectacular objects will remain on display.)

Also on the second floor is the renovated **O. Orkin Insect Zoo.** Visitors can view all manner of creepy crawlies, from bees to tarantulas, and even crawl through a termite mound. (And yes it's named after the pest control magnate; he donated money for the zoo's renovation.)

If you've always wished you could get your hands on the objects behind the glass, stop by the Discovery Room and the Naturalist Center. The **Discovery Room,** in the northwest corner of the second floor, is for families and children. Here elephant tusks, petrified wood, seashells, rocks, feathers, and other items from the natural world can be handled. The **Naturalist Center** on the ground floor houses a "research collection," meaning visitors—at least 12 years old—can pull out drawer after drawer of minerals, bones, preserved animals, and dried flowers and examine them. Docents guide you through your study, and if you've brought something you'd like to learn about—a rock, a fossil, an egg, whatever—they'll help you identify it. *Madison Dr. between 9th and 12th Sts. NW, tel. 202/357–2700, TDD 202/ 357–1729. Admission free. Open daily 10–5:30; closed Dec. 25. Discovery Room open weekdays noon–2:30, weekends 10:30–3:30; in spring and summer free passes are distrib-*

*uted starting at 11:45 weekdays, 10:15 weekends. Natural-
ist Center open Mon.–Sat. 10:30–4. Extended spring and
summer hrs determined annually.*

❽ The **National Museum of American History**—the next
building to the west, toward the Washington Monument—
explores America's cultural, political, technical, and scientific past. It opened in 1964 as the National Museum of History and Technology and was renamed in 1980. The
incredible diversity of artifacts here helps the Smithsonian
live up to its nickname as "the Nation's attic." This is the
museum that displayed Muhammed Ali's boxing gloves, the
Fonz's leather jacket, and the Bunkers' living room furniture from "All in the Family." Visitors can wander for hours
on the museum's three floors. The exhibits on the first floor
emphasize the history of science and technology and include such items as farm machines, antique automobiles,
early phonographs, and a 280-ton steam locomotive. The
second floor is devoted to U.S. social and political history
and features an exhibit on everyday American life just after
the Revolution. After a 4½-year conservation project the
gowns of the First Ladies are on display again. This new
permanent exhibit, "First Ladies: Political Role and Public
Image," goes beyond fashion to explore the women behind
the satin, lace, and brocade. The third floor has installations on ceramics, money, graphic arts, musical instruments, photography, and news reporting.

Be sure to check out Horatio Greenough's statue of the first
president (by the west-wing escalators on the second floor).
Commissioned by Congress in 1832, the statue was intended to grace the Capitol Rotunda. It was there for only a
short while, however, since the toga-clad likeness proved
shocking to legislators who grumbled that it looked as if the
father of our country had just emerged from a bath. The
statue was first banished to the east grounds of the Capitol,
then given to the Smithsonian in 1908. And if you'd like a
more interactive visit, stop by the **Hands On History Room**
behind the Star Spangled Banner display. Visitors can ride
on a high-wheeler bike, try harnessing a mule, or sort mail
as it was done on the railroads in the 1870s. *Madison Ave.
between 12th and 14th Sts. NW, tel. 202/357–2700, TDD
202/357–1729. Admission free. Open daily 10–5:30; closed
Dec. 25. Hands On History Room open Tues.–Sat. noon–3.
Extended spring and summer hrs determined annually.*

To continue the loop of the Mall, head south on 14th Street.
From here you'll be able to view the length of the Mall from
its western end, this time seeing the Capitol from afar. Instead of turning east on Jefferson Drive, continue south on
14th Street. On the right you'll pass a turreted, castle-like
structure called the **Auditor's Building.** Built in 1879, it was
the first building dedicated exclusively to the work of printing America's money. It was renovated in 1991 and is now
home to the Forest Service.

❾ Next door is the new **United States Holocaust Memorial Museum,** designed by James Ingo Freed. It is an atypical museum, since it doesn't celebrate the best that humanity can achieve, but instead illustrates the worst. The museum tells the story of the 11 million Jews, Gypsies, Jehovah's Witnesses, homosexuals, political prisoners, and others killed by the Nazis between 1933 and 1945. The museum's graphic presentation is as atypical as its subject matter: Upon arrival, each visitor punches his or her sex and age into a computer and is issued an "identity card" containing biographical information on a real person from the Holocaust. As visitors move through the museum, their cards are updated. The museum recounts the Holocaust in almost cinematic fashion, with documentary films, videotaped oral histories, and a collection that includes such items as a German freight car, used to transport Jews from Warsaw to the Treblinka death camp, and the Star of David patches that Jewish prisoners were made to wear. Like the history it covers, the museum can be profoundly disturbing; it is not recommended for visitors under 12. After this powerful— even wrenching—experience, the adjacent **Hall of Remembrance** provides a space for quiet reflection. *100 Raoul Wallenberg Pl. SW (enter from either Raoul Wallenberg Pl. or 14th St. SW), tel. 202/488-0400. Admission free. Open daily 10–5:30. Closed Yom Kippur and Christmas.*

❿ In 1914 the country's money-making operation moved from the Auditor's Building to the **Bureau of Engraving and Printing.** All the paper currency in the United States, as well as stamps, military certificates, and presidential invitations, is printed in this huge building. Despite the fact that there are no free samples, the 20-minute, self-guided tour of the bureau—which takes visitors past presses that turn out some $22.5 million a day—is one of the city's most popular. *14th and C Sts. SW, tel. 202/874-3019. Open weekdays 9–2; closed Dec. 25. During peak tourist season, passes for timed entry are issued on day of tour, starting at 8:30 AM.*

⓫ Return to 14th Street and turn east onto Independence Avenue. Continuing down Independence Avenue back toward the Capitol, you'll walk between the two buildings of the **Department of Agriculture.** The older building on your left was started in 1905 and was the first building to be constructed by order of the McMillan Commission on the south side of the Mall. The cornices on the north side of this white-marble building feature depictions of forests and of grains, flowers, and fruits—some of the plants the department keeps an eye on. The newer building south of Independence Avenue, to your right, covers three city blocks (an example, perhaps, of big government).

⓬ A few steps farther up Independence Avenue, across 12th Street, is the **Freer Gallery of Art,** a gift from Detroit industrialist Charles L. Freer, who retired in 1900 and devoted the rest of his life to collecting Asian treasures. The Freer opened in 1923, four years after its benefactor's death. Its collection includes more than 26,000 works of art from the Far and Near East, including Asian porcelains, Japanese screens, Chinese paintings and bronzes, Korean stoneware, and examples of Islamic art. Freer's friend James McNeill Whistler introduced him to Asian art, and the American painter is represented in the vast collection. On display in Gallery 12 is the "Peacock Room," a blue-and-gold dining room decorated with painted leather, wood, and canvas and designed by Whistler for a British shipping magnate. Freer paid $30,000 for the entire room and moved it from London to the United States in 1904. The works of other American artists Freer felt were influenced by the Orient also are on display. The Freer reopened in 1993 after a $26-million renovation that was begun in 1988. Additions include three floors of underground space, more storage space, a gift shop, and an auditorium. The spectacular Peacock Room also received a sprucing up. *12th St. and Jefferson Dr. SW, tel. 202/357–2700, TDD 202/357–1729. Admission free. Open daily 10–5:30.*

Just beyond the Freer turn left off of Independence Avenue into the **Enid Haupt Memorial Garden.** This 4-acre Victorian-style garden is built largely on the rooftops of two Smithsonian museums, the Arthur M. Sackler Gallery and the National Museum of African Art, both of which opened in 1987 and sit underground like inverted pyramids.

When Charles Freer endowed the gallery that bears his name, he insisted on a few conditions: Objects in the collection could not be loaned out, nor could objects from outside the collections be put on display. Because of these restrictions it was necessary to build a second, complementary, ⓭ Oriental art museum. The result was the **Arthur M. Sackler Gallery.** A wealthy medical researcher and publisher who began collecting Asian art as a student, Sackler allowed Smithsonian curators to select 1,000 items from his ample collection and pledged $4 million toward the construction of the museum. The collection includes works from China, the Indian subcontinent, Persia, Thailand, and Indonesia. Articles in the permanent collection include Chinese ritual bronzes, jade ornaments from the third millenium BC, Persian manuscripts, and Indian paintings in gold, silver, lapis lazuli, and malachite. *1050 Independence Ave. SW, tel. 202/ 357–2700, TDD 202/357–1729. Admission free. Open daily 10–5:30; closed Dec. 25.*

The other half of the Smithsonian's underground museum ⓮ complex is the **National Museum of African Art.** Founded in 1964 as a private educational institution, the museum became part of the Smithsonian in 1979. Dedicated to the collection, exhibition, and study of the traditional arts of sub-Saharan Africa, the museum has a permanent collection of more than 6,000 objects representative of hundreds of African cultures. Objects on display include masks, carvings, textiles, and jewelry, all made from materials such as wood, fiber, bronze, ivory, and fired clay. A new permanent exhibit explores the personal objects—chairs, pipes, cups, snuff containers—that were a part of daily life in 19th- and early 20th-century Africa. These items show how aesthetics are integrated with utility to create works of peculiar beauty. Because many pieces of African art are made of organic materials, the museum also runs a conservation laboratory, where curators work to arrest the decay of the valuable collection. *950 Independence Ave. SW, tel. 202/ 357–4600, TDD 202/357–4814. Admission free. Open daily 10–5:30; closed Dec. 25.*

You'll find the nearest Metro station, Smithsonian, on Jefferson Drive in front of the Freer Gallery.

Tour 2: The Monuments

Numbers in the margin correspond to points of interest on the Tour 2: The Monuments map.

Washington is a city of monuments. In the middle of traffic circles, on tiny slivers of park, and at street corners and intersections, statues, plaques, and simple blocks of marble honor the generals, politicians, poets, and statesmen who helped shape the nation. The monuments dedicated to the most famous Americans are west of the Mall on ground reclaimed from the marshy flats of the Potomac. This is also the location of Washington's cherry trees, gifts from Japan and focus of a festival each spring.

On this tour we'll walk clockwise among the monuments and through the cherry trees. This can be a leisurely, half-day walk, depending on the speed you travel and the time you spend at each spot. If it's an extremely hot day you may want to hop a Tourmobile bus and travel between the monuments in air-conditioned comfort.

❶ We'll start in front of the tallest of them all, the **Washington Monument** (nearest Metro stop, Smithsonian). Located at the western end of the Mall, the Washington Monument punctuates the capital like a huge exclamation point. Visible from nearly everywhere in the city, it serves as a landmark for visiting tourists and lost motorists alike.

Congress first authorized a monument to General Washington in 1783. In his 1791 plan for the city, Pierre L'Enfant selected a site (the point where a line drawn west from the Capitol crossed one drawn south from the White House), but it wasn't until 1833, after years of quibbling in Congress, that a private National Monument Society was formed to select a designer and to search for funds. Robert Mills's winning design called for a 600-foot-tall decorated obelisk rising from a circular colonnaded building. The building at the base was to be an American pantheon,

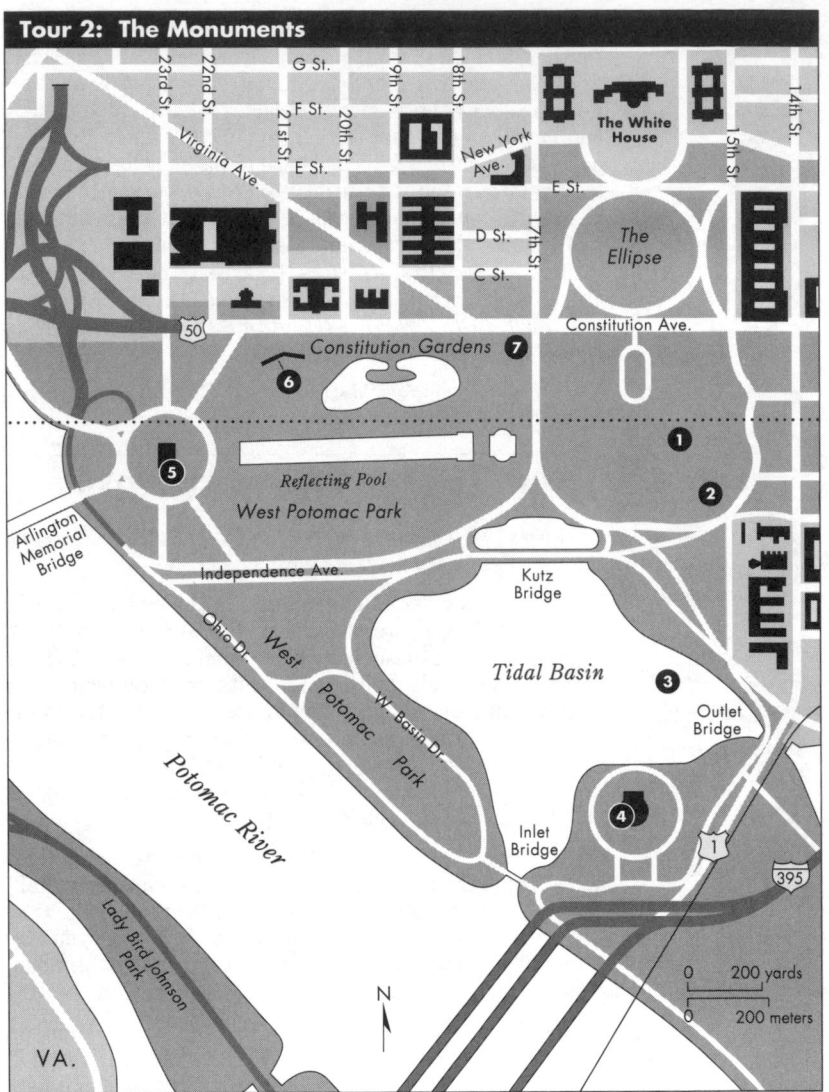

Tour 2: The Monuments

Jefferson Memorial, **4**
Lincoln Memorial, **5**
Lock keeper's house, **7**
Sylvan Theater, **2**
Tidal Basin, **3**

Vietnam Veterans
Memorial and
Constitution
Gardens, **6**
Washington
Monument, **1**

adorned with statues of national heroes and a massive statue of Washington riding in a chariot pulled by snorting horses.

Because of the marshy conditions of L'Enfant's original site, the position of the monument was shifted to firmer ground 100 yards southeast. (If you walk a few steps north of the monument you can see the stone marker that denotes L'Enfant's original axis.) The cornerstone was laid in 1848 with the same Masonic trowel Washington himself had used to lay the Capitol's cornerstone 55 years earlier. The Monument Society continued to raise funds after construction was begun, soliciting subscriptions of one dollar from citizens across America. It also urged states, organizations, and foreign governments to contribute memorial stones for the construction. Problems arose in 1854, when members of the anti-Papist "Know Nothing" party stole a block donated by Pope Pius IX, smashed it, and dumped its shards into the Potomac. This action, a lack of funds, and the onset of the Civil War kept the monument at a fraction of its final height, open at the top, and vulnerable to the rain. A clearly visible ring about a third of the way up the obelisk testifies to this unfortunate stage of the monument's history: Although all of the marble in the obelisk came from the same Maryland quarry, that used for the second phase of construction came from a different stratum and is of a slightly different shade.

In 1876 Congress finally appropriated $200,000 to finish the monument, and the Army Corps of Engineers took over construction, thankfully simplifying Mills's original design. Work was finally completed in December 1884, when the monument was topped with a 7½-pound piece of aluminum, then one of the most expensive metals in the world. Four years later the monument was opened to visitors, who rode to the top in a steam-operated elevator. (Only men were allowed to take the 20-minute ride; it was thought too dangerous for women, who as a result had to walk up the stairs if they wanted to see the view.)

At 555 feet 5 inches, the Washington Monument is the world's tallest masonry structure. The view from the top takes in most of the District and parts of Maryland and Virginia. Visitors are no longer permitted to climb the 898 steps leading to the top. (Incidents of vandalism and a disturbing number of heart attacks on the steps convinced the Park Service that letting people walk up on their own wasn't such a good idea.) Most weekends at 10 and 2 there are walk-down tours, with a volunteer guide describing the monument's construction and showing the 193 stone and metal plaques that adorn the inside. (The tours are sometimes canceled due to lack of staff. Call the day of your visit to confirm.)

There is usually a wait to take the minute-long elevator ride up the monument's shaft. The Park Service rangers standing at the head of the line are good at estimating how long you'll have to wait. Figure on a wait of approximately 10–15 minutes for each side of the monument that is lined with people. If the line goes all the way around the monument, you'll be in line anywhere from 40 minutes to an hour. *Constitution Ave. at 15th St. NW, tel. 202/426–6840. Admission free. Open Apr.–Labor Day, daily 8 AM–midnight; Sept.–Mar., daily 9–5.*

After your ascent and descent, walk on the path that leads south from the monument. On your right you'll pass the ❷ open-air **Sylvan Theater,** scene of a variety of musical performances during the warmer months. Continue south and cross Independence Avenue at 15th Street. Just south of the redbrick **Auditors Building** (the first building constructed by the federal government to print money) is the new **United States Holocaust Memorial Museum** (*see* Tour 1: The Mall, *above*). Beyond that is the colonnaded **Bureau of Engraving and Printing.**

Carefully cross Maine Avenue at the light and walk down to ❸ the **Tidal Basin.** This placid pond was part of the Potomac until 1882, when portions of the river were filled in to improve navigation and create additional parkland, including that upon which the Jefferson Memorial was later built. Paddleboats have been a fixture on the Tidal Basin for years. You can rent one at the boathouse on the east side of the basin, southwest of the Bureau of Engraving. *Northeast bank of Tidal Basin, tel. 202/484–0206. Paddleboat rentals $7 an hour, $1.75 each additional 15 min. Children under 16 must be accompanied by an adult. Open daily 10–6, weather permitting.*

Continue down the path that skirts the Tidal Basin and ❹ cross the Outlet Bridge to get to the **Jefferson Memorial,** the southernmost of the major monuments in the District. Congress decided that Jefferson deserved a monument positioned as prominently as those in honor of Washington and Lincoln, and this spot directly south of the White House seemed ideal. Jefferson had always admired the Pantheon in Rome—the rotundas he designed for the University of Virginia and his own Monticello were inspired by the dome of the Pantheon—so architect John Russell Pope drew from the same source when he designed this memorial to our third president. Dedicated in 1943, it houses a statue of Jefferson. Its walls are lined with inscriptions based on his writings. One of the best views of the White House can be seen from the memorial's top steps, although the view may be obstructed on your visit by the scaffolding that will surround the memorial while it undergoes a three- to five-year renovation. *Tidal Basin, south bank, tel. 202/426–6821. Admission free. Open daily 8 AM–midnight.*

After viewing the Jefferson Memorial, continue along the sidewalk that hugs the Tidal Basin. You'll see two grotesque sculpted heads on the sides of the **Inlet Bridge.** The inside walls of the bridge also sport two other interesting sculptures: bronze, human-headed fish that spout water from their mouths. The bridge was refurbished in the 1980s at the same time the chief of the park—a Mr. Jack Fish—was retiring. Sculptor Constantine Sephralis played a little joke: These fish heads are actually Fish's head.

Once you cross the bridge, you have a choice: You can walk to the left, along the Potomac, or continue along the Tidal Basin to the right. The latter route is somewhat more scenic, especially when the cherry trees are in bloom. The first batch of these trees arrived from Japan in 1909. The trees were infected with insects and fungus, however, and the Department of Agriculture ordered them destroyed. A diplomatic crisis was averted when the United States politely asked the Japanese for another batch, and in 1912 Mrs. William Howard Taft planted the first tree. The second was planted by the wife of the Japanese ambassador. About 200 of the original trees still grow near the Tidal Basin. (The Tidal Basin's cherry trees are the single-flowering Akebeno and Yoshino variety. Double-blossom Fugenzo and Kwanzan trees grow in East Potomac Park and flower about two weeks after their more famous cousins.)

The trees are now the centerpiece of Washington's Cherry Blossom Festival, held each spring. The festivities are kicked off by the lighting of a ceremonial Japanese lantern that rests on the north shore of the Tidal Basin, not far from where the first tree was planted. The once-simple celebration has grown over the years to include concerts, fashion shows, and a parade. Park Service experts try their best to predict exactly when the buds will pop. The trees are usually in bloom for about 10–12 days at the beginning of April. When winter refuses to release its grip, the parade and festival are held anyway, without the presence of blossoms, no matter how inclement the weather. And when the weather complies, and the blossoms are at their peak at the time of the festivities, Washington rejoices.

West Potomac Park, the green expanse to the west of the Tidal Basin, is a pleasant place to sit and rest for a while, to watch the paddleboats skim the surface of the Tidal Basin, and to feed the squirrels that usually approach looking for handouts. The character of West Potomac Park will change over the next few years as the $47.2 million Franklin Delano Roosevelt Memorial is constructed. FDR asked for a simple memorial (in fact, one already sits on a wedge of grass in front of the National Archives) but boosters have for years been pushing for something more grandiose. When it's completed the memorial will comprise a long sequence of walkways and shaded, exterior "rooms" containing sculptures and inscriptions about the 32nd president. To get to our next stop, the Lincoln Memorial, walk northwest along West Basin Drive, then cut across to Ohio Drive. Cross Independence Avenue at the light; the traffic here can be dangerous.

As you walk north along Ohio Drive you'll pass a series of playing fields. Softball has become as competitive a sport as politics in Washington, and the battle to secure a field here or elsewhere in the city starts long before the season. Further along Ohio Drive, directly south of the Lincoln Memorial, is a granite sculpture honoring **John Ericsson,** builder of the ironclad *Monitor,* which took on the Confederate *Merrimac* at Hampton Roads off the coast of Virginia during the Civil War.

A memorial to veterans of the Korean War will soon be erected between Independence Avenue and the Lincoln Memorial, in a grove of trees called Ash Woods. Scheduled to be dedicated on July 27, 1995—the 42th anniversary of the Korean War armistice—**the Korean War Veterans Memorial** will consist of 19 soldiers marching toward an American flag, along with a reflecting pool and a granite wall etched with war scenes.

⑤ The **Lincoln Memorial** is considered by many to be the most inspiring monument in the city. It would be hard to imagine Washington without the Lincoln and Jefferson memorials, though they were both criticized when first built. The Jefferson Memorial was dubbed "Jefferson's muffin"; critics lambasted the design as outdated and too similar to that of the Lincoln Memorial. Some also complained that the Jefferson Memorial blocked the view of the Potomac from the White House. Detractors of the Lincoln Memorial thought it inappropriate that the humble Lincoln be honored with what amounts to a modified but nonetheless rather grandiose Greek temple. The white Colorado-marble memorial was designed by Henry Bacon and completed in 1922. The 36 Doric columns represent the 36 states in the Union at the time of Lincoln's death; the names of the states appear on the frieze above the columns. Above the frieze are the names of the 48 states in the Union when the memorial was dedicated. (Alaska and Hawaii are noted by an inscription on the terrace leading up to the memorial.)

Daniel Chester French's somber statue of the seated president is in the center of the memorial and gazes out over the Reflecting Pool. While French's 19-foot-high sculpture looks as if it were cut from one huge block of stone, it actually comprises 28 interlocking pieces of Georgia marble. (The memorial's original design called for a 10-foot-high sculpture, but experiments with models revealed that a statue that size would be lost in the cavernous space.) Inscribed on the south wall is the Gettysburg Address, and on the north wall is Lincoln's second inaugural address. Above each inscription is a mural painted by Jules Guerin. On the south wall is an angel of truth freeing a slave; the unity of North and South are depicted on the opposite wall. The memorial served as a fitting backdrop for Martin Luther King's "I have a dream" speech in 1963.

Many visitors look only at the front and inside of the Lincoln Memorial, but there is much more to explore. On the lower level to the left is a display that chronicles the memorial's construction. There is also a set of windows that look onto the huge structure's foundation. Stalactites (hanging from above) and stalagmites (growing from below) have formed underneath the marble tribute to Lincoln. Some parts of the Lincoln Memorial may be off-limits when you visit. Like the Jefferson, the Lincoln is shrouded in scaffolding as it undergoes a three- to five-year program to repair the effects of acid rain, insects, jet fuel, and other destructive elements.

Although visiting the area around the Lincoln Memorial during the day allows you to take in an impressive view of the Mall to the east, the best time to see the memorial itself is at night. Spotlights illuminate the outside while inside, light and shadows play across Lincoln's gentle face. *West end of Mall, tel. 202/426–6895. Admission free. Open 24 hrs a day; staffed daily 8 AM–midnight.*

Walk down the steps of the Lincoln Memorial and to the left **6** to get to the **Vietnam Veterans Memorial** and **Constitution Gardens.** Constitution Gardens, the area south of Constitution Avenue between 17th and 23rd streets, was once home to "temporary" buildings erected by the Navy before World War I and not removed until after World War II. Many ideas were proposed to develop the 50-acre site. President Nixon is said to have favored something resembling Copenhagen's Tivoli Gardens. The final design was a little plainer, with paths winding through groves of trees and a tiny island paying tribute to the signers of the Declaration of Independence, their signatures carved into a low stone wall.

The Vietnam Veterans Memorial is another landmark that encourages introspection. The concept came from Jan Scruggs, a former infantry corporal who had served in Vietnam. The stark design by Maya Ying Lin, a 21-year-old Yale architecture student, was selected in a 1981 competition. Upon its completion in 1982, the memorial was decried by some veterans as a "black gash of shame." With the addition of Frederick Hart's statue of three soldiers and a flagpole just south of the wall, most critics were won over.

The wall is one of the most visited sites in Washington, its black granite panels reflecting the sky, the trees, and the faces of those looking for the names of friends or relatives who died in the war. The names of more than 58,000 Americans are etched on the face of the memorial in the order of their deaths. Directories at the entrance and exit to the wall list the names in alphabetical order. (It was recently discovered that because of a clerical error the names of some two dozen living vets are carved into the stone as well.) For help in finding a specific name, ask a ranger at the blue-and-white hut near the entrance. Thousands of offerings are left at the wall each year: letters, flowers, medals, uniforms, snapshots. The National Park Service collects these and stores them in a warehouse in Lanham, Maryland, where they are fast becoming another memorial. Veterans groups often have tents set up near the wall; some provide information on soldiers who remain missing in action, and others are on call to help fellow vets deal with the sometimes powerful emotions that overtake them when visiting the wall for the first time. *Constitution Gardens, 23rd St. and Constitution Ave. NW, tel. 202/634–1568. Admission free. Open 24 hrs a day; staffed 8 AM–midnight.*

After years of debate over its design and necessity, the **Vietnam Women's Memorial**—in honor of the women who served in that conflict—was scheduled to be dedicated on Veterans Day 1993. The monument—two uniformed women caring for a wounded male soldier while a third woman kneels nearby—will sit in Constitution Gardens, southeast of the Vietnam Veterans Memorial.

The FDR, Korean War, and Vietnam Women's memorials—as well as proposed memorials to military women, black patriots, and George Mason—have troubled some Washingtonians. They feel the city is entering an unnecessary monument-building boom in the 1990s. Each veterans' and special-interest group seems to want its own separate memorial and there's concern that too many grandiose designs (each group, of course, wants its to be the biggest) are clogging Washington's monumental core.

Time Out   At the circular **snack bar** just west of the Constitution Gardens lake you can get hot dogs, potato chips, candy bars, soft drinks, and beer at prices lower than those charged by most street vendors.

Walk north to Constitution Avenue and head east. The
➐ stone **lockkeeper's house** at the corner of Constitution Avenue and 17th Street is the only remaining monument to Washington's unsuccessful experiment with a canal. L'Enfant's design called for a canal to be dug from the Tiber—a branch of the Potomac that extended from where the Lincoln Memorial is now—across the city to the Capitol and then south to the Anacostia River. (L'Enfant even envisioned the president's riding in a ceremonial barge from the White House to the Capitol.) The City Canal became more nuisance than convenience, and by the Civil War it was a foul-smelling cesspool that often overran its banks. The stone building at this corner was the home of the canal's lockkeeper until the 1870s, when the waterway was covered over with B Street, which was renamed Constitution Avenue in 1932.

The nearest Metro station is Federal Triangle, five blocks to the east on 12th Street.

Tour 3: The White House Area

Numbers in the margin correspond to points of interest on the Tour 3: The White House Area map.

In a city full of immediately recognizable images, perhaps none is more familiar than the White House. This is where the buck stops and where the nation turns in times of crisis. On this tour we'll visit the White House, then strike out into the surrounding streets to explore the president's neighborhood, which includes some of the oldest houses in the city.

To reach the start of our tour, take the Metro to the Mc-Pherson Square station. We'll begin our exploration in front of 1600 Pennsylvania Avenue. Pierre L'Enfant called it the President's House; it was known formally as the Executive Mansion; and in 1902 Congress officially proclaimed it the **White House,** though, contrary to popular belief, it had been given that nickname even before its white sandstone exterior was painted to cover the fire damage it suffered during the War of 1812. Irishman James Hoban's plan, based on the Georgian design of Leinster Hall near Dublin and of other Irish country homes, was selected in a contest, in 1792. The building wasn't ready for its first occupant until 1800, so George Washington never lived here. Completed in 1829, it has undergone many structural changes since then: Thomas Jefferson, who had entered his own design in the contest under an assumed name, added terraces to the east and west wings. Andrew Jackson installed running water. James Garfield put in the first elevator. Between 1948 and 1952, Harry Truman had the entire structure gutted and restored, adding a second-story porch to the south portico. Each family that has called the White House home has left its imprint on the 132-room mansion. George Bush installed a horseshoe pit. Most recently, Bill Clinton had a customized jogging track put in.

Tuesday through Saturday mornings (except holidays), from 10 AM to noon, selected public rooms on the ground floor and first floor of the White House are open to visitors. Expect a long line, but the wait is worthwhile if you're interested in a firsthand look at what is perhaps the most important building in the city. Most of the year you can simply join the line that forms along East Executive Avenue, between the White House and the Treasury Building. Between Memorial Day and Labor Day, however, you'll need tickets to tour the mansion. During the summer months there is a blue-and-green ticket booth on the **Ellipse** just south of the White House, open between 8 AM and noon, Tuesday through Saturday,

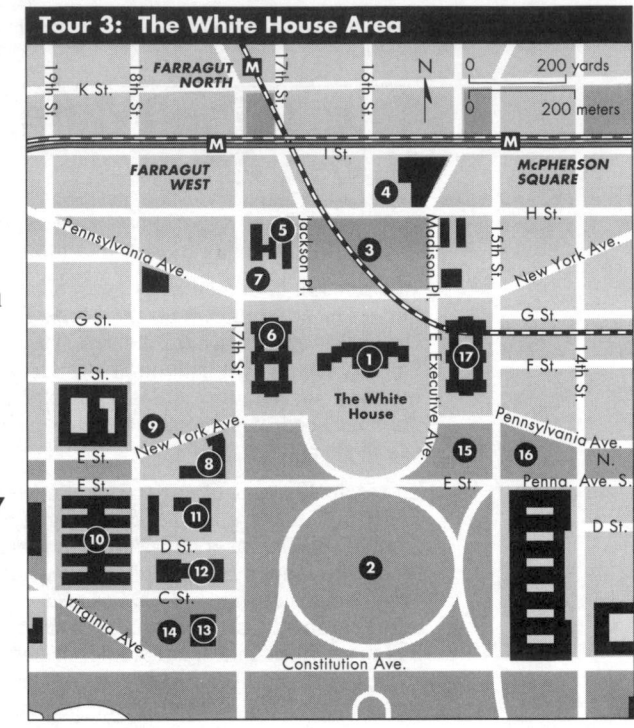

Tour 3: The White House Area

dispensing tickets on a first-come, first-served basis. (Tickets
are often gone by 9 AM.) Your ticket will show the approxi-
mate time of your tour. There is seating on the Ellipse for
those waiting to see the White House. Volunteer marching
bands, drill teams, and other musical groups usually perform
here, entertaining those who are stuck in line. If you write
your representative or senator's office well in advance of your
trip, you can receive special VIP passes for tours between 8
and 10 AM. On selected weekends in April and October, the
White House is open for garden tours. In December it's decorated for the holidays.

The **Ellipse** is bounded by Constitution Avenue, E Street,
15th Street, and 17th Street. From this vantage point you
can see the Washington Monument and the Jefferson Memorial to the south and the red-tile roof of the Department
of Commerce to the east, with the tower of the Old Post Office Building sticking up above it. To the north you have a
good view of the back of the White House; the rounded portico and Harry Truman's second-story porch are clearly
visible. The south lawn of the White House serves as a heli-
port for *Marine One*, the president's helicopter. Each Monday after Easter the south lawn is also the scene of the
White House Easter Egg Roll. The **National Christmas
Tree** grows on the northern edge of the Ellipse. Each year
in mid-December it is lighted by the president during a fes-

tive ceremony that marks the beginning of the holiday season.

You'll enter the White House through the East Wing lobby on the ground floor, walking past the Jacqueline Kennedy Rose Garden. Your first stop is the large white-and-gold **East Room,** the site of presidential news conferences. In 1814 Dolley Madison saved the room's full-length portrait of George Washington from torch-carrying British soldiers by cutting it from its frame, rolling it up, and spiriting it out of the White House. (No fool she, Dolley also rescued her own portrait.) A later occupant, Teddy Roosevelt, allowed his children to ride their pet pony in the East Room.

The Federal-style **Green Room,** named for the moss-green watered silk that covers its walls, is used for informal receptions and "photo opportunities" with foreign heads of state. Notable furnishings in this room include a New England sofa that once belonged to Daniel Webster and portraits of Benjamin Franklin, John Quincy Adams, and Abigail Adams. The president and his guests are often shown on TV sitting in front of the Green Room's English Empire mantel, engaging in what are invariably described as "frank and cordial" discussions.

The elliptical **Blue Room,** the most formal space in the White House, is furnished with a gilded Empire-style settee and chairs that were ordered by James Monroe. (Monroe asked for plain wooden chairs, but the furniture manufacturer thought such unadorned furnishings too simple for the White House and took it upon himself to supply chairs more in keeping with their surroundings.) The White House Christmas tree is placed in this room each year. Another well-known elliptical room, the president's **Oval Office,** is in the semidetached West Wing of the White House, along with other executive offices.

The **Red Room** is decorated as an American Empire–style parlor of the early 19th century, with furniture by the New York cabinetmaker Charles-Honoré Lannuier. You'll recognize the marble mantel as the twin of the mantel in the Green Room.

The **State Dining Room,** second in size only to the East Room, can seat 140 guests. The room is dominated by G.P.A. Healy's portrait of Abraham Lincoln, painted after the president's death. The stone mantel is inscribed with a quotation from one of John Adams's letters: "I pray heaven to bestow the best of blessings on this house and all that shall hereafter inhabit it. May none but honest and wise men ever rule under this roof." In Teddy Roosevelt's day a stuffed moose head hung over the mantel. *1600 Pennsylvania Ave. NW, tel. 202/755–7798, 202/456–7041 (recording), or 202/619–7222 (Park Service). Admission free. Open Tues.–Sat. 10–noon. The White House is occasionally*

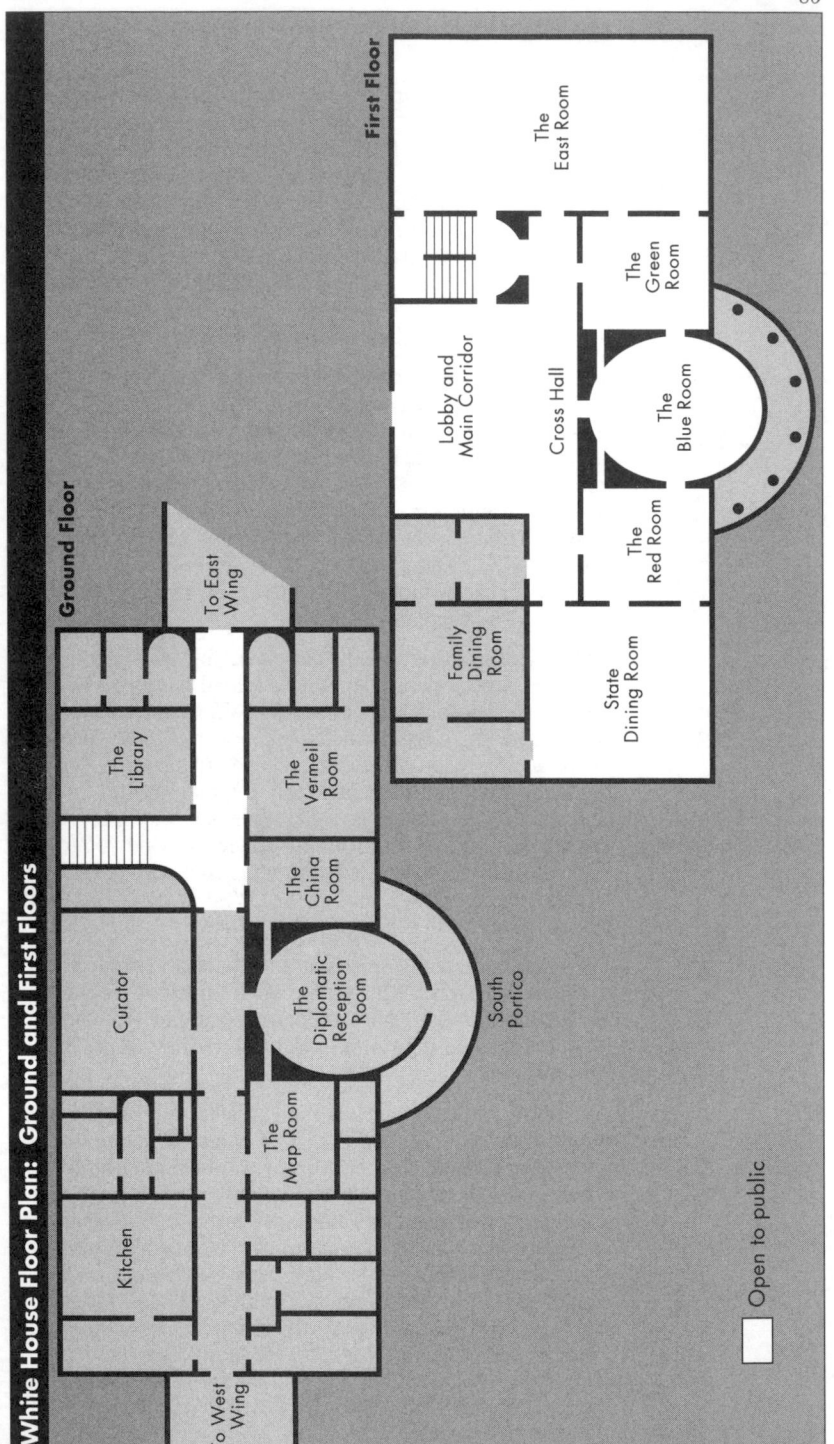

*closed without notice for official functions. Baby strollers
are not allowed on the tour.*

❸ **Lafayette Square,** bordered by Pennsylvania Avenue, Madison Place, H Street, and Jackson Place, is an intimate oasis in the midst of downtown Washington. With such an important resident living across the street, National Capital Park Service gardeners lavish extra attention on the square's trees and flower beds.

When Pierre L'Enfant proposed the location for the Executive Mansion, the only building north of what is today Pennsylvania Avenue was the Pierce family farmhouse, which stood at the northeast corner of what is today Lafayette Square. An apple orchard and a family burial ground were the area's two other main features. During the construction of the White House, workers' huts and a brick kiln were set up, and soon private residences began popping up around the square (though sheep would continue to graze on it for years). L'Enfant's original plan for the city designated this area as part of "President's Park"; in essence it was the president's front yard, just as what is now the Ellipse was once the president's backyard. The egalitarian Thomas Jefferson, concerned that large, landscaped White House grounds would give the wrong impression in a democratic country, ordered that the area be turned into a public park. Soldiers camped in the square during the War of 1812 and the Civil War, turning it at both times into a muddy pit. Today, protesters set their placards up in Lafayette Square, jockeying for positions that face the White House. While the National Park Service can't restrict the protesters' freedom of speech, it does try to restrict the size of their signs.

Standing in the center of the park—and dominating the square—is a large **statue of Andrew Jackson.** Erected in 1853 and cast from bronze cannon that Jackson had captured during the War of 1812, this was the first equestrian statue made in America. (An exact duplicate faces St. Louis Cathedral in New Orleans's Jackson Square.)

Jackson's is the only statue of an American in the park. The other statues are of foreign-born soldiers who helped in America's fight for independence. In the southeast corner is the park's namesake, the **Marquis de Lafayette,** the young French nobleman who came to America to fight in the Revolution. When Lafayette returned to the United States in 1824 he was given a rousing welcome: He was wined and dined in the finest homes and showered with gifts of cash and land.

Head north on **Madison Place.** The colonnaded building across the street at the corner of Pennsylvania Avenue is an annex to the Treasury Department. The modern redbrick building at 717 Madison Place houses a variety of judicial offices. Its design—with the squared-off bay windows—is echoed in the taller building that rises behind it and is mirrored in the **New Executive Office Building** on the other side of Lafayette Square. Planners in the '20s recommended that the private homes on Lafayette Square, many built in the Federal period, be torn down and replaced with a collection of uniform neoclassical-style government buildings. A lack of funds kept the neighborhood intact, and in the early '60s John and Jacqueline Kennedy worked to save the historic town houses.

The next house down, yellow with a second-story ironwork balcony, was built in 1828 by Benjamin Ogle Tayloe. During the McKinley administration, Ohio Senator Marcus Hanna lived here, and the president's frequent visits earned it the nickname the "Little White House." Dolley Madison lived in the next-door Cutts-Madison House after her husband died. Both the Tayloe and Madison houses are now part of the Federal Judicial Center.

Continue down Madison Place. The next statue is that of **Thaddeus Kosciuszko,** the Polish general who fought alongside American colonists against the British. If you head east on H Street for half a block, you'll come to the **United States Government Bookstore** (1510 H St. NW, tel. 202/653–5075), the place to visit if you'd like to buy a few pounds of the millions of tons of paper the government churns out each year. Here is where you'll find a copy of the latest federal budget or *The Surgeon General's Report on Nutrition and Health.*

Time Out Presidential adviser Bernard Baruch used to eat his lunch in Lafayette Park, and you can, too. **Loeb's Restaurant** (around the corner at 15th and I streets NW) is a New York–style deli that serves up salads and sandwiches to eat there or to go.

---

❹ On H Street is the golden-domed **St. John's Episcopal Church,** the so-called "Church of the Presidents." Every president since Madison has visited the church, and many worshiped here on a regular basis. Built in 1816, the church was the second building on the square. Benjamin Latrobe, who worked on both the Capitol and the White House, designed it in the form of a Greek cross, with a flat dome and a lantern cupola. The church has been altered somewhat since then; later additions include the Doric portico and the cupola tower. You can best sense the intent of Latrobe's design while standing inside under the saucer-shaped dome of the original building. Not far from the center of the church is pew 54, where visiting presidents are seated. The kneelers of many of the pews are embroidered with the presidential seal and the names of several chief executives. Brochures are available inside for those who would like to take a self-guided tour. *16th and H Sts. NW, tel. 202/ 347–8766. Admission free. Open Mon.–Sat. 8–4. Tours after 11 AM Sun. service and by appointment.*

Just east of the church is the four-story **St. John's Parish House,** built in 1836 by Matthew St. Clair Clark, clerk of the House of Representatives. The house's most famous resident was Lord Alexander Baring Ashburton, the British Minister who lived here in 1842 while negotiating a dispute over the position of the U.S.-Canadian border. The house later served as the British legation.

Across 16th Street stands the **Hay-Adams Hotel,** one of the most opulent hostelries in the city and a favorite with Washington insiders and visiting celebrities. It takes its name from a double house, owned by Lincoln biographer John Hay and historian Henry Adams, that stood on this spot. Next to it is the **Chamber of Commerce of the United States,** its neoclassical facade typical of the type of building that might have surrounded Lafayette Park had JFK not intervened. The statue at the northwest corner of Lafayette Square is of **Baron von Steuben,** the Prussian general who drilled Colonial troops during the Revolution.

⑤ The redbrick, Federal-style **Decatur House** on the corner of H Street and Jackson Place was the first private residence on President's Park (the White House doesn't really count as *private*). Designed by Benjamin Latrobe, the house was built for naval hero Stephen Decatur and his wife, Susan, in 1819. Decatur had earned the affection of the nation in battles against the British and the Barbary pirates. Planning to start a political career, he used the prize money Congress awarded him for his exploits to build this home near the White House. Tragically, only 14 months after he moved in, Decatur was killed in a duel with James Barron, a disgruntled former Navy officer who held Decatur responsible for his court-martial. Later occupants of the house included Henry Clay, Martin Van Buren, and the Beales, a prominent family from the West whose modifications of the building include a parquet floor showing the state seal of California. The house is now operated by the National Trust. The first floor is furnished as it was in Decatur's time. The second floor is furnished in the Victorian style favored by the Beale family, who owned it until 1956 (thus making Decatur House both the first and *last* private residence on Lafayette Square). The National Trust store around the corner (entrance on H Street) sells a variety of books, postcards, and gifts. *748 Jackson Pl. NW, tel. 202/ 842–0920. Open Tues.–Fri. 10–3, weekends noon–4. Admission: $3 adults, $1.50 senior citizens and students under 12, free to children under 5 and National Trust members. Tours on the hr and ½ hr.*

Head south on **Jackson Place.** Many of the row houses on this stretch date from the pre–Civil War or Victorian periods; even the more modern additions, though—such as those at 718 and 726—are designed in a style that blends with their more historic neighbors. **Count Rochambeau,** aide to General Lafayette, is honored with a statue at the park's southwest corner.

Directly across Pennsylvania Avenue, to the right of the ❻ White House, is the **Old Executive Office Building,** which has gone from being one of the most detested buildings in the city to one of the most beloved. It was built between 1871 and 1888 and originally housed the War, Navy, and State departments. Its architect, Alfred B. Mullett, patterned it after the Louvre, but detractors quickly criticized the busy French Empire design—with its mansard roof, tall chimneys, and 900 freestanding columns—as an inappropriate counterpoint to the Greek Revival Treasury Building that sits on the other side of the White House. Numerous plans to alter the facade foundered due to lack of money. The granite edifice may look like a wedding cake, but its high ceilings and spacious offices make it popular with occupants, who include members of the executive branch. Dan Quayle had his office in here; Albert Gore, Jr., is a little closer to the action, in the West Wing of the White House, just down the hall from the president. The Old Executive Office Building has played host to numerous historic events. It was here that Secretary of State Cordell Hull met with Japanese diplomats after the bombing of Pearl Harbor, and it was here that Oliver North and Fawn Hall shredded Iran-contra documents.

The green canopy at 1651 Pennsylvania Avenue marks the entrance to **Blair House,** the residence used by heads of state visiting Washington. Harry S Truman lived here from 1948 to 1952 while the White House was undergoing its much-needed renovation. A plaque on the fence honors White House policeman Leslie Coffelt, who died in 1950 when Puerto Rican separatists attempted to assassinate President Truman at this site.

Head west on Pennsylvania Avenue. At the end of the block, with the motto "Dedicated to Art" engraved above ❼ the entrance, is the **Renwick Gallery.** The French Second Empire–style building was designed by Smithsonian Castle architect James Renwick in 1859 to house the art collection of Washington merchant and banker William Wilson Corcoran. Corcoran was a Southern sympathizer who spent the duration of the Civil War in Europe. While he was away his unfinished building was pressed into service by the government as a Quartermaster's General post. In 1874 the Corcoran, as it was then called, opened as the first private art museum in the city. Corcoran's collection quickly outgrew the building and in 1897 it was moved to a new gallery a few blocks south on 17th Street (described below). After a stint as the U.S. Court of Claims, this building was restored to its former glory, renamed after its architect, and opened in 1972 as the Smithsonian's museum of American decorative arts. While crafts were once the poor relations of the art world—handwoven rugs and delicately carved tables were considered somehow less "artistic" than, say, oil paintings and sculptures—they have recently come into their own. The Renwick has been at the forefront of the crafts movement and its collection includes exquisitely designed and made utilitarian items, as well as objects created out of such traditional craft media as fiber and glass. Not everything at the museum is Shaker furniture and enamel jewelry, though. The second-floor Grand Salon is still furnished in the opulent Victorian style Corcoran favored when his collection adorned its walls. Paintings are hung in tiers, one above the other, and in Corcoran's portrait the Renwick itself is visible in the background. *Pennsylvania Ave. and 17th St. NW, tel. 202/357-2700, TDD 202/357-1729. Admission free. Open daily 10-5:30; closed Dec. 25.*

Head south on 17th Street. You'll pass the **Winder Building** (604 17th St.), erected in 1848 as one of the first office blocks in the capital and used during the Civil War as the headquarters of the Union Army. Down another block on the right, at the corner of 17th Street and New York Avenue, is the **Corcoran Gallery of Art,** one of the few large museums in Washington outside the Smithsonian family. The Beaux Arts–style building, its copper roof green with age, was designed by Ernest Flagg and completed in 1897. The gallery's permanent collection numbers more than 11,000 works, including paintings by the first great American portraitists John Copley, Gilbert Stuart, and Rembrandt Peale. The Hudson River School is represented by such works as *Mount Corcoran* by Albert Bierstadt and Frederic Church's *Niagara*. There are also portraits by John Singer Sargent, Thomas Eakins, and Mary Cassatt. European artwork is included in the Walker Collection (late-19th- and early 20th-century paintings, including works by Gustave Courbet, Monet, Pissarro, and Renoir) and the Clark Collection (Dutch, Flemish, and French Romantic paintings, and the restored entire 18th-century Grand Salon of the Hotel d'Orsay in Paris). Be sure to see Samuel Morse's *Old House of Representatives* and Hiram Powers's *Greek Slave*, which scandalized Victorian society. (The latter, a statue of a nude woman with her wrists chained, was considered so shocking by Victorian audiences that separate viewing hours were established for men and women, and children under 16 were not allowed to see it at all.) Photography and works by contemporary American artists are also among the Corcoran's strengths. The adjacent Corcoran School is the only four-year art college in the Washington area. *17th St. and New York Ave. NW, tel. 202/638-1439 (recording), 202/638-3211. Suggested donation: $3 adults, $1 students and senior citizens, $5 for family groups. Open Mon., Wed., and Fri.–Sun. 10–5, Thurs. 10–9. Closed Tues., Dec. 25, Jan. 1. Tours of the permanent collection are offered daily (except Tues.) at 12:30, Thurs. at 7:30 PM.*

Time Out **The Cafe at the Corcoran** has a lunch menu that includes a selection of salads, light entrées, desserts, and a refreshing assortment of fruit and vegetable shakes. The café also serves a Continental breakfast, an English tea complete with scones and clotted cream, and dinner on Thursday, when the museum is open late.

⑨ A block up New York Avenue, at the corner of 18th Street, is the **Octagon House,** completed in 1801 for John Tayloe III, a wealthy Virginia plantation owner. Designed by William Thornton, the Octagon House actually has only six sides, not eight. Thornton chose the unusual shape to conform to the acute angle formed by L'Enfant's intersection of New York Avenue and 18th Street.

After the White House was burned in 1814 the Tayloes invited James and Dolley Madison to stay in the Octagon House. It was in a second-floor study that the Treaty of Ghent, ending the War of 1812, was signed. By the late 1800s the building was used as a rooming house. In this century the house served as the headquarters of the American Institute of Architects before the construction of AIA's rather unexceptional building behind it.

The Octagon's first restoration, in the 1960s, revealed intricate plaster molding and the original 1799 Coade stone mantels (made using a now-lost method of casting crushed stone). It is currently in the midst of a far more thorough, $4 million restoration that will return it to its 1815 appearance. The exterior work is finished, topped off by a new, and historically accurate, cypress-shingle roof, complete with parapet. Work continues inside, though the second-floor galleries—home to changing exhibits on architecture, city planning, and Washington history—are open to the public. *1799 New York Ave. NW, tel. 202/638–3105, TDD 202/638–1538. Suggested donation: $2 adults, $1 senior citizens and students, 50 cents children. Open Tues.–Fri. 10–4, weekends noon–4; closed Christmas and New Year's Day.*

⑩ A block south on 18th Street is the **Department of the Interior** building, designed by Waddy B. Wood. At the time of its construction in 1937 it was the most modern government building in the city and the first with escalators and central air-conditioning. The outside of the building is somewhat plain, but much of the interior is decorated with paintings that reflect the Interior Department's work. Hallways feature heroic oil paintings of dam construction, panning for gold, and cattle drives. You'll pass some of these if you visit the **Department of the Interior Museum** on the first floor. (You can enter the building at its E Street or C Street doors; adults must show photo ID.) Soon after it opened in 1938, the museum became one of the most popular attractions in Washington; evening hours were maintained even during the Second World War. The small museum tells the story of

the Department of the Interior, a huge agency dubbed the
"Mother of Departments" because from it grew the Departments of Agriculture, Labor, Education, and Energy. Today Interior oversees most of the country's federally owned
land and natural resources, and exhibits in the museum outline the work done by the Bureau of Land Management, the
U.S. Geological Survey, the Bureau of Indian Affairs, the
National Park Service, and other Interior branches. The
museum retains much of its New Deal–era flavor—including meticulously created dioramas depicting various historical events and American locales—and is, depending on
your tastes, either quaint or outdated. Still, it's a nice contrast to the high-tech video museums of today. It is in the
process of getting a facelift that promises to modernize it.
The Indian Craft Shop across the hall from the museum
sells Native American pottery, dolls, carvings, jewelry,
baskets, and books. It, too, has been part of the Department of the Interior since 1938. *C and E Sts. between 18th
and 19th Sts. NW, tel. 202/208–4743. Admission free. Open
weekdays 8–5; closed federal holidays. Call at least 2 wks
ahead for a tour of the building's architecture and murals.*

Back on 17th Street (walk east on E Street) are the three
⓫ buildings that house the headquarters of the **American Red
Cross.** The main building, a neoclassical structure of blind-
ing white marble built in 1917, commemorates the service
and devotion of the women who cared for the wounded on
both sides during the Civil War. The building's Georgian-
style board of governors hall features three stained-glass
windows designed by Louis Tiffany. *430 17th St. NW, tel.
202/737–8300. Admission free. Open weekdays 8:30–4.*

⓬ A block south is **Memorial Continental Hall,** headquarters
of the Daughters of the American Revolution. This beaux
arts building was the site each year of the DAR's congress
until the larger Constitution Hall was built around the corner. An entrance on D Street leads to the **DAR Museum.** Its
50,000-item collection includes fine examples of Colonial
and Federal silver, china, porcelain, stoneware, earthen-
ware, and glass. Thirty-three period rooms are decorated
in styles representative of various U.S. states, ranging
from an 1850 California adobe parlor to a New Hampshire
attic filled with toys from the 18th and 19th centuries. *1776
D St. NW, tel. 202/879–3240. Admission free. Open weekdays 8:30–4, Sun. 1–5. Docents available for tours weekdays 10:30–2:30.*

Just across C Street to the south of Continental Hall is the
⓭ House of the Americas, the headquarters building of the Organization of American States. The interior of this building
features a cool patio adorned with a pre-Columbian–style
fountain and lush tropical plants. This tiny rain forest is a
good place to rest when Washington's summer heat is at its
most oppressive. The upstairs Hall of Flags and Heroes
contains, as the name implies, busts of generals and states-

men from the various OAS member countries as well as each country's flag. *17th St. and Constitution Ave. NW, tel. 202/458–3000. Admission free. Open weekdays 9–5:30.*

⓮ Behind the House of the Americas is the **Art Museum of the Americas,** with its entrance on 18th Street. The small gallery is in a building that formerly served as the residence for the secretary general of the OAS. It hosts changing exhibits highlighting 20th-century Latin American artists. *201 18th St. NW, tel. 202/458–6016. Admission free. Open Tues.–Sat. 10–5.*

Next, head east on Constitution Avenue and take the first left, following the curving drive that encircles the Ellipse. The rather weather-beaten **gate house** at the corner of Constitution Avenue and 17th Street once stood on Capitol Hill. It was designed in 1828 by Charles Bulfinch, the first native-born American to serve as architect of the Capitol, and was moved here in 1874 after the Capitol grounds were redesigned by Frederick Law Olmsted. A twin of the gate house stands at Constitution Avenue and 15th Street.

Across E Street to the northeast of the Ellipse, in a small park bounded by E Street, 15th Street, East Executive Avenue, and Alexander Hamilton Place, stands the massive
⓯ **William Tecumseh Sherman Monument.** Just north of this memorial is the southern facade of the Treasury Building, its entrance guarded by a **statue of Alexander Hamilton,** the department's first secretary.

⓰ Across 15th Street to the east is **Pershing Park,** a quiet, sunken garden that honors General "Blackjack" Pershing, commander of the American expeditionary force in World War I. Engravings on the stone walls recount pivotal campaigns from that war. Ice skaters glide on the square pool in the winter.

One block to the north is the venerable **Hotel Washington** (515 15th St., tel. 202/638–5900). Its lobby is narrow and unassuming, but the view from the rooftop Sky Top Lounge—open May to October—is one of the best in the city.

⓱ To your left is the long side of the **Treasury Building,** the largest Greek Revival edifice in Washington. Pierre L'Enfant had intended for Pennsylvania Avenue to stretch in a straight, unbroken line from the White House to the Capitol. This plan was ruined by the construction of the Treasury Building on this site just east of the White House. Robert Mills, the architect responsible for the Washington Monument and the Patent Office (now the National Museum of American Art), designed the grand colonnade that stretches down 15th Street. Construction of the Treasury Building started in 1836 and, after several additions, was finally completed in 1869. Guided 90-minute tours are given every Saturday, except holiday weekends, and take visitors past the Andrew Johnson suite, used by Johnson as the executive office while Mrs. Lincoln moved out of the White House; the two-story marble Cash Room; and a 19th-century burglarproof vault lining that saw duty when the Treasury once stored currency. *15th St. between Pennsylvania and New York Aves. NW, tel. 202/622–0896, TDD 202/622–0692. Admission free. Register at least a week ahead for the tour; visitors must provide name, date of birth, and Social Security number, and show photo ID at the start of the tour.*

Time Out A glittering urban mall, **The Shops** (in the National Press Building, F and G Sts. between 13th and 14th Sts. NW) is home to table-service restaurants such as the **American Cafe** and the **Boston Seafood Company,** as well as faster and cheaper fare in its top-floor Food Hall.

Continue up 15th Street. The luxurious **Old Ebbitt Grill** (675 15th St. NW, tel. 202/347–4800) is a popular watering spot for journalists and television news correspondents.

The corner of 15th Street and Pennsylvania Avenue has been dubbed Washington's Wall Street. Adjacent to the imposing Treasury are brokerage firms and buildings belonging to Riggs Bank and Crestar Bank. The location is especially fitting for banks, since this stretch of 15th Street is pictured on the back of every $10 bill. (And if you're wondering what that car is that drives past the Treasury Building on the back of every sawbuck, it's a 1926 Hupmobile.)

The Metro stations nearest to the end of this tour are McPherson Square, at 15th and I streets, and Metro Center, three blocks east on G Street.

Tour 4: Capitol Hill

Numbers in the margin correspond to points of interest on the Tour 4: Capitol Hill map.

The people who live and work on "the Hill" do so in the shadow of the edifice that lends the neighborhood its name: the gleaming white Capitol building. More than just the center of government, however, the Hill also includes charming residential blocks lined with Victorian row houses and a fine assortment of restaurants, bars, and shops. Capitol Hill's boundaries are disputed: It's bordered to the west, north, and south by the Capitol, Union Station, and I Street, respectively. Some argue that Capitol Hill extends east to the Anacostia River, others that it ends at 11th Street near Lincoln Park. The neighborhood does in fact seem to grow as members of Capitol Hill's active historic-preservation movement restore more and more 19th-century houses.

Start your exploration of the Hill inside the cavernous main ➊ hall of **Union Station,** which sits on Massachusetts Avenue north of the Capitol. In 1902 the McMillan Commission—

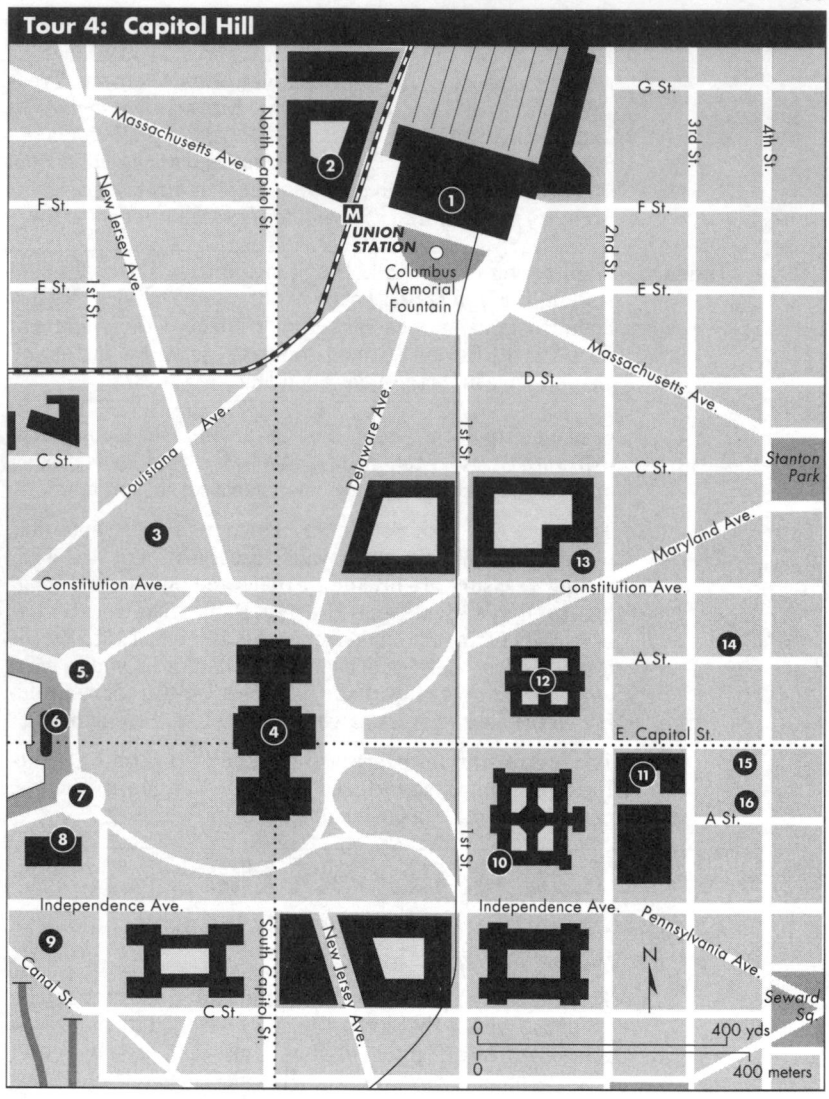

Tour 4: Capitol Hill

Bartholdi Fountain, **9**
Capitol, **4**
Folger Shakespeare
Library, **11**
Frederick Douglass
Townhouse, **14**
Grant Memorial, **6**
James Garfield
Memorial, **7**

Library of
Congress/Jefferson
Building, **10**
National Postal
Museum, **2**
Peace Monument, **5**
Robert A. Taft
Memorial, **3**
Sewall-Belmont
House, **13**

South side of East
Capitol Street, **15**
Supreme Court
Building, **12**
326 A Street, **16**
Union Station, **1**
United States Botanic
Gardens, **8**

charged with suggesting ways to improve the appearance of the city—recommended that the many train lines that sliced through the capital share one main depot. Union Station was opened in 1908 and was the first building completed under the commission's plan. Chicago architect and commission member Daniel H. Burnham patterned the station after the Roman Baths of Diocletian.

For many visitors to Washington, the capital city is first seen framed through the grand station's arched doorways. In its heyday, during World War II, more than 200,000 people swarmed through the station daily. By the '60s, however, the decline in train travel had turned the station into an expensive white-marble elephant. It was briefly, and unsuccessfully, transformed into a visitors center for the Bicentennial; but by 1981 rain was pouring in through the neglected station's roof, and passengers boarded trains at a ramshackle depot behind the station.

The Union Station you see today is the result of a restoration completed in 1988, an effort intended to be the beginning of a revival of Washington's east end. It's hoped the shops, restaurants, and nine-screen movie theater in Union Station will draw more than just train travelers to the beaux arts building. The jewel of the structure remains its meticulously restored main waiting room. With its 96-foot-high coffered ceiling gilded with eight pounds of gold leaf, it is one of the city's great spaces and is used for inaugural balls and other festive events. Forty-six statues of Roman legionnaires, one for each state in the Union when the station was completed, ring the grand room. The statues were the subject of controversy when the building was first opened. Pennsylvania Railroad president Alexander Cassatt (brother of artist Mary) ordered sculptor Louis Saint-Gaudens to alter the statues, convinced that the legionnaires' skimpy outfits would scandalize female passengers. The sculptor obligingly added a shield to each figure, obscuring any offending body parts.

The east hall, now filled with vendors, was once an expensive restaurant. It is decorated with Pompeian tracery and plaster walls and columns painted to look like marble. At one time the station also featured a secure presidential waiting room, now restored. The private waiting room was by no means a frivolous addition: Twenty years before Union Station was built, President Garfield was assassinated in the public waiting room of the old Baltimore and Potomac terminal on 6th Street. Group tours of Union Station are available by appointment (tel. 202/289–1908).

Time Out On Union Station's lower level you'll find more than 20 food stalls, offering everything from pizza to sushi. On the main level are Capitol Hill favorite the **American Cafe,** the trendy Italian restaurant **Sfuzzi,** and **America,** which offers a menu as expansive as its name: everything from Albu-

querque blue corn enchiladas to New York Reuben sandwiches.

As you walk out Union Station's front doors, glance to the
right. At the end of a long succession of archways is the
Washington **City Post Office,** also designed by Daniel
Burnham and completed in 1914. Nostalgic odes to the noble mail carrier are inscribed on the exterior of the marble
building; one of them characterizes mail carriers as the
"Messenger of sympathy and love, servant of parted
friends, consoler of the lonely, bond of the scattered family,
enlarger of the common life." After extensive renovation,
② the building reopened in 1993 as the **National Postal Museum,** the newest member of the Smithsonian family. Exhibits underscore the important part the mail played in the
development of America and include horse-drawn mail
coaches, railway mail cars, actual airmail planes, every
U.S. stamp issued, many foreign stamps, and a collection of
philatelic rarities. The National Museum of Natural History may have the Hope Diamond, but the National Postal
Museum has in its collection the container used to mail the
priceless gem to the Smithsonian. *2 Massachusetts Ave.
NE, tel. 202/357–2700. Admission free. Open daily 10–
5:30; closed Dec. 25.*

Return to Union Station and walk to the plaza in front. At
the center of the plaza is the **Columbus Memorial Fountain,**
designed by Lorado Taft. A caped, steely-eyed Christopher Columbus stares into the distance, flanked by a hoary,
bearded figure (the Old World) and an Indian brave (the
New).

Head south from the fountain, away from Union Station,
cross Massachusetts Avenue, and walk down Delaware Avenue. On the left you'll pass the **Russell Senate Office Building.** Note the delicate treatment below the second-story
windows that resembles twisted lengths of fringed cloth.
Completed in 1909, this was the first of the Senate office
buildings. Beyond it are the Dirksen and Hart office buildings. To the right, sticking up above the trees, is a **memorial**
③ **to Robert A. Taft,** son of the 27th president and longtime
Republican senator. The monolithic carillon is rather unat-
tractive, resembling nothing so much as a huge room de-
odorizer.

④ Cross Constitution Avenue and enter the **Capitol** grounds,
landscaped in the late-19th century by Frederick Law Olmsted, Sr., who, along with Calvert Vaux, created New York
City's Central Park. On these 68 acres you will find both the
tamest squirrels in the city and the highest concentration of
television news correspondents, jockeying for a good position in front of the Capitol for their "stand-ups." A few hundred feet northeast of the Capitol are two cast-iron car
shelters, left over from the days when horse-drawn trolleys

Ceremonial Office of the Vice President, **3**

Congresswomen's Suite, **13**

Democratic Cloakrooms, **6**

East Front, **12**

House Chamber, **17**

House Document Room, **14**

House Reception Room, **16**

Marble Room (Senators' Retiring Room), **2**

Old Senate Chamber, **9**

Prayer Room, **11**

President's Room, **1**

Representatives' Retiring Rooms, **18**

Republican Cloakrooms, **7**

Rotunda, **10**

Senate Chamber, **5**

Senators' Conference Room, **8**

Senators' Reception Room, **4**

Statuary Hall, **15**

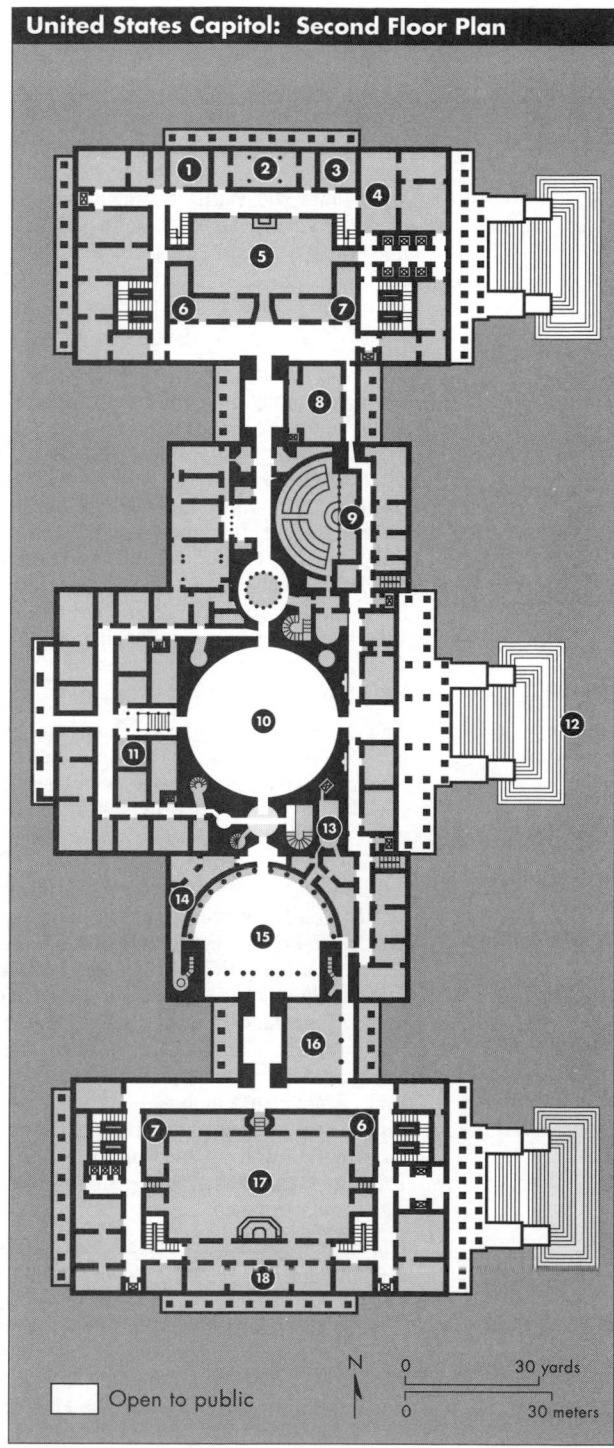

United States Capitol: Second Floor Plan

Open to public

N

0   30 yards

0   30 meters

served the Hill. Olmsted's six pinkish, bronze-topped lamps directly east from the Capitol are a treat, too.

When planning the city, Pierre L'Enfant described the gentle rise on which the Capitol sits, known then as Jenkins Hill, as "a pedestal waiting for a monument." The design of this monument was the result of a competition held in 1792; the winner was William Thornton, a physician and amateur architect from the West Indies. With its central rotunda and dome, Thornton's Capitol is reminiscent of Rome's Pantheon, a similarity that must have delighted the nation's founders, who felt the American government was based on the principles of the Republic of Rome.

The cornerstone was laid by George Washington in a Masonic ceremony on September 18, 1793, and in November 1800, both the Senate and the House of Representatives moved down from Philadelphia to occupy the first completed section of the Capitol: the boxlike portion between the central rotunda and today's north wing. (Subsequent efforts to find the cornerstone Washington laid have been unsuccessful, though when the east front was extended in the 1950s, workmen found a knee joint thought to be from a 500-pound ox that was roasted at the 1793 celebration.) By 1806 the House wing had been completed, just to the south of what is now the domed center, and a covered wooden walkway joined the two wings.

The Congress House grew slowly and suffered a grave setback on August 24, 1814, when British troops led by Sir George Cockburn marched on Washington and set fire to the Capitol, the White House, and numerous other government buildings. (Cockburn reportedly stood on the House Speaker's chair and asked his men, "Shall this harbor of Yankee democracy be burned?" The question was rhetorical; the building was torched.) The wooden walkway was destroyed and the two wings gutted, but the walls were left standing after a violent rainstorm doused the flames. Fearful that Congress might leave Washington, residents raised money for a hastily built "Brick Capitol" that stood where the Supreme Court is today. Architect Benjamin Henry Latrobe supervised the rebuilding of the Capitol, adding such American touches as the corn-cob-and-tobacco-leaf capitals to columns in the east entrance to the Senate wing. He was followed by Boston-born Charles Bulfinch, and in 1826 the Capitol, its low wooden dome sheathed in copper, was finally finished.

North and south wings were added in the 1850s and '60s to accommodate a growing government trying to keep pace with a growing country. The elongated edifice extended farther north and south than Thornton had planned, and in 1855, to keep the scale correct, work began on a tall cast-iron dome. President Lincoln was criticized for continuing this expensive project while the country was in the throes of the bloody Civil War, but he called the construction "a sign we intend the Union shall go on." This twin-shelled dome, a marvel of 19th-century engineering, rises 285 feet above the ground and weighs 9 million pounds. It expands and contracts up to 4 inches a day, depending on the outside temperature. The figure on top of the dome, often mistaken for Pocahontas, is called *Freedom*. Sculptor Thomas Crawford had first planned for the 19-foot-tall bronze statue to wear the cloth liberty cap of a freed Roman slave, but southern lawmakers, led by Jefferson Davis, objected. An "American" headdress composed of a star-encircled helmet surmounted with an eagle's head and feathers was substituted. After being plucked from the dome by helicopter, *Freedom* received a much needed sprucing up in 1993.

The Capitol has continued to grow. In 1962 the east front was extended 34 feet, creating 100 additional offices. Preservationists have fought to keep the west front from being extended, since it is the last remaining section of the Capitol's original facade. A compromise was reached in 1983, when it was agreed that the facade's crumbling sandstone blocks would simply be replaced with stronger limestone.

Guided tours of the Capitol usually start beneath the dome in the Rotunda, but if there's a crowd you may have to wait in a line that forms at the top of the center steps on the east side. If you want to forgo the tour, which is brief but informative, you may look around on your own. Enter through one of the lower doors to the right or left of the main steps. Start your exploration under Constantino Brumidi's *Apotheosis of Washington*, the fresco in the center of the dome. Working as Michelangelo did in the Sistine Chapel, applying paint to wet plaster, Brumidi completed this fresco in 1865. The figures in the inner circle represent the 13 original states of the Union; those in the outer ring symbolize arts, sciences, and industry. The flat, sculpture-style frieze around the rim of the Rotunda depicting 400 years of American history was started by Brumidi. While painting Penn's treaty with the Indians, the 74-year-old artist slipped on the 58-foot-high scaffold and almost fell off. Brumidi managed to hang on until help arrived, but he died a few months later from shock brought on by the incident. The work was continued by another Italian, Filippo Costaggini, but the frieze wasn't finished until American Allyn Cox added the final touches in 1953.

Notice the Rotunda's eight immense oil paintings of scenes from American history. The four scenes from the Revolutionary War are by John Trumbull, who served alongside George Washington and painted the first president from life. Twenty-six people have lain in state in the Rotunda, including nine presidents, from Abraham Lincoln to Lyndon Baines Johnson. Underneath the Rotunda, above an empty crypt that was designed to hold the remains of George and Martha Washington, is an exhibit chronicling the construction of the Capitol.

South of the Rotunda is Statuary Hall, once the legislative chamber of the House of Representatives. The room has an interesting architectural feature that maddened early legislators: A slight whisper uttered on one side of the hall can be heard on the other. (Don't be disappointed if this parlor trick doesn't work when you're visiting the Capitol; sometimes the hall is just too noisy.) When the House moved out, Congress invited each state to send statues of two great deceased citizens for placement in the former chamber. Because the weight of the accumulated statues threatened to cave the floor in, some of the sculptures were dispersed to various other spots throughout the Capitol.

To the north, on the Senate side, you can visit the chamber once used by the Supreme Court as well as the splendid Old Senate Chamber, both of which have been restored. Also be sure to see the Brumidi Corridor on the ground floor of the Senate wing. Frescoes and oil paintings of birds, plants, and American inventions adorn the walls and ceilings, and an intricate, Brumidi-designed bronze stairway leads to the second floor. The Italian artist also memorialized several American heroes, painting them inside trompe l'oeil frames. Trusting that America would continue to produce heroes long after he was gone, Brumidi left some frames empty. The most recent one to be filled, in 1987, honors the crew of the space shuttle *Challenger*.

If you want to watch some of the legislative action in the **House** or **Senate chambers** while you're on the Hill you'll have to get a gallery pass from the office of your representative or senator. (To find out where those offices are, ask any Capitol police officer, or dial 202/224–3121.) In the chambers you'll notice that Democrats sit to the right of the presiding officer, Republicans to the left—the opposite, it's often noted, of their political leanings. You may be disappointed by watching from the gallery. Most of the day-to-day business is conducted in the various legislative committees, many of which meet in the congressional office buildings. The *Washington Post*'s daily "Today in Congress" lists when and where the committees are meeting. To get to a house or Senate office building, go to the Capitol's basement and ride the miniature subway used by legislators. *East end of the Mall, tel. 202/224–3121. For guide service, tel. 202/225–6827. Admission free. Open daily 9–4:30; summer hrs determined annually.*

Time Out   A meal at a **Capitol cafeteria** may give you a glimpse of a well-known politician or two. A public dining room on the first floor, Senate-side, is open 7:30 AM–3:30 PM (reserved for staff only 11:30–1). A favorite with legislators is the Senate bean soup, made and served every day since 1901 (no one is sure exactly why, though the menu, which you can take with you, outlines a few popular theories).

When you're finished exploring the inside of the Capitol, make your way to the west side. In 1981, Ronald Reagan broke with tradition and moved the presidential swearing-in ceremony to this side of the Capitol, which offers a dramatic view of the Mall and monuments below and can accommodate more guests than the east side, where all previous presidents took the oath of office. Walk down the northernmost flight of steps and follow the red-and-black path that leads to Pennsylvania Avenue. The white-marble memorial in the center of the traffic circle in front of you is

⑤ the **Peace Monument,** which depicts America, grief-stricken over sailors lost at sea, weeping on the shoulder of History. Cross First Street carefully and walk to the left along the **Capitol Reflecting Pool.** As you continue south you'll

⑥ pass the **Grant Memorial.** At a length of 252 feet, it's the largest sculpture group in the city. The statue of Ulysses S. Grant on horseback is flanked by Union artillery and cavalry. Further south, in the intersection of First Street and

⑦ Maryland Avenue SW, is the **James Garfield Memorial.** The 20th president of the United States, Garfield was assassinated in 1881 after only a few months in office.

⑧ Across Maryland Avenue is the **United States Botanic Gardens,** a peaceful, plant-filled oasis between Capitol Hill and the Mall. The conservatory includes a cactus house, a fern house, and a subtropical house filled with orchids. Seasonal displays include blooming plants at Easter, chrysanthemums in the fall, and Christmas greens and poinsettias in December and January. Brochures just inside the doorway offer helpful gardening tips. *1st St. and Maryland Ave. SW, tel. 202/225–8333. Admission free. Open May–July, daily 9–8; Aug.–Apr., daily 9–5.*

When you exit the Botanic Gardens, walk away from the Capitol, take the first left along the pebbled sidewalk, and cross Independence Avenue. To the right is the **Hubert H. Humphrey Building,** home of the Department of Health and Human Services. The beige building gets a much-needed splash of color from *Shorepoints I,* the red abstract sculpture by James Rosati that sits in front of it.

Walk east on Independence Avenue. On the right, in a park

⑨ that is part of the Botanic Garden, you'll pass the **Bartholdi Fountain.** Frédéric-Auguste Bartholdi, sculptor of the more famous—and much larger—Statue of Liberty, created this delightful fountain for the Philadelphia Centennial Exhibition of 1876. With its aquatic monsters, sea nymphs, tritons, and lighted globes (once gas, now electric), the fountain represents the elements of water and light. The U.S. government purchased the fountain after the exhibition and placed it on the grounds of the old Botanic Garden on the Mall. It was moved to its present location in 1932.

Cross 1st Street SW and continue east on Independence Avenue past the **Rayburn, Longworth,** and **Cannon House**

office buildings. At Independence Avenue and 1st Street SE is the green-domed **Jefferson Building** of the **Library of Congress.** Like many buildings in Washington that seem a bit overwrought (the Old Executive Office Building is another example), the library was criticized when it was completed, in 1897. Some detractors felt its Italian Renaissance design was a bit too florid. Congressmen were even heard to grumble that its dome—topped with the gilt "Flame of Knowledge"—competed with that of their Capitol. It is certainly decorative, with busts of Dante, Goethe, Hawthorne, and other great writers perched above its entryway. *The Court of Neptune,* Roland Hinton Perry's fountain at the base of the front steps, rivals some of Rome's best fountains.

Provisions for a library to serve members of Congress were originally made in 1800, when the government set aside $5,000 to purchase and house books that legislators might need to consult. This small collection was housed in the Capitol but was destroyed in 1814, when the British burned the city. Thomas Jefferson, then in retirement at Monticello, offered his personal library as a replacement, noting that "there is, in fact, no subject to which a Member of Congress may not have occasion to refer." Jefferson's collection of 6,487 books, for which Congress eventually paid him $23,950, laid the foundation for the great national library. (Sadly, another fire in 1851 wiped out two-thirds of Jefferson's books.) By the late 1800s it was clear the Capitol building could no longer contain the growing library, and the Jefferson Building was constructed. The **Adams Building,** on 2nd Street behind the Jefferson, was added in 1939. A third structure, the **James Madison Building,** opened in 1980; it is just south of the Jefferson Building, between Independence Avenue and C Street.

The **Library of Congress** today holds some 90 million items, of which 30 million are books. Also part of the library is the Congressional Research Service, which, as the name implies, works on special projects for senators and representatives.

The Jefferson and Adams buildings are nearing the end of an extensive renovation and some parts may be closed on your visit. The gem of the Jefferson Building is the richly decorated Great Hall, adorned with mosaics, paintings, and curving marble stairways. The grand, octagonal Main Reading Room, its central desk surrounded by mahogany readers' tables, is either inspiring or overwhelming to researchers. Computer terminals have replaced the wooden card catalogues, but books are still retrieved and dispersed the same way: Readers (18 years or older) hand request slips to librarians and wait patiently for their materials to be delivered. Researchers aren't allowed in the stacks and only members of Congress can check books out.

But books are only part of the story. Family trees are explored in the Local History and Genealogy Reading Room. In the Folklife Reading Room, patrons can listen to LP recordings of American Indian music or hear the story of B'rer Rabbit read in the Gullah dialect of Georgia and South Carolina. Items from the library's collection—which includes a Gutenberg Bible—are often on display in the Jefferson and Madison buildings. Classic films are shown for free in the 64-seat Mary Pickford Theater (tel. 202/707–5677 for information). *Jefferson Bldg., 1st St. and Independence Ave. SE, tel. 202/707–8000. Admission free. Most reading rooms open Mon., Wed., and Thurs. 8:30–9:30, Tues., Fri., and Sat. 8:30–5, Sun. 1–5. Tel. 202/707–6400 for special hours. Tours leave weekdays at 10, 1, and 3 from the Madison Bldg., Independence Ave. between 1st and 2nd Sts. SE; groups of 10 or more should call ahead for reservations.*

⑪ Behind the Jefferson Building stands the **Folger Shakespeare Library.** The Folger Library's collection of works by and about Shakespeare and his times is second to none. The white-marble art deco building, designed by architect Paul Philippe Cret, is decorated with scenes from the Bard's plays. Inside is a reproduction of an inn-yard theater, which is the setting for performances of chamber music, baroque opera, and other events appropriate to the surroundings, and a gallery, designed in the manner of an Elizabethan Great Hall, which hosts rotating exhibits from the library's collection. *201 E. Capitol St. SE, tel. 202/544–4600. Admission free. Open Mon.–Sat. 10–4.*

Walk back down East Capitol Street and turn right onto 1st
⑫ Street. The stolid **Supreme Court Building** faces 1st Street here. The justices arrived in Washington in 1800 along with the rest of the government but were for years shunted around various rooms in the Capitol; for a while they even met in a tavern. It wasn't until 1935 that the court got its own building, this white-marble temple with twin rows of Corinthian columns, designed by Cass Gilbert. William Howard Taft, the only man to serve as both president and chief justice, was instrumental in getting the court a home of its own, though he died before it was completed.

The Supreme Court convenes on the first Monday in October and remains in session until it has heard all of its cases and handed down all its decisions (usually the end of June). For two weeks of each month (Monday through Wednesday), the justices hear oral arguments in the velvet-swathed court chamber. Visitors who want to listen can choose from two lines. One is a "three-to-five-minute" line, which shuttles visitors through, giving them a quick impression of the court at work. The other is for those who'd like to stay for the whole show. If you choose the latter, it's best to be in line by 8:30 AM. The main hall of the Supreme Court is lined with busts of former chief justices; the courtroom itself is decorated with allegorical friezes. Perhaps the most interesting appurtenance in the imposing building, however, is a basketball court on one of the upper floors (it's been called the highest court in the land). *1st and E. Capitol Sts. NE, tel. 202/479–3000. Admission free. Open weekdays 9– 4:30.*

One block north of the Supreme Court, at the corner of Constitution Avenue and 2nd Street, is the redbrick **⑬ Sewall-Belmont House,** built in 1800 by Robert Sewall. Part of the house dates to 1680, making it the oldest home on Capitol Hill. From 1801 to 1813 Secretary of the Treasury Albert Gallatin lived here. He finalized the details of the Louisiana Purchase in his front-parlor office. The house became the only private residence burned in Washington during the British invasion of 1814, after a resident fired on advancing British troops from an upper-story window. (It was, in fact, the only resistance the British met. The rest of the country was disgusted at Washington's inability to defend itself.) The house is now the headquarters of the National Woman's Party and features a museum that chronicles the early days of the women's movement. The museum is filled with period furniture, and portraits and busts of suffrage movement leaders, such as Lucretia Mott, Elizabeth Cady Stanton, and Alice Paul. *144 Constitution Ave. NE, tel. 202/546–3989. Admission free. Open Jan.– Feb., Tues.–Fri. 10–3, Sat. 10–4; Mar.–Dec., Tues.–Fri. 10–3, Sat. 10–4, Sun. noon–4.*

After seeing the Sewall-Belmont House, continue east on Maryland Avenue, past the headquarters of the **Veterans of Foreign Wars.** Only three blocks from the Capitol, the Hill's residential character asserts itself. At Stanton Square turn right onto 4th Street NE, walk south two blocks, and then turn right onto A Street. The gray house with the mansard **⑭** roof at 316 A Street is the **Frederick Douglass Townhouse** (not open to the public). The first Washington home of the famous abolitionist and writer, this structure housed the Museum of African Art until 1987, when the museum was moved to a new building on the Mall (*see* Tour 1, *above*).

Walk back to 4th Street and down another block to East Capitol Street, the border between the northeastern and southeastern quadrants of the city. The orange and yellow trash cans, emblazoned with the silhouette of an Indian, are reminders that East Capitol street is a main thoroughfare to RFK Stadium, home turf of the Washington Redskins. (A new stadium is set to be built next to the old one.) In the '50s there was a plan to construct government office buildings on both sides of East Capitol Street as far as Lincoln Park, seven blocks to the east. The neighborhood's active historic-preservation supporters successfully fought the **⑮** proposal. The houses on the **south side of East Capitol Street** are a representative sampling of homes on the Hill. The corner house, No. 329, has a striking tower with a bay window and stained glass. Next door are two Victorian houses with iron trim below the second floor. A pre–Civil War, Greek-Revival frame house sits behind a trim garden at No. 317.

⑯ At **326 A St.,** in a quiet neighborhood behind the Library of Congress's Adams Building, is the stucco house that artist Constantino Brumidi lived in while he was working on the Capitol.

Time Out **Sherrill's Bakery** (233 Pennsylvania Ave. SE) is known as much for its taciturn, no-nonsense waitresses as for its tasty pastries and cookies. Either way, it's a Hill institution.

Turn right on Pennsylvania Avenue and head back toward the Capitol's familiar white dome. The south side of the street is lined with restaurants and bars frequented by those who live and work on the Hill.

You'll find the nearest Metro stop, Capitol South, on the corner of 1st and D streets SE.

Tour 5: Old Downtown and Federal Triangle

Numbers in the margin correspond to points of interest on the Tour 5: Old Downtown and Federal Triangle map.

Just because Washington is a planned city doesn't mean the plan was executed flawlessly. Pierre L'Enfant's design has been alternately shelved and rediscovered several times in the last 200 years. Nowhere have the city's imperfections been more visible than on L'Enfant's grand thoroughfare, Pennsylvania Avenue. By the early '60s it had become a national disgrace, the dilapidated buildings that lined it home to pawn shops and cheap souvenir stores. While riding up Pennsylvania Avenue in his inaugural parade, a disgusted John F. Kennedy is said to have turned to an aide and said, "Fix it!" Washington's downtown—once within the diamond formed by Massachusetts, Louisiana, Pennsylvania, and New York avenues—had its problems, too, many as a result of the riots that rocked the capital in 1968 after the assassination of Martin Luther King, Jr. In their wake, many downtown businesses left the area and moved north of the White House.

In recent years developers have rediscovered "old downtown," and buildings are now being torn down or remodeled at an amazing pace. After several false starts Pennsylvania Avenue is shining once again. This tour explores the old downtown section of the city, then swings around to check the progress on the monumental street that links the Congress House—the Capitol—with the President's House.

❶ Start your exploration in front of the **Pension Building,** on F Street between 4th and 5th streets. (Nearest Metro stop,

Tour 5: Old Downtown and Federal Triangle

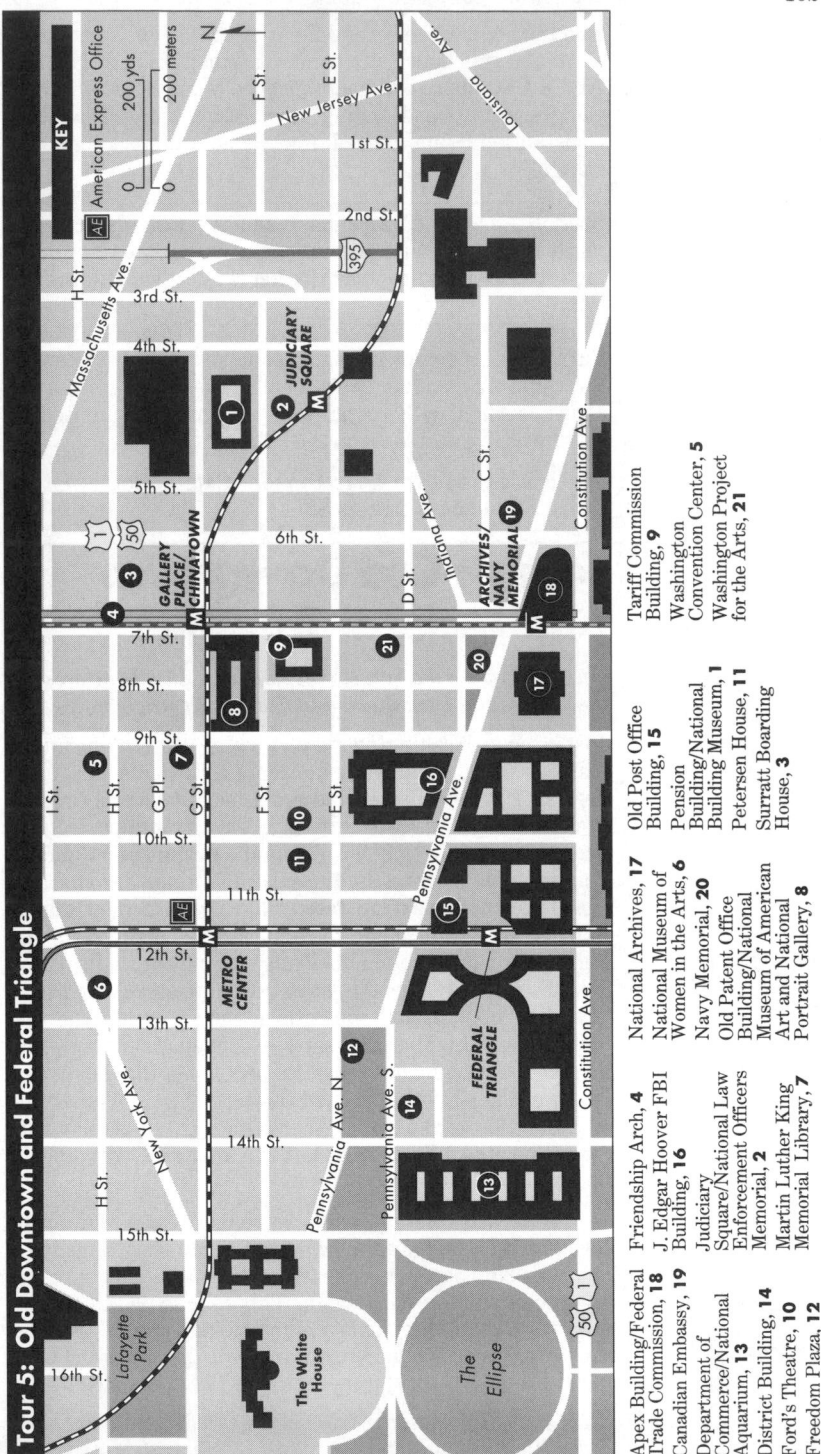

KEY

AE American Express Office

N

0 200 yds
0 200 meters

Lafayette Park

The White House

The Ellipse

FEDERAL TRIANGLE

METRO CENTER

GALLERY PLACE/CHINATOWN

JUDICIARY SQUARE

ARCHIVES/NAVY MEMORIAL

Apex Building/Federal
Trade Commission, **18**
Canadian Embassy, **19**
Department of
Commerce/National
Aquarium, **13**
District Building, **14**
Ford's Theatre, **10**
Freedom Plaza, **12**

Friendship Arch, **4**
J. Edgar Hoover FBI
Building, **16**
Judiciary
Square/National Law
Enforcement Officers
Memorial, **2**
Martin Luther King
Memorial Library, **7**

National Archives, **17**
National Museum of
Women in the Arts, **6**
Navy Memorial, **20**
Old Patent Office
Building/National
Museum of American
Art and National
Portrait Gallery, **8**

Old Post Office
Building, **15**
Pension
Building/National
Building Museum, **1**
Petersen House, **11**
Surratt Boarding
House, **3**

Tariff Commission
Building, **9**
Washington
Convention Center, **5**
Washington Project
for the Arts, **21**

Judiciary Square.) The massive redbrick edifice was built between 1882 and 1887 to house workers who processed the pension claims of veterans and their survivors, an activity that intensified after the Civil War. The architect was U.S. Army Corps of Engineers General Montgomery C. Meigs, who took as his inspiration the Italian Renaissance–style Palazzo Farnese in Rome.

Before entering the building, walk down its F Street side. The terra-cotta frieze by Caspar Buberl between the first and second floors depicts soldiers marching and sailing in an endless procession around the building. Architect Meigs lost his oldest son in the Civil War, and, though the frieze depicts Union troops, he intended it as a memorial to all who were killed in the bloody war. Meigs designed the Pension Building with workers' comfort in mind, long before anyone knew that cramped, stuffy offices could cause "sick building syndrome." Note the three "missing" bricks under each window that helped keep the building cool by allowing air to circulate.

The open interior of the building is one of the city's great spaces and has been the site of inaugural balls for more than 100 years. (The first ball was for Grover Cleveland in 1885; because the building wasn't finished at the time, a temporary wooden roof and floor were erected.) The eight central Corinthian columns are the largest in the world, rising to a height of 75 feet. Though they look like marble, each is made of 75,000 bricks, covered with plaster and painted to resemble Siena marble. Each year NBC tapes its "Christmas in Washington" TV special in the breathtaking hall.

The Pension Building now houses the **National Building Museum,** devoted to architecture and the building arts. "Washington: Symbol and City" is a permanent exhibit that outlines the capital's architectural history, from monumental core to residential neighborhoods. Recent temporary exhibits have explored the construction of the Statue of Liberty, the history of Washington's apartment buildings, and the Pension Building itself. *F St. between 4th and 5th Sts. NW, tel. 202/272-2448. Admission free. Open Mon.– Sat. 10–4, Sun. noon–4; closed Thanksgiving, Christmas, New Year's Day. Tours weekdays at 12:30, weekends at 12:30 and 1:30.*

Two blocks east and a block north is another redbrick building, though one on a smaller scale. The Federal Revival-style **Old Adas Israel Synagogue** is the oldest synagogue in Washington. Built in 1876 at 6th and G streets NW, it was moved to its present location in 1969 to make way for an office building. Exhibits in the Lillian and Albert Small Jewish Museum inside explore Jewish life in Washington. *3rd and G Sts. NW, tel. 202/789-0900. Suggested donation: $2 adults, $1 children. Open Sun.–Thurs. 11–3, Fri. by appointment.*

② Back across F Street from the Pension Building is **Judiciary Square.** As the name implies, this is the District's judicial core, with both city and federal courthouses arranged around it. The **National Law Enforcement Officers Memorial** was dedicated here in October 1991. A 3-foot-high wall bears the names of more than 15,000 American police officers killed in the line of duty since 1794. On the third line of panel 13W are the names of six officers killed by William Bonney, better known as Billy the Kid. J.D. Tippit, the Dallas policeman killed by Lee Harvey Oswald, is honored on line 9 of panel 63E. Given the dangerous nature of police work, it will be one of the few memorials to which names will continue to be added. Two blocks away is a visitors center with exhibits on the history of the memorial and computers that allow you to look up officers by name, date of death, state, and department. A small shop sells souvenirs. *Free guided tours Apr.–Oct., Sat. 11 and 2. Call 202/737–3400. Visitors Center-605 F St. NW. Admission free. Open weekdays 9–5, Sat. 10–5, Sun. noon–5.*

Head west on F Street. After you cross 5th Street, look back at the Pension Building. It's easier to see the interesting roof from this distance. The prison block–like structure north of the Pension Building houses the General Accounting Office.

Turn right on 6th Street and walk two blocks north. The Chinese characters on the street signs signal that you're entering Washington's compact **Chinatown,** bordered by G, E, 5th, and 8th streets. The area is somewhat down-at-the-heels—you'll find boarded-up buildings and graffiti-covered walls—but this is the place to go for Chinese food in the District. Nearly every restaurant has a roast duck hanging in the window, and the shops here sell a wide variety of Chinese goods, from paperback books to traditional medicines.

Time Out   If the smells of Chinese cooking have activated your taste buds, try the highly rated **Mr. Yung's** (740 6th St. NW). It specializes in Cantonese cuisine, and if you're lucky enough to be in the neighborhood between 11 and 3, be sure to sample the *dim sum.*

---

③ Turn left off 6th Street onto H Street. The **Surratt Boarding House,** where John Wilkes Booth and his co-conspirators plotted the assassination of Abraham Lincoln, is at 604 H Street NW. (It's now a Chinese restaurant called Go-Lo's.) **④** The colorful and ornate 75-foot-wide **Friendship Arch** that spans H Street at 7th Street is a reminder of Washington's sister-city relationship with Beijing.

⑤ To the west, at 9th and H streets, is the **Washington Convention Center.** Opened in 1983, the center pumped much-needed life into this part of downtown and spurred the development of nearby hotels and office buildings.

A block up 9th Street is the shiny Techworld complex. In the go-go '80s this was envisioned as a place for high-tech companies to show their stuff. The recession dulled that dream, though one small gallery shows its faith in the future: **Tech 2000** focuses on how computer software, hardware, and other multimedia technologies can be creatively and usefully integrated. The emphasis is on education—what computers can do in the classroom—but there's some fun stuff here, too: a 3-D driving simulator that approaches virtual reality, a computer program that allows visitors to put out a fire on an F–14, and the holdings of the National Gallery of Art on interactive videodisc. *800 K St. NW, tel. 202/842–0500. Admission: $5 adults, $4 students, $4 children under 13. Open weekdays by appointment only, though generally open in the summer Tues.–Sat. 11–5.*

❻ Continue west on H Street and turn right on 13th Street. At 13th and New York Avenue is the **National Museum of Women in the Arts,** a showcase of works by prominent female artists from the Renaissance to the present. The beautifully restored 1907 Renaissance Revival building was designed by Waddy Wood and, ironically, was once a men-only Masonic temple. When the museum opened in 1987 some questioned the wisdom of segregating artists by sex. Since then its acclaimed exhibitions have won over most nay-sayers. In addition to displaying traveling shows, the museum houses a permanent collection that includes paintings, drawings, sculpture, prints, and photographs by such artists as Georgia O'Keeffe, Mary Cassatt, Élisabeth Vigée-Lebrun, Frida Kahlo, and Judy Chicago. *1250 New York Ave. NW, tel. 202/783–5000. Suggested donation: $3 adults; $2 students, senior citizens, and children. Open Mon.–Sat. 10–5, Sun. noon–5.*

Across the street, at 1300 New York Avenue, is the **InterAmerican Development Bank Cultural Center.** Founded in 1959, the IADB is an international bank that finances economic and social development in Latin America and the Caribbean. Its small cultural center hosts changing exhibits of paintings, sculptures, and artifacts from member countries. *1300 New York Ave. NW, tel. 202/623–3287. Admission free. Open weekdays 11–6.*

Head south on 12th Street. Two of the Washington area's largest department stores are nearby—Woodward & Lothrop, at 11th and F, and Hecht's, at 12th and G. Turn left on G Street.

❼ The squat black building at 9th and G streets is the **Martin Luther King Memorial Library,** designed by Mies van der Rohe and the largest public library in the city. A mural on the first floor depicts events in the life of the Nobel Prize-winning civil rights activist. Used books are almost always on sale at bargain prices in the library's gift shop. *801 G St. NW, tel. 202/727–1111. Open Mon.–Thurs. 9–9, Fri.–Sat. 9–5:30, Sun. 1–5.*

Across G Street is the Tudor-style St. Patrick's Parish House, home to the **Paul VI Institute for the Arts.** Though it's part of the Catholic Archdiocese of Washington, this three-room gallery doesn't display what are usually considered "religious" works. Instead, it's a home for art in which the "spirituality" of the artist is exposed. Exhibits have ranged from watercolors by a Japanese Carmelite nun to a survey of contemporary Native American art. There are an Irish festival each March and a display of creches every Christmas. *924 G St. NW, tel. 202/347–1450. Admission free. Open Tues.–Sat. 10–5. Closed most religious holidays.*

Across 9th Street, on the block bounded by F, G, 7th, and 9th, stands the **Old Patent Office Building,** which now houses two Smithsonian museums: the **National Portrait Gallery** on the south and the **National Museum of American Art** on the north. Construction on the south wing, which was designed by Washington Monument architect Robert Mills, started in 1836. When the huge Greek-Revival quadrangle was completed in 1867 it was the largest building in the country. Many of its rooms housed glass display cabinets filled with the models that inventors were required to submit with their patent applications.

During the Civil War, the Patent Office, like many other buildings in the city, was turned into a hospital. Among those caring for the wounded here were Clara Barton and Walt Whitman. In the 1950s the building was threatened with demolition to make way for a parking lot, but the efforts of preservationists saved it. The Smithsonian opened it to the public in 1968.

The first floor of the National Museum of American Art holds displays of early American art and art of the West, as well as a gallery of painted miniatures. Be sure to see *The Throne of the Third Heaven of the Nations' Millennium General Assembly,* by James Hampton. Discarded materials, such as chairs, bottles, and light bulbs, are sheathed in aluminum and gold foil in this strange and moving work of religious art. On the second floor are works by the American Impressionists, including John Henry Twachtman and Childe Hassam. There are also plaster models and marble sculptures by Hiram Powers, including the plaster cast of his famous work *The Greek Slave,* the original of which is housed in the Corcoran Gallery (*see* Tour 3, *above*). Just outside the room containing Powers's work is a copy of a sculpture Augustus Saint-Gaudens created for Henry Adams. Adams's wife had committed suicide and the original of this moving, shroud-draped figure sits above her grave in Rock Creek Cemetery. Also on this floor are massive landscapes by Albert Bierstadt and Thomas Moran. The third floor is filled with modern art, including works by Leon Kroll and Edward Hopper that were commissioned during the '30s by the federal government. The Lincoln

Gallery—site of the receiving line at Abraham Lincoln's 1865 inaugural ball—has been restored to its original appearance and contains modern art by Jasper Johns, Robert Rauschenberg, Milton Avery, Kenneth Noland, and others. *8th and G Sts. NW, tel. 202/357-2700, TDD 202/357-1729. Admission free. Open daily 10-5:30; closed Dec. 25.*

You can enter the National Portrait Gallery from any floor of the National Museum of American Art or walk through the courtyard between the two wings. The best place to start a circuit of the Portrait Gallery is on the restored third floor. The mezzanine level of the wonderfully busy room features a **Civil War exhibition,** with portraits, photographs, and lithographs of such wartime personalities as Julia Ward Howe, Frederick Douglass, Ulysses S. Grant, and Robert E. Lee. There are also life casts of Abraham Lincoln's hands and face. The gallery has been restored to its American Victorian Renaissance–style splendor, complete with colorful tile flooring and a stained-glass skylight. Highlights of the Portrait Gallery's second floor include the **Hall of Presidents** (featuring a portrait or sculpture of each chief executive) and the George Washington "Lansdowne" portrait. The first floor features portraits of well-known American athletes and performers. *Time* magazine gave the museum its collection of Person of the Year covers and many other photos and paintings that the magazine has commissioned over the years. Parts of this collection are periodically on display. *8th and F Sts. NW, tel. 202/357-2700, TDD 202/357-1729. Admission free. Open daily 10-5:30; closed Dec. 25.*

Time Out The **Patent Pending** restaurant, between the two museums, serves an ample selection of salads, sandwiches, hot entrées, and other treats. Tables and chairs in the large museum courtyard make sitting outside the thing to do when the weather is pleasant.

If you leave the pair of museums in the Patent Office Building by way of the National Portrait Gallery's F Street doors, you'll come upon another of Washington's beautiful views. Directly ahead, four blocks away in the Federal Triangle, is the **National Archives** building. To the east is the green barrel-roof of **Union Station,** and to the west you can see the **Treasury Department Building.** Just across the F Street pedestrian mall and to the left is the **Tariff Commission Building,** designed by Robert Mills and finished in 1866. When the Capitol was burned by the British in 1814, Congress met temporarily in a hotel that stood on this site. Another earlier building on the site housed the nation's first public telegraph office, operated by Samuel F.B. Morse.

The block of F Street between 9th and 10th streets has long been a center of shopping in the District. It's dotted with cut-rate electronics stores, pawn shops, and lingerie

stores, and the sidewalks are usually crowded with shoppers looking over the wares of street vendors, who hawk
everything from sweatshirts and sunglasses to perfumes
and panty hose. Many residents fear that developers' new
found interest in old downtown may threaten this lively
part of the city.

Turn left off F Street onto 10th Street. Halfway down the
⑩ block on the left is **Ford's Theatre.** In 1861, Baltimore theater impresario John T. Ford leased the First Baptist
Church building that stood on this site and turned it into a
successful music hall. The building burned down late in
1862, and Ford rebuilt it. The events of April 14, 1865,
would shock the nation and close the theater. On that night,
during a production of *Our American Cousin*, John Wilkes
Booth entered the presidential box and assassinated Abraham Lincoln. The stricken president was carried across the
street to the house of tailor William Petersen. Charles Augustus Leale, a 23-year-old doctor, attended to the president, whose injuries would have left him blind had he ever
regained consciousness. To let Lincoln know that someone
was nearby, Leale held his hand throughout the night. Lin-
⑪ coln died in the **Petersen House** (516 10th St. NW, tel. 202/
426–6830; open daily 9–5) the next morning. Visitors can
see the restored front and back parlors of the house, as well
as the bedroom where the president died. Most of the furnishings are not original, but the pillow and bloodstained
pillowcases are those used on that fateful night.

The federal government bought Ford's Theatre in 1866 for
$100,000 and converted it into office space. It was remod-
eled as a Lincoln museum in 1932 and was restored to its
1865 appearance in 1968. The basement museum—with artifacts such as Booth's pistol and the clothes Lincoln was
wearing when he was shot—reopened in 1990 after a complete renovation. The theater itself continues to present a
complete schedule of plays. *A Christmas Carol* is an annual
holiday favorite. *511 10th St. NW, tel. 202/426–6924. Admission free. Open daily 9–5. Theater closed when rehear-
sals or matinees are in progress (generally Thurs. and
weekends); Lincoln Museum in basement remains open at
these times. Closed Christmas.*

Continue south on 10th Street and turn right on E Street.
Most people would consider this E Street, but you'll notice
that some of the buildings on this stretch—including both
the Warner Theatre and the National Theatre—boast
"Pennsylvania Avenue" on their entrances. There's a certain cachet to sharing a street with the president.

Time Out   The **Hard Rock Cafe** (999 E St. NW, tel. 202/737–7625)
opened its Washington branch in 1989, bringing hearty
American food, a modest selection of beers, and lots of
those famous T-shirts (the Hard Rock's gift shop opened a
full year before the restaurant did). This is a popular spot

for tourists, so if you're not up to waiting in line, try to arrive early for lunch or dinner.

---

⑫ Freedom Plaza is bounded by 13th, 14th, and E streets and Pennsylvania Avenue. Its east end is dominated by a **statue of General Casimir Pulaski,** the Polish nobleman who led an American cavalry corps during the Revolutionary War and was mortally wounded in 1779 at the Siege of Savannah. He gazes over a plaza that is inlaid with a detail from L'Enfant's original 1791 plan for the Federal City. Bronze markers outline the President's Palace and the Congress House; the Mall is represented by a green lawn. Cut into the edges are quotations about the capital city, not all of them complimentary. To compare L'Enfant's vision with today's reality, stand in the middle of the map's Pennsylvania Avenue and look west. L'Enfant had planned an unbroken vista from the Capitol to the White House, but the Treasury Building, constructed in 1842, ruined the view. Turning to the east you'll see the U.S. Capitol sitting on Jenkins Hill like an American Taj Mahal.

There's a lot to see and explore in the blocks near Freedom Plaza. The beaux arts **Willard Hotel** is on the corner of 14th Street and Pennsylvania Avenue. There was a Willard Hotel on this spot long before this ornate structure was built in 1901. The original Willard was the place to stay in Washington if you were rich or influential (or wanted to give that impression). Abraham Lincoln stayed there while waiting to move into the nearby White House. Julia Ward Howe stayed there during the Civil War and wrote "The Battle Hymn of the Republic" after gazing down from her window to see Union troops drilling on Pennsylvania Avenue. It's said the term "lobbyist" was coined to describe the favor seekers who would buttonhole President Ulysses S. Grant in the hotel's public rooms. The second Willard, with its mansard roof dotted with circular windows, was designed by Henry Hardenbergh, architect of New York's Plaza Hotel. Although it was just as opulent as the hotel it replaced, it fell on hard times after the second World War. In 1968 it closed, standing empty until 1986, when it reopened, amid much fanfare, after an ambitious restoration. The Willard's rebirth is one of the most visible successes of the Pennsylvania Avenue Development Corporation, the organization charged with reversing the decay of America's Main Street.

Just north of Freedom Plaza, on F Street between 13th and 14th streets, are **The Shops,** a collection of stores in the National Press Building, itself home to dozens of domestic and foreign media organizations. **The Shops** features sit-down restaurants, such as the **American Cafe** and the **Boston Seafood Company,** as well as fast food in its upstairs Food Hall. Washington's oldest stage, the **National Theatre,** also overlooks the plaza. This National has been here since 1922, though there has been a theater on this spot since 1835. After seeing her first play here at the age of six, Helen Hayes vowed to become an actress. If you plan ahead you can take a free tour of the historic theater that takes in the house, stage, backstage, wardrobe room, dressing rooms, the area under the stage, the Helen Hayes Lounge, and the memorabilia-filled archives. *1321 Pennsylvania Ave. NW, tel. 202/783–3370. Admission free. Minimum of 6 people on tour; make reservations at least a month ahead.*

To the south of Freedom Plaza is **Federal Triangle,** the mass of government buildings constructed from 1929 to 1938 between 15th Street, Pennsylvania Avenue, and Constitution Avenue. Before Federal Triangle was developed, government workers were scattered throughout the city, largely in rented offices. Looking for a place to consolidate this work force, city planners hit on the area south of Pennsylvania Avenue, then composed of a notorious collection of rooming houses, taverns, tattoo parlors, and brothels known as "Murder Bay." A uniform classical architectural style, with Italianate red-tile roofs and interior plazas reminiscent of the Louvre, was chosen for the building project.

The base of Federal Triangle, and the first part completed, ⑬ is the **Department of Commerce** building, between 14th and 15th streets. When it opened in 1932 it was the world's largest government office building. In addition to the Commerce Department, the building houses the **National Aquarium.** Established in 1873, it's the oldest public aquarium in the United States. Displays feature tropical and freshwater fish, moray eels, frogs, turtles, piranhas, even sharks. A "touch tank" allows visitors to handle sea creatures such as crabs and oysters. *14th St. and Pennsylvania Ave. NW, tel. 202/482–2825. Admission: $2 adults, 75¢ children 4–12 and senior citizens. Open daily 9–5; closed Dec. 25. Sharks are fed Mon., Wed., Sat. at 2; piranhas Tues., Thurs., Sun. at 2.*

Federal Triangle's planners envisioned interior courts filled with plazas and parks, but the needs of the motor car foiled any such grand plans. The park that was planned for the spot of land between 13th and 14th streets across from the Commerce Building is now an immense parking lot. A federal office building containing an international cultural ⑭ and trade center is being built here. The beaux arts **District Building,** at the corner of 14th Street and Pennsylvania Avenue, is the seat of the city's government. It was erected in 1908, and, though it didn't fit in with the original 1929 Federal Triangle plans, it survived.

This tour continues east on Pennsylvania Avenue, against the direction taken by newly inaugurated presidents on their way to the White House. Thomas Jefferson started the parade tradition in 1805 after taking the oath of office for his second term. He was accompanied by a few friends and a handful of congressmen. Four years later James Madison made things official by instituting a proper inaugural celebration. The flag holders on the lamp posts are clues that Pennsylvania Avenue remains the city's most important parade route. With the Capitol at one end and the White House at the other, the avenue symbolizes both the distance and the connection between these two branches of government.

Such symbolism may have been lost on early inhabitants of Washington. When Pennsylvania Avenue first opened in 1796, it was an ugly and dangerous bog. Attempts by Jefferson to beautify the road by planting poplar trees were only partially successful: Many were chopped down for firewood. In the mid–19th century, crossing the rutted thoroughfare was a dangerous proposition, and rainstorms often turned the street into a river. The avenue was finally paved with wooden blocks in 1871.

The **Postal Service** stands on the southeast corner of Pennsylvania Avenue and 13th Street. Farther down, across 12th Street, is the Romanesque **Old Post Office Building.** When it was completed, in 1899, it was the largest government building in the District, the first with a clock tower, and the first with an electric power plant. Despite these innovations, it earned the sobriquet "old" after only 18 years, when a new District post office was constructed near Union Station. When urban planners in the '20s decided to impose a uniform design on Federal Triangle, the Old Post Office was slated for demolition (some critics said it stood out like an "old tooth"). First a lack of money during the Depression, then the intercession of preservationists, headed by Nancy Hanks of the National Endowment for the Arts, saved the fanciful granite building. Major renovation was begun in 1978, and in 1984 the public areas in the Old Post Office Pavilion—an assortment of shops and restaurants inside the airy central courtyard—were opened. Other shops and restaurants were added to the pavilion's three-story, glass-enclosed East Atrium in 1992, along with City Golf, an indoor miniature golf course and bar.

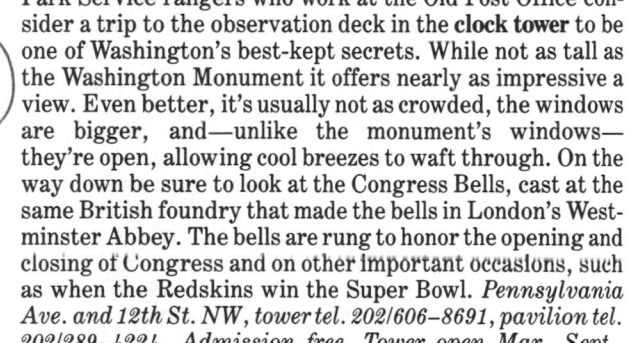

Park Service rangers who work at the Old Post Office consider a trip to the observation deck in the **clock tower** to be one of Washington's best-kept secrets. While not as tall as the Washington Monument it offers nearly as impressive a view. Even better, it's usually not as crowded, the windows are bigger, and—unlike the monument's windows—they're open, allowing cool breezes to waft through. On the way down be sure to look at the Congress Bells, cast at the same British foundry that made the bells in London's Westminster Abbey. The bells are rung to honor the opening and closing of Congress and on other important occasions, such as when the Redskins win the Super Bowl. *Pennsylvania Ave. and 12th St. NW, tower tel. 202/606–8691, pavilion tel. 202/289–4224. Admission free. Tower open Mar.–Sept., daily 9 AM–11 PM; Oct.–Feb., daily 10–6.*

Time Out The waffle-cone ice-cream confections available at **Scoops Homemade Cones,** on the lower level of the Post Office Pavilion, are especially refreshing on a hot, humid day.

As you cross 10th Street look to your left at the delightful trompe l'oeil mural on the side of the **Lincoln Building,** two blocks up on 10th Street. It looks as if there's a hole in the building. There's also a portrait of the building's namesake. Closer to Pennsylvania Avenue on 10th Street is an example of one of Washington's strangest and most popular architectural conceits: a "façadamy." The multi-arched, redbrick facade of a 1909 building has been retained—like a bug stuck in amber—on the front of a massive shop-and-office block.

Continuing down Pennsylvania Avenue, the next big building on the right is the **Department of Justice.** Like the rest of Federal Triangle, it boasts some art deco features, including the cylindrical aluminum torches outside the doorways, adorned with bas-relief figures of bison, dolphins, and birds.

16 Across from Justice is the **J. Edgar Hoover Federal Bureau of Investigation Building.** A hulking presence on the avenue, it was decried from birth as hideous. Even Hoover himself is said to have called it the "ugliest building I've ever seen." Opened in 1974, it hangs over 9th Street like a poured-concrete Big Brother. One thing is certain, it is secure. The tour of the building remains one of the most popular tourist activities in the city. Exhibits outline famous past cases and illustrate the Bureau's fight against organized crime, terrorism, bank robbery, espionage, and extortion. The tour ends with a live-ammo firearms demonstration. *10th St. and Pennsylvania Ave. NW (tour entrance on E St. NW), tel. 202/324–3447. Admission free. Tours weekdays 8:45–4:15. Closed federal holidays. At peak times, there may be an hour wait for the tour.*

17 The classical **National Archives** building fills the area between 7th and 9th streets and Pennsylvania and Constitution avenues. Beside it is a small park with a modest **memorial to Franklin Roosevelt.** The desk-sized piece of marble on the sliver of grass is exactly what the president asked for (though this hasn't stopped fans of the 32nd president in their successful efforts to secure a grander memorial to FDR in West Potomac Park, due to be completed in 1995). Designed by John Russell Pope, the Archives building was erected in 1935 on the site of the old Center Market. This large block between 7th and 9th streets had been a center of commerce since the early 1800s, when barges plying the City Canal (which flowed where Constitution Avenue is now) were loaded and unloaded here. A vestige of this mercantile past lives on in the name given to the two semicircular developments across from the Archives—**Market**

Square. City planners hope the residential development will enliven this stretch of Pennsylvania Avenue.

Turn right onto 9th Street and head to the Constitution Avenue side of the Archives. All the sculpture that adorns the building was carved on the site, including the two statues that flank the flight of steps facing the Mall, *Heritage* and *Guardianship*, by James Earle Fraser. Fraser also carved the scene on the pediment, which represents the transfer of historic documents to the recorder of the Archives. (Like nearly all pediment decorations in Washington, the scene is bristling with electric wires designed to thwart the advances of destructive pigeons.)

The Declaration of Independence, the Constitution, and the Bill of Rights are on display in the Rotunda of the Archives building, in a case made of bulletproof glass, illuminated with green light, and filled with helium gas (to protect the irreplaceable documents). At night and on Christmas—the only day the Archives are closed—the documents are lowered into a vault. *Constitution Ave. between 7th and 9th Sts. NW, tel. 202/501–5000. Admission free. Open Apr.–Labor Day, daily 10–9:30; Sept.–Mar., daily 10–5:30. Behind-the-scenes tours by reservation weekdays at 10:15 and 1:15, tel. 202/501–5205 well in advance.*

Continuing down Constitution Avenue you'll come to the tip of Federal Triangle. The **Apex Building,** completed in 1938, is the home of the **Federal Trade Commission.** The artwork that adorns this triangular building depicts various aspects of trade. Note the relief decorations representing *Agriculture* (the harvesting of grain, by Concetta Scaravaglione) and *Trade* (two men bartering over an ivory tusk, by Carl Schmitz) over the doorways on the Constitution Avenue side. Two heroic statues by Michael Lantz on either side of the rounded eastern portico, each depicting a muscular, shirtless workman wrestling with a wild horse, represent *Man Controlling Trade.* Just across 6th Street is a three-tier fountain decorated with the signs of the zodiac; it is a memorial to Andrew Mellon, who as secretary of the treasury oversaw construction of the $125 million Federal Triangle. The impressive white-stone-and-glass building across Pennsylvania Avenue from Mellon's fountain is the **Canadian Embassy,** designed by Arthur Erickson and completed in 1988. Inside, a museum periodically displays exhibits on Canadian culture and history. *501 Pennsylvania Ave. NW, tel. 202/682–1740. Admission free. Open weekdays 10–5.*

Backtrack a bit by circling the rounded end of the Federal Trade Commission Building, crossing Pennsylvania Avenue, and heading west. Pioneering photographer **Mathew Brady** had his studio in the twin-towered building at 625 Pennsylvania Avenue. He's thought to have snapped some of his pictures of the city from the building's upper windows. For years after that it was better known as the home of Apex Liquors. Sears, Roebuck and Co. now owns the building, which serves as the huge retailer's Washington lobbying office.

There is a multitude of statues and monuments at this confluence of 7th Street and Pennsylvania and Indiana avenues. The **Grand Army of the Republic** memorial pays tribute to the men who won the Civil War. Less conventional is the nearby stork-surmounted **Temperance Fountain.** It was erected in the 19th century by a teetotaling physician named Cogswell who hoped the fountain, which once dispensed ice-cold water, would lure people from the evils of drink.

Across 7th Street, close by a memorial to **General Winfield Scott,** is the **Navy Memorial,** a massive granite map of the world with a statue of a lone sailor. In the summer, the memorial's concert stage is the site of military band performances. To the northeast, in the Market Square Development, is the memorial's visitors center, complete with gift shop and "Navy Memorial Log Room," where visitors can use computers to look up the service records of sailors entered into the log. There's also the 250-seat, widescreen Arleigh & Roberta Burke Theater, home of continuous screenings of the 30-minute, 70-mm film *At Sea.* Produced by the same company that made the IMAX hit *To Fly, At Sea* is a visually stunning look at life aboard a modern aircraft carrier. *701 Pennsylvania Ave. NW, tel. 202/ 737–2300. Visitor center open Mon.–Sat. 10–6, Sun. noon–5 (closes daily at 5 Nov.–Feb.). Admission to* At Sea: *$3 adults, $2.50 senior citizens, $2 children under 12; advance tickets available from Ticketmaster, tel. 202/432– 7328.*

The redevelopment that has rejuvenated Pennsylvania Avenue hasn't been confined solely to that famous street. **Pennsylvania Quarter** is the name given to the mix of condominiums, apartments, retail spaces, and restaurants in the blocks bounded by Pennsylvania Avenue and 6th, 9th, and G streets. The area includes the Lansburgh complex, at the corner of 8th and E streets. Built around three existing buildings (including the defunct Lansburgh department store), the complex includes the Shakespeare Theatre, which in 1992 moved from its former home in the Folger Library to this state-of-the-art, 447-seat space.

The **Washington Project for the Arts** shows the challenging work of contemporary artists, many of them from the Washington area. The two floors of gallery space usually include displays of avant-garde media (photography and video) as well as visual art (paintings and sculpture). WPA's **Bookworks** sells an exhaustive selection of art books—both books about art and limited edition books created by artists that are works of art themselves. *400 7th St. NW (entrance on D St.), tel. 202/347–4813, Bookworks tel. 202/347–4590. Admission free. Open Mon.–Sat. 11–6, Sun. noon–5.*

To reach public transportation, walk up 7th Street, then turn left on F Street and right on 9th to the Gallery Place Metro station. Or you can walk back down 7th to the National Archives station.

Tour 6: Georgetown

Numbers in the margin correspond to points of interest on the Tour 6: Georgetown map.

Long before the District of Columbia was formed, Georgetown, Washington's oldest neighborhood, was a separate city that boasted a harbor full of ships and warehouses filled with tobacco. Washington has filled in around Georgetown over the years, but the former tobacco port retains an air of aloofness. Its narrow streets, which refuse to conform to Pierre L'Enfant's plan for the Federal City, make up the capital's wealthiest neighborhood and are the nucleus of its nightlife.

The area that would come to be known as George (after George II), then George Towne and, finally, Georgetown, was part of Maryland when it was settled in the early 1700s by Scottish immigrants, many of whom were attracted to the region's tolerant religious climate. Georgetown's position at the farthest point up the Potomac one could reach by boat made it an ideal transit-and-inspection point for farmers who grew tobacco in Maryland's interior. In 1789 the state granted the town a charter, but two years later Georgetown—along with Alexandria, its counterpart in Virginia—was included by George Washington in the Territory of Columbia, site of the new capital.

While Washington struggled, Georgetown thrived. Wealthy traders built their mansions on the hills overlooking the river; merchants and the working class lived in more modest homes closer to the water's edge. In 1810 a third of Georgetown's population was black—both freedmen and slaves. The **Mt. Zion Church** on 29th Street is the oldest black church in the city and was a stop on the Underground Railroad. Georgetown's rich history and success instilled in citizens of both colors feelings of superiority that many feel linger today. (When Georgetowners thought the dismal capital was dragging them down, they asked to be given back to Maryland, the way Alexandria was given back to Virginia in 1845). Tobacco eventually became a less important commodity, and Georgetown became a milling center, using water power from the Potomac. When the Chesapeake & Ohio Canal was completed in 1850, the city intensified its milling operations and became the eastern end of a waterway that stretched 184 miles to the west. The canal took up some of the slack when Georgetown's harbor began to fill with silt and the port lost business to Alexandria and Baltimore, but the canal never became the success it was meant to be.

In the years that followed, Georgetown was a far cry from the fashionable spot it is today. Clustered near the water were a foundry, a fishmarket, paper and cotton mills, and a power station for the city's streetcar system, all of which made Georgetown a smelly industrial district. It still had its Georgian, Federal, and Victorian homes, though, and when the New Deal and World War II brought a flood of newcomers to Washington, Georgetown's tree-shaded streets and handsome brick houses were rediscovered. Pushed out in the process were Georgetown's blacks, most of whom rented the houses they lived in.

Today some of Washington's most famous citizens call Georgetown home, including *Washington Post* matriarch Katherine Graham, former *Post* editor Ben Bradlee, celebrity biographer Kitty Kelley, and political insider Pamela Churchill Harriman. Georgetown's historic preservationists are among the most vocal in the city. Part of what the activists want protection from is the crush of people who descend on their community every night. This is Washington's center for restaurants, bars, nightclubs, and trendy boutiques. On M Street and Wisconsin Avenue, visitors can indulge just about any taste and take home almost any up-market souvenir. Harder to find is a parking place. The lack of a Metro station in Georgetown—apocryphally attributed to residents' desires to keep out the riffraff— means you'll have to take a bus or walk to this part of Washington. It's about a 15-minute walk from the Dupont Circle or Foggy Bottom Metro station. (Or you can take a bus: The G2 Georgetown University bus goes from Dupont Circle west along P Street. The 34 and 36 Friendship Heights buses leave from 22nd and Pennsylvania and deposit you at 31st and M.)

Georgetown owes some of its charm and separate growth to geography. This town-unto-itself is separated from Washington to the east by Rock Creek. On the south it's bordered by the Potomac, on the west by Georgetown University. How far north does Georgetown reach? Probably not much farther than the large estates and parks above R Street, though developers and real estate agents would be happy to take Georgetown right up to the Canadian border if it increased the value of property along the way.

❶ Start your exploration of Georgetown in front of the **Old Stone House** (M Street between 30th and 31st streets), thought to be Washington's only surviving pre-Revolutionary building. Begun in 1764 by a cabinetmaker named Christopher Layman, this fieldstone house was used as both a residence and a place of business by a succession of occupants. Five of the house's rooms are furnished with the sort of sturdy beds, spinning wheels, and simple tables associated with middle-class Colonial America. The National Park Service maintains the house and its lovely gardens in the rear, which are planted with fruit trees and seasonal

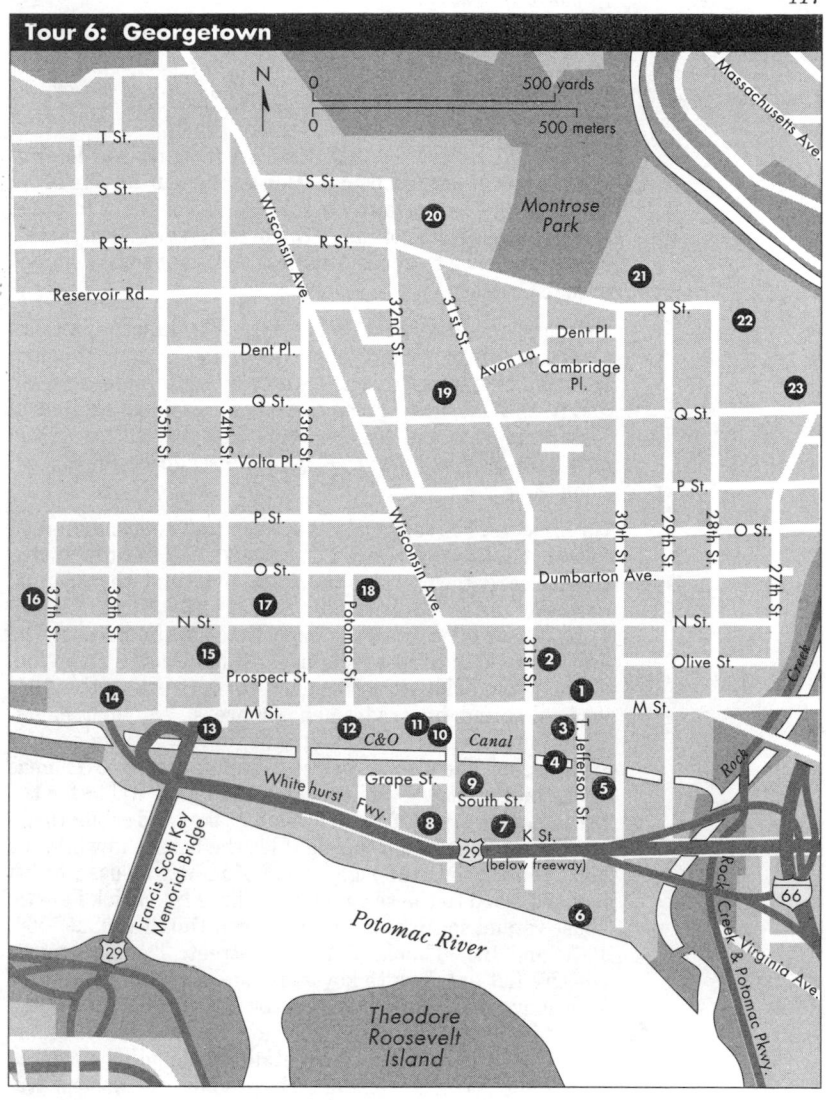

Tour 6: Georgetown

N

0   500 yards

0   500 meters

Massachusetts Ave.

T St.

S St.   S St.

R St.   R St.

Montrose Park

Reservoir Rd.

Wisconsin Ave.

32nd St.

31st St.

Avon La.

Dent Pl.   Dent Pl.

Cambridge Pl.

R St.

Q St.

P St.

Dent Pl.

Q St.

35th St.

34th St.

33rd St.

Volta Pl.

P St.

Wisconsin Ave.

30th St.

29th St.

28th St.

O St.

Dumbarton Ave.

O St.

16

37th St.

36th St.

17

18

N St.

Potomac St.

31st St.

N St.

Olive St.

27th St.

Rock Creek

15

Prospect St.

2

14

M St.   1   M St.

13   12   C&O   11   10   Canal   3

White hurst Fwy.   Grape St.   9   South St.   4   T. Jefferson St.   5

8   7   K St.

29   (below freeway)

6

Francis Scott Key Memorial Bridge

29

Potomac River

66

Rock Creek & Potomac Pkwy.

Virginia Ave.

Theodore Roosevelt Island

Chesapeake & Ohio Canal, **4**

Cox's Row, **17**

Customs House, **2**

Dodge Warehouse, **8**

Dumbarton House, **23**

Dumbarton Oaks, **20**

Evermay, **22**

Exorcist steps, **14**

Foundry Mall, **5**

Francis Scott Key Memorial Park, **13**

Georgetown Park, **11**

Georgetown University, **16**

Grace Episcopal Church, **9**

Halcyon House, **15**

Markethouse, **12**

Masonic lodge, **3**

Oak Hill Cemetery, **21**

Old Stone House, **1**

St. John's Church, **18**

Suter's Tavern plaque, **7**

Tudor Place, **19**

Vigilant Firehouse, **10**

Washington Harbour, **6**

blooms. Costumed guides answer questions about the house and its history. *3051 M St. NW, tel. 202/426-6851. Admission free. Open Wed.-Sun. 8-4:30; closed major holidays.*

Around the corner, at 1221 31st Street, is the old Renaissance Revival–style **Customs House.** Built in 1858 to serve the port of Georgetown, it's been transformed into the Georgetown branch of the U.S. Postal Service, and there's really no reason to go inside unless you want to buy stamps or mail postcards.

On the other side of 31st Street is the **Alif Gallery.** The nonprofit Arab American Cultural Foundation runs the one-room gallery, which displays works by contemporary Arab and Arab-American artists as well as occasional exhibits of historic objects and textiles. *1204 31st St. NW., tel. 202/337-9670. Admission free. Open weekdays 10-6, Sat. noon-6.*

Go back to M Street and cross over to Thomas Jefferson Street (between 30th and 31st streets). For most of its history, Georgetown was a working city, and the original names of its streets—Water Street, The Keys, Fishing Lane—bear witness to the importance of the harbor. The area south of M Street (originally called Bridge Street because of the bridge that spanned Rock Creek to the east) was inhabited by tradesmen, laborers, and merchants. Their homes were modest and close to Georgetown's industrial heart. The two-story brick building at **1083 Thomas Jefferson Street** was built around 1865 as a stable for the horses and hearses of a nearby undertaker and cabinetmaker. The wide doors on the right let the horses in while the hoist beam above the right-most window was used to lift hay and wood to the second floor. Three fine brick Federal houses stand south of the Georgetown Dutch Inn, at 1069, 1067, and 1063 Thomas Jefferson Street. The last has attractive flat lintels with keystones and a rounded keystone arch above the doorway. Across the street, at No. 1058, is a two-story brick structure built around 1810 as a **Masonic lodge.** It features interesting detailing, including a pointed facade and recessed central arch, proof of the Masons' traditional attachment to the building arts.

As you walk south on Thomas Jefferson Street, you'll pass over the **Chesapeake & Ohio Canal,** the waterway that kept Georgetown open to shipping after its harbor had filled with silt. George Washington was one of the first to advance the idea of a canal linking the Potomac with the Ohio River across the Appalachians. Work started on the C & O Canal in 1828, and when it opened in 1850, its 74 locks linked Georgetown with Cumberland, Maryland, 184 miles to the northwest (still short of its intended destination). Lumber, coal, iron, wheat, and flour moved up and down the canal, but it was never as successful as its planners had hoped it would be. Many of the bridges spanning the canal in Georgetown were too low to allow anything other than fully loaded barges to pass underneath, and competition from the Baltimore & Ohio Railroad eventually spelled an end to profitability. Today the canal is a part of the National Park system, and walkers follow the towpath once used by mules while canoers paddle the canal's calm waters. Between April and October you can go on a leisurely, mule-drawn trip aboard the *Georgetown* canal barge. Tickets are available across the canal, in the **Foundry Mall**. The mall gets its name from an old foundry that overlooked the canal at 30th Street. Around the turn of the century it was turned into a veterinary hospital that cared for mules working on the canal. Today it's a restaurant. *1055 Thomas Jefferson St., NW, tel. 202/472–4376 or 202/653–5844 for group reservations and rates. Admission: $5 adults, $3.50 senior citizens and children under 13. 90-min barge trips mid-Apr.–mid-Oct., Wed.–Sun. 10:30, 1, and 3; Sat. 10:30, 1, 3, and 5.*

6 Continue south, across K Street, and into **Washington Harbour,** a glittering, postmodern riverfront development designed by Arthur Cotton Moore that includes restaurants, offices, apartments, and upscale shops. The plazas around its large central fountain and gardens are dotted with the eerily realistic sculptures of J. Seward Johnson, Jr. From the edge of Washington Harbour you can see the Watergate complex and Kennedy Center to the east.

Georgetown's **K Street** is lined with the offices of architects, ad agencies, and public relations companies. In many of these offices you can hear the rumble of cars on the Whitehurst Freeway, the elevated road above K Street that leads to the Francis Scott Key Memorial Bridge. Though you'll probably have to peer through a vine-covered fence to see it, at the corner of 31st and K streets is a **plaque 7** commemorating **Suter's Tavern.** In March 1791, in the one-story hostelry that once stood on this spot, George Washington met with the men who owned the tobacco farms and swampy marshes to the east of Georgetown and convinced them to sell their land to the government so construction of the District of Columbia could begin.

At the foot of Wisconsin Avenue is another legacy from the area's mercantile past. The last three buildings on the west side were built around 1830 by trader and merchant **Francis Dodge.** Note the heavy stone foundation of the southern-**8** most **warehouse,** its star-end braces and the broken hoist in the gable end. According to an 1838 newspaper ad, Georgetown shoppers could visit Dodge's grocery to buy such items as "Porto Rico Sugar, Marseilles soft-shelled Almonds and Havanna Segars."

Halfway up Wisconsin Avenue, on the other side of the **9** street, stands the Gothic Revival **Grace Episcopal Church.** In the mid- to late-19th century this church served the boatmen and workers from the nearby C & O Canal. At the time this was one of the poorest sections of Georgetown. (There are no "poor" sections in Georgetown anymore.)

Walking farther up Wisconsin Avenue you'll again cross the C & O Canal, this time via the only bridge that remains from the 19th century. On the north side is a simple granite obelisk honoring the men who built the waterway. A memorial of a more poignant sort can be found at the 1840 ⑩ **Vigilant Firehouse,** north of the canal at 1066 Wisconsin Avenue. A plaque set in the wall reads: "Bush, the Old Fire Dog, died of Poison, July 5th, 1869, R.I.P."

The intersection of Wisconsin Avenue and M Street is the heart of boisterous Georgetown. This spot—under the gleaming, golden dome of Riggs Bank on the northeast corner—is mobbed every weekend.

Turning left on M Street you'll come to the entrance to ⑪ **Georgetown Park** (3222 M St. NW), a multilevel shopping extravaganza that answers the question "If the Victorians had invented shopping malls, what would they look like?" Such high-ticket stores as FAO Schwarz, Williams-Sonoma, Polo/Ralph Lauren, and Godiva Chocolates can be found within this artful, skylit mass of polished brass, tile flooring, and potted plants. If you've always looked down your nose at mall architecture, Georgetown Park might win you over.

Time Out   **Pizzeria Uno** (3211 M St. NW) has brought Chicago-style pizza to the heart of Georgetown. The deep-dish pies take a while to cook, but the wait is worth it. Those in a hurry may want to order the "personal-sized" pizza: It's ready in five minutes and costs less than $5.

A stroll up either M Street or Wisconsin Avenue will take you past a dizzying array of merchandise, from expensive bicycling accessories to ropes of gold, from antique jewelry and furniture to the latest fashions in clothes and records. Walking west on M Street to Potomac Street you'll come to ⑫ the **Markethouse,** an 1865 brick building that once housed a market filled with victual stalls. There has been some sort of market on this spot since 1795, and in 1993 Dean & DeLuca, the trendy Manhattan specialty grocer, moved in. In addition to expensive meats and cheeses, espressos, lattés, and cappuccinos, are available, along with sandwiches and pastries.

M Street to the west leads to the **Key Bridge** into Rosslyn, Virginia. A house owned by Francis Scott Key, author of the national anthem, was demolished in 1947 to make way for the bridge that would bear his name.

⑬ The **Francis Scott Key Memorial Park** (on M Street between 34th Street and Key Bridge) honors the Washington attorney who "by dawn's early light" penned the national anthem. A replica of the 15-star, 15-stripe flag that inspired

Key in 1814 flies over the park 24 hours a day. It's a noisy spot for a park, hard by busy Key Bridge, washed in the sounds of jets thundering into National Airport. Here Georgetown's quaint demeanor contrasts with the silvery skyscrapers of Rosslyn, Virginia, across the Potomac.

The heights of Georgetown to the north above N Street contrast with the busy jumble of the old waterfront. To reach the higher ground you can walk up M Street past the old brick streetcar barn at No. 3600 (now a block of offices), turn right, and climb the 75 **steps** that figured prominently in the eerie climax of the movie *The Exorcist*. If you prefer a less demanding climb, walk up 34th Street instead.

14

15 **Halcyon House,** at the corner of 34th and Prospect streets, was built in 1783 by Benjamin Stoddert, first secretary of the Navy. The object of many subsequent additions and renovations, the house is now a concatenation of architectural styles. Prospect Street gets its name from the fine views it affords of the waterfront and the river below.

The sounds of traffic diminish the farther north one walks **16** from the bustle of M Street. To the west is **Georgetown University,** the oldest Jesuit school in the country. It was founded in 1789 by John Carroll, first American bishop and first archbishop of Baltimore. About 12,000 students attend Georgetown, known now as much for its perennially successful basketball team as for its fine programs in law, medicine, and the liberal arts. When seen from the Potomac or from Washington's high ground, the Gothic spires of Georgetown's older buildings give the university an almost medieval look.

Architecture buffs, especially those interested in Federal and Victorian houses, enjoy wandering along the redbrick sidewalks of upper Georgetown. The average house here has two signs on it: a brass plaque notifying passersby of the building's historic interest and a window decal that warns burglars of its state-of-the-art alarm system. To get a representative taste of the houses in the area, continue north for a block on 34th Street and turn right onto N Street. The group of five Federal houses between 3339 and **17** 3327 N Street are known collectively as **Cox's Row,** after John Cox, a former mayor of Georgetown, who built them in 1817.

The flat-fronted, redbrick Federal house at **3307 N Street** was the home of then-Senator John F. Kennedy and his family before the White House beckoned. Turn left onto Potomac Street and walk a block up to O Street. O Street still has two leftovers from an earlier age: cobblestones and streetcar tracks. Residents are proud of the cobblestones, and you'll notice that even some of the concrete patches **18** have been scored to resemble the paving stones. **St. John's Church** (3240 O St. NW, tel. 202/338–1796) was built in 1809 and is attributed to Dr. William Thornton, architect of the

Capitol. Later alterations have left it looking more Victorian than Federal. At the corner of the churchyard is a memorial to Colonel Ninian Beall, the Scotsman who received the original patent for the land that would become Georgetown.

Georgetown's largest estates sit farther north, commanding fine views of Rock Creek to the east and of the old tobacco town spread out near the river below. Depending on your mood, you can walk north either on Wisconsin Avenue (the bustling commercial route) or a block east, on 31st Street (a quieter residential street). Strolling 31st Street will give you a chance to admire more of the city's finest houses.

Whichever way you go, make your way to Q Street between 31st and 32nd streets. Through the trees to the north, at ❶⑨ the top of a sloping lawn, you'll see the neoclassical **Tudor Place,** designed by Capitol architect William Thornton and completed in 1816. The house was built for Thomas Peter, son of Georgetown's first mayor, and his wife, Martha Custis, Martha Washington's granddaughter. It was because of this connection to the president's family that Tudor Place came to house many items from Mount Vernon. The yellow stucco house is interesting for its architecture—especially the dramatic, two-story domed portico on the south side—but its familial heritage is even more remarkable: Tudor Place stayed in the same family for 178 years, until 1983, when Armistead Peter III died. Before his death, Peter established a foundation to restore the house and open it to the public. On a house tour you'll see chairs that belonged to George Washington, Francis Scott Key's desk, and spurs of members of the Peter family who were killed in the Civil War (although the house was in Washington, the family was true to its Virginia roots and fought for Dixie). The grounds contain many specimens planted in the early 19th century. *1644 31st St. NW, tel. 202/965-0400. Suggested donation: $5. Tours Tues.–Sat. 10, 11:30, 1, and 2:30. Reservations required.*

❷⓪ **Dumbarton Oaks**—not to be confused with the nearby Dumbarton House—is on 32nd Street, north of R Street. Career diplomat Robert Woods Bliss and his wife, Mildred, heiress to the Fletcher's Castoria fortune, bought the property in 1920 and set about taming the sprawling grounds and removing 19th-century additions that had marred the Federal lines of the 1801 mansion. In 1940 the Blisses conveyed the estate to Harvard University, which maintains world-renowned collections of Byzantine and pre-Columbian art there. Both are small but choice, reflecting the enormous skill and creativity going on at roughly the same time on two sides of the Atlantic. The Byzantine collection includes beautiful examples of both religious and secular items executed in mosaic, metal, enamel, and ivory. Pre-Columbian works—artifacts and textiles from Mexico and Central and South America by such peoples as the Aztec,

Maya, and Olmec—are arranged in an enclosed glass pavilion designed by Philip Johnson. Also on view to the public are the lavishly decorated music room and selections from Mrs. Bliss's collection of rare, illustrated garden books. Events at Dumbarton Oaks have not been confined to the study of the past. In 1944 representatives of the United States, Great Britain, China, and the Soviet Union met in the music room here to lay the groundwork for the United Nations.

Anyone with even a mild interest in flowers, shrubs, trees—anything that grows out of the ground—will enjoy a visit to Dumbarton Oaks' 10 acres of formal gardens, one of the loveliest spots in all of Washington (enter via R Street). Designed by noted landscape architect Beatrix Farrand, the gardens incorporate elements of traditional English, Italian, and French styles. A full-time crew of a dozen gardeners toils to maintain the stunning collection of terraces, geometric gardens, tree-shaded brick walks, fountains, arbors, and pools. Plenty of well-positioned benches make this a good place for resting weary feet, too. *Art collections: 1703 32nd St. NW, tel. 202/338–8278 (recorded information) or 202/342–3200. Suggested donation: $1. Open Tues.–Sun. 2–5. Gardens: 31st and R Sts. NW. Admission: Apr, 1–Oct. 31, $2 adults, $1 senior citizens and children under 12, senior citizens free on Wed; Nov.1–Mar. 31, free. Open Apr. 1–Oct. 31, daily 2 –6; Nov. 1–Mar. 31, daily 2–5. Gardens and collections are closed on national holidays and Christmas eve.*

Three other sylvan retreats lie north of R Street in upper Georgetown. Originally part of the Bliss estate, **Dumbarton Oaks Park** sprawls to the north and west. **Montrose Park** lies to the east of the estate. Further east is ㉑ **Oak Hill Cemetery,** its funerary obelisks, crosses, and gravestones spread out like an amphitheater of the dead on a hill overlooking Rock Creek. Near the entrance is an 1850 Gothic-style chapel designed by Smithsonian Castle architect James Renwick. Across from the chapel is the resting place of actor, playwright, and diplomat John H. Payne, who is remembered today primarily for his song "Home Sweet Home." A few hundred feet to the north is the circular tomb of William Corcoran, founder of the Corcoran Gallery of Art. *30th and R Sts. NW, tel. 202/337–2835. Admission free. Open weekdays 10–4; closed major holidays.*

㉒ Walking south on 28th Street you'll pass **Evermay** (1623 28th St. NW). The Georgian manor house, built around 1800 by real estate speculator Samuel Davidson, is almost hidden by its black-and-gold gates and high brick wall. Davidson wanted it that way. He sometimes took out advertisements in newspapers warning sightseers to avoid his estate "as they would a den of devils or rattlesnakes." The mansion is in private hands, but its grounds are often opened for garden tours.

㉓ A few steps east of 28th Street on Q Street is **Dumbarton House,** the headquarters of the National Society of the Colonial Dames of America. Its symmetry and the two bow wings on the north side make Dumbarton, built around 1800, a distinctive example of Georgian architecture. The man who built the house, Joseph Nourse, was registrar of the U.S. Treasury. Other well-known Americans have spent time at the house, including Dolley Madison, who is said to have stopped here when fleeing Washington in 1814. One hundred years later, the house was moved 50 feet up the hill, when Q Street was cut through to the Dumbarton Bridge.

Eight rooms inside Dumbarton House have been restored to their Colonial splendor and are decorated with period furnishings, such as mahogany American Chippendale chairs, hallmark silver, Persian rugs, and a breakfront cabinet filled with rare books. Notable items include a 1789 Charles Willson Peale portrait of Benjamin Stoddert's children (with an early view of Georgetown harbor in the background), Martha Washington's traveling cloak, and a British redcoat's red coat. *2715 Q St. NW, tel. 202/337–2288. Suggested donation: $3. Open Tues.–Sat. 9:30–12:30. Group tours by appointment. Occasionally closed weekends for private events.*

Tour 7: Dupont Circle

Numbers in the margin correspond to points of interest on the Tour 7: Dupont Circle map.

Three of Washington's main thoroughfares intersect at Dupont Circle: Connecticut, New Hampshire, and Massachusetts avenues. With a handsome small park and a splashing fountain in the center, Dupont Circle is more than a deserted island around which traffic flows, making it an exception among Washington circles. The activity on the circle spills over into the surrounding streets, one of the liveliest, most vibrant neighborhoods in Washington.

Development near Dupont Circle started during the post–Civil War boom of the 1870s. As the city increased in stature, the nation's wealthy and influential citizens began building their mansions near the circle. The area underwent a different kind of transformation in the middle of this century, when the middle and upper classes deserted Washington for the suburbs, and in the '60s the circle became the starting point for marches sponsored by various counterculture groups. Today the neighborhood is once again fashionable, and its many restaurants, off-beat shops, and specialty bookstores lend it a distinctive, cosmopolitan air.

❶ Start your exploration in **Dupont Circle** itself (Metro stop, Dupont Circle). Originally known as Pacific Circle, this hub was the westernmost circle in Pierre L'Enfant's original design for the Federal City. The name was changed in 1884, when Congress authorized construction of a bronze statue honoring Civil War hero Admiral Samuel F. Dupont. The statue fell into disrepair, and Dupont's family—who had never liked it anyway—replaced it in 1921 with the fountain you see today. The marble fountain, with its allegorical figures Sea, Stars, and Wind, was created by Daniel Chester French, the sculptor of Lincoln's statue in the Lincoln Memorial.

As you look around the circumference of the circle, you'll be able to see the special constraints within which architects in Washington must work. Since a half dozen streets converge on Dupont Circle, the buildings around it are, for the most part, wedge shaped and set on oddly shaped plots of land like massive slices of pie.

Only two of the great houses that stood on the circle in the early 20th century remain today. The Renaissance-style house at **15 Dupont Circle,** next to P Street, was built in 1903 for Robert W. Patterson, publisher of the *Washington Times-Herald.* Patterson's daughter, Cissy, who succeeded him as publisher of the paper, was known for hosting parties that attracted such notables as William Randolph Hearst, Douglas MacArthur, and J. Edgar Hoover. In 1927, while Cissy was living in New York City and the White House was being refurbished, Calvin Coolidge and his family stayed in this Dupont Circle home. The Coolidges received American flyer Charles Lindbergh here; some of the most famous photographs of Lindy were taken as he stood on the house's balcony and smiled down at the crowds below. After Patterson's death the house was bought by the Washington Club. The **Sulgrave Club,** at the corner of Massachusetts Avenue, was also once a private home and is now likewise a club. Neither is open to the public.

Cross the traffic circle carefully and head south on New Hampshire Avenue. A block down on the left is the impressive **Heurich Mansion,** whose dark sandstone walls and stolid countenance provide quite a contrast to the two gay houses on the circle. This severe Romanesque Revival mansion was the home of Christian Heurich, a German orphan who made his fortune in this country in the beer business. Heurich's brewery was located in Foggy Bottom, where the Kennedy Center stands today. Brewing was a dangerous business in the 19th century, and fires had more than once reduced Heurich's beer factory to ashes. Perhaps because of this he insisted that his home, completed in 1894, be fireproof. Although 17 fireplaces were installed—some with onyx facings, one with the bronze image of a lion staring out from the back—not a single one ever held a fire.

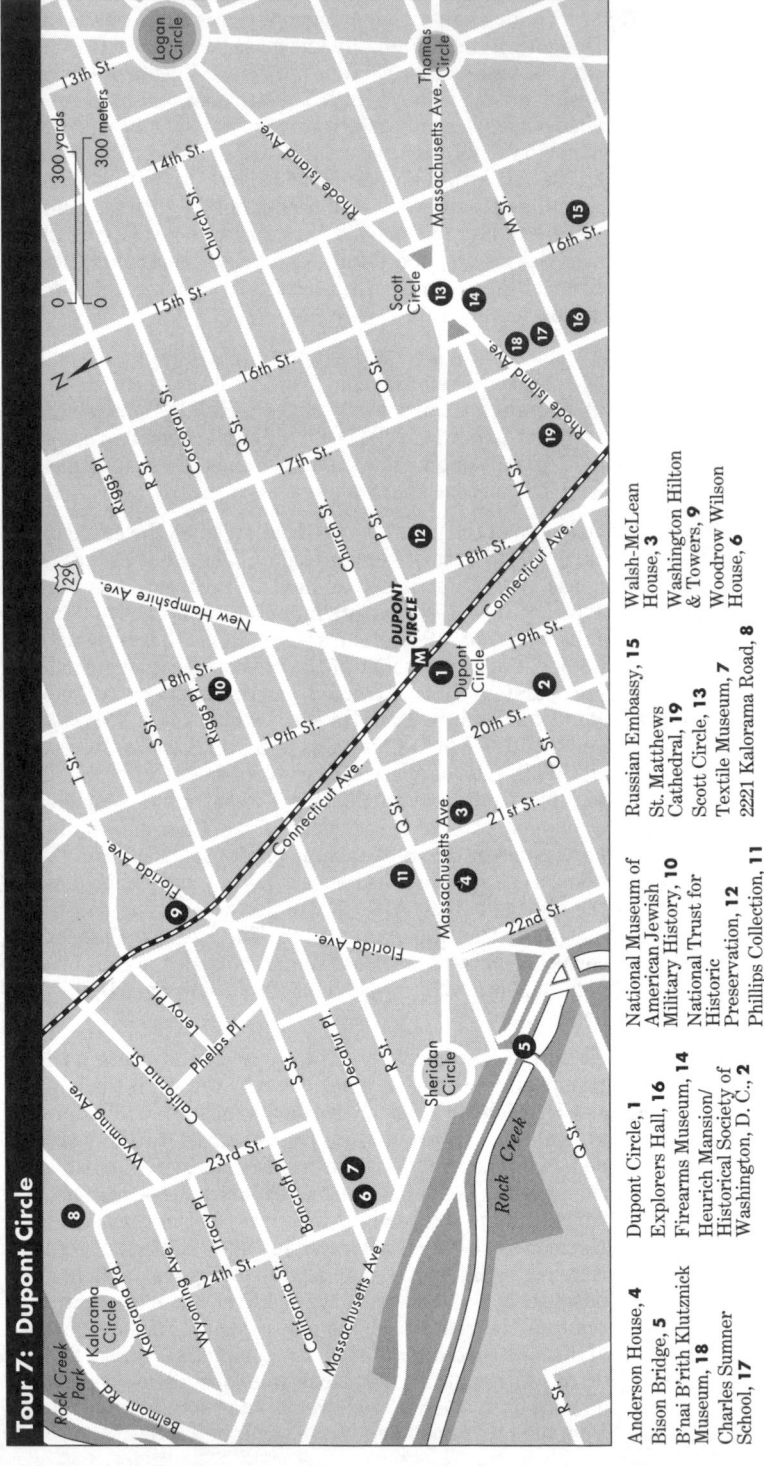

Tour 7: Dupont Circle

N

300 yards
300 meters
0
0

Logan Circle

Thomas Circle

Massachusetts Ave. Circle

Scott Circle

Rock Creek Park

Kalorama Circle

Sheridan Circle

DUPONT CIRCLE M

Dupont Circle

Rock Creek

Anderson House, **4**
Bison Bridge, **5**
B'nai B'rith Klutznick Museum, **18**
Charles Sumner School, **17**

Dupont Circle, **1**
Explorers Hall, **16**
Firearms Museum, **14**
Heurich Mansion/ Historical Society of Washington, D. C., **2**

National Museum of American Jewish Military History, **10**
National Trust for Historic Preservation, **12**
Phillips Collection, **11**

Russian Embassy, **15**
St. Matthews Cathedral, **19**
Scott Circle, **13**
Textile Museum, **7**
2221 Kalorama Road, **8**

Walsh-McLean House, **3**
Washington Hilton & Towers, **9**
Woodrow Wilson House, **6**

After Heurich's widow died, in 1955, the house was turned over to the **Historical Society of Washington, D.C.** Today it serves as the group's headquarters and houses its voluminous archives. All the furnishings in the house were owned and used by the Heurichs. The interior of the house is an eclectic Victorian treasure trove filled with plaster detailing, carved wooden doors, and painted ceilings. The downstairs breakfast room, where Heurich, his wife, and their three children ate most of their meals, is decorated like a rathskeller and is adorned with such German sayings as "A good drink makes old people young."

Heurich must have taken the German proverbs seriously. He drank his beer every day, had three wives (not all at once), and lived to be 102. (In 1986 Heurich's grandson Gary started brewing the family beer again. Though it's made in Utica, New York, he vows to someday build another Heurich brewery near Washington.) Docents who give tours of the house are adept at answering questions about other Washington landmarks, too. *1307 New Hampshire Ave. NW, tel. 202/785–2068. Admission: $3 adults, $1.50 senior citizens, children through 12th grade free. Open Wed.–Sat. noon–3.*

Cross New Hampshire Avenue and turn left on O Street. The row houses on this block are a little less impressive than Heurich's castle, but they are examples of what makes Dupont Circle so attractive to Washington's young professionals: spacious brick Victorian town houses close to nightlife, offices, and public transportation.

Turn north on 21st Street and cross P Street. This area has a high concentration of restaurants and bars and is crowded and boisterous at night. It also serves as an informal crossroads for Washington's gay community. (There are several gay night spots farther up P Street.)

Time Out This Dupont Circle location is one of three branches of **Pan Asian Noodles & Grill** (2020 P St. NW, tel. 202/872–8889) in Washington. All offer reasonably priced noodle dishes from around the Orient.

At the corner of Massachusetts Avenue and 21st Street is ❸ the opulent **Walsh-McLean House.** Tom McLean was an Irishman who made a fortune with a Colorado gold mine and came to Washington to show his wealth. Washington was the perfect place to establish a presence for America's late-19th-century nouveau riche. It was easier to enter "society" in the nation's planned capital than in New York or Philadelphia, and wealthy industrialists and lucky entrepreneurs flocked to the city on the Potomac. Walsh announced his arrival with this 60-room mansion. His daughter, Evalyn Walsh-McLean, the last private owner of the Hope Diamond (now in the Smithsonian's Museum of Natural History), was one of the city's leading hostesses.

Today the house is used as an embassy by the Indonesian government. The **Jockey Club** restaurant in the redbrick Ritz-Carlton Hotel across the street is a favorite lunching spot of Washington power brokers.

Head west on Massachusetts Avenue. The palatial home at No. 2118 is a mystery even to many longtime Washingtonians, who assume it's just another embassy. **Anderson House** is not an embassy, though it does have a link to the diplomatic world. Larz Anderson was a diplomat whose career included postings to Japan and Belgium. Anderson and his heiress wife, Isabel, toured the world, picking up objects that struck their fancy. They filled their residence, which was constructed in 1905, with the booty of their travels, including choir stalls from an Italian Renaissance church, Flemish tapestries, and a large—if spotty—collection of Asian art. All this remains in the house, for visitors to see.

In accordance with Anderson's wishes, the building also serves as the headquarters of a group he belonged to: the **Society of the Cincinnati.** The oldest patriotic organization in the country, the society was formed in 1783 by a group of officers who had served with George Washington during the Revolutionary War. The group took the name Cincinnati from Cincinnatus, a distinguished Roman who, circa 500 BC, led an army against Rome's enemies and later quelled civil disturbances in the city. After each instance he returned to the simple life on his farm. The story impressed the American officers, who saw in it a mirror of their own situation: They too would leave the battlefields behind to get on with the business of forging a new nation. (One such member went on to name the city in Ohio.) Today's members are direct descendants of those American revolutionaries.

Many of the displays in the society's museum focus on the Colonial period and the Revolutionary War. One room— painted in a marvelous trompe l'oeil style that deceives visitors into thinking the walls are covered with sculpture—is filled with military miniatures from the United States and France. (Because of the important role France played in defeating the British, French officers were invited to join the society. Pierre L'Enfant, "Artist of the Revolution" and planner of Washington, designed the society's eagle medallion.)

The house is often used by the federal government to entertain visiting dignitaries. Amid the glitz, glamour, beauty, and patriotic spectacle of the mansion are two delightful painted panels in the solarium that depict the Andersons' favorite motor-car sightseeing routes around Washington. *2118 Massachusetts Ave. NW, tel. 202/785–2040. Admission free. Open Tues.–Sat. 1–4.*

Across the street at 2121 Massachusetts Avenue is the **Cosmos Club,** founded in 1878 and perhaps the most exclusive private club in the city. Neither money nor influence will get you on the membership rolls. It takes brains. Different rooms in the club celebrate members who have won Nobel Prizes or appeared on postage stamps. The formerly men-only club started accepting women in 1988. Judith Martin (aka Miss Manners) was one of the first admitted.

Head west on Q Street, past a row of expensive town houses, to the **Bison Bridge.** Tour guides at the Smithsonian's Museum of Natural History are quick to remind visitors that America never had buffalo; the big animals that roamed the plains were bison. Though many maps and guidebooks call this the Buffalo Bridge, the four bronze statues by A. Phimister Proctor are of bison. Officially called the **Dumbarton Bridge,** the structure stretches across Rock Creek Park into Georgetown. Its sides are decorated with busts of Native Americans, the work of architect Glenn Brown, who, along with his son Bedford, designed the bridge in 1914. The best way to see the busts is to walk the footpath along Rock Creek or to lean over the green railings beside the bison and peer through the trees.

Walking north on 23rd Street you'll pass between two more embassies, those of Turkey and Romania, both of which sit on **Sheridan Circle** and are topped with antennae as big as trampolines used to send messages back to the homeland.

Turn left on Massachusetts Avenue. Although the entire Dupont Circle area is dotted with embassies, the stretch of Massachusetts Avenue on either side of Sheridan Circle is known as Embassy Row proper. The area is rife with delegations from foreign countries, and a stroll down the street will provide you with an opportunity to test your knowledge of the world's flags.

Continue west on Massachusetts Avenue. The **Cameroon Embassy** is housed in the mansion at 2349 Massachusetts Avenue. This fanciful castle, with its conical tower, bronze weathervane, and intricate detailing around the windows and balconies, is the westernmost of the beaux arts–style mansions built along Massachusetts Avenue in the late-19th and early 20th centuries.

Turn right on S Street. The statue on the left commemorates Irish patriot **Robert Emmet;** it was dedicated in 1966 to mark the 50th anniversary of Irish independence. A small reproduction can be found in the **Woodrow Wilson House,** a few hundred feet down S Street. Wilson is the only president who stayed in Washington after leaving the White House. (He's also the only president buried in the city, inside the Washington Cathedral.) He and his second wife, Edith Bolling Wilson, retired in 1920 to this Georgian Revival house designed by Washington architect Waddy B. Wood. (Wood also designed the Department of the Interior

Building on C Street.) The house had been built in 1915 for a carpet magnate, and on the first and third floors you can still see the half-snaps that run along the edges of the floors to hold down the long-gone wall-to-wall carpeting.

President Wilson suffered a stroke toward the end of his second term, in 1919, and he lived out the last few years of his life on this quiet street. Edith made sure he was comfortable; she had a bed constructed that was the same dimensions as the large Lincoln bed Wilson had slept in in the White House. She also had the house's trunk lift electrified so the partially paralyzed president could move from floor to floor. When the streetcars stopped running in 1962 the elevator stopped working. It had received its electricity directly from the streetcar line.

After Edith died, in 1961, the house and its contents were bequeathed to the National Trust for Historic Preservation. On view inside are such items as a Gobelins tapestry, a baseball signed by King George V, and the shell casing from the first shot fired by U.S. forces in World War I. The house also contains memorabilia related to the history of the short-lived League of Nations, including the colorful flag Wilson hoped would be adopted by that organization. *2340 S St. NW, tel. 202/387-4062. Admission: $4 adults, $2.50 senior citizens and students, children under 7 free. Open Tues.-Sun. 10-4; closed major holidays.*

❼ Just next door, in a house that was also designed by Waddy Wood, is the **Textile Museum.** In the 1890s, founder George Hewitt Myers purchased his first Oriental rug for his dorm room at Yale and subsequently collected more than 12,000 textiles and 1,500 carpets. An heir to the Bristol-Myers fortune, Myers and his wife lived two houses down from Wilson, at 2310 S Street, in a home designed by John Russell Pope, architect of the National Archives and Jefferson Memorial. Myers bought the house next door, at No. 2320, and opened his museum to the public in 1925. Rotating exhibits are taken from a permanent collection of historic and ethnographic items that include Coptic textiles, Kashmir embroidery, Turkman tribal rugs, and pre-Columbian textiles from Central and South America. At least one show of modern textiles—such as quilts or fiber art—is mounted each year. *2320 S St. NW, tel. 202/667-0441. Suggested donation: $5. Open Mon.-Sat. 10-5, Sun. 1-5; closed major holidays. Highlight tours: Sept.-May; Wed., Sat., and Sun. at 2.*

S Street is an informal dividing line between the Dupont Circle area to the south and the exclusive **Kalorama** neighborhood to the north. The name for this peaceful, tree-filled enclave—Greek for "beautiful view"—was contributed by politician and writer Joel Barlow, who bought the large tract in 1807. Kalorama is filled with embassies and luxurious homes. Walk north on 23rd Street until it dead-ends at

❽ the Tudor mansion at **2221 Kalorama Road.** This imposing house was built in 1911 for mining millionaire W.W. Lawrence, but since 1936 it has been the residence of the French ambassador. For a taste of the beautiful view that so captivated Barlow, walk west on Kalorama Road, then turn right on Kalorama Circle. At the bottom of the circle you can look down over Rock Creek Park, the finger of green that pokes into northwest Washington.

Walk back down 23rd Street then left down Kalorama. The large, beige institutional building on the left near Connecticut Avenue is the Chinese Embassy. Turn right and walk south down Connecticut Avenue. On the left at 1919 Connecticut is the **Washington Hilton & Towers,** home of the largest ballroom on the East Coast and site of John Hinckley's 1981 assassination attempt on Ronald Reagan.

⑩ Two blocks off Connecticut to the left is the **National Museum of American Jewish Military History.** The message here is that Jews in this country are first and foremost American citizens and have served in every war the nation has fought. It is primarily a military museum, with displays of weapons, uniforms, medals, recruitment posters, and other memorabilia. The few specifically religious items—a camouflage yarmulke, rabbinical supplies fashioned from shell casings and parachute silk—underscore the strange demands placed on religion during war. *1811 R St. NW, tel. 202/265–6280. Admission free. Open weekdays 9–5, Sun. 1–5; closed Sat. and federal and Jewish holidays.*

On R street on the other side of Connecticut is the **Fondo Del Sol Visual Art and Media Center,** a nonprofit center devoted to the cultural heritage of the Americas. Changing exhibitions cover contemporary, pre-Columbian, and folk art. The center also offers a program of lectures, concerts, poetry readings, exhibit tours, and an annual summer festival featuring salsa and reggae music. *2112 R St. NW, tel. 202/483–2777. Admission: $2, children under 13 free. Open Wed.–Sat. 12:30–5.*

Walk south on 21st Street. Many private art galleries—selling the work of local, national, and international artists—have sprung up around here, perhaps to bask in the glow of our next stop.

⑪ Washington has many museums that are the legacy of one great patron, but the **Phillips Collection,** at 21st and Q streets, is among the most beloved. In 1918 Duncan Phillips, grandson of a founder of the Jones and Laughlin Steel Company, started to collect art for a museum that would stand as a memorial to his father and brother, who had died within 13 months of each other. Three years later what was first called the Phillips Memorial Gallery opened in two rooms of this Georgian-Revival home near Dupont Circle. It was the first permanent museum of modern art in the country.

Not interested in a painting's market value or its faddishness, Phillips searched for works that impressed him as outstanding products of a particular artist's unique vision. Holdings include works by George Braque, Paul Cézanne, Paul Klee, Henri Matisse, John Henry Twachtman, and the largest museum collection in the country of the work of Pierre Bonnard. The exhibits change regularly. The collection's best-known paintings include Renoir's *Luncheon of the Boating Party, Repentant Peter*s by both Goya *and* El Greco, *A Bowl of Plums* by 18th-century artist Jean-Baptiste Siméon Chardin, Degas's *Dancers at the Bar,* Van Gogh's *Entrance to the Public Garden at Arles,* and Cézanne's self-portrait, the painting Phillips said he would save first if his gallery caught fire. During the '20s, Phillips and his wife, Marjorie, started to support American Modernists such as John Marin, Georgia O'Keeffe, and Arthur Dove.

The Phillips is a comfortable museum. Works of a favorite artist are often grouped together in "exhibition units," and unlike most other galleries (where uniformed guards appear uninterested in the masterpieces around them) the Phillips employs students of art, many of whom are artists themselves, to sit by the paintings and answer visitors' questions.

The Phillips family moved out of the house in 1930. An addition was built in 1960 and renovated and renamed the Goh Annex in 1989. It gave the Phillips 50% more exhibit space and is host to traveling exhibits and rotating selections from the museum's permanent collection. *1600–1612 21st St. NW, tel. 202/387–2151. Admission: weekends, $6.50 adults, $3.25 students and senior citizens; suggested donation weekdays, $6.50 adults, $3.25 students and senior citizens, under 19 free. Open Mon.–Sat. 10–5, Sun. noon–7. Tours Wed. and Sat. at 2. Gallery talks 1st and 3rd Thurs. at 12:30.*

After visiting the Phillips, walk east on Q Street and turn south on Connecticut Avenue.

Time Out Connecticut Avenue above and below Dupont Circle is chockablock with restaurants that will satisfy any craving. The **Chesapeake Bagel Bakery** (1636 Connecticut Ave.) is a low-key lunchroom that features a wide variety of bagel sandwiches. **Ferrara** (just above the Q Street entrance to the Dupont Circle Metro) is part of the invasion of specialty coffee shops. In addition to espressos and cappuccinos, it offers Italian pastries such as cannoli and biscotti, as well as muffins and cookies. There aren't many tables inside, but you can take your treats to Dupont Circle, a block away.

Skirt the circle and walk east on Massachusetts Avenue. The **National Trust for Historic Preservation** sits at the corner of 18th Street and Massachusetts Avenue in, naturally, a building that has been historically preserved. The building once housed some of the most luxurious apartments in the city. The beaux arts–style McCormick Apartments, designed by Jules H. de Sibour, were built in 1917 and contained only six apartments, one on each floor, each with 11,000 square feet of space. Some of Washington's most prominent citizens lived here, including hostess Perle Mesta and Andrew Mellon, secretary of the treasury under three presidents, whose top-floor flat contained many of the paintings that would later go to the National Gallery of Art. During World War II the building was converted to office space, and in 1977 it was bought by the National Trust. The building is closed to the public, but a quick peek at the circular lobby will give you an idea of the lavish world its onetime residents inhabited.

Continue down Massachusetts Avenue. On the left is the **Brookings Institution,** one of dozens of think tanks in Washington that offer their partisan and nonpartisan advice to whoever is in power or whoever would like to be. Farther east on the left you'll spot the **Australian Embassy,** containing a gallery that periodically shows works of art of an antipodean nature. *1601 Massachusetts Ave. NW, tel. 202/797–3000. Admission free. Open weekdays 8:30–4:30.*

⓭ **Scott Circle** is at the center of the intersections of Massachusetts and Rhode Island avenues and 16th Street. The equestrian statue of **General Winfield Scott** was cast from cannon captured in the Mexican War. On the west side of Scott Circle there is a statue of fiery orator **Daniel Webster.** If you walk to the south side of the circle and look down 16th Street you'll get a familiar view of the columns of the White House, six blocks away. Across the circle is an interesting memorial to **S.C.F. Hahnemann,** his statue sitting in a recessed wall, his head surrounded by a mosaic of colorful tiles. (Who, you ask, was S.C.F. Hahnemann? He was the founder of the homeopathic school of medicine. Washington is a city of monuments, not all of them to people whose names are household words.)

The headquarters of the National Rifle Association is also near the circle. There are dozens of guns on display in the **⓮** NRA's **Firearms Museum,** from muzzle-loading flintlocks used in the Revolutionary War to high-tech pistols used by Olympic shooting teams. Also on display are weapons that once belonged to presidents, such as Teddy Roosevelt's .32-caliber Browning pistol and a Winchester rifle used by Dwight Eisenhower. *1600 Rhode Island Ave. NW, tel. 202/ 828–6253. Admission free. Open Mon.–Sat. 10–4; closed major holidays.*

One block south on 16th Street stands the **Jefferson Hotel.** Designed by Jules H. de Sibour, the man responsible for the McCormick Apartments, it too started out as apartments but was converted to a hotel in the '50s. It has a reputation for luxury and discretion and is a favorite temporary

home for White House cabinet members awaiting confirmation. Farther down 16th Street, the red, white, and blue
⓯ flag of Russia flies before the **Russian Embassy** (1125 16th St. NW), housed in an ornate mansion that was built for the widow of George Pullman of railroad-car fame. It first did diplomatic duty as the Imperial Russian Embassy, then became the Soviet Embassy, and now it's Russian once again. The rest of the ex-Soviet republics were left scrambling for their own embassies after the breakup of the USSR in 1991.

Turn right onto M Street. On the southwest corner of 16th and M streets sits the headquarters of the **National Geographic Society.** Founded in 1888, the society is best known for its yellow-bordered magazine, found in family rooms and attics across the country. The society has sponsored numerous expeditions throughout its 100-year history, including those of Admirals Peary and Byrd and underwater
⓰ explorer Jacques Cousteau. **Explorers Hall,** entered from 17th Street, is the magazine come to life. Recently renovated, Explorers Hall invites visitors to learn about the world in a decidedly interactive way. You can experience everything from a minitornado to video "touch-screens" that explain various geographic concepts and then quiz you on what you've learned. The most dramatic events take place in Earth Station One, a 72-seat amphitheater that sends the audience on a journey around the world. The centerpiece is a hand-painted globe, 11 feet in diameter, that floats and spins on a cushion of air, showing off different features of the planet. *17th and M Sts., tel. 202/857–7588 (recorded information), 202/857–7689 (group tour information). Admission free. Open Mon.–Sat. and holidays 9–5, Sun. 10–5.*

⓱ Across M Street is the **Charles Sumner School,** built in 1872 for the education of black children in the city. It takes its name from the Massachusetts senator who delivered a blistering attack against slavery in 1856 and was savagely caned as a result by a congressman from South Carolina. The building was designed by Adolph Cluss, who created the Arts and Industries Building on the Mall. It is typical of the District's Victorian-era public schools. Beautifully restored in 1986, the school serves mainly as a conference center, though it hosts changing art exhibits and houses a permanent collection of memorabilia relating to the city's public school system. *1201 17th St. NW, tel. 202/727–3419. Admission free. Open weekdays 10–5. Often closed for conferences; call ahead to arrange tours.*

Further up 17th Street, at the corner of Rhode Island Ave-
⓲ nue, is the **B'nai B'rith Klutznick Museum,** devoted to the history of the Jewish people. The museum's permanent exhibits span 20 centuries and highlight Jewish festivals and the rituals employed to mark the various stages of life. A wide variety of Jewish decorative art, adorning such items as spice boxes and Torah wrappers, is on display. Changing

exhibits highlight the work of contemporary Jewish artists. *1640 Rhode Island Ave. NW, tel. 202/857–6583. Admission free. Open Sun.–Fri. 10–5; closed Sat. and federal and Jewish holidays.*

Half a block west on Rhode Island Avenue, across from a memorial to nuns who served as nurses during the Civil War, is **St. Matthew's Cathedral,** the seat of Washington's Catholic archbishop. John F. Kennedy frequently worshiped in this Renaissance-style church, and in 1963 his funeral mass was held within its richly decorated walls. Set in the floor, directly in front of the main altar, is a memorial to the slain president: "Here rested the remains of President Kennedy at the requiem mass November 25, 1963, before their removal to Arlington where they lie in expectation of a heavenly resurrection." *1725 Rhode Island Ave. NW, tel. 202/347–3215. Admission free. Open weekdays and Sun. 6:30–6:30, Sat. 7:30–6:30. Tours Sun. 2:30–4:30.*

You are now between two Metro stations. Dupont Circle is two blocks north on Connecticut Avenue, and Farragut North is one block south.

Tour 8: Foggy Bottom

Numbers in the margin correspond to points of interest on the Tour 8: Foggy Bottom map.

The Foggy Bottom area of Washington—bordered roughly by the Potomac and Rock Creek to the west, 20th Street to the east, Pennsylvania Avenue to the north, and Constitution Avenue to the south—has three main claims to fame: the State Department, the Kennedy Center, and George Washington University. In 1763 a German immigrant named Jacob Funk purchased this land, and a community called Funkstown sprang up on the Potomac. This nickname is only slightly less amusing than the present one, an appellation that owes its derivation to the wharves, breweries, lime kilns, and glassworks that were built near the water. Smoke from these factories combined with the swampy air of the low-lying ground to produce a permanent fog along the waterfront.

The smoke-belching factories ensured work for the hundreds of German and Irish immigrants who settled in Foggy Bottom in the 19th century. By the 1930s, however, industry was on the way out, and Foggy Bottom had become a poor, predominantly black part of Washington. The opening of the State Department headquarters in 1947 reawakened middle-class interest in the neighborhood's modest row houses. Many of them are now gone, and Foggy Bottom today suffers from a split personality, and tiny, one-room-wide row houses sit next to large, mixed-use developments.

❶ Start your exploration near the Foggy Bottom Metro station on 23rd Street near I Street. The campus of **George Washington University** covers much of Foggy Bottom south of Pennsylvania Avenue between 19th and 24th streets. George Washington had always hoped the capital would be home to a world-class university. He even left 50 shares of stock in the Potowmack Canal Co. to endow it. Congress never acted upon his wishes, however, and it wasn't until 1822 that the university that would eventually be named after the first president began to take shape. The private Columbian College in the District of Columbia opened that year with the aim of training students for the Baptist ministry. In 1904, the university shed its Baptist connections and changed its name to George Washington University. In 1912, it moved to its present location and since that time has become the second largest landholder in the District (after the federal government). Students have ranged from J. Edgar Hoover to Jacqueline Kennedy Onassis. In addition to modern university buildings GWU occupies many 19th-century houses.

❷ Walk west from the Metro station on the I Street pedestrian mall, then turn left on New Hampshire Avenue. Across Virginia Avenue is the **Watergate,** possibly the world's most notorious apartment/office complex, famous for the events that took place here on June 17, 1972. As Nixon aides E. Howard Hunt, Jr., and G. Gordon Liddy sat in the Howard Johnson Motor Lodge across the street, five men were caught trying to bug the headquarters of the Democratic National Committee on the sixth floor of 2600 Virginia Avenue. (There's a marketing company in that space today.)

Even before the break-in, the Watergate—which first opened in 1965—was well known in the capital. Within its distinctive curving lines and behind its "toothpick" balusters have lived some of Washington's famous, including John Mitchell and Rose Mary Woods of Nixon White House fame, and such politicians as Jacob Javits, Alan Cranston, and Robert and Elizabeth Dole. The embassies of Qatar, the United Arab Emirates, Sweden, and Yemen are also in the Watergate. The suffix "-gate" is attached to any political scandal nowadays, but the Watergate itself was named after a monumental flight of steps leading down to the Potomac behind the Lincoln Memorial. The original Watergate was the sight of band concerts until airplane noise from nearby National Airport made the site impractical.

❸ Walk south on New Hampshire Avenue, past the Saudi Arabian Embassy, to the **John F. Kennedy Center for the Performing Arts.** The opening of the Kennedy Center in 1971 established Washington as a cultural city to be reckoned with. Concerts, ballets, opera, musicals, and drama are presented in the center's five theaters, and movies are screened almost every night in the theater of the American Film Institute.

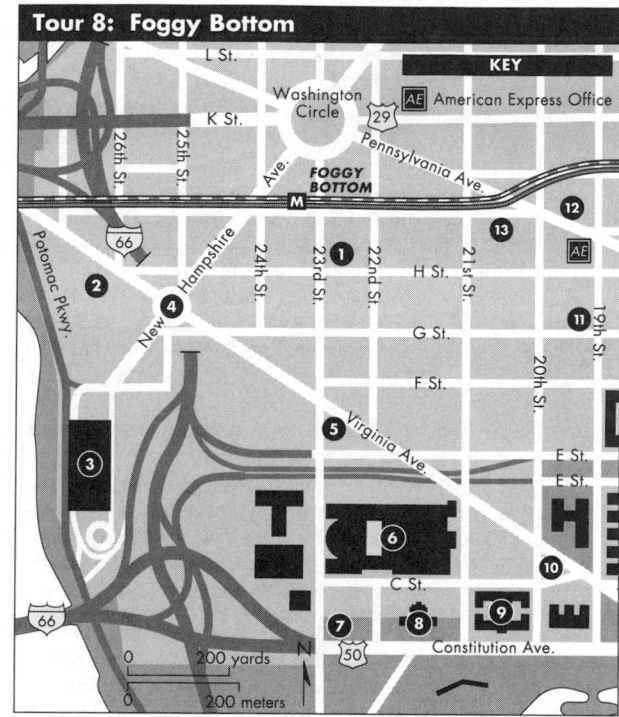

Tour 8: Foggy Bottom

The idea for a national cultural center had been proposed by President Eisenhower in 1958. John F. Kennedy had also strongly supported the idea, and after his assassination it was decided to dedicate the center to him as a living memorial. Some critics have called the center's square design unimaginative—it's been dubbed the cake box that the more decorative Watergate came in—but no one has denied that the building is immense. The Grand Foyer, lighted by 18 one-ton Orrefors crystal chandeliers, is 630 feet long. (Even at this size it is mobbed at intermission.) Many of the center's furnishings were donated by foreign countries: The chandeliers came from Sweden, the Matisse tapestries outside the Opera House came from France, and the 3,700 tons of white Carrara marble for the interior and exterior of the building were a gift from Italy. Flags fly in the Hall of Nations and the Hall of States, and in the center of the foyer is a seven-foot-high bronze bust of Kennedy by sculptor Robert Berks.

The Library of Congress maintains a **Performing Arts Library** on the roof terrace level, mounting periodic theatrical and musical exhibits (original Mozart manuscripts were a recent offering). If you can tolerate the sound of jets screaming up the Potomac to National Airport, you can get one of the city's better views from the rooftop terrace: To the north are Georgetown and the National Cathedral; to the west Theodore Roosevelt Island and Rosslyn, Virginia; and to the south the Lincoln and Jefferson memorials. *New Hampshire Ave. and Rock Creek Pkwy. NW, tel. 202/467-4600. Admission free. Open daily 10 AM–9 PM (or until last show lets out). Box office open Mon.–Sat. 10–9, Sun. and holidays noon–9. Free tours daily 10–1, tel. 202/416–8341 for tour information. Performing Arts Library, tel. 202/707-6245. Open Tues.–Fri. 11–8:30, Sat. 10–6.*

Time Out   There are two restaurants on the top floor of the Kennedy Center. The **Roof Terrace Restaurant** is the most expensive, with a lunch menu that offers open-faced sandwiches and salads. The **Encore Café** has soups, chili, salads, and hot entrées starting at under $5.

Walk back up New Hampshire Avenue; then turn right on G Street, right on Virginia Avenue (follow the outstretched ❹ arm of the **statue of Benito Juárez,** the famed Mexican ❺ statesman) and right on 23rd Street. The **Pan American Health Organization,** American headquarters of the World Health Organization, is at 23rd Street and Virginia Avenue, in the building that looks like a huge car air filter.

❻ Two blocks down is the massive **Department of State building.** On the top floor are the opulent **Diplomatic Reception Rooms,** decorated in the manner of great halls of Europe and the rooms of Colonial American plantations. The museum-quality furnishings include a Philadelphia Highboy, a Paul Revere bowl, and the desk on which the Treaty of Paris was signed. The largest room boasts a specially loomed carpet so heavy and large it had to be airlifted in by helicopter. The rooms are used 15–20 times a week to entertain foreign diplomats and heads of state; you can see them, too, but you need to register for a tour well in advance of your visit. *23rd and C Sts. NW, tel. 202/647–3241. Admission free. Tours weekdays at 9:30, 10:30, and 2:45 (not recommended for children under 12). Summer tours must be booked up to 3 months in advance.*

Across C Street is the **U.S. Naval Medical Command.** In an early sketch of Washington, Thomas Jefferson placed the Capitol atop this hill. One of the federal government's earliest scientific installations was a naval observatory built here in 1844. By the 1880s, however, Foggy Bottom's smoke and haze forced officials to move the observatory to higher ground, in northwest Washington.

Continue down 23rd Street and turn left onto Constitution Avenue. On the south side of Constitution are the Lincoln and Vietnam Veterans memorials (*see* Tour 2: The Monuments, *above*). The **American Pharmaceutical Association** ❼ building is on the corner of Constitution Avenue and 23rd Street. This white-marble building was designed by John Russell Pope and completed in 1934. The APA is one of more than 3,000 trade and professional associations (as obscure as the Cast Iron Soil Pipe Institute and as well-known as the National Association of Broadcasters) that have chosen Washington for their headquarters, eager to represent their members' interests before the government.

⑧ One block east is the **National Academy of Sciences.** Inscribed in Greek under the cornice is a quotation from Aristotle on the value of science. Inside, there are often free art exhibits—not all of them relating to science. In front of the academy is Robert Berks's **sculpture of Albert Einstein,** done in the same lumpy, mashed-potato style as the artist's bust of JFK in the Kennedy Center. *2101 Constitution Ave. NW, tel. 202/334–2000. Admission free. Open weekdays 8:30–5.*

⑨ The **Federal Reserve Building** (designed by Folger Library architect Paul Cret) is on Constitution Avenue between 21st and 20th streets. The imposing marble edifice, its bronze entryway topped by a massive eagle, seems to say, "Your money's safe with us." Even so, there isn't any money here. Fort Knox and New York's Federal Reserve Bank hold most of the Federal Reserve System's gold. The stolid building is a bit more human inside, with a varied collection of artwork and four special art exhibitions every year. A 45-minute tour includes a film that attempts to explain exactly what it is that "the Fed" does. *Enter on C St., between 20th and 21st Sts., tel. 202/452–3686. Admission free. Open weekdays 11:30–2. Tours Thurs. at 2:30, tel. 202/452–2526.*

Turn left on 20th Street. The fountain one block up in
⑩ **Robert Owen Park** is perfect for cooling hot and tired feet. Crossing Virginia Avenue and continuing north on 20th Street will take you back onto the campus of George Washington University. Foggy Bottom's immigrant past is apparent in the **United Church** at 20th and G streets. Built in 1891 for blue-collar Germans in the neighborhood, the church still conducts services in German the first and third Sunday of every month.

A block away at 19th and G is the **International Monetary Fund Visitors Center.** Exhibits and a number of films outline the origin and functions of the IMF. International photographs, paintings, and sculpture are on display. The center also hosts cultural events—readings, recitals, and films—with an international flavor. *700 19th St. NW, tel. 202/623–6869. Admission free. Open weekdays 10–6. Films usually shown between noon and 2. Closed federal holidays.*

Walk two blocks north to Pennsylvania Avenue. To the left—near No. 1901—are the only two survivors of a string
⑫ of 18th-century row houses known as the **Seven Buildings.** One of the five that have been demolished had served as President Madison's executive mansion after the British burned the White House in 1814. The two survivors are now dwarfed by the taller office block behind them.

A similar fate befell a row of residences further west on Pennsylvania Avenue between 20th and 21st streets. These Victorian houses have been hollowed out and refurbished and serve as the entryway for a modern glass office building **⓭** at **2000 Pennsylvania Avenue.** The backs of the buildings are under the sloping roof of the new development, preserved as if in an urban terrarium.

To get to the Foggy Bottom Metro station, walk three blocks west on I Street.

Tour 9: Cleveland Park and the National Zoo

Numbers in the margin correspond to points of interest on the Tour 9: Cleveland Park and the National Zoo map.

Cleveland Park, a tree-shaded neighborhood in northwest Washington, owes its name to onetime summer resident Grover Cleveland and its development to the streetcar line that was laid along Connecticut Avenue in the 1890s. President Cleveland and his wife, Frances Folson, escaped the heat of downtown Washington in 1886 by establishing a summer White House on Newark Street between 35th and 36th streets. Many prominent Washingtonians followed suit. When the streetcar came through in 1892, construction in the area snowballed. Developer John Sherman hired local architects to design houses and provided amenities such as a fire station and a streetcar-waiting lodge to entice home buyers out of the city and into "rural" Cleveland Park. Today the neighborhood's attractive houses and suburban character are popular with Washington professionals.

Start your exploration at the Cleveland Park Metro station at Connecticut Avenue and Ordway Street NW. The colo-**❶** nial-style **Park and Shop** on the east side of Connecticut Avenue has the distinction of being the first shopping center with off-street parking in the city. Built in 1930, it was at the time one of only a handful of shopping centers on the East Coast to offer this convenience. Off-street parking was then a rather revolutionary notion, and business and architectural publications of the day followed the center's progress with interest. A 1930 industry magazine explained, "Customers can leave their cars here without fear of violating traffic regulations," and the *Washington Post* gushed that the development was "modern to the nth degree." The Park and Shop sat empty for several years in the 1980s as the very active Cleveland Park Historical Society—fearful that the building might be torn down and replaced with a high rise—lobbied to preserve it in some way. They were successful, and in 1991 the restored Park and Shop, with new green awnings and a tasteful addition, reopened with such modern-day draws as a bagel bakery and a video store.

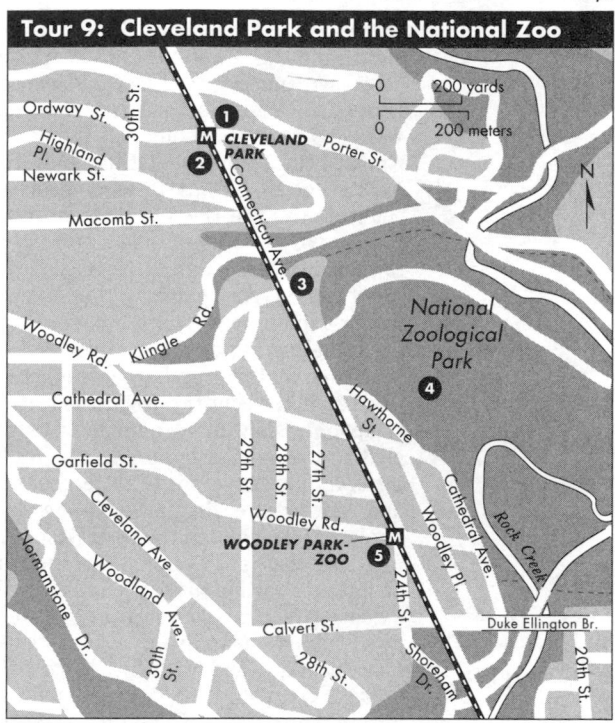

Tour 9: Cleveland Park and the National Zoo

❷ Half a block to the south is the **Cineplex Odeon Uptown**
(3426 Connecticut Ave. NW, tel. 202/966–5400), a marvelous vintage-1936 art deco movie house. Although many other big-screen theaters in the city have been chopped up and
transformed into "multiplexes," the Uptown still has a single huge screen and an inviting balcony. The **Calliope Used
Bookshop** next door (3424 Connecticut Ave. NW, tel. 202/
364–0111) does a brisk business selling to Uptown theater
patrons waiting for the next show. It specializes in literary
fiction, poetry, philosophy, and art.

Continue south on Connecticut Avenue. You'll cross over a
finger of Rock Creek Park via a span decorated with eight
art deco bridge lights. Beyond the bridge on the left is the
city's finest Art Deco apartment house, the
❸ **Kennedy-Warren** (3133 Connecticut Ave. NW). Opened in
1931, it features such period detailing as decorative aluminum panels and a streamlined entryway, stone griffins under the pyramidal copper roof, and stylized carved eagles
flanking the driveways. Perhaps in keeping with its elegant
architecture, the Kennedy-Warren is one of the last apartment buildings in town to still have a doorman.

❹ On the same side of Connecticut Avenue is the **National
Zoological Park,** part of the Smithsonian Institution and
one of the foremost zoos in the world. Created by an Act of
Congress in 1889, the 160-acre zoo was designed by land-

scape architect Frederick Law Olmsted, the man who designed the U.S. Capitol grounds. (Before the zoo opened in 1890, live animals used as taxidermists' models had been kept on the Mall.) For years the zoo's most famous residents were giant pandas Hsing-Hsing and Ling-Ling, gifts from China in 1972. But female Ling-Ling died of heart failure in 1993 at age 23. Sympathy cards poured in from all over the country, the zoo tried in vain to fertilize some of Ling-Ling's extracted eggs, and her body was donated to the Smithsonian's Museum of Natural History. Hsing-Hsing is now the only giant panda in the United States. The zoo has had breeding success with numerous other species, however, including red pandas, Pere David's deer, golden lion tamarins, and pygmy hippopotamuses. The only Komodo dragons in the country are at the National Zoo. Innovative compounds show many animals in naturalistic settings, including the Great Flight Cage—a walk-in aviary in which birds fly unrestricted. Giant crabs, octopuses, cuttlefish, and worms are displayed in an invertebrate exhibit. Zoolab, Herplab, and the Bird Resource Center all feature activities that teach young visitors about biology. The most ambitious addition to the zoo is Amazonia, a reproduction of a South American rain forest ecosystem. Such fish as twig cats and arowanas swim behind glass walls, while overhead, monkeys and birds flit from tree to tree. The temperature is a constant 85 degrees, with 85% humidity. Also new to the zoo is the Cheetah Conservation Area, a grassy compound that's home to a family of the world's fastest cats. Amazonia and the Cheetah Conservation Area are the most visible attempts by the zoo to show animals in more naturalistic settings and heighten visitors' appreciation of those environments. *3001 Connecticut Ave. NW, tel. 202/673–4800 or 202/673–4717. Admission free. Open May 1–Sept. 15, daily: grounds 8–8, animal buildings 9–6; Amazonia 10–5:30; Sept. 16–Apr. 30: grounds 8–6, animal buildings 9–4:30; Amazonia 10–4; closed Dec. 25. Limited paid parking is available.*

The stretch of Connecticut Avenue south of the zoo is bordered by more venerable apartment buildings. Passing Cathedral Avenue (the first cross-street south of the zoo) you enter a part of town known as **Woodley Park.** Like Cleveland Park to the north, Woodley Park grew as the streetcar advanced into this part of Washington. In 1800 Philip Barton Key, uncle of Francis Scott Key, built Woodley, a Georgian mansion on Cathedral Avenue between 29th and 31st streets. The white stucco mansion was the summer home of four presidents: Van Buren, Tyler, Buchanan, and Cleveland. It is now owned by the private Maret School.

At the corner of Connecticut Avenue and Woodley Road is the cross-shaped **Wardman Tower.** The Georgian-style tower was built by developer Harry Wardman in 1928 as a luxury apartment building to accompany a now-demolished luxury hotel he had built nearby 10 years earlier. Washingtonians called the project "Wardman's Folly," convinced no one would want to stay in a hotel so far from the city. The Wardman Tower was famous for its well-known residents, who included Dwight D. Eisenhower, Herbert Hoover, Clare Booth Luce, Dean Rusk, Earl Warren, and Caspar Weinberger. It is now part of the Sheraton Washington Hotel (*see* Northwest/Upper Connecticut Avenue in Chapter 8).

Wardman's success spurred the development of the neighborhood's other large hotel, the **Omni Shoreham** (*see* Northwest/Upper Connecticut Avenue in Chapter 8) on Calvert Street west of Connecticut Avenue. The Shoreham was known for the entertainers who appeared here, including Rudy Vallee, who performed at its grand opening in 1930. The Shoreham and the nearby Sheraton Washington are two of the city's main convention hotels; you'll notice that many of the people on the streets around you have a plastic name badge pinned to their lapel.

The nearest Metro station is Woodley Park/Zoo, at Connecticut Avenue and Woodley Road.

Tour 10: Adams-Morgan

To the young, the hip, the cool, and the postmodern, Washington has the reputation of being a rather staid town, more interested in bureaucracy than boogie, with all the vitality of a seersucker suit. It may have the Hope Diamond, these detractors say, but that's about the only thing that really sparkles. What these people are saying, of course, is that Washington isn't New York City. And thank goodness, say Washingtonians, who wouldn't want to give up their clean subway, comfortable standard of living, or place in the political spotlight, even if it did mean being able to get a decent corned beef sandwich or a double espresso at three in the morning. Besides, Washington does have **Adams-Morgan**. It may not be Greenwich Village, but it's close enough in spirit to satisfy all but the most hardened black-clad, shade-sporting cynics.

Adams-Morgan (roughly, the blocks north of Florida Avenue, between Connecticut Avenue and 16th Street NW) is Washington's most ethnically diverse neighborhood. And as is so often the case, that means it's one of Washington's most interesting areas, home to a veritable United Nations of cuisines, offbeat shops, and funky bars and clubs. The name itself, fashioned in the 1950s by neighborhood civic groups, serves as a symbol of the area's melting pot character: It's a conjunction of the names of two local schools, the predominantly white Adams School and the largely black Morgan School. Today Adams-Morgan is home to every shade in-between, too, with large Latino and West African populations.

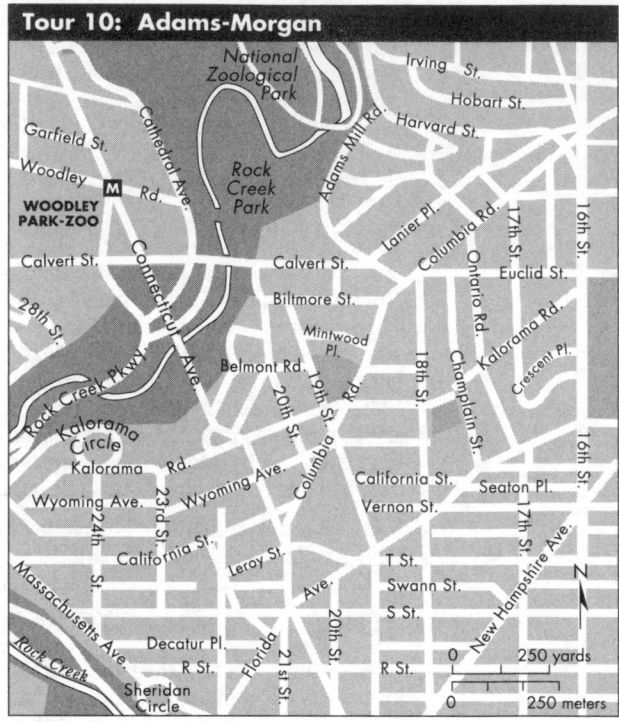

Tour 10: Adams-Morgan

The neighborhood's grand 19th-century apartment buildings and row houses and its bohemian atmosphere have also attracted young urban professionals, in turn attracting the businesses that cater to them, the attendant parking and crowd problems, and the inevitable climb in real estate values. It's all caused some longtime Adams-Morganites to wonder if their neighborhood is in danger of mutating into another Georgetown.

Adams-Morgan already has one thing in common with Georgetown: There's no Metro stop. It's a 15-minute walk from the Woodley Park/Zoo Metro station: Walk south on Connecticut, then turn left on Calvert Street, and cross over Rock Creek Park on the Duke Ellington Bridge. When you come to the crossroads of Adams Mill Road, Columbia Road, and 18th Street you're in the heart of Adams-Morgan.

What follows is more of a leisurely ramble than a tour. Visitors may want to deviate from the path described here and make their own discoveries, in a spirit in keeping with the serendipity of this fascinating area.

Turn left on **Columbia Road**. At tables stretched along the street, vendors hawk watches, leather goods, knockoff perfumes, cassette tapes (blank and prerecorded), sneakers, clothes, and handmade jewelry. The store signs—Casa

Lebrato, Urgente Express (the latter the name of a business that specializes in shipping to and from Central America)—are a testament to the area's Latin flavor; on these blocks you'll hear as much Spanish as English.

Cross Columbia at Ontario Road and backtrack. If you'd rather see the neighborhood on two wheels than two feet, turn left onto Champlain Street and rent a bicycle at **City Bikes** (2501 Champlain St. NW, tel. 202/265–1564; call ahead to reserve a bike on weekends).

Continue west on Columbia Road to its intersection with 18th Street. On Saturday mornings a **market** springs up on the plaza in front of the Crestar bank, at the southwest corner of 18th and Columbia, with vendors selling fruits, vegetables, flowers, and breads.

If Columbia Road east of 18th is Adams-Morgan's Latin Quarter, 18th Street south of Columbia is its restaurant corridor. In the next few blocks you'll pass—beside McDonald's—restaurants serving the cuisines of China, Mexico, India, El Salvador, Ethiopia, France, the Caribbean, Thailand, Argentina, Italy, Vietnam, and, believe it or not, America. If you can't make up your mind, there's even a palm reader who can help decide what your future has in store.

You can also feed your hunger for the outré or offbeat with the funky shops on 18th Street. Here you'll find the mission-style furniture, Russell Wright crockery and Fiestaware, aerodynamic art deco armchairs, Bakelite telephones, massive chromium toasters, kidney-shaped Formica-topped coffee tables, skinny neckties, and tacky salt-and-pepper shakers that, through time and television reruns, have been transformed from kitsch into collectible. Among stores carrying these are **Homeworks** (2405 18th St. NW, tel. 202/483–5857), **Retrospective** (2324 18th St. NW, tel. 202/483–8112), and **Wake Up Little Suzie** (2316 18th St. NW, tel. 202/328–7577).

Once you've had your fill of Jetsons lunchboxes and gloopy lava lamps, proceed to the souklike **Bazaar Atlas** (2405 18th St. NW, no phone), located above Homeworks and specializing in ethnic goods such as geometric-patterned sweaters from Ecuador and Bolivia and leather, carved wood, rugs, and hammered metal from Morocco. Nearby is **Kobos** (2444 18th St. NW, tel. 202/332–9580), owned by a Ghanaian immigrant who sells African carvings, jewelry, and clothes fashioned from colorful kente cloth.

Down the block is **Bick's Books** (2309 18th St. NW, tel. 202/328–2356), a "serious" bookstore with a good selection of modern and classic fiction, poetry, philosophy, literary criticism, and literary anthologies and journals. Across the street, **Idle Time Books** (2410 18th St. NW, tel. 202/232–4774) stocks used and out-of-print titles.

The west side of 18th Street is home to a gamut of antiques shops, from the bargain-priced used furniture of **Ruff & Ready** (2220 18th St. NW, tel. 202/667–7833) to the more classic goods at **Chenonceau Antiques** (2314 18th St. NW, tel. 202/667–1651). Antiques shoppers should also keep an eye out for secondhand shops set up in alleys or warehouses here.

Nearby is the **District of Columbia Arts Center** (DCAC), a combination art gallery/performance space. DCAC exhibits the cutting-edge work of local artists and is the home of off-beat plays, including that uncategorizable category known as "performance art." *2438 18th St. NW, tel. 202/462–7833. Gallery admission free, performance costs vary. Open Thurs.–Fri. 6–10 PM, weekends 4–10 PM.*

Of course, the measure of any neighborhood is the tone it takes when the sun goes down. In the spring and summer, restaurants open their windows or set out tables on the sidewalks. Those lucky enough to have rooftop seating find diners lining up to eat under the stars. (Washington can be notoriously hot in the summer, but one of Adams-Morgan's charms has always been that its slight elevation wraps it in cooling breezes.)

Although the neighborhood's bar and club scene isn't as varied as its restaurant scene, there are some standouts. Tap dancers use the bar as a stage Friday and Saturday evenings at the decidedly Gallic jazz club **Café Lautrec** (2431 18th St. NW, tel. 202/265–6436). **Chief Ike's Mambo Room** (1725 Columbia Rd. NW, tel. 202/332–2211) is as eclectic as its name, with DJs playing everything from R&B to disco and a mural of its namesake, Dwight Eisenhower, in an Indian headdress. Locals cue them up at **Bedrock Billiards** (1841 Columbia Rd. NW, tel. 202/667–7665), a pool hall with eight tables and a '50s fashion sense. **Club Heaven** is upstairs from a bar named **Hell** (2327 18th St. NW, tel. 202/667–4355) and features dancing to live and recorded synth-pop music. More in keeping with Adams-Morgan's international flavor is **Bukom Cafe** (2442 18th St. NW, tel. 202/265–4600), home on weekends to West African music.

Remember that the last trains leave the Woodley Park Metro station at around midnight, so if you can't tear yourself away, be prepared to take a cab. For more on Adams-Morgan shops, restaurants, and nightlife, *see* Chapters 5, 7, and 9.

Tour 11: Arlington

Numbers in the margin correspond to points of interest on the Tour 11: Arlington map.

The Virginia suburb of Arlington County was once part of the District of Columbia. Carved out of the Old Dominion when Washington was created, it was returned to Virginia along with the rest of the land west of the Potomac in 1845. Washington hasn't held a grudge, though, and there are three attractions in Arlington—each linked to the military—that should be a part of any complete visit to the nation's capital: Arlington National Cemetery, the U.S. Marine Corps War Memorial, and the Pentagon. All are accessible by Metro, and a trip across the Potomac makes an enjoyable half day of sightseeing.

Begin your exploration in **Arlington National Cemetery.** To get there, you can take the Metro to the Arlington Cemetery station, travel on a Tourmobile bus (*see* Staying in Washington in Chapter 1), or walk across Memorial Bridge from the District (southwest of the Lincoln Memorial). If you're driving, there's a large paid parking lot at the skylit

1 **Visitors Center** on Memorial Drive. Stop at the center for a free brochure with a detailed map of the cemetery's 612 acres. (If you're looking for a specific grave, the staff will consult microfilm records and give you directions on how to find it. You should know the deceased's full name and, if possible, his or her branch of service and year of death.) *Tel. 703/692–0931. Admission free. Open Apr.–Sept., daily 8–7; Oct.–Mar., daily 8–5. Parking lot open Apr.–Sept., daily 8–8; Oct.–Mar., daily 8–6. Parking $1/hr for first 3 hrs, $2/hr thereafter.*

Tourmobile tour buses leave from just outside the Visitors Center mid-June–early September, daily 8:30–6:30; early September–mid-June, daily 8:30–4:30. You can buy tickets here (adults $2.75, children $1.25) for the 40-minute tour of the cemetery, which includes stops at the Kennedy grave sites, the Tomb of the Unknowns, and Arlington House. Touring the cemetery on foot means a fair bit of hiking, but it will give you a closer look at some of the 200,000 graves spread over these rolling Virginia hills. If you decide to walk, head west from the Visitors Center on Roosevelt Drive and then turn right on Weeks Drive.

While you are at Arlington you will probably hear the clear, doleful sound of a trumpet playing taps or the sharp reports of a gun salute. Approximately 15 funerals are held here daily. It is projected the cemetery will be filled in 2020. Although not the largest cemetery in the country, Arlington is certainly the best known, a place where visitors can trace America's history through the aftermath of its battles.

2 The **Kennedy graves** are located just west of the Visitors Center. John F. Kennedy is buried under an eternal flame near two of his children who died in infancy. Across from the graves is a low wall engraved with quotations from Kennedy's inaugural address. JFK's grave was opened to the public in 1967 and since that time has become the most-visited grave site in the country. Nearby, marked by a simple white cross, is the grave of his brother Robert Kennedy.

Tour 11: Arlington

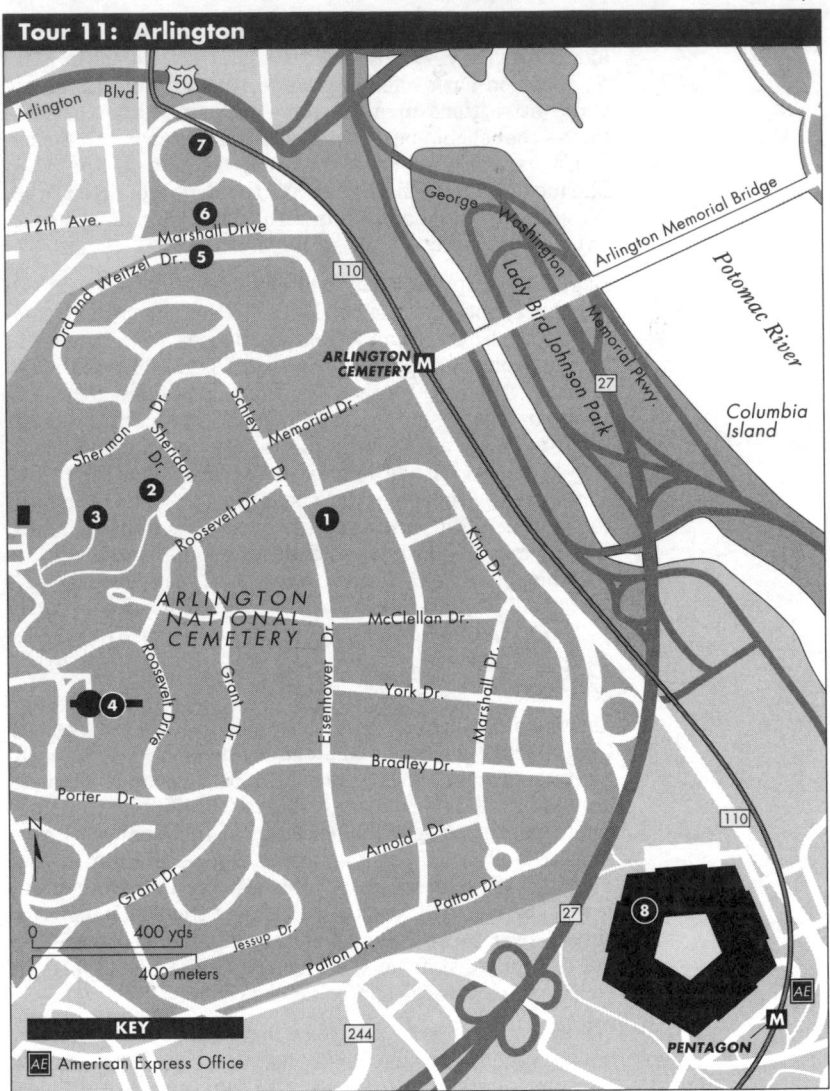

KEY

AE American Express Office

Arlington House, **3**
Kennedy graves, **2**
Netherlands
Carillon, **6**
Pentagon, **8**
Section 27, **5**
Tomb of the
Unknowns, **4**

United States Marine
Corps War
Memorial, **7**
Visitors Center, **1**

This somber plot of land hasn't always been a cemetery. It was in Arlington that the two most famous names in Virginia history—Washington and Lee—became intertwined. George Washington Parke Custis—raised by Martha and George Washington, his grandmother and step-grandfa-

❸ ther—built **Arlington House** (also known as the Custis-Lee Mansion) between 1802 and 1817 on his 1,100-acre estate overlooking the Potomac. After his death, the property went to his daughter, Mary Anna Randolph Custis. In 1831, Mary Custis married Robert E. Lee, a recent graduate of West Point. For the next 30 years the Custis-Lee family lived at Arlington House.

In 1861, Lee was offered command of the Union forces. He declined, insisting that he could never take up arms against his native Virginia. The Lees left Arlington House that spring, never to return. Union troops soon occupied the estate, making it the headquarters of the officers who were charged with defending Washington. When Mrs. Lee was unable to appear in person to pay a $92.07 property tax the government had assessed, the land was confiscated and a portion set aside as a military cemetery.

Its heavy Doric columns and severe pediment make Arlington House one of the area's best examples of Greek Revival architecture. The plantation home was designed by George Hadfield, a young English architect who for a while supervised construction of the Capitol. The view of Washington from the front of the house is superb. In 1955 Arlington House was designated a memorial to Robert E. Lee. It looks much as it did in the 19th century, and a quick tour will take you past objects once owned by the Custises and the Lees. *Between Lee and Sherman Drs., tel. 703/557-0613. Admission free. Open Apr.–Sept., daily 9:30–6; Oct.–Mar., daily 9:30–4:30; closed Dec. 25 and New Year's Day.*

In front of the house, next to a flag that flies at half staff whenever there is a funeral in the cemetery, is the flat-topped grave of Pierre L'Enfant, designer of the Federal City. L'Enfant died in 1825, a penniless, bitter man who felt he hadn't been recognized for his planning genius. He was originally buried in Maryland, but his body was moved here with much ceremony in 1909.

After visiting Arlington House and the Kennedy graves, walk south on Crook Walk past the seemingly endless rows of simple white headstones—arranged like soldiers on pa-

❹ rade—and follow the signs to the **Tomb of the Unknowns**. The first burial at the Tomb of the Unknowns was on November 11, 1921, when the Unknown Soldier from World War I was interred under the large white-marble sarcophagus. Unknown servicemen killed in World War II and Korea were buried in 1958. The unknown serviceman killed in Vietnam was laid to rest on the plaza on Memorial Day 1984. Soldiers from the Army's U.S. 3rd Infantry ("The Old

Guard," portrayed in the movie *Gardens of Stone*) keep watch over the tomb 24 hours a day, regardless of weather conditions. Each sentinel marches exactly 21 steps, then faces the tomb for 21 seconds, symbolizing the 21-gun salute, America's highest military honor. The guard is changed with a precise ceremony during the day—every half-hour from April 1 to September 30 and every hour the rest of the year. At night the guard is changed every two hours. The **Memorial Amphitheater** west of the tomb is the scene of special ceremonies on Veterans Day, Memorial Day, and Easter. Decorations awarded to the unknowns by foreign governments and U.S. and foreign organizations are displayed in an indoor trophy room.

Across from the amphitheater are memorials to the astronauts killed in the *Challenger* shuttle explosion and to the servicemen killed in 1980 while trying to rescue American hostages in Iran. Rising beyond that is the mast from the USS *Maine*, the American ship that was sunk in Havana Harbor in 1898, killing 299 men and sparking the Spanish-American War.

Below the Tomb of the Unknowns is **section 7A,** where you can find the graves of many distinguished veterans, including boxing champ Joe Louis, ABC newsman Frank Reynolds, actor Lee Marvin, and World War II fighter pilot Col. "Pappy" Boyington.

To reach the sites at the northern end of the cemetery and to make your way into the city of Arlington, first walk north along Roosevelt Drive to Schley Drive (you'll pass the Memorial Gate), then turn right on Custis Walk to the Ord ❺ & Weitzel Gate. On your way you'll pass **section 27,** where 3,800 former slaves are buried. They lived at Freedman's Village, established at Arlington in 1863 to provide housing, education, and employment training for ex-slaves who had traveled to the capital. The headstones are marked with their names and the word "Civilian" or "Citizen." Buried at grave 19 in the first row of section 27 is William Christman, a Union private who died of peritonitis in Washington on May 13, 1864. He was the first soldier interred at Arlington National Cemetery during the Civil War. *West end of Memorial Bridge, Arlington, VA, tel. 703/692–0931. Admission free. Open Apr.–early Sept., daily 8–7; mid-Sept.–Mar., daily 8–5.*

Leaving the cemetery through the Ord & Weitzel Gate, ❻ cross Marshall Drive carefully, and walk to the **Netherlands Carillon.** The 49-bell carillon was presented to the United States by the Dutch people in 1960 as thanks for aid received during World War II. A performance season featuring guest carillonneurs begins Easter Sunday. For one of the most inclusive views of Washington, look to the east across the Potomac. From this vantage point, the Lincoln Memorial, the Washington Monument, and the Capitol are bunched together in a side-by-side formation. *Carillon in-*

formation, tel. 703/285–2598. Free performances Apr., May, Sept., Sat. 2; Easter Sunday starting at 6 AM; June–Aug., Sat. 6:30 PM.

7 To the north is the **United States Marine Corps War Memorial,** honoring marines who have given their lives since the corps was formed in 1775. The memorial statue, sculpted by Felix W. de Weldon, is based on Joe Rosenthal's Pulitzer Prize—winning photograph of five marines and a Navy corpsman raising a flag atop Mount Suribachi on Iwo Jima on February 19, 1945. By executive order, a real flag flies 24 hours a day from the 78-foot-high memorial. On Tuesday evenings at 7 from late May to late August there is a Marine Corps sunset parade on the grounds of the memorial. On parade nights a free shuttle bus runs from the Arlington Cemetery visitor parking lot (for information, tel. 202/433–6060). A word of caution: It is dangerous to visit the memorial after dark.

The Arlington neighborhood of Rosslyn is north of the memorial. Like parts of downtown Washington and Crystal City further to the south, Rosslyn is almost empty at night once the thousands of people who work there have gone home. Its tall buildings do provide the preternaturally horizontal Washington with a bit of a skyline, but this has come about not without some controversy: Some say the silvery, wing-shaped Gannett Buildings are too close to the flight path followed by jets landing at National Airport.

8 To get to the **Pentagon,** take the Metro to the Pentagon station, which is right alongside the humongous office building. The headquarters of the Department of Defense, the Pentagon was completed in 1943 after just two years of construction. The five-sided building is an exercise in immensity: 23,000 military and civilian employees work here; it is as wide as three Washington Monuments laid end to end; inside are 17½ miles of corridors, 7,754 windows, and 691 drinking fountains. The 75-minute tour of the Pentagon takes you past only those areas that are meant to be seen by outside visitors. In other words, you won't see situation rooms, communications centers, or gigantic maps outlining U.S. and foreign troop strengths. A uniformed serviceman or -woman (who conducts the entire tour walking backward, lest anyone slip away down a corridor) will take you past hallways lined with the portraits of past and present military leaders, scale models of Air Force planes and Navy ships, and the Hall of Heroes, where the names of all the Congressional Medal of Honor winners are inscribed. Occasionally you will catch a glimpse through an interior window of the Pentagon's 5-acre interior courtyard. In the center—at ground zero—is a hotdog stand. *Pentagon, off I–395, Arlington, VA, tel. 703/695–1776. Admission free. Tours weekdays every ½ hr 9:30–3:30. Photo I.D. required. Closed federal holidays.*

Tour 12: Alexandria

*Numbers in the margin correspond to points of interest on
the Tour 12: Alexandria map.*

Just a short Metro ride (or bike ride) away from Washington, Old Town Alexandria today attracts visitors seeking a break from the monuments and hustle-and-bustle of the District and interested in an encounter with America's Colonial heritage. Founded in 1749 by Scottish merchants eager to capitalize on the booming tobacco trade, Alexandria emerged as one of the most important ports in Colonial America. The city's history is linked to the most significant events and personages of the Colonial and Revolutionary periods. This colorful past is still alive in restored 18th- and 19th-century homes, churches, and taverns; on the cobbled streets; and on the revitalized waterfront, where clipper ships dock and artisans display their wares.

The quickest way to get to Old Town is to take the Metro to the King Street stop (about 25 minutes from Metro Center). If you're driving you can take either the George Washington Memorial Parkway or Jefferson Davis Highway (Route 1) south from Arlington.

The best place to start a tour of Old Town is at the
❶ **Alexandria Convention & Visitors Bureau,** which is in **Ramsay House,** the home of the town's first postmaster and lord mayor, William Ramsay. The structure is believed to be the oldest house in Alexandria. Ramsay was a Scotsman, as a swatch of his tartan on the door proclaims. Travel counselors here provide information, brochures, and self-guided walking tours of the town. *221 King St. 22314, tel. 703/838–4200, TDD 703/838–6494. Open daily 9–5; closed Thanksgiving, Dec. 25, and New Year's Day. Out-of-towners are given a 24-hr courtesy parking permit that allows them to park free at any 2-hr metered spot.*

Across the street, at the corner of Fairfax and King streets,
❷ is the **Stabler-Leadbeater Apothecary,** the second-oldest apothecary in the country. It was patronized by George Washington and the Lee family, and it was here, on October 17, 1859, that Lt. Col. Robert E. Lee received orders to move to Harper's Ferry to suppress John Brown's insurrection. The shop now houses a small museum of 18th-century apothecary memorabilia, including one of the finest collections of apothecary bottles in the country (some 800 bottles in all). *105–107 S. Fairfax St., tel. 703/836–3713. Suggested donation: $1. Open Mon.–Sat. 10–4; closed Thanksgiving, Dec. 25, Jan. 1.*

Two blocks south on Fairfax Street, just beyond Duke
❸ Street, stands the **Old Presbyterian Meeting House.** Built in 1774, this was an important meeting place for Scotts patriots during the Revolution. Eulogies for George Washington were delivered here on December 29, 1799. In a corner of

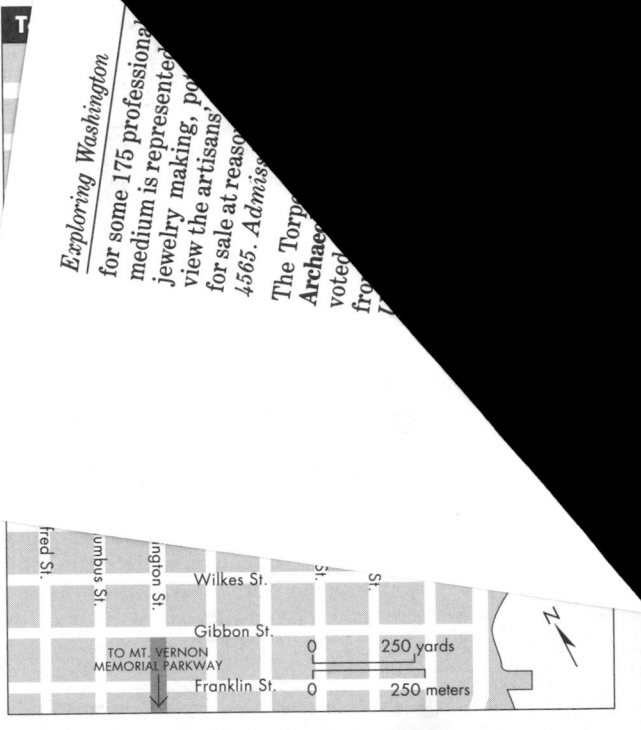

the churchyard you'll find the **Tomb of the Unknown Soldier of the American Revolution.** *321 S. Fairfax St., tel. 703/549–6670. Admission free. Church open weekdays 8:30–4:30; graveyard always open.*

Next walk back up Fairfax Street one block and turn right on Prince Street. The block between Fairfax and Lee streets is known as **Gentry Row.** One of the most noteworthy structures in the city is the **Athenaeum,** at the corner of Prince and Lee streets. The striking, reddish-brown Greek Revival edifice was built as a bank in the 1850s.

The next block of Prince Street to the east (between Lee and Union streets) is known as **Captain's Row** because this was where many of the city's sea captains built their homes. The cobblestones in the street were allegedly laid by Hessian mercenaries who fought for the British during the Revolutionary War and who were being held in Alexandria as prisoners of war.

Continuing east on Prince Street you'll come to Alexandria's lively waterfront. Two blocks to the north up Union Street (at the foot of King Street) is one of the most popular destinations in the city, the **Torpedo Factory Arts Center.** This former munitions plant (yes, naval torpedoes were actually manufactured here during World War I and World War II) has now been converted into studios and galleries

artists. Almost every imaginable
, from printmaking and sculpture to
tery, and stained glass. Visitors can
workshops, and most of the artworks are
able prices. *105 N. Union St., tel. 703/838–*
on free. Open daily 10–5.

do Factory complex also houses the **Alexandria**
ology Program, a city-operated research facility de-
to urban archaeology and conservation. Artifacts
excavations dug in Alexandria are on display. *105 N.*
nion St., tel. 703/838–4399. Admission free. Open Tues.–
Thurs. 10–3, Fri.–Sat. 10–5, Sun. 1–5.

Moving back into the town, walk two blocks up Cameron
Street to reach the grandest of the older houses in the town,
⑧ **Carlyle House,** at the corner of North Fairfax Street. Patterned after a Scottish country manor house, the structure
was completed in 1753 by Scottish merchant John Carlyle.
This was General Braddock's headquarters and the place
where he met with five royal governors in 1755 to plan the
strategy and funding of the early campaigns of the French
and Indian War. *121 N. Fairfax St., tel. 703/549–2997. Ad-*
mission: $3 adults, $1 students 11–17, children under 11
free. Open Tues.–Sat. 10–4:30, Sun. noon–4:30. Tours ev-
ery ½ hr.

⑨ One block west on Royal Street is **Gadsby's Tavern Museum,**
housed in the old City Tavern and Hotel, which was a center
of political and social life in the late 18th century. George
Washington attended birthday celebrations in the ballroom
here. A tour of the facilities takes you through the taproom,
game room, assembly room, ballroom, and communal bedrooms. *134–138 N. Royal St., tel. 703/838–4242. Admis-*
sion: $3 adults, $1 students 11–17, children under 11 free.
Open Tues.–Sat. 10–5, Sun. 1–5. Tours at quarter to and
quarter after the hr.

Continue west on Cameron Street for three blocks and turn
right on Washington Street. The corner of Washington and
Oronoco streets (three blocks north) is known as **Lee Cor-**
ner because at one time a Lee-owned house stood on each of
⑩ the four corners. Two survive. One is the **Lee-Fendall**
House, the home of several illustrious members of the Lee
family, including Richard Henry Lee, signer of the Declaration of Independence, and cavalry commander "Light
Horse Harry" Lee. *614 Oronoco St., tel. 703/548–1789. Ad-*
mission: $3 adults, $1 students 11–17, children under 11
free. Open Tues.–Sat. 10–4, Sun. noon–4. Occasionally
closed weekends for private events.

⑪ Directly across the street is the **boyhood home of Robert E.**
Lee, a fine example of a 19th-century town house. It features Federal architecture and antique furnishings and
paintings. *607 Oronoco St., tel. 703/548–8454. Admission:*
$3 adults, $1 students 11–17, children under 11 free. Open

Mon.–Sat. 10–4, Sun. 1–4; closed Dec. 15–Feb. 1 except on Sun. closest to Jan. 19 for Lee's birthday celebration. Occasionally closed weekends for private events.

Alexandria's history isn't all Washingtons and Lees, however. The federal census of 1790 recorded 52 free blacks living in the city, and the port town was one of the largest slave exportation points in the South, with at least two bustling slave markets. The history of African Americans in Alexandria and Virginia from 1749 to the present is recounted at the **Alexandria Black History Resource Center,** two blocks north and two blocks west of Lee's boyhood home. *638 North Alfred St., tel. 703/838–4356. Admission free. Open Tues.–Sat. 10–4.*

Head back to Washington Street and move south now all the way to the corner of Queen Street. Here you'll find the **Lloyd House,** a fine example of Georgian architecture. Built in 1797, it is now operated as part of the Alexandria Library and houses a collection of rare books and documents relating to city and state history. *220 North Washington St., tel. 703/838–4577. Admission free. Open Mon.–Sat. 9–5.*

At the corner of Cameron and Washington streets, one block south, stands **Christ Church,** where both Washington and Lee were pewholders (Washington paid 36 pounds and 10 shillings, a lot of money in those days, for Pew 60). Built in 1773, it is a fine example of an English, Georgian country-style church. The interior features a fine Palladian window, interior balcony, and a wrought-brass-and-crystal chandelier brought from England at Washington's expense. *118 N. Washington St., tel. 703/549–1450. Admission free. Open weekdays 9–4, Sat. 9–noon, Sun. 2–4:30. Occasionally closed weekends for private events.*

From Christ Church, walk two blocks south to the **Lyceum** at the corner of Washington and Prince streets. Built in 1839, the structure served alternately as the Alexandria Library, a Civil War hospital, a residence, and an office building. It was restored in the 1970s and now houses two art galleries, a gift shop, and a museum devoted to the area's history. A limited amount of travel information for the entire state is also available here. *201 S. Washington St., tel. 703/838–4994. Admission free. Open Mon.–Sat. 10–5, Sun. 1–5; closed Thanksgiving, Dec. 25, and New Year's Day.*

The **Confederate Statue** stands in the middle of Washington and Prince streets, the point from which the 800 soldiers from Alexandria's garrison assembled and marched out of town to join the Confederate Army when the city was occupied by Union forces in 1861. In 1885, Confederate veterans proposed a memorial honoring their fallen comrades. This statue, based on John A. Elder's painting *Appomattox*, is of a lone soldier glumly surveying the battlefields after General Robert E. Lee's surrender. The names of 100 Alexandria Confederate dead are carved on the base.

Two blocks to the west on South Alfred Street is the ⓰ **Friendship Fire Company.** The building was recently renovated and is now outfitted like a typical 19th-century firehouse. *107 S. Alfred St., tel. 703/838–3891. Suggested donation: $1. Open Thurs.–Sat. 10–4, Sun. 1–4.*

⓱ A little far to walk but well worth visiting is the **George Washington Masonic National Memorial** on Callahan Drive at King Street, a mile west of the center of the city. (You can take a #2 or #5 DASH bus west on King Street to the memorial.) The memorial's spire dominates the surroundings, and from the entryway visitors get a spectacular view of Alexandria and Washington in the distance. Among other things, the building contains furnishings from the first Masonic lodge in Alexandria, in which George Washington was Worshipful Master at the same time he served as president. *101 Callahan Dr., tel. 703/683–2007. Admission free. Open daily 9–5; closed Thanksgiving, Dec. 25, and New Year's Day. Free guided tours of the building and observation deck daily 9:15–4:10.*

Washington for Free

Visitors will have a hard time finding attractions and events in Washington that are *not* free. There are no admission fees to any of the Smithsonian museums—including the National Zoo—and entry to many other museums and galleries is also without charge. The ride to the top of the Washington Monument used to cost a dime, but today, like admission to the rest of the memorials, that's free, too.

Concerts **Fort Dupont Summer Theater** (Minnesota Ave. and F St. SE, tel. 202/426–7723) hosts well-known jazz artists Friday and Saturday evenings at 8:30 during the summer.

The National Building Museum's impressive Pension Building (F St. between 4th and 5th Sts. NW, tel. 202/272–2448) is the site of lunchtime concerts the last Wednesday of each month.

The National Gallery Orchestra offers free classical concerts at the National Gallery of Art (6th St. and Constitution Ave. NW, tel. 202/842–6941) Sunday evenings from October to June. Admission is free, but on a first-come basis.

The National Symphony Orchestra (tel. 202/416–8100) presents free concerts on the West Lawn of the Capitol on Memorial Day and Labor Day weekends and on July 4th.

The National Theatre (1321 Pennsylvania Ave. NW, tel. 202/783–3372) hosts a wide-ranging free performance series of music, dance, readings, and one-act plays most Monday nights from October to April. "Monday Night at the National" performances are held at 7 PM and 8:30 PM.

The Sylvan Theater (tel. 202/619–7222), on the grounds of the Washington Monument, is the site of numerous military and big-band concerts from mid-June to August.

Festivals **Adams-Morgan Day** (tel. 202/332–3292), in September, is a street festival with the music and cuisine of Africa, Latin America, and the Caribbean.

The Festival of American Folklife, a celebration of home-grown crafts, music, and food, is sponsored by the Smithsonian and is held on the Mall each year in late June or early July (tel. 202/ 357–2700).

Lectures **The Library of Congress** (tel. 202/707–5394 or 202/707–2905) sponsors periodic literary lectures and poetry readings by well-known poets, usually on Thursday evenings.

The Martin Luther King Memorial Library's "Lunchtime Author Series" (901 G St. NW, tel. 202/727–1186) features readings and discussions with local and national authors every Tuesday at noon, except during the months of July and August.

The Smithsonian Institution (tel. 202/357–2700) offers free lectures, demonstrations, and gallery talks by both visiting scholars and Smithsonian fellows at many of its museums on and off the Mall.

The "Weekend" section in Friday's *Washington Post* and the free weekly *City Paper* are excellent sources of other free events in and around the District.

Off the Beaten Track

Anacostia Neighborhood Museum. Exhibits in this Smithsonian museum deal with African-American history and culture. *1901 Fort Pl. SE, tel. 202/287–3369. Admission free. Open daily 10–5. Closed Dec. 25.*

The Ansel Adams Collection, a permanent exhibit of the famed photographer's most important landscapes, is on display at the Wilderness Society's headquarters. *900 17th St. NW, tel. 202/833–2300. Open weekdays 10–5; closed major holidays and day after Thanksgiving. Large groups should call ahead. Metro stops, Farragut North and Farragut West.*

Bethune Museum-Archives. Mary McLeod Bethune founded Florida's Bethune-Cookman College, established the National Council of Negro Women, and served as an adviser to President Franklin D. Roosevelt. Exhibits in the museum focus on the achievements of black women. The museum also hosts free weekly concerts as part of its "Black Women in Jazz" series, March through June and September through December. *1318 Vermont Ave. NW, tel. 202/332–1233. Admission free. Open weekdays 10–4:30. Metro stop, McPherson Square.*

College Park Airport Museum. Opened in 1909, College Park is the world's oldest operating airport and was the site

of numerous aviation firsts. Orville and Wilbur Wright
tested military planes here and their presence is evident in
the museum's early aviation memorabilia. The airport's Air
Fair every September features antique airplanes, hot-air
balloons, and a Wright Brothers look-alike contest. *6709
Cpl. Frank Scott Dr., College Park, MD, tel. 301/864–1530.
Admission free. Open Wed.–Fri. 11–3, weekends 11–5.*

Frederick Douglass National Historic Site. Cedar Hill, the
Anacostia home of noted abolitionist Frederick Douglass,
was the first place designated by Congress as a Black National Historic Site. Douglass, an ex-slave who delivered fiery abolitionist speeches at home and abroad, resided here
from 1877 until his death in 1895. The house has a wonderful
view of the Federal City, across the Anacostia, and contains
many of Douglass's personal belongings. A short film on
Douglass's life is shown at a nearby visitors center. *1411 W
St. SE, tel. 202/426–5961. Admission free. Open mid-Oct.–
mid-Apr., daily 9–4; mid-Apr.–mid-Oct., daily 9–5. Tours
given on the hour. Metro stop, Anacostia.*

Eastern Market. Built in 1873, Eastern Market has always
been a bustling center of activity on Capitol Hill. It was designed by Adolph Cluss, the architect of the Smithsonian
Arts and Industries Museum. Inside are shops, restaurants, and galleries. There is a flea market outside on weekends. *7th and C Sts. SE. Metro stop, Eastern Market.*

The Flying Circus Airshow bills itself as the only remaining
barnstorming show in the country. Operating out of a Virginia aerodrome about 90 minutes outside Washington, the
Flying Circus features stunt flying, wing walking, and
open cockpit biplane rides for the public, on Sunday from
May through early November. *On Rte. 17 in Bealeton, VA,
between Fredericksburg and Warrenton, tel. 703/439–8661.
Admission: $8 adults, $3 children 3–12. Group rates un-
available.*

Paul E. Garber Facility. This collection of Smithsonian
warehouses in suburban Maryland is where flight-related
artifacts are stored and restored prior to their display at
the National Air and Space Museum on the Mall. Among
the 160 objects on view here are such historic craft as a Soviet MiG-15 from the Korean War and a Battle of Britain-
era Hawker Hurricane IIC, as well as model satellites and
assorted engines and propellers. A behind-the-scenes look
at how the artifacts are preserved is included on the three-
hour walking tour. Note: The tour is for ages 14 and up, and
there is no heating or air-conditioning at the facility, so plan
accordingly. *Old Silver Rd. at St. Barnabas Rd., Suitland,
MD, tel. 202/357–1400. Free tours weekdays at 10 AM, weekends at 10 AM and 1 PM. Reservations required at least 3–8
wks in advance.*

Goddard Space Flight Center. Space flight is brought down
to earth at this NASA museum, located in the suburban

Maryland complex where scientists and technicians monitor spaceships circling the Earth, the solar system, and beyond. Local model rocket clubs send their handiwork skyward the first and third Sundays of each month. *Baltimore–Washington Pkwy. and Greenbelt Rd., Greenbelt, MD, tel. 301/286–8981. Admission free. Open daily 10–4. Tours Wed.–Sat. at 11:30 and 2:30.*

Hillwood Museum. Hillwood House, the 40-room Georgian mansion of cereal heiress Marjorie Merriweather Post, contains a large collection of 18th- and 19th-century French and Russian decorative art that includes gold and silver work, icons, lace, tapestries, china, and Fabergé eggs. Also on the estate are a dacha filled with Russian objects and an Adirondacks-style cabin that houses an assortment of Native American artifacts. The grounds are composed of lawns, formal French and Japanese gardens, and paths that wind through plantings of azaleas, laurels, and rhododendrons. *4155 Linnean Ave. NW, tel. 202/686–5807. Admission to house and grounds: $10, children under 12 not admitted on house tour. Admission to grounds only: $2. House open by reservation only; grounds open 11–3. House and grounds closed Feb. Make reservations well in advance to tour the house. Metro stop, Van Ness/UDC.*

Intelsat, the international satellite cooperative, has its headquarters in a striking glass building that looks as if it itself had come down from space. Although no tours of the building are given, a brief film about the work of the organization is shown by appointment in the high-tech Visitors Center. Visitors see models of rockets, satellites, and control centers where satellite traffic is monitored. Space buffs will enjoy the visit. *Connecticut Ave. and Van Ness St. NW, tel. 202/944–7500. Admission free. Reservations required. Metro stop, Van Ness/UDC.*

The Maine Avenue Seafood Market is a reminder that Washington isn't far from the Chesapeake Bay, the Atlantic Ocean beyond that, and the bounty of both. The market bustles with activity as more than a dozen vendors sell fresh crabs, fish, shrimp, squid, clams, and other types of seafood. If you work up an appetite there are seven restaurants stretched out along Maine Avenue, including local seafood powerhouse **Phillips Flagship.** All have terraces overlooking the Washington Channel and the motorboats, houseboats, and sailboats that are moored there. *Maine Ave. SW. Metro stop, Waterfront.*

Marine Corps Barracks. Each Friday evening at 8:45 from May to September the Marine Corps Drum and Bugle Corps, the Marine Band, and the Silent Drill Team present a dress parade filled with martial music and precision marching. *8th and I Sts. SE, tel. 202/433–6060. Admission free. Reservations required. Call 3 wks in advance. Metro stop, Eastern Market.*

Meridian House and the White-Meyer House. Meridian International Center, a nonprofit institution promoting international understanding, now owns these two handsome mansions designed by John Russell Pope. The 30-room Meridian House was built in 1920 by Irwin Boyle Laughlin, scion of a Pittsburgh steel family and former ambassador to Spain. The Louis XVI–style home features parquet floors, ornamental iron grillwork, handsome moldings, period furniture, tapestries, and a garden planted with European linden trees. Next door is the Georgian-style house built for Henry White (former ambassador to France) that was later the home of the Meyer family, publishers of the *Washington Post*. The first floors of both houses are open to the public and are the scene of periodic art exhibits with an international flavor. *1630 and 1624 Crescent Pl. NW, tel. 202/667–6800. Admission free. Open Wed.–Sun. 2–5.*

Mexican Cultural Institute. This museum is in a glorious 1911 Italianate house that was once the Embassy of Mexico. Inside are highlights of 19th- and 20th-century Mexican art, including the works of Diego Rivera, José Clemente Orozco, David Alfaro, Sigueiros, and Juan O'Gorman. *2829 16th St. NW, tel. 202/728–1628. Admission free. Open Tues.–Sat. 11–5.*

National Capital Trolley Museum. Some of the capital's historic trolleys have been rescued and restored and are now on display at this suburban Maryland museum, along with streetcars from Europe and elsewhere in America. For a nominal fare you can go on a 2-mile ride through the country. *Bonifant Rd. between Layhill Rd. and New Hampshire Ave., Wheaton, MD, tel. 301/384–6088. Trolley-ride fare: $2 adults, $1.50 children 2–18, children under 2 free. Open Jan.–Nov., weekends and Memorial Day, July 4, and Labor Day noon–5; Dec., weekends 5–9 PM for "Holly Trolley Illuminations"; July and Aug., Wed. noon–4.*

National Museum of Health and Medicine. Opened more than 125 years ago, the medical museum features exhibits that illustrate medicine's fight against injury and disease. Included are displays on the Lincoln and Garfield assassinations and one of the world's largest collections of microscopes. Because some exhibits are fairly graphic (the wax surgical models and various organs floating in alcohol, for example), the museum may not be suitable for young children or the squeamish. *Walter Reed Army Medical Center, 6825 16th St. NW, tel. 202/576–2348. Admission free. Open daily 10–5:30. Closed Dec. 25.*

National Weather Service Science and History Center. Opened in 1990 in suburban Maryland, this museum displays the tools of the National Oceanic and Atmospheric Administration, including remote data collectors, weather satellites, and "TOTO," a robotlike Totable Tornado Observatory used to study twisters. There's also the actual 1891 Cairo, Illinois, U.S. Weather Bureau office, complete with the original furniture, record books, and meteorological instruments. *1325 East-West Hwy., Silver Spring, MD, tel. 301/427-2153. Admission free. Open weekdays 8:30-5. Metro stop, Silver Spring.*

Washington Dolls' House and Toy Museum. Founded in 1975 by a dollhouse historian, this compact museum contains a collection of American and imported dolls, dollhouses, toys, and games, most from the Victorian period. Miniature accessories, dollhouse kits, and antique toys and games are on sale in the museum's shops. *5236 44th St. NW, tel. 202/244-0024. Admission: $3 adults, $2 senior citizens, $1 children under 14. Open Tues.-Sat. 10-5, Sun. noon-5. Metro stop, Friendship Heights.*

Washington Navy Yard. The yard is the Navy's oldest shore establishment, authorized in 1799. The facility is now a supply and administrative center, but four attractions make it a must-see for anyone interested in military history. (Eastern Market is the closest Metro station to the Navy Yard.) The **Navy Museum,** in a former weapons factory, chronicles the history of the U.S. Navy from the Revolution to the present. Exhibits range from the fully rigged foremast of the USS *Constitution* (better known as "Old Ironsides") to a U.S. Navy Corsair fighter plane dangling from the ceiling. All around are models of fighting ships, displays on battles, and portraits of the sailors who fought them. Children especially enjoy peering through the operating periscopes and pretending to launch torpedoes at the display ship *Barry* floating a few hundred yards away in the Anacostia River. In front of the museum is a collection of guns, cannons, and missiles. An annex is full of unusual submarines. *9th and M Sts. SE, Bldg. 76, tel. 202/433-4882. Admission free. Open weekdays 9-4 (Memorial Day-Labor Day 9-5), weekends and holidays 10-5. Call ahead to schedule free weekday highlights tour.*

The **Marine Corps Museum** tells the story of the corps from its inception in 1775 to its role in Desert Storm. A variety of artifacts—uniforms, weapons, documents, photographs—outline the growth of the corps, including its embrace of amphibious assault and the strategy of "vertical envelopment" (helicopters, to you and me). *9th and M Sts. SE, Bldg. 58, tel. 202/433-3534. Admission free. Open fall-spring, Mon.-Sat. 10-4, Sun. noon-5; summer, weekdays 10-8, Sat. 10-4, Sun. noon-5; closed Dec. 25 and Jan. 1.*

The one-room **Navy Art Gallery** hosts rotating exhibits of Navy-related paintings, sketches, and drawings, many created during combat by Navy artists. The bulk of the collection illustrates World War II. *9th and M Sts. SE, Bldg. 67, tel, 202/433-3815. Admission free. Open Labor Day-Memorial Day, Wed.-Fri. 9-4, weekends 10-4; Memorial Day-Labor Day, Wed.-Fri. 9-5, weekends 10-5; closed federal holidays.*

Moored in the Anacostia River nearby and on permanent display is the *Barry,* a decommissioned U.S. Navy destroyer open for tours. *Tel. 202/433–3377. Admission free. Open Mar.–Aug., daily 10–5; Sept.–Feb., daily 10–4.*

From June through August the Navy and Marines put on a multimedia Summer Pageant at an amphitheater across from the Navy Museum. For free reservations, call 202/ 433–2218.

Sightseeing Checklists

Historic Buildings and Sites

This is a list of the principal buildings and sites mentioned in the Exploring section. For other attractions not listed here, see Off the Beaten Track, above.

American Red Cross (Tour 3: The White House Area). The neoclassical headquarters of the Red Cross. *Metro stop, Farragut West.*
Anderson House (Tour 7: Dupont Circle). The headquarters of the Society of the Cincinnati, filled with trompe l'oeil paintings, Asian art, and military miniatures. *Metro stop, Dupont Circle.*
Blair House (Tour 3: The White House Area). Foreign dignitaries stay here when visiting the president. *Metro stop, McPherson Square.*
Cox's Row (Tour 6: Georgetown). Fine examples of Federal architecture.
Customs House (Tour 6: Georgetown). Renaissance Revival–style Customs House is now a post office.
Decatur House (Tour 3: The White House Area). Federal- and Victorian-style home of naval hero Stephen Decatur. *Metro stop, McPherson Square.*
District (of Columbia) Building (Tour 5: Old Downtown and Federal Triangle). Washington's mayor and city council toil in this beaux arts building. *Metro stop, Federal Triangle.*
Dumbarton House. (Tour 6: Georgetown). The Georgian headquarters of the National Society of Colonial Dames of America.
Evermay (Tour 6: Georgetown). An 1800 Georgian private manor house.
Folger Shakespeare Library (Tour 4: Capitol Hill). Items from the library's vast collection are often on display. *Metro stop, Capitol South.*
Ford's Theatre (Tour 5: Old Downtown and Federal Triangle). The scene of Lincoln's assassination is still a working theater. *Metro stop, Metro Center.*
Heurich Mansion/Historical Society of Washington, D.C. (Tour 7: Dupont Circle). Beer baron's mansion houses a collection of Washingtoniana. *Metro stop, Dupont Circle.*
House of the Americas/Organization of American States (Tour 3: The White House Area). The United Nations of this

hemisphere features a cooling interior fountain and atrium. *Metro stop, Farragut West.*

J. Edgar Hoover FBI Building (Tour 5: Old Downtown and Federal Triangle). Exhibits on how agents solved cases and a live-ammo demonstration are part of this building's popular tour. *Metro stop, Federal Triangle.*

John F. Kennedy Center for the Performing Arts (Tour 8: Foggy Bottom). The city's premier cultural center. *Metro stop, Foggy Bottom.*

Martin Luther King Memorial Library (Tour 5: Old Downtown and Federal Triangle). The only Ludwig Mies van der Rohe–designed building in the city and its largest public library. *Metro stop, Gallery Place.*

Library of Congress, Jefferson Building (Tour 4: Capitol Hill). Holds some 90 million items in one of the most ornate spaces in town. *Metro stop, Capitol South.*

National Archives (Tour 5: Old Downtown and Federal Triangle). The Declaration of Independence, Bill of Rights, and Constitution are displayed here. *Metro stop, Archives/Navy Memorial.*

Octagon House (Tour 3: The White House Area). The treaty ending the War of 1812 was signed here; now used for architectural exhibitions. *Metro stop, Farragut West.*

Old Executive Office Building (Tour 3: The White House Area). Executive branch offices in a building patterned after the Louvre. *Metro stop, Farragut West.*

Old Post Office Building (Tour 5: Old Downtown and Federal Triangle). A pavilion of shops and restaurants with a scenic view from the clock tower. *Metro stop, Federal Triangle.*

Old Stone House (Tour 6: Georgetown). The oldest house in the city, with some parts dating back to 1764.

Sears House (Tour 5: Old Downtown and Federal Triangle). Civil War photographer Mathew Brady had his studios here. *Metro stop, Archives.*

Sewall-Belmont House (Tour 4: Capitol Hill). The early days of the women's movement are chronicled in this 1800 house. *Metro stop, Union Station.*

Charles Sumner School (Tour 7: Dupont Circle). The Adolph Cluss–designed school, now home to administrative offices and galleries, was built for the education of black children. *Metro stop, Farragut North.*

Supreme Court of the United States (Tour 4: Capitol Hill). The highest court in the land meets here October through June. *Metro stop, Capitol South.*

Treasury Building (Tour 3: The White House Area). Treasury Department headquarters. *Metro stop, McPherson Square.*

Union Station (Tour 4: Capitol Hill). Trains, shops, and restaurants are in this beautifully restored beaux arts station. *Metro stop, Union Station.*

United States Capitol (Tour 4: Capitol Hill). Congress meets here, surrounded by some of the city's finest artwork. *Metro stop, Capitol South or Union Station.*

White House (Tour 3: The White House Area). The most famous home in the country. *Metro stop, McPherson Square.*
Willard Hotel (Tour 5: Old Downtown and Federal Triangle). An elegant 1901 hostelry. *Metro stops, Federal Triangle and Metro Center.*
Woodrow Wilson House (Tour 7: Dupont Circle). The 28th president retired here; today it's a museum to his accomplishments. *Metro stop, Dupont Circle.*

Museums and Galleries

The Smithsonian dominates the public museum and gallery scene in Washington, but there are also many private art galleries that show and sell the work of local, national, and international artists. These galleries are concentrated near Dupont Circle, in Georgetown, and on 7th Street north of Pennsylvania Avenue. For an overview of the day's events at Smithsonian museums, call **Dial-a-Museum** (tel. 202/357–2020).

Art Museum of the Americas (Tour 3: The White House Area). The work of contemporary Latin American artists is shown in this gallery behind the Organization of American States. *Metro stop, Farragut West.*
Arts and Industries Building (Tour 1: The Mall). This Smithsonian museum features a re-creation of an 1876 Centennial exhibition. *Metro stop, Smithsonian.*
Australian Embassy (Tour 7: Dupont Circle). Aboriginal and antipodean art are on display. *Metro stop, Dupont Circle.*
B'nai B'rith Klutznick Museum (Tour 7: Dupont Circle). Works by Jewish artists are on display. *Metro stop, Farragut North.*
Canadian Embassy (Tour 5: Old Downtown and Federal Triangle). The embassy hosts concerts and exhibits of Canadian art. *Metro stop, Archives/Navy Memorial.*
Corcoran Gallery of Art (Tour 3: The White House Area). This venerable Washington institution boasts a strong collection of European and American art and photography. *Metro stop, Farragut West.*
Daughters of the American Revolution Museum (Tour 3: The White House Area). America's Colonial past is explored at this museum. *Metro stop, Farragut West.*
Department of the Interior Museum (Tour 3: The White House Area). A quaint museum outlines the accomplishments of this agency. *Metro stop, Farragut West.*
Dumbarton Oaks (Tour 6: Georgetown). Harvard University administers two world-class museums of Byzantine art and pre-Columbian artifacts.
Explorers Hall/National Geographic Society (Tour 7: Dupont Circle). Geography and the natural world are the focus of the famous magazine's museum. *Metro stop, Farragut North.*
Firearms Museum/National Rifle Association (Tour 7:

Dupont Circle). All manner of famous firearms are on display here. *Metro stop, Farragut North.*

Freer Gallery of Art (Tour 1: The Mall). Asian art and James McNeill Whistler's stunning *Peacock Room* highlight this Smithsonian museum. *Metro stop, Smithsonian.*

Joseph H. Hirshhorn Museum and Sculpture Garden (Tour 1: The Mall). Modern art is housed in this circular building; the sculpture garden holds one of the largest public collections of works by Henry Moore. *Metro stop, Smithsonian.*

National Air and Space Museum (Tour 1: The Mall). The city's most popular museum has everything from the Wright Brothers' *Flyer* to a model of the USS *Enterprise* from "Star Trek." *Metro stop, Smithsonian.*

National Aquarium (Tour 5: Old Downtown and Federal Triangle). The oldest public aquarium in the country. *Metro stop, Federal Triangle.*

National Building Museum (Tour 5: Old Downtown and Federal Triangle). Museum on architecture and the building arts. *Metro stop, Judiciary Square.*

National Gallery of Art (Tour 1: The Mall). One of the world's best collections of art. *Metro stop, Archives.*

National Museum of African Art (Tour 1: The Mall). Carvings, textile, and jewelry from sub-Saharan Africa are on display. *Metro stop, Smithsonian.*

National Museum of American Art (Tour 5: Old Downtown and Federal Triangle). The collection stretches from the earliest days of American art through such lights of modernism as Jasper Johns and Robert Rauschenberg. *Metro stop, Gallery Place.*

National Museum of American History (Tour 1: The Mall). The history of the country is traced in this Smithsonian museum. *Metro stop, Smithsonian.*

National Museum of Natural History (Tour 1: The Mall). The Hope Diamond is just one of the attractions at this most diverse Smithsonian museum. *Metro stop, Smithsonian. Open Mon.–Sat. 10–5.*

National Portrait Gallery (Tour 5: Old Downtown and Federal Triangle). Likenesses of famous Americans and portraits of every U.S. president are on display here. *Metro stop, Gallery Place.*

National Postal Museum (Tour 4: Capitol Hill). The newest Smithsonian museum in Washington celebrates stamps and more. *Metro stop, Union Station.*

Phillips Collection (Tour 7: Dupont Circle). The collection includes works by Cézanne and O'Keeffe and Renoir's *Luncheon of the Boating Party. Metro stop, Dupont Circle.*

Renwick Gallery (Tour 3: The White House Area). This Smithsonian museum is devoted to American arts and crafts. *Metro stop, McPherson Square.*

Sackler Gallery (Tour 1: The Mall). Treasures from the Orient are part of this Smithsonian museum's collection. *Metro stop, Smithsonian.*

Smithsonian Institution Castle (Tour 1: The Mall). The

Smithsonian's information center. *Metro stop, Smithsonian.*

Textile Museum (Tour 7: Dupont Circle). Oriental rugs, Coptic textiles, pre-Columbian weavings, and modern fiber art are on display here. *Metro stop, Dupont Circle.*

United States Holocaust Memorial Museum (Tour 1: The Mall). The story of the Holocaust is told at this new museum. *Metro stop, Smithsonian.*

Washington Project for the Arts (Tour 5: Old Downtown and Federal Triangle). The works of area artists are shown at this gallery. The bookstore is a favorite with local bohemians. *Metro stops, National Archives or Gallery Place.*

Churches, Temples, and Mosques

All Souls' Unitarian Church. The design of this church, erected in 1924, is based on that of St. Martin-in-the-Fields in London. *16th and Harvard Sts. NW, tel. 202/332–5266.*

Franciscan Monastery and Gardens. Not far from the **Shrine of the Immaculate Conception,** this Byzantine-style monastery contains facsimiles of such Holy-Land shrines as the Grotto of Bethlehem and the Holy Sepulcher. Underground are reproductions of the catacombs of Rome. The gardens are especially beautiful, planted with roses that bloom in the summer. *14th and Quincy Sts. NE, tel. 202/ 526–6800. Open daily 9–5. Tours of catacombs on the hr (except noon) Mon.–Sat. 9–4, Sun. 1–4. Metro stop, Brookland–Catholic University.*

Grace Episcopal Church (Tour 6: Georgetown).

Islamic Mosque and Cultural Center. The Moslem faithful are called to prayer five times a day from atop this mosque's 162-foot-high minaret. Each May, the Moslem Women's Association sponsors a bazaar, with crafts, clothing, and food for sale. *2551 Massachusetts Ave. NW, tel. 202/332–8343. Center open daily 10–5; mosque open for all 5 prayers, dawn–past sunset. Women must wear a scarf to cover their head.*

Metropolitan African Methodist Episcopal Church. Completed in 1886, this Gothic-style church became one of the most influential black churches in the city. Abolitionist orator Frederick Douglass worshiped here and Bill Clinton chose the church as the setting for his inaugural prayer service. *1518 M St. NW, tel. 202/331–1426. Metro stop, Farragut North.*

Mt. Zion United Methodist Church (Tour 6: Georgetown).

National Shrine of the Immaculate Conception. This is the largest Catholic church in the United States, begun in 1920 and built with funds contributed by every parish in the country. Dedicated in 1959, the shrine is a blend of Romanesque and Byzantine styles, with a bell tower that reminds many of St. Mark's in Venice. *Michigan Ave. and 4th St. NE, tel. 202/526–8300. Open spring and summer, daily 7–7; fall and winter, daily 7–6. Sunday mass at 7:30, 9,*

10:30, noon, 1:30 (in Latin), and 4:30. Metro stop, Brookland–Catholic University.

Old Adas Israel Synagogue (Tour 5: Old Downtown and Federal Triangle). This redbrick, Federal Revival–style building is the oldest synagogue in Washington.

St. John's Episcopal Church (Tour 3: The White House Area) *Metro stop, McPherson Square.*

St. Matthew's Cathedral (Tour 7: Dupont Circle) *Metro stop, Farragut North.*

Saint Sophia Cathedral. This Greek Orthodox cathedral is noted for the handsome mosaic work on the interior of its dome. Saint Sophia holds a festival of Greek food and crafts each May and October. *Massachusetts Ave. and 36th St. NW, tel. 202/333–4730.*

Scottish Rite Temple. This dramatic Masonic shrine is patterned after the Mausoleum of Halicarnassus. Tours available weekdays on request. *1733 16th St. NW, tel. 202/232–3579.*

Washington National Cathedral. Construction of this stunning Gothic church—the sixth-largest cathedral in the world—started in 1907 and was finished on September 30, 1990, when the cathedral was consecrated. Like its 14th-century counterparts, the National Cathedral (officially Washington's Cathedral Church of St. Peter and St. Paul) has flying buttresses, naves, transepts, and barrel vaults that were built stone by stone. It is adorned with fanciful gargoyles created by skilled stone carvers. The tomb of Woodrow Wilson, the only president buried in Washington, is on the south side of the nave. The expansive view of the city from the Pilgrim Gallery is exceptional. The cathedral is under the governance of the Episcopal church but has played host to services of many denominations. *Wisconsin and Massachusetts Aves. NW, tel. 202/537–6200. Open fall, winter, and spring, daily 10–4:30; May 1–Labor Day, weekdays 10–9, weekends 10–4:30. Sun. services at 8, 9, 10, 11, 6:30; evensong at 4 PM. Tours Mon.–Sat. 10–3:15, Sun. 12:45–2:45. Tour information: tel. 202/537–6207.*

Temple of the Church of Jesus Christ of Latter-Day Saints. This striking Mormon temple in suburban Maryland—one of its white towers is topped with a golden statue of the Mormon angel and prophet, Moroni—has become a Washington landmark. It is closed to non-Mormons, but a visitors center offers a lovely view of the white-marble church and has a film about the temple and what takes place inside. Tulips, dogwoods, and azaleas bloom in the 57-acre grounds each spring. *9900 Stoneybrook Dr., Kensington, MD, tel. 301/587–0144. Grounds and visitors center open daily 10–9.*

Statues and Monuments

Washington, perhaps more than any other city in the United States, is filled with allegorical outdoor art. Examples can be found in the middle of traffic circles and on dozens of neoclassical public buildings. *The Outdoor Sculpture of Washington, D.C.*, by architectural historian James M. Goode, provides readable histories of the well-known and little-known works to be found in the nation's capital.

The Awakening. Children love this giant sculpture of a bearded man emerging from the ground near Hains Point. Adults are captivated, too. *Hains Point, East Potomac Park.*

Bartholdi Fountain (Tour 4: Capitol Hill) *Metro stop, Federal Center SW.*

Boy Scouts Memorial. Just east of the Ellipse stands this group of heroic statuary: a uniformed Boy Scout flanked by a male figure representing patriotism and a female figure who holds the light of faith. *East of the Ellipse, near 15th St. NW. Metro stop, McPherson Square.*

Columbus Memorial Fountain (Tour 4: Capitol Hill) *Metro stop, Union Station.*

Confederate Statue (Tour 12: Alexandria).

Dumbarton Bridge (Tour 7: Dupont Circle) *Metro stop, Dupont Circle.*

Dupont Circle/Fountain (Tour 7: Dupont Circle) *Metro stop, Dupont Circle.*

Albert Einstein (Tour 8: Foggy Bottom) *Metro stop, Foggy Bottom.*

Freedmen's Memorial. This bronze statue of Abraham Lincoln standing above a newly freed slave who has just broken his chains was dedicated on April 14, 1876, the 11th anniversary of the president's assassination. Money for its construction was donated by hundreds of ex-slaves. *Lincoln Park, Massachusetts Ave. between 11th and 13th Sts. NE.*

Albert Gallatin (Tour 4: Capitol Hill) *Metro stop, McPherson Square.*

James Garfield Memorial (Tour 4: Capitol Hill) *Metro stop, Capitol South.*

Grand Army of the Republic (Tour 5: Old Downtown and Federal Triangle) *Metro stop, Archives/Navy Memorial.*

Grant Memorial (Tour 4: Capitol Hill) *Metro stop, Federal Center SW.*

Alexander Hamilton (Tour 3: The White House Area) *Metro stop, Federal Triangle.*

Andrew Jackson (Tour 3: The White House Area) *Metro stop, McPherson Square.*

Jefferson Memorial (Tour 2: The Monuments).

John F. Kennedy (Tour 8: Foggy Bottom) *Metro stop, Foggy Bottom.*

Thaddeus Kosciuszko (Tour 3: The White House Area) *Metro stop, McPherson Square.*

Marquis de Lafayette (Tour 3: The White House Area) *Metro stop, McPherson Square.*

Lincoln Memorial (Tour 2: The Monuments).

Marine Corps War Memorial (Tour 11: Arlington) *Metro stop, Arlington Cemetery.*

National Law Enforcement Officers Memorial (Tour 5: Old

Downtown and Federal Triangle). *Metro stop, Judiciary Square.*

Navy Memorial (Tour 5: Old Downtown and Federal Triangle) *Metro stop, Archives.*

The Peace of God that Passeth Understanding. Henry Adams commissioned Augustus Saint-Gaudens to create this memorial to Adams's wife, who had committed suicide. Known by the nickname "Grief," this figure of a shroud-draped woman is thought by many to be the most moving sculpture in the city. *In Rock Creek Cemetery, Rock Creek Rd. and Webster St. NW.*

Peace Monument (Tour 4: Capitol Hill) *Metro stop, Union Station.*

Comte de Rochambeau (Tour 3: The White House Area) *Metro stop, McPherson Square.*

General Casimir Pulaski (Tour 5: Old Downtown and Federal Triangle) *Metro stop, Federal Triangle.*

Franklin Delano Roosevelt Memorial (Tour 5: Old Downtown and Federal Triangle) *Metro stop, Archives.*

General Winfield Scott (Tour 7: Dupont Circle) *Metro stop, Dupont Circle;* (Tour 5: Old Downtown and Federal Triangle) *Metro stop, Archives/Navy Memorial.*

General Philip Sheridan (Tour 7: Dupont Circle) *Metro stop, Dupont Circle.*

General William Tecumseh Sherman Monument (Tour 3: The White House Area) *Metro stop, Federal Triangle.*

Baron von Steuben (Tour 3: The White House Area) *Metro stop, McPherson Square.*

Temperance Fountain (Tour 5: Old Downtown and Federal Triangle) *Metro stop, Archives/Navy Memorial.*

Vietnam Veterans Memorial (Tour 2: The Monuments) *Metro stop, Foggy Bottom.*

Vietnam Women's Memorial (Tour 2: The Monuments) *Metro stop, Foggy Bottom.*

Washington Monument (Tour 2: The Monuments) *Metro stop, Federal Triangle or Smithsonian.*

Zoos

National Aquarium (Tour 5: Old Downtown and Federal Triangle). Housed in the Department of Commerce Building and featuring tropical and freshwater fish, this is the nation's oldest public aquarium. *Metro stop, Federal Triangle.*

National Zoological Park (Tour 9: Cleveland Park and the National Zoo). One of the foremost zoos in the world, the 160-acre zoo is known for its giant panda, Hsing-Hsing, and ambitious Amazonia ecosystem. Many animals are shown in naturalistic settings. *Metro stops, Cleveland Park and Woodley Park/Zoo.*

4 Washington for Children

By John F. Kelly It's easy to pigeonhole Washington as the archetypal grown-up place. After all, running the government of the most important country in the world is serious stuff. But the city that has the White House, the Capitol, and the Supreme Court also has the National Museum of Natural History, the Capital Children's Museum, and the National Zoo, three places children especially love. And while not every kid is wowed by the Jefferson Memorial, there hasn't been one born yet who won't enjoy a ride to the top of the Washington Monument. What's more, history that seems dry and dusty in the classroom comes alive for children in Washington, as they visit the landmarks they've seen on the evening news. And in this age of belt-tightening, the capital has one more thing going for it: most of the attractions are free.

Despite its kid-friendliness, Washington isn't bursting at the seams with hotels and restaurants that cater to families. It's not that they don't like kids; it's just that they're more accustomed to catering to their parents. Most hotels can help find a baby-sitter though, and at some time during your stay you'll probably want to take advantage of the sitting services, because for Washingtonians a night out at a fashionable eatery is usually a night away from the kids— their own and other peoples'.

Even adults can get tired traipsing around the large Smithsonian museums, so a stroller is a good idea for younger kids who may wear out easily (and the parents who'd then have to carry them). Keep in mind, though, that you'll have to leave your stroller at the entrances to the White House and the Washington Monument.

For kid-oriented fare, consult the Friday *Washington Post* "Weekend" section. Its "Carousel" listings include information on plays, puppet shows, concerts, story-telling sessions, nature programs, and other events just for families. And if you find yourself stuck in traffic in a rental car, tune to WKDL, 1050 AM. The first radio station just for families in the Washington area, WKDL has music and features of interest to children and their parents.

Exploring

Pierre L'Enfant didn't design Washington's Mall with children in mind, but his central monumental core couldn't be better for them. With most of the Smithsonian museums arranged around it, and the Washington Monument and Tidal Basin a few steps away, it should be every family's base camp. Even its name can help parents coax reluctant children out for a day of sightseeing: Just tell them you're going "to the Mall."

Many of Washington's museums have exhibits designed especially for—or appealing especially to—children. On the Mall are the **Discovery Room, Dinosaur Hall,** and **O. Orkin**

Insect Zoo at the National Museum of Natural History and the Hands On History Room at the National Museum of American History. Just about everything at the National Air and Space Museum is cool to kids. There's an old-time carousel in front of the Arts and Industries Building. You know when there are kids at the Navy Museum because the sound of the submarine dive claxon reverberates through its halls. (Youngsters love pushing it and looking through the museum's operating periscopes.) The Touch Tank at the National Aquarium is usually thronged by young oceanographers, and the National Geographic Explorers Hall is an interactive museum that tests youngsters' knowledge of Planet Earth. (*See* Chapter 3, Exploring Washington.)

Many Washington museums have special printed children's guides to their collections, allowing kids to, for example, take pencil in hand and go on "scavenger hunts" to pick out the shapes and patterns in a work of modern art. Ask at the information desks.

The following Smithsonian museums have diaper-changing facilities in both men's and women's rooms: the Smithsonian Castle, the National Museum of Natural History, the National Museum of American History, the National Air and Space Museum, the Renwick Gallery, and the National Museum of American Art. Metro stations have no rest rooms at all.

Here are some other Washington attractions tailor-made for family visits.

Museums, Monuments, and Exhibits

Capital Children's Museum. A former convent three blocks from Union Station is the site of this sprawling, decidedly hands-on museum. Everything is at kid level and just about everything is meant to be touched. That means children may take apart old typewriters, use pulleys and levers to hoist cinder blocks, create their own old-time animations, weave their way through a maze, and fill a room with huge soap bubbles. Volunteer docents guide children and parents to different activity areas and oversee their young charges as they engage in such play as cooking tortillas or making paper flowers. The museum strives to show how people in other cultures live, so there is an international flavor to many of the exhibits. Unlike the glitzier Smithsonian offerings, this museum seems a bit frayed around the edges. But it's a comfortable sort of wear and tear, achieved through the inquisitive hands of countless young visitors, and it makes the Capital Children's Museum seem like one huge playroom. *800 3rd St. NE, tel. 202/543-8600. Open daily 10-5. Closed Thanksgiving, Dec. 25, Jan. 1, Easter. Admission: $6, children under 2 free. Metro stop, Union Station.*

Bureau of Engraving and Printing (*see* Tour 1: The Mall in Chapter 3, Exploring Washington). Any kid who gets an allowance will enjoy watching money roll off the presses here.

DAR Museum (*see* Tour 3: The White House Area in Chapter 3). Exhibits frequently touch on how families lived in Colonial times, and youngsters may not be entranced by all the displays. However, they'll love the free "Colonial Adventure" tours that are usually held the first and third Sundays of the month from 2 to 3. Costumed docents lead children aged five through seven through the museum, explaining the exhibits and describing life in Colonial America. Make reservations at least 10 days in advance by calling 202/879–3239. *Metro stop, Farragut West.*

The National Zoo (*see* Tour 9: Cleveland Park and the National Zoo in Chapter 3). One of the nation's best zoos is a must-see for families. Rental strollers are available for when little legs wear out. *Metro stops, Cleveland Park and Woodley Park/National Zoo.*

Washington Dolls' House and Toy Museum (*see* Off the Beaten Track in Chapter 3). Antique toys and doll houses are on display, and accessories and kits are available for purchase. Most of the collection is behind glass, disappointing younger visitors; older kids will enjoy it more. *Metro stop, Friendship Heights.*

The Washington Monument (*see* Tour 2: The Monuments in Chapter 3). You can't really say you've been to Washington until you've taken in the view from atop this 555-foot-tall obelisk. *Metro stops, Federal Triangle and Smithsonian.*

Shopping

Young visitors to Washington can leave with a lot more than they came with, from souvenir T-shirts to paper models of the White House. Shoppers shouldn't overlook the merchandise on the Mall. The Smithsonian museums have creatively stocked shops, and many of the items have the benefit of actually being educational.

Favorite Smithsonian shops include those in the **National Museum of American History** (books, games), the **National Museum of Natural History** (dinosaur models, stuffed animals), and the **National Air and Space Museum.** The last is where you'll find something kids seem incapable of resisting: astronauts' freeze-dried ice cream sandwiches in foil pouches. (Warning to grown-ups: They're messy and not particularly tasty.)

As for more traditional finds, there's **F.A.O. Schwarz,** the upscale toy store; the **Kid's Closet,** a children's clothing store in downtown DC; and the **Cheshire Cat,** a bookstore just for children (*see* Chapter 5, Shopping). The Cheshire Cat also has occasional reading and story-telling sessions, and well-known children's book authors sometimes stop by to meet and talk with their readers.

The Great Train Store (Union Station, 40 Massachusetts Ave. NE, tel. 202/371–2881) has all manner of train sets, engineer's hats, and other choo-choo-related toys and memorabilia. **Al's Magic Shop** (1012 Vermont Ave. NW, tel. 202/789-2800) has been catering to both magicians and pranksters for more than 50 years. **All Wound-Up** (Old Post Office Pavilion, 1100 Pennsylvania Ave. NW, tel. 202/842-0635) has a name that says it all: close to 70 different types of wind-up toys. At the **ReUse** store (418 S Washington St., Alexandria, VA, tel. 703/549-0111) you'll find scraps of wood, old egg cartons, empty coffee cans, bits of yarn, bags of bottle caps, and other cast-off items designed to be recycled into children's art projects. And kids who want to be famous, or pretend that they are, can get their likeness computer superimposed on the cover of *National Geographic* (at **National Geographic Explorers Hall,** 17th and M Sts. NW, tel. 202/857-7689) or on a postage stamp, a $100 bill, or Mount Rushmore (at the **National Museum of American History,** 12th St. and Constitution Ave. NW, tel. 202/357-2700). ·

Parks and Playgrounds

Washington prides itself on the trees that line its streets, and that green thumb extends to the city's parks. You won't need to venture far to find a patch of grass for running on or a pool of water for dipping hot feet into.

The biggest stretch of parkland is **Rock Creek Park** (*see* The Outdoors in Chapter 6). Start at the **Nature Center** (5200 Glover Rd. NW, tel. 202/426-6829), where easily hiked trails lead off in all directions. The Nature Center has a small room filled with pelts, bones, feathers, and shells for naturalists-in-training to handle and another with stuffed animals representative of the mid-Atlantic. (That's also where you'll find Noel, the great horned owl who, since breaking a wing, has called the Nature Center home.) There are special activities every weekend at the center. At 11 Saturdays and Sundays rangers show a nature film, and at 2 they give a "live animal" talk. The center's 70-seat planetarium introduces young visitors to the night sky at 1 PM, with a show for ages four and up, and at 4 PM, with a show for ages seven and up. Children also like the falling water of **Pierce Mill** (Tilden St. and Park Rd. NW), where rangers grind grain into flour.

Running parallel to the Potomac is the Chesapeake & Ohio Canal, a favorite spot for jogging and bicycling. Kids especially like the **mule-drawn barge rides,** which depart spring through early autumn from Georgetown, and the Great Falls Tavern Visitors Center in Maryland (*see* The Outdoors in Chapter 6).

There's a small play area close to the Capitol: The new **judicial office building beside Union Station** (2nd and E Sts. NE) has a modest but choice selection of play equipment behind it. The new type of playground—with lots of tubes and bridges—hasn't found its way into Washington yet, but there are two in suburban Maryland worth a trip. Both **Cabin John Regional Park** (7400 Tuckerman La., Rockville, MD, tel. 301/299–4555) and **Wheaton Regional Park** (2000 Shorefield Rd., Wheaton, MD, tel. 301/946–7033) boast modern, terraced playgrounds with corkscrewing plastic slides, bouncing wooden bridges, sandboxes, and mazes. An added bonus: Both have ice rinks and trains that operate seasonally, and there's even a carousel at Wheaton. About 20 miles from downtown is the **Discovery Zone** (Rte. 355 and Middlebrook Rd., Germantown, MD, tel. 301/540–2424), an indoor fitness play center with tunnels, ball bins, padded cubes, and more; there's a $5.99-per-two-hours admission charge.

Kite flyers can be found most windy weekends near the Washington Monument grounds. (Buy a kite at the National Air and Space Museum if you want to join them.) One of the oldest **miniature golf courses** in the country operates during the summer in East Potomac Park (see The Outdoors in Chapter 6). **City Golf** is an indoor course at the Old Post Office Pavilion (1100 Pennsylvania Ave. NW, tel. 202/898–7888). A good way to tire out rambunctious offspring is to set them adrift in the **Tidal Basin** (*see* Tour 2: The Monuments in Chapter 3) at the helm of a paddleboat.

Young Brian Boitanos and Kristy Yamaguchis can practice their moves at two **ice rinks** close to the Mall: **The Sculpture Garden Outdoor Rink** (Constitution Ave. between 7th and 9th Sts. NW, tel. 202/371–5340) and the **Pershing Park Ice Rink** (Pennsylvania Ave. between 14th and 15th Sts. NW, tel. 202/737–6938). Rental skates are available. Both rinks operate seasonally.

There are no beaches in Washington, but **Wild World** (13710 Central Ave., Largo, MD, tel. 301/249–1500) is a 115-acre water theme park in suburban Maryland that operates late May through August. It has a wave pool, roller coaster, children's rides, and water slides.

Dining

When Washingtonians go out for a nice meal at a trendy downtown restaurant they usually leave the kids at home. That doesn't mean you need to check your children at the door, just that you shouldn't be surprised if you're one of the few obvious parents in attendance, especially in such neighborhoods as Adams-Morgan and Dupont Circle, where the restaurants cater to a young, single crowd. Most restaurants, however, stock booster seats and high chairs for kids who need a lift, and well-behaved babies are generally fawned over wherever they go.

Inside the Beltway For your own peace of mind you might want to eat somewhere with a loud dining room (the well-reviewed **Red Sage** and **Primi Piatti** have noisy atmospheres) or at just about any Chinese restaurant (whose staffs seem especially tolerant of children).

Some other suggestions: **The American Cafe** chain, with many locations in the Washington area (*see* Chapter 7, Dining), has been keeping parents sane since it opened in 1979, with a children's menu kids can draw on (they provide the crayons). Similarly, **Hamburger Hamlet** (5225 Wisconsin Ave. NW, tel. 202/244–2037) also lets kids express themselves on placemats. Both **E.E. Wolensky's** (2000 Pennsylvania Ave. NW, tel. 202/463–0050) and **T.G.I. Friday's** (2100 Pennsylvania Ave. NW, tel. 202/872–4344) are down-to-earth restaurants offering hearty American fare in children's portions. **Geppetto** (2917 M St. NW, tel. 202/333–2602) is an Italian restaurant with irresistible carved marionettes as part of the decor. **Swensen's** (4200 Wisconsin Ave. NW, tel. 202/244–5544) prides itself on being a family restaurant and scoops up its own brand of ice cream for dessert. Teens and teens-in-training will enjoy the music and memorabilia of the **Hard Rock Cafe** (999 E St. NW, tel. 202/737–7625) and the funky clothing store/restaurant at **Boogie's Diner** (1229 Wisconsin Ave. NW, tel. 202/298–7469). For fast food a shade more interesting than hamburgers and fries, check out the food courts at Washington's three main malls: **Union Station** (50 Massachusetts Ave. NW), **The Shops at National Place** (13th and F Sts. NW), and **The Pavilion at the Old Post Office** (12th St. and Pennsylvania Ave. NW).

Suburban Washington Restaurants in the suburbs are generally kid friendlier, with a few standouts. **The Calvert Grille** (3106 Mount Vernon Ave., Alexandria, VA, tel. 703/836–8425), specializing in barbecued baby-back ribs, seats families in a back room that's equipped with toys and butcher paper–covered tables for kids to draw on. The often crowded '50s-style, meat-and-potatoes **Silver Diner** (11806 Rockville Pike, Rockville, MD, tel. 301/770–2828) boasts a basket of crayons and a pile of connect-the-dot placemats at the cash register. And for interactive dining for the Nintendo generation, there's **Chuck E. Cheese** (several locations, including 6303 Richmond Hwy., Alexandria, VA, tel. 703/660–6800).

Lodging

Washington has hotels for everyone, from the sightseer on a budget to the big spender on a junket. Luckily for families, children under 16 stay free in most hotels. Here are some things to keep in mind when deciding on lodging with the little ones: Staying at an all-suite hotel will allow you to spread out and, if you prepare your meals in a kitchenette, keep costs down. A pool may be essential for a stay with kids; game rooms are a plus. Major convention hotels, and those on Capitol Hill and the waterfront, don't see as many families as those downtown, in Foggy Bottom, uptown, or in the Maryland and Virginia suburbs. The closer you are to a Metro stop, the quicker you'll be able to hit the sightseeing trail.

Baby-sitting Services Most larger hotels and those with concierges can arrange baby-sitting with one of Washington's licensed, bonded child-care agencies. Rates are usually per hour, with a four-hour minimum, and you may need to pay the sitter's transportation costs. The average cost is around $10 an hour for one child, with additional children about $1 more per hour; some agencies charge more to sit for additional nonrelated children. Most agencies are happy to provide references, and some sitters will even take kids sightseeing. A tip: Though most agencies can arrange last-minute child care, they appreciate as much notice as you can give them.

WeeSit (10681 Oak Thrust Ct., Burke, VA 22015, tel. 703/764-1542) works with many of the city's largest hotels. **Chevy Chase Babysitters** (10771 Middleboro Dr., Damascus, MD 20872, tel. 301/942-2931) has been in business for 33 years. **Mothers' Aides Inc.** (Box 7088, Fairfax Station, VA 22039, tel. 703/250-0700) counts schoolteachers among its sitters. **Helpers Plus Inc.** (4700 Auth Pl., Suite 401, Camp Springs, MD 20746, tel. 301/894-7200) employs certified nursing assistants.

Hotels that families should consider include the **Sheraton Washington** and the **Omni Shoreham;** both are within walking distance of the National Zoo, and the latter features a weekend matinee cabaret for children. The **Days Inn Connecticut Avenue** is only one Metro stop from the zoo and away from the bustle of downtown. Several all-suite hotels are clustered in Foggy Bottom, including the **Embassy Suites** and two **Guest Quarters** hotels.

The Arts

Washington has a lively arts scene for young and old alike. The museum community and the Kennedy Center serve as a mecca for traveling troupes, and the home-grown talent isn't bad either, with children's concerts and plays staple entertainment for many a Washington family. Museums often host programs related to their exhibitions—African trickster stories at the National Museum of African Art, for example—and "serious" groups such as the National Symphony Orchestra and the Washington Chamber Symphony have special programs to woo young fans.

Check the "Carousel" listings in the *Washington Post* "Weekend" section for special events that crop up during the year. For example, the **Ringling Bros. and Barnum & Bailey Circus** usually moves into the D.C. Armory for two weeks each April, and Wolf Trap Farm Park hosts the three-day **International Children's Festival,** with performers from around the world, each Labor Day weekend.

The **Kennedy Center** (tel. 202/467–4600) is the setting for more than 80 family events each year, including the two-day **Imagination Celebration** each April. Year-round offerings include dance, music, story-telling, plays, and concerts for prekindergarten to eighth-grade kids. It's also the home base of the **National Symphony Orchestra,** whose Family Concerts are for children as young as three. Other concerts, which include "instrument petting zoos," are for youngsters six and up.

The **Hirshhorn Museum** (7th St. and Independence Ave. SW, tel. 202/357–2700) screens free children's movies and cartoons most Saturday mornings at 11.

Adventure Theater (7300 MacArthur Blvd., Glen Echo, MD, tel. 301/320–5331) produces such traditional plays and musicals as *Charlotte's Web, Robin Hood,* and *Aesop's Fables* weekends year-round at Glen Echo Park. Plays are aimed at children ages four to 12 and are presented in a 192-seat theater. The audience sits on carpeted steps, perfect for sprawling families. Reservations suggested.

Discovery Theater (900 Jefferson Dr. SW, tel. 202/357–1500), in the west hall of the Smithsonian's Arts and Industries Building, is the setting for plays, puppet shows, and storytellers October through June. Most presentations are for those in preschool through second grade, but some offerings are for children as old as 12.

Now This! (Omni Shoreham Hotel, Marquee Lounge, 2500 Calvert St. NW, tel. 202/745–1023) is a musical comedy improvisation group that brings things down to kid level for Saturday matinees. Children shout out suggestions to help the actors keep the show rolling.

At the **Puppet Co. Playhouse** (7300 MacArthur Blvd., Glen Echo, MD, tel. 301/320–6668) in Glen Echo Park, skilled puppeteers manipulate marionettes in classic plays and stories.

Saturday Morning at the National (1321 Pennsylvania Ave. NW, tel. 202/783–3372) is a performance series for youngsters that has featured such acts as mimes, puppet shows, dance troupes, magicians, and children's theater groups. The performances are free, on a first-come, first-seated basis, at the National Theater, Saturdays at 9:30 AM and 11 AM from October through April.

The **Washington Chamber Symphony** (tel. 202/452–1321) is especially good at turning children on to classical music by providing workbooks, bringing kids on stage, marching the orchestra down the aisles, or having kids sing along with the proceedings. Its "Family Series" programs are for children as young as four; "Concerts for Young People" are for ages six and up. Most performances are at the Kennedy Center.

A few suburban dinner theaters have recently started mounting children's weekend matinees to supplement their nighttime adult offerings. The plays—such favorites as *Jack and the Beanstalk*, *Little Red Riding Hood*, and *Beauty and the Beast*—usually include lunch or a snack. Among the theaters: **West End Dinner Theatre** (4615 Duke St., Alexandria, VA, tel. 703/370-2500), **Burn Brae Dinner Theatre** (U.S. 29 at Blackburn Rd., Burtonsville, MD, tel. 301/384-5800), and **Petrucci's Dinner Theatre** (312 Main St., Laurel, MD, tel. 301/725-5226).

5 Shopping

By Deborah Papier
Updated by
Jeanne Cooper

Not long ago, a shopping trip in the Washington area really was a trip—a long trek to one of the suburban shopping malls, which offered far more than could be found in town. It is still true that some major national retailers have bypassed the city, so that a visitor wanting to check out Bloomingdale's, Nordstrom, or Macy's has to venture to Montgomery Mall or White Flint Mall in Bethesda, Maryland (the latter near the White Flint stop on Metrorail's red line), the twin megamalls in Tysons Corner, Virginia (reachable by bus but not subway), or the Fashion Centre mall at Pentagon City (on the blue and yellow Metrorail lines). In recent years, however, the city's own shopping scene has been revitalized. Washington department stores have upgraded both their facilities and their merchandise, many of the smaller one-of-a-kind shops have managed to survive urban renewal, designer boutiques are increasing, and interesting specialty shops and minimalls are popping up all over town. Weekdays downtown and most days in Georgetown and Adams-Morgan, street vendors offer a funky mix of jewelry, brightly patterned ties, buyer-beware watches, sunglasses, and African-inspired clothing, accessories, and art. Of course, T-shirts and Capital City souvenirs are always in plentiful supply, especially on the streets ringing *the* Mall.

On the discount scene, several major outlet centers are within 45 minutes of the city (including Potomac Mills, the mile-long mall off I–95 that bills itself as Virginia's leading tourist attraction); closer to the District, the off-price Nordstrom Rack and other discount shops are clustered in City Place mall, which opened in 1992 in downtown Silver Spring, Maryland, on Metro's red line.

Store hours vary greatly, so it is safest to call ahead. In general, Georgetown stores are open late and on Sunday; stores in the downtown district that cater to office workers close at 6 PM and may not be open at all on Saturday or Sunday. Some stores extend their hours on Thursday.

Sales tax is 6% (9% for restaurant fare), and the major credit cards are accepted virtually everywhere.

Shopping Districts

Georgetown remains Washington's favorite shopping area. Though it is not on a subway line, and parking is impossible, people still flock here. The attraction (aside from the lively street scene) is the profusion of specialty shops in a charming, historic neighborhood. In addition to tony antiques, elegant crafts, and high-style shoe and clothing boutiques, the area offers wares attracting students and other less-well-heeled shoppers: books, records, and fashions from popular chain stores, such as the Gap and Benetton.

The hub of Georgetown is the intersection of Wisconsin Avenue and M Street, with most of the stores lying to the east

Ann Taylor, **7, 60, 72**
Appalachian
Spring, **71**
Bally, **59**
Beadazzled, **30**
Betsy Fisher, **37**
Bick's Books, **16**
Big Time Antiques, **17**
Britches of
Georgetown, **41**
Britches Great
Outdoors, **45**

Brooks Brothers, **8, 53**
Burberrys, **47**
Chanel Boutique, **65**
Chapters, **61**
Charles Schwartz
& Son, **4**
Chenonceau
Antiques, **18**
Cherishables, **29**
The Cheshire Cat, **11**
Church's, **52**
Crown Books, **9, 14,
39, 49, 55, 68**

Earl Allen, **57**
Fahrney's, **64**
The Farrell
Collection, **13**
Hecht's, **67**
Hugo Boss, **10, 43**
Indian Craft Shop, **58**
J. Press, **51**
John B. Adler, **63**
Kemp Mill Music, **6,
28, 31, 54**
The Kid's Closet, **44**
Kitchen Bazaar, **12**

Kobos, **19**
Kramerbooks, **32**
Lammas Books, **33**
Les Gals, **62**
Lord & Taylor, **2**
Marston Luce, **38**
Maybe Baby, **20**
Mazi Jewelry
Design, **74**
Moon, Blossoms and
Snow, **73**
Music Box Center, **70**
Mystery Books, **15**

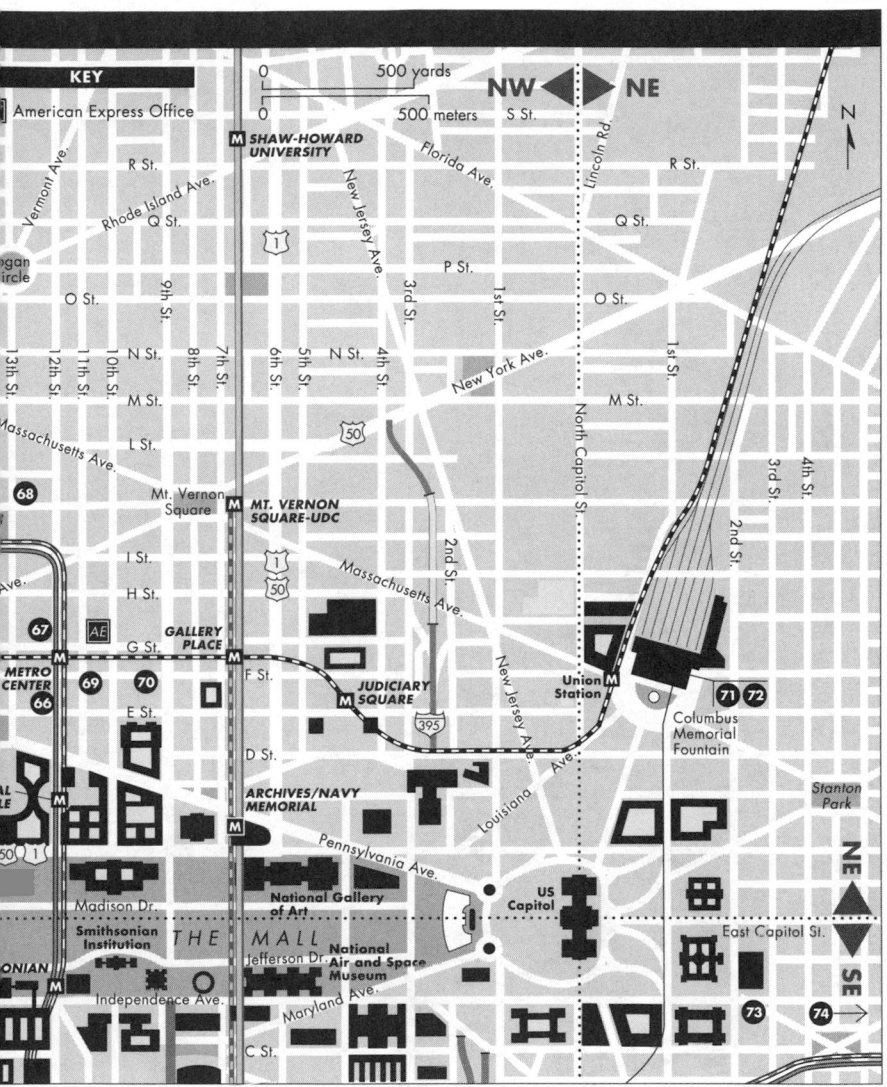

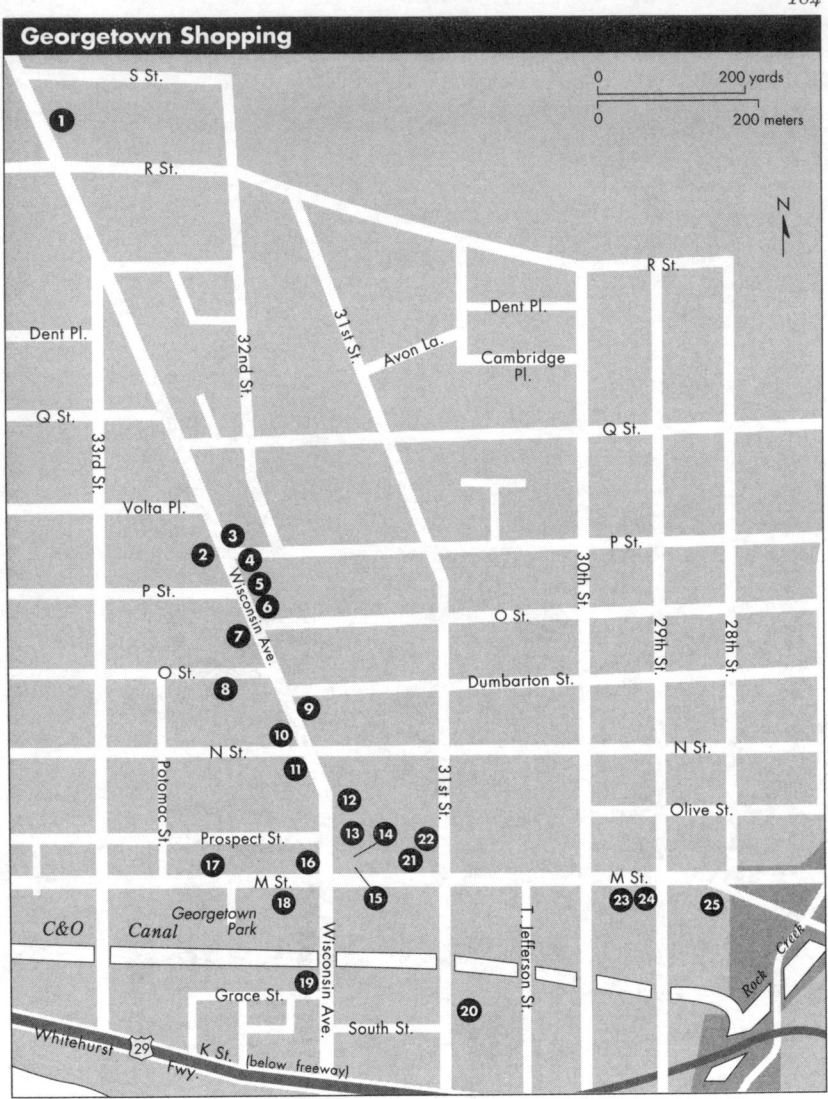

Georgetown Shopping

S St.

R St.

Dent Pl.

Q St.

33rd St.

32nd St.

31st St.

Avon La.

Dent Pl.

Cambridge Pl.

R St.

Q St.

Volta Pl.

P St.

Wisconsin Ave.

30th St.

P St.

O St.

O St.

Dumbarton St.

29th St.

28th St.

Potomac St.

N St.

Prospect St.

31st St.

N St.

Olive St.

M St.

T. Jefferson St.

M St.

C&O Canal

Georgetown Park

Wisconsin Ave.

Grace St.

South St.

Whitehurst Fwy.

K St. (below freeway)

Rock Creek

N

0 ——— 200 yards
0 ——— 200 meters

The American
Hand, **24**
Ann Taylor, **18**
Appalachian Spring, **6**
Betsey Johnson, **9**
Boogie's Diner, **14**
Britches Great
Outdoors, **15**
Britches of
Georgetown, **12**
The Coach Store, **16**
Commander
Salamander, **7**

Earl Allen, **21**
F.A.O. Schwarz, **18**
Georgetown Antiques
Center, **23**
Georgetown Leather
Design, **17**
G.K.S. Bush, **25**
Hugo Boss, **3**
Indian Craft Shop, **19**
Kemp Mill Music, **11**
Little Caledonia, **5**
Martin's, **10**
Miller & Arney
Antiques, **1**

Old Print Gallery, **22**
Olsson's Books &
Records, **13**
Opportunity Shop, **4**
The Phoenix, **2**
Susquehanna, **8**
Yes!, **20**

and west on M Street and to the north on Wisconsin. Near that intersection, at 3222 Wisconsin Avenue, is **Georgetown Park** (tel. 202/298-5577), a three-level mall that looks like a Victorian ice-cream parlor inside. Georgetown Park is anchored by Conran's (tel. 202/298-8300), which features reasonably priced, well-designed housewares, including furniture. The other stores in the posh mall draw international tourists in droves. Next door to the mall, New York City's premier gourmet food store, Dean & DeLuca (3272 M St. NW), attracts visitors and residents alike.

Dupont Circle has some of the same flavor as Georgetown. Here, too, there is a lively mix of shops and restaurants, with most of the action on the major artery of Connecticut Avenue. There are many book and record stores in the neighborhood, as well as stores selling coffees, stationery, and bric-a-brac. The street scene here is grittier than Georgetown's, with fewer teens and older shoppers and more twenty- and thirty-somethings.

In **Adams-Morgan,** scattered among the dozens of Latin, Ethiopian, and Caribbean restaurants in this most bohemian of Washington neighborhoods, are a score of the city's most eccentric shops. It's a mine field of quality, but great fun for the bargain hunter. A word of caution—call ahead to verify hours. Adams-Morganites are often not clockwatchers, but you can be sure a weekend afternoon stroll will find a good representation of the shops open and a great few hours of browsing. Most of the shops are on 18th Street NW, between Columbia Road and California Avenue.

The city's department stores can be found in the "new" downtown, which is still being built. Its fulcrum is **Metro Center,** which spans 11th and 12th streets NW along G Street. The Metro Center subway stop takes you directly into the basements of downtown's two major department stores, Woodward & Lothrop, familiarly called "Woodies," and Hecht's. Take the 11th and G streets exit to Woodies; for Hecht's, follow the signs to the 12th or 13th street exits.

Now open on weekends, **The Shops at National Place** (by Metro Center, 13th and F Sts. NW, tel. 202/783-9090), takes up three levels, one of which is devoted to food stands. The Shops is oriented primarily to younger consumers. This is a good place to drop off teenagers weary of the Smithsonian and more in the mood to buy compact discs or T-shirts. Banana Republic, Victoria's Secret, and The Sharper Image are three of the catalogue stores that have outlets here.

Although Washington doesn't have anything on the order of Boston's Faneuil Hall, it does have **The Pavilion at the Old Post Office** (12th St. NW and Pennsylvania Ave., tel. 202/289-4224), a renovated building dating from the last century. In 1992 The Pavilion added an atrium with 29 specialty stores to its already more than 30 small shops, such as

Caswell & Massey (for toiletries and perfumes) and All Wound-Up (selling wind-up toys). An observation deck in the building's clock tower offers an excellent view of the city.

One of the most delightful shopping enclaves in the city is **Union Station** (tel. 202/371–9441), at Massachusetts Avenue NE, near North Capitol Street on the Metrorail red line. Resplendent with marble floors and gilded, vaulted ceilings, it's now both a working train station and a mall with three levels of stores, including one level of food stands. The east hall, reminiscent of London's Covent Garden, is filled with vendors of expensive and ethnic wares in open stalls. Christmas is an especially pleasant time to shop here.

As the **Capitol Hill** area has become gentrified, additional unique shops and boutiques have sprung up here. Many are clustered around the 1873 building known as **Eastern Market** (7th and C Sts. SE, one block north of Metrorail's Eastern Market stop on the orange and blue lines). Inside are produce and meat counters, plus the Market Five art gallery; outside are a farmer's market (on Saturdays) and a flea market (on weekends). Across 7th Street are Mission Traders, Antiques on the Hill, and the Eastern Market Emporium, which contains antiques stores and the Harmattan Arts of Africa gallery.

The final major shopping district is on the outskirts of the city, on Wisconsin Avenue straddling the Maryland border. Here is the **Mazza Gallerie** (5300 Wisconsin Ave. NW, tel. 202/966–6114), a four-level mall anchored by the ritzy Neiman Marcus department store. Its other stores include Williams-Sonoma's kitchenware and Laura Ashley Home. The mall is accessible directly from the Friendship Heights station on the Metrorail red line. Three other department stores are close by: Lord & Taylor, Woodward & Lothrop, and Saks Fifth Avenue (*see* Department Stores, *below*).

Across from Mazza Gallerie is the newer, similarly upmarket **Chevy Chase Pavilion** (5335 Wisconsin Ave. NW, tel. 202/686–5335). Its exclusive women's clothing stores include Joan & David, Oilily, and Steilmann European Selection (which carries Karl Lagerfeld's sportier KL line). Other specialty shops of note here are La Bottega Fine Papers, Curious Kids toys, and Rock Creek, a two-store chain selling high-quality, fashionable men's and women's athletic clothing and shoes.

Department Stores

Hecht's (12th and G Sts. NW, tel. 202/628–6661). When the Hecht company decided to abandon its store on 7th Street and build a new one, it did the job right. The new downtown Hecht's is bright and spacious, and its sensible groupings and attractive displays of merchandise make shopping relatively easy on the feet and the eyes. The clothes sold here are a mix of conservative and trendy lines, with the men's department assuming increasing importance. Cosmetics, lingerie, and housewares are also strong departments.

Lord & Taylor (5255 Western Ave. NW, tel. 202/362–9600). Lord & Taylor lets other stores be all things to all people while it focuses on nonutilitarian housewares and classic clothing by such designers as Anne Klein and Ralph Lauren. All of the clothing is American designed and manufactured.

Neiman Marcus (Mazza Gallerie, tel. 202/966–9700). If you have to ask how much it costs, you probably shouldn't shop at Neiman Marcus, which caters to the customer who values quality above all. The carefully selected merchandise includes couture clothes, furs, precious jewelry, crystal, and silver.

Saks Fifth Avenue (5555 Wisconsin Ave., tel. 301/657–9000). Though not strictly a Washington department store, since it is located just over the Maryland line, Saks is nonetheless a Washington institution. The major draw is the wide selection of European and American couture clothes; other attractions are the shoe, jewelry, fur, and lingerie departments.

Woodward & Lothrop (11th and F Sts. NW, tel. 202/347–5300). The largest of the downtown stores, Woodies has eight floors of merchandise that can accommodate just about any need or whim. There are two floors of women's clothing in a variety of styles and price ranges, another floor for juniors, one floor for men, and a large children's department. In addition, just about anything you could need for the home can be found here, including gourmet food. There is also a branch across the Maryland border at the Friendship Heights Metrorail station (Wisconsin and Western Aves., tel. 301/654–7600).

Specialty Stores

Antiques and Collectibles   **Big Time Antiques** (2102 18th St. NW, tel. 202/462–1171). Mostly 20th-century American toys, signs, commercial display cases, and vending machines. Seasonal offerings include Christmas ornaments and American Flyer trains.

Chenonceau Antiques (2314 18th St. NW, tel. 202/667–1651). Two floors of mostly American 19th- and 20th-century pieces selected by a buyer with an exquisite eye, including beautiful 19th-century paisley scarves from India and from Scotland, and French travel posters from the '30s. Closed Monday–Wednesday.

Cherishables (1608 20th St. NW, tel. 202/785–4087). American 18th- and 19th-century furniture and decorative arts, with emphasis on the Federal period.

Georgetown Antiques Center (2918 M St. NW, tel. 202/338–3811). Two dealers share space in this Victorian town house: Cherub Gallery (tel. 202/337–2224) specializes in art glass and Icart etchings, and Michael Getz Antiques (tel. 202/338–3811) sells fireplace equipment and silverware.

G.K.S. Bush (2828 Pennsylvania Ave. NW, tel. 202/965–0653). Formal American furniture from the 18th and early 19th centuries, plus related American antiques and works of art.

Marston Luce (1314 21st St. NW, tel. 202/775–9460). The specialty here is American folk art, including quilts, weather vanes, and hooked rugs. There are also home and garden furnishings, primarily American, but some English and French as well.

Miller & Arney Antiques (1737 Wisconsin Ave. NW, tel. 202/338–2369). English, American, and European furniture and accessories from the 18th and early 19th centuries, plus Oriental porcelain.

Old Print Gallery (1220 31st St. NW, tel. 202/965–1818). The area's largest collection of old prints and maps, including Washingtoniana.

The Opportunity Shop of the Christ Child Society (1427 Wisconsin Ave. NW, tel. 202/333–6635). This Georgetown thrift shop sells vintage housewares, accessories, and other fine collectibles at moderate prices, and clothing on consignment; 30% goes to charity. Closed Sunday.

Retrospective (2324 18th St. NW, tel. 202/483–8112). A small shop crammed with high-quality furniture and accessories, mostly from the '40s and '50s. Here you can still buy the princess phone that lit up your nightstand in 1962 and the plates your mother served her meat loaf on. Closed Tuesday.

Ruff and Ready (2220 18th St. NW, tel. 202/667–7833). It could be called Adams-Morgan's most venerable used-furniture store except that the word "used" seems out of place in this jumble of styles and quality. There's a great selection of estate sale furniture that moves out of the store almost as fast as it moves in—and the prices make the reason clear. Mostly 20th-century with a few 19th-century pieces, and a good assortment of bric-a-brac from the Deco period onward. Closed Monday–Thursday.

Susquehanna (3216 O St. NW, tel. 202/333–1511). The largest antiques shop in Georgetown, specializing in American furniture and paintings.

Uniform (2318 18th St. NW, tel. 202/483–4577). The best of the vintage clothing and household accessories shops in Adams-Morgan, an assortment from the '50s and '60s that makes it seem like the entire country transferred to the moon for 20 years. The mix varies, but in addition to the obligatory lava lamps you'll find three-button suits and pillbox hats, feathered mules with Lucite heels, and plates, lamps, and dishes that could have been props for the Jetsons. Closed Monday.

Books **Bick's Books** (2309 18th St. NW, tel. 202/328–2356). An emphasis on literature, small presses, black studies, green politics, and philosophy characterizes this neighborhood bookstore.

Chapters (1512 K St. NW, tel. 202/347–5495). Calling itself a "literary bookstore," Chapters eschews cartoon collections and diet guides, filling its shelves instead with the sort of books that are meant to be read—serious contemporary fiction, classics, and poetry.

The Cheshire Cat (5512 Connecticut Ave. NW, tel. 202/244–3956). A bookstore for children, with a selection of records, cassettes, posters, and books on parenting.

Crown Books (1200 New Hampshire Ave. NW, tel. 202/822–8331; 3131 M St. NW, tel. 202/333–4493; 2020 K St. NW, tel. 202/659–2030; 1275 K St. NW, tel. 202/289–7170; 1155 19th St. NW, tel. 202/659–4172; 3335 Connecticut Ave. NW, tel. 202/966–7232; 4301 Connecticut Ave. NW, tel. 202/966–2576; 4400 Jenifer St. NW, tel. 202/966–8784; 1710 G St. NW, tel. 202/789–2277). This large local chain sells hardback best-sellers at significant discounts, and even lowers paperback and newsstand prices.

Kramerbooks (1517 Connecticut Ave. NW, tel. 202/387–1400). Sharing space with a café that offers late-night dining and weekend entertainment, Kramer's has a small but well-selected stock.

Lammas Books (1426 21st St. NW, tel. 202/775–8218). Women's and gay literature, with a selection of women's music.

Mystery Books (1715 Connecticut Ave. NW, tel. 202/483–1600). Washington's largest collection of detective, crime, suspense, and spy fiction, as well as mystery-related gifts, can be found here.

Olsson's Books & Records (1239 Wisconsin Ave. NW, tel. 202/338–9544; 1307 19th St. NW, tel. 202/785–1133; 1200 F St. NW, tel. 202/347–3686). With its large and varied collection, this is undoubtedly the area's preeminent general bookstore. Hours vary significantly from store to store.

Second Story Books (2000 P St. NW, tel. 202/659–8884). Hours of browsing are possible at this used-books (and records) emporium on Dupont Circle.

Vertigo Books (1337 Connecticut Ave. NW, tel. 202/429–9272). Just south of Dupont Circle, this store specializes in political and progressive literature, nonfiction, and journals.

Yawa (2206 18th St. NW, tel. 202/483–6805). The large collection of African and African-American fiction and nonfiction, magazines, and children's books is supplemented by ethnic jewelry, crafts, and greeting cards.

Yes! (1035 31st St. NW, tel. 202/338–7874). A bookstore geared to self-development, Yes! has an unusual stock of volumes on spiritual growth, psychology, mythology, and travel.

Children's Clothing and Toys **F.A.O. Schwarz** (in Georgetown Park, 3222 M St. NW, tel. 202/342–2285). The most upscale of toy stores, carrying such items as a toy car (a Mercedes, of course) that costs almost as much as the real thing. Among the other imports are stuffed animals (many larger than life), dolls, and children's perfumes.

The Kid's Closet (1226 Connecticut Ave. NW, tel. 202/429–9247). The downtown choice for baby clothes and shower gifts, plus some togs for older children.

Maybe Baby (1840 18th St. NW, tel. 202/986–0995). New and vintage ('40s–'70s) children's gear, including antique pint-size chairs.

Crafts and Gifts **The American Hand** (2906 M St. NW, tel. 202/965–3273). One-of-a-kind functional and nonfunctional pieces from America's foremost ceramic artists, plus limited edition objects for home and office, such as architect-designed dinnerware.

Appalachian Spring (1415 Wisconsin Ave. NW, tel. 202/337–5780, and Union Station, tel. 202/682–0505). Traditional and contemporary crafts, including quilts, jewelry, weavings, pottery, and blown glass.

Beadazzled (1522 Connecticut Ave. NW, tel. 202/265–2323). A truly dazzling array of ready-to-string beads and jewelry.

Fahrney's (1430 G St. NW, tel. 202/628–9525). Fahrney's started out as a pen bar in the Willard Hotel, a place to fill your fountain pen before embarking on the day's business. Today it offers pens in silver, gold, and lacquer by the world's leading manufacturers.

The Farrell Collection (2633 Connecticut Ave. NW, tel. 202/483–8334). An assortment of moderately priced American pottery, fiber, and glass.

Indian Craft Shop (1050 Wisconsin Ave. NW, tel. 202/342–3918; Dept. of Interior, 1800 C St. NW, tel. 202/208–4056). Handicrafts, including jewelry, pottery, sand paintings, weavings, and baskets, from a dozen Native American tribal traditions.

Moon, Blossoms and Snow (225 Pennsylvania Ave. SE, tel. 202/543–8181). Wearable art is the specialty of this Capitol Hill store. In addition to hand-painted, hand-woven garments, the store sells contemporary American ceramics, glass, jewelry, and wood.

Music Box Center (918 F St. NW, tel. 202/783–9399). Choose from more than 500 melodies played by boxes made of marble, glass, porcelain, metal, and wood.

Nomad (2407 18th St. NW, tel. 202/332–2998). Reasonably priced clothing, artifacts, and jewelry with an ethnic flair.

The Phoenix (1514 Wisconsin Ave. NW, tel. 202/338–4404). Mexican crafts, including folk art, masks, silver jewelry, fabrics, and native garments.

Skynear and Company (1800 Wyoming Ave. NW, tel. 202/797–7160). Undoubtedly the most bizarre assortment of home accessories, gifts, and objects in Washington. The owners, an Egyptian husband and Native American wife, travel the world for the unusual, and the result is an extravagant assortment of rich materials and brilliant colors. Lighting, textiles, art, and furniture are options.

Wake Up Little Suzie (2316 18th St. NW, tel. 202/328–7577). New knickknacks that look like vintage '50s, as well as hip, modern bric-a-brac. Closed Monday.

Jewelry   **Charles Schwartz & Son** (Mazza Gallerie, tel. 202/363–5432). A full-service jeweler specializing in precious stones in traditional and modern settings. Fine watches are also offered.

Mazi Jewelry Design (311 7th St. SE, tel. 202/547–2555). Modern jewelry is custom-made on the premises.

Pampillonia Jewelers (Mazza Gallerie, tel. 202/363–6305; 1213 Connecticut Ave. NW, tel. 202/628–6305). Traditional designs in 18-karat gold and platinum, including many pieces for men.

The Tiny Jewel Box (1143 Connecticut Ave. NW, tel. 202/393–2747). A well-chosen collection of estate jewelry.

Kitchenware   **Kitchen Bazaar** (4401 Connecticut Ave. NW, tel. 202/244–1550). This emporium (headquarters of a local chain) carries just about everything one could possibly need to equip a kitchen.

Little Caledonia (1419 Wisconsin Ave. NW, tel. 202/333–4700). A "Tom Thumb department store" for the home, this old Georgetown store consists of nine rooms crammed with thousands of unusual and imported items; candles, cards, fabrics, and lamps round out the stock of decorative kitchenware.

Martin's (1304 Wisconsin Ave. NW, tel. 202/338–6144). A long-established Georgetown purveyor of china, crystal, and silver, including antique silver.

Leather Goods   **The Coach Store** (1214 Wisconsin Ave. NW, tel. 202/342–1772). The complete line of Coach's rugged, well-made handbags, briefcases, belts, and wallets.

Georgetown Leather Design (3265 M St. NW, tel. 202/333–9333; 1150 Connecticut Ave. NW, tel. 202/223–1855). A full line of leather goods, most of them made for the store, including jackets, briefcases, wallets, gloves, and handbags.

Men's Clothing   **Britches of Georgetown** (1247 Wisconsin Ave. NW, tel. 202/338–3330; 1219 Connecticut Ave. NW, tel. 202/347–8994). Britches carries an extensive selection of traditional but trend-conscious designs in natural fibers.

Brooks Brothers (1840 L St. NW, tel. 202/659–4650; 5500 Wisconsin Ave., tel. 301/654–8202). The oldest men's store in America, Brooks Brothers has offered traditional formal and casual clothing since 1818. It is the largest men's specialty store in the area and has a small women's department as well.

Hugo Boss (1201 Connecticut Ave. NW, tel. 202/887–5081; 1517 Wisconsin Ave. NW, tel. 202/338–0120; 5454 Wisconsin Ave., tel. 301/907–7806). The Washington area has the only U.S. collection of clothes from this German designer and manufacturer, noted for his classic fabrics and unique silhouettes.

J. Press (1801 L St. NW, tel. 202/857–0120). Founded in 1902 as a custom shop for Yale University, J. Press is a stalwartly traditional clothier. Shetland wool sportcoats are a specialty.

Men's and Women's Clothing

John B. Adler (901 15th St. NW, tel. 202/842–4432). This longtime Washington clothier offers what used to be called the Ivy League look in suits, sportcoats, and formal and casual wear.

Boogie's Diner (1229 Wisconsin Ave. NW, tel. 202/298–7469). Taking the place of the old Esprit superstore in location and spirit is this combination restaurant and clothing store for the teen crowd.

Britches Great Outdoors (1225 Wisconsin Ave. NW, tel. 202/333–3666; 1801 M St. NW, tel. 202/775–8983). This casual version of Britches of Georgetown has filled many Washington closets with rugby shirts and other sportswear.

Burberrys (1155 Connecticut Ave. NW, tel. 202/463–3000). It made its reputation with the trench coat, but this British company also manufactures traditional men's and women's apparel.

Commander Salamander (1420 Wisconsin Ave. NW, tel. 202/333–9599). This is about as funky as Washington gets— leather, chains, silver skulls. As much entertainment as shopping, it's open till 11 on weekends.

Kobos (2444 18th St. NW, tel. 202/332–9580). A rainbow of clothing and accessories imported from West Africa, plus a small selection of African music.

Records

Kemp Mill Music (1260 Wisconsin Ave. NW, tel. 202/333–1392; 1518 Connecticut Ave. NW, tel. 202/332–8247; 2459 18th St. NW, tel. 202/387–1011; 1900 L St. NW, tel. 202/223–5310; 4000 Wisconsin Ave. NW, tel. 202/364–9704). This local chain store concentrates on CDs and cassettes of popular music and keeps its prices low.

Olsson's Books & Records (1239 Wisconsin Ave. NW, tel. 202/338–6712; 1307 19th St. NW, tel. 202/785–2662; 1200 F St. NW, tel. 202/393–1853). A full line of compact discs and cassettes, plus books.

Serenade Record Shop (1800 M St. NW, tel. 202/452–0075; 1710 Pennsylvania Ave. NW, with an annex at 1713 G St. NW, tel. 202/638–6648). A full-catalogue record store with a strong classical collection.

Tower Records (2000 Pennsylvania Ave. NW, tel. 202/331–2400). With 16,000 square feet of selling space, Tower offers the area's best selection of music in all categories. Open daily until midnight.

Shoes

Bally (1020 Connecticut Ave. NW, tel. 202/429–0604). The Swiss manufacturer of high-quality leather goods has expanded its line of women's shoes, but the focus is still on footwear for men, primarily European-style loafers. The store also sells handbags, briefcases, and belts.

Church's (1742 L St. NW, tel. 202/296-3366). Church's is an English company whose handmade men's shoes are noted for their comfort and durability.

Shoe Scene (1330 Connecticut Ave. NW, tel. 202/659-2194). A good selection of moderately priced, fashionable shoes for women.

Women's Clothing   **Ann Taylor** (1720 K St. NW, tel. 202/466-3544; 3222 M St. NW, tel. 202/338-5290; 5300 Wisconsin Ave. NW, tel. 202/244-1940; Union Station, tel. 202/371-8010). Sophisticated fashions for the woman who has broken out of the dress-for-success mold. Ann Taylor also has an excellent shoe department.

Betsey Johnson's (1319 Wisconsin Ave. NW, tel. 202/338-4090). Fanciful frocks from the British designer for the young and restless.

Betsy Fisher (1350 Connecticut Ave. NW, tel. 202/785-1975).Tasteful, rather than conservative, clothing appealing to women of all ages.

Chanel Boutique (1455 Pennsylvania Ave. NW, tel. 202/638-5055). Shoes, scarves, handbags, belts, and suits from the legendary house of fashion fill this boutique in the Willard Hotel annex.

Earl Allen (3109 M St. NW, tel. 202/338-1678; 1825 I St. NW, tel. 202/466-3437). Earl Allen caters to the professional woman, offering conservative but distinctive dresses and sportswear, much of it made exclusively for this shop.

Les Gals (1000 Vermont Ave. NW, tel. 202/371-0289). Spunky work and workout clothes, plus shoes and hosiery, appeal to the downtown work force.

Rizik Bros. (1100 Connecticut Ave. NW, tel. 202/223-4050). A Washington institution, Rizik's combines designer clothing and accessories with expert service. The sales staff is trained to find styles and prices that meet customers' desires from the large inventory, over half of which is in the stockroom. Take the elevator up from the northwest corner of Connecticut and L Street.

6 Sports and the Outdoors

Sports

Updated by John F. Kelly

When conversation turns to America's great sports towns, Washington isn't often high on the list. The honors usually go to New York, Los Angeles, or Boston. Nevertheless, Washington is home to an impressive variety of opportunities for both spectators and participants. According to national surveys, the residents of metropolitan Washington are more active than the nation as a whole. Washingtonians jog, cycle, swim, fish, lift weights, play tennis, and sail more than the residents of any other major city in the United States. One reason may be that Washington's climate is generally mild year-round. Another reason is the plentitude of parks, trails, and athletic facilities throughout the area that entices the active population.

Whether you're coming to Washington for a few days of sightseeing or a few days of business, bring your sweats. There is more to the District than national monuments and boardrooms.

Participant Sports and Fitness

Bicycling Bicycling is one of the most popular activities in Washington for locals and visitors alike. The numerous trails in the District and the surrounding areas are well maintained and clearly marked, which makes for pleasant bike touring. Most of the paths described below in the section on jogging—the Mall, the Chesapeake & Ohio Canal, the Mount Vernon Trail, and Rock Creek Park—are also well suited for use by bikers.

Routes and Trails For scenery, you can't beat the towpath that runs along the **C & O Canal** (*see* Parks and Woodlands in The Outdoors, *below*), starting in Georgetown. You could pedal to the end of the canal, 184 miles away in Cumberland, Maryland, but most cyclists are content to roll to Great Falls, 15 miles from where the canal starts. The towpath is a gravel-and-packed-down-dirt surface and occasionally bumpy, but along the way you'll pass abundant flora and fauna and 19th-century locks remaining from the canal's working days.

Cyclists interested in serious training might want to try the 3-mile loop around the golf course in **East Potomac Park,** Hains Point (entry is near the Jefferson Memorial). This is a favorite training course for dedicated local racers and would-be triathletes. A note of caution, though: Restrict your workouts to the daytime; the area is not safe after dark.

Rentals Bicycles can be rented at the following locations:

Bicycle Exchange (1506-C Belle View Blvd., Alexandria, VA, tel. 703/768–3444), near the Mount Vernon Trail.
Big Wheel Bikes (1034 33rd St. NW, Georgetown, tel. 202/

337-0254, near the C & O Canal Towpath; 315 7th St. SE, tel. 202/543-1600, near Capitol Hill; 2 Prince St., Alexandria, VA, tel. 703/739-2300, near the Mount Vernon Trail).
City Bikes (2501 Champlain St., NW, tel. 202/265-1564), near the Rock Creek bike path.
Fletcher's Boat House (C & O Canal Towpath, near Reservoir Rd. NW, tel. 202/244-0461).
Metropolis Bike & Scooter (709 8th St. SE, Capitol Hill, tel. 202/543-8900) also rents rollerblades.
Proteus Bicycle Shop (2422 18th St. NW, Adams-Morgan, tel. 202/332-6666; 7945 MacArthur Blvd., NW, tel. 301/229-5900, near the C & O Canal).
Thompson's Boat Center (Virginia Ave. and Rock Creek Park, behind Kennedy Center, tel. 202/333-4861).
Tow Path Cycle (823 S. Washington St., Alexandria, VA, tel. 703/549-5368) also rents rollerblades.

Information and Organizations The **Greater Washington Area Bicyclist Association** (1819 H St. NW, Suite 640, 20006, tel. 202/872-9830) offers information and publications on cycling in the nation's capital. Two invaluable local cycling guides are *The Greater Washington Area Bicycle Atlas*, published by the American Youth Hostels Association, and Michael Leccese's *Short Bike Rides in and Around Washington, D.C.*

Boating Canoeing, sailing, and powerboating are all popular in the region. There are several places to rent boats along the **Potomac River** north and south of the city. You can dip your oars just about anywhere along the Potomac for canoeing in the C & O Canal, sailing in the widening river south of Alexandria, even kayaking in the raging rapids at Great Falls. Although it is not widely known, Washington is home to some of the best white-water kayakers and white-water canoeists in the country. On weekends they can be seen practicing below Great Falls in **Mather Gorge,** a canyon carved by the Potomac River just north of the city, above Chain Bridge. The water is deceptive and dangerous, and only top-level kayakers should consider a run there. It is, however, safe to watch the experts at play from a post above the gorge. For information, call the ranger stations at Great Falls, Virginia (tel. 703/285-2966), or Great Falls, Maryland (tel. 301/443-0024).

Boat Rentals The two boat houses listed here are convenient for tourists.

Fletcher's Boat House (tel. 202/244-0461), about 2 miles north of Georgetown on the C & O Canal, rents rowboats and canoes for use in the canal.
Thompson's Boat Center (tel. 202/333-4861), at Virginia Avenue and Rock Creek Parkway behind the Kennedy Center, rents canoes, rowboats, rowing shells, and sailboards.

Paddle boats are available during the summer on the east side of the **Tidal Basin** (tel. 202/619-7222) in front of the Jefferson Memorial. The **Washington Sailing Marina** (tel. 703/548-9027), just south of National Airport on the George

Washington Parkway, and the **Belle Haven Marina** (tel. 703/ 768–0018), just south of Old Town Alexandria on the George Washington Parkway, rent Sunfish, Windsurfers, and larger boats to those qualified to charter.

Sailing If you're really interested in sailing, consider taking a day trip to Annapolis, Maryland (about an hour's drive from the District). Annapolis is one of the best sailing centers on the East Coast, and the Chesapeake Bay is without a doubt one of the great sailing basins of the world. The **Annapolis Sailing School** (tel. 410/267–7205) is a world-renowned school and charter company.

Fishing The Potomac River is something of an environmental success story. Once dangerously polluted, it has rebounded in recent years, to the benefit of local fish and, therefore, local fisherman. Largemouth bass, striped bass, shad, and white and yellow perch are all down there somewhere, willing to take your bait.

Fishing Spots A 5-mile stretch of the Potomac River—roughly from the Wilson Memorial Bridge in Alexandria south to Fort Washington National Park—is one of the country's best spots for largemouth bass fishing. It has, in fact, become something of an East Coast mecca for anglers in search of this particular fish. The area around Fletcher's Boat House on the C & O Canal is one of the best spots for perch.

Fishing Guides and Tackle Shops The simple act of renting a boat and going fishing in Washington is complicated by the fact that this stretch of the Potomac is divided among three jurisdictions: Virginia, Maryland, and the District of Columbia. It's not always easy to determine in whose water you're fishing or which licenses you should have. The best solution is to hire a guide. **Life Outdoors Unlimited** (tel. 301/937–0010), run by nationally known fisherman and conservationist Ken Penrod, is an umbrella group of area freshwater fishing guides. A dozen of the area's best guides are listed with Penrod, and for about $250 a day a guide will take care of all your needs, from tackle to boats, and advise you on which licenses are required. Penrod's guides are all professionals and will both teach novices or guide experts.

The two best tackle shops in the area are both in Alexandria, Virginia: **Delta Tackle** (1435 Powhatan St., tel. 703/ 549–5729) and **Potomac Sports Center** (5954 Richmond Hwy., tel. 703/960–0662).

Information **Gene Mueller,** a nationally known hunting and fishing writer, has a column three times a week (Monday, Wednesday, and Friday) in the *Washington Times*. He takes readers' telephone calls Thursday mornings at 202/636–3268. The "Fish Lines" column in Friday's *Washington Post* "Weekend" outlines where the fish are biting, from the Potomac to the Chesapeake Bay.

Golf Serious golfers must resign themselves to driving out of the District to find a worthwhile course. There are three public courses in town: East Potomac, Langston, and Rock Creek. Rock Creek is the best, but none could be considered among the country's top public courses. Still, people line up to play here and at other local public courses, sometimes arriving as early as 2 AM to snare a tee time. (Some courses allow you to call ahead to reserve a tee time; call for details.)

Public Courses All three of the public courses in the District have the same *within the District* greens fees: $11 for 18 holes on weekdays, $6 for nine; weekends it's $13 and $7, respectively.

The **Hains Point course** (tel. 202/863–9007) in East Potomac Park near the Jefferson Memorial is a flat, wide, featureless 6,303-yard, par-72 course. Its greatest claim to fame is that professional golfer and Washington resident Lee Elder got his start there. It also has two 9-hole courses and a driving range. One of the country's oldest miniature golf courses operates here during the summer.

Langston Golf Course (26th St. and Benning Rd. NE, tel. 202/397–8638) is a par-72, 6,300-yard course. Its greens and fairways are poorly maintained, but holes 8 and 9, hard by the Anacostia River, are challenging, and the course is sufficiently popular that when construction of a new Redskins stadium threatened to displace it, local golfers rallied to Langston's defense.

Rock Creek Park (16th and Rittenhouse Sts. NW, tel. 202/882–7332) is a 4,798-yard, par-65 course with an easy front nine but challenging back. Its tight, rolling, well-treed back nine make it the most attractive public course in the city of Washington.

Public Courses in There are several excellent suburban public courses within *Nearby Suburbs* a half hour of downtown.

Reston South (11875 Sunrise Valley Dr., Reston, VA, tel. 703/620–9333) is a four-star, 6,480-yard, par-71 course widely considered the best public course in the metropolitan area. Well maintained, it is heavily wooded but not too difficult for the average player. The fee is $18 on weekdays and $25 weekends.

Also 30 minutes from town is **Northwest Park** (15701 Layhill Rd., Wheaton, MD, tel. 301/598–6100). This 6,732-yard, par-72 course is extremely long and windy, making for slow play, but it is immaculately groomed and fair. It also has a short-nine course. The fee for 18 holes is $16.50 weekdays, $18 weekends; the short-nine course is $8.50 and $9.50.

Maryland's 6,209-yard, par-72 **Enterprise** (2802 Enterprise Rd., Mitchellville, MD, tel. 301/249–2040), near the Beltway in Prince Georges County, has the reputation as the best-manicured public course in the area. Its well-landscaped layout gives it a country-club feel. The fee for 18 holes is $15 weekdays, $18 weekends.

If you are flying into or out of Dulles Airport and want to fit in a round of golf, try **Penderbrook** (at Rte. 50 and I–66, tel. 703/385–3700). A short but imaginative 5,927-yard, par-72 course, it is one of the best public greens in the area. The 5th, 11th, 12th, and 15th holes are exceptional. The weekday fee is $24 and the weekend fee is $32 for 18 holes. Tee times are given three days in advance.

Health Clubs The number of health clubs in the area has been on the increase in recent years. All of the clubs in Washington require that you be a member—or at least a member of an affiliated club—in order to use their facilities. Some hotels, however, have made private arrangements with neighboring health clubs to enable hotel guests to use the club's facilities (in some cases guests pay a daily fee). Check with your hotel when making reservations.

A number of downtown hotels are associated with the **fitness center at the ANA Hotel.** All you need to do is show your hotel room key to the center's employees and pay a $20 daily fee. One of the fanciest fitness centers in Washington, the ANA is the place where celebrities like Cybill Sheperd, Holly Hunter, and Arnold Schwarzenegger come to sweat (ANA Hotel, 2401 M St. NW, tel. 202/457–5070).

Card-carrying members of the **International Racquet Sports Association (IRSA)** can use the facilities at one of the many member clubs in Washington for a daily fee. You must present your membership card from your home club. The IRSA "Passport" lists member clubs.

The **National Capital YMCA** (1711 Rhode Island Ave. NW, tel. 202/862–9622) offers just about everything a body could want, from basketball, weights, racquetball, squash, and swimming to exercise equipment. Some downtown hotels offer their guests free one-day passes to the YMCA—check with your concierge. Members of an out-of-town Y must show their membership card and pay a usage fee ranging from $5 to $15 per visit, depending on the time of day.

Horseback Riding **Rock Creek Park Horse Center** (Military Rd. and Glover Rd. NW, tel. 202/362–0117) is open all year offering lessons and trail rides. The guided trail rides, for beginning riders 12 and up, are an hour long; the hours vary according to season.

Ice Skating The **Sculpture Garden Outdoor Rink** (Constitution Ave. between 7th and 9th Sts. NW, tel. 202/371–5340) appears each winter with the cold weather. **Pershing Park Ice Rink** (Pennsylvania Ave. between 14th and 15th Sts. NW, tel. 202/737–6938) is also popular. Skates can be rented at both locations. **Fort Dupont Park** (37th and Ely Pl. SE, tel. 202/581–0199) has a beautiful rink; the park itself, though, is in a less-than-wonderful section of town. Two indoor, year-round suburban rinks you might try are at **Mount Vernon Recreation Center** (2017 Belle View Blvd., Alexandria, VA, tel. 703/768–3222) and **Cabin John Regional Park** (10610

Westlake Dr., Rockville, MD, tel. 301/365–0585). They, too, have rentals.

Jogging If you really want to see the people who run Washington, go for a jog. Congressmen, senators, and Supreme Court justices can often be spotted on the Mall, running loops around the monuments. Georgetown power brokers hoof it along the towpaths of the C & O Canal or on the meandering trails in Rock Creek Park. At lunchtime in Arlington, the Pentagon empties out along the Mount Vernon Trail. Even Mr. Clinton jogs, though it's usually on the White House's custom-built jogging track.

Routes, Trails, Downtown Washington and nearby northern Virginia offer
and Tracks some of the most scenic running trails in the country, and running is one of the best ways to take in the vistas of the city. The most popular paths are presented below. A word of caution: Joggers unfamiliar with the city should not go out at night, and, even in daylight, it's best to run in pairs if you venture beyond the most public areas and the more heavily used sections of the trails.

The Mall. The loop around the Capitol and past the Smithsonian museums, the Washington Monument, the Reflecting Pool, and the Lincoln Memorial is the most popular of all Washington running trails. At any time of day, hundreds of joggers, speed walkers, bicyclists, and tourists can be seen making their way along the gravel pathways of this 4.5-mile loop. If you're looking for a longer run, you can veer south of the Mall on either side of the Tidal Basin and head for the Jefferson Memorial and East Potomac Park, the site of many races. Monday, Wednesday, and Thursday evenings at 6:30 the **Capitol Hill Runners** (tel. 301/283–0821) set off on a 2- to 8-mile run from the 1st Street SW entrance of the Rayburn House Office Building.

The Mount Vernon Trail. Just across the Potomac in Virginia, this trail is another favorite with Washington runners. The northern (shorter) section begins near the pedestrian causeway leading to Theodore Roosevelt Island (directly across the river from the Kennedy Center) and goes past National Airport and on to Old Town Alexandria. This stretch is approximately 3.5 miles one way. You can get to the trail from the District by crossing either the Theodore Roosevelt Bridge (at the Lincoln Memorial) or the Rochambeau Memorial Bridge (also known as the 14th Street Bridge, at the Jefferson Memorial). South of National Airport, the trail runs down to the Washington Marina. The final mile of the trail's northern section meanders through protected wetlands before ending in the heart of Old Town Alexandria. The longer, southern section of the trail (approximately 9 miles) takes you along the banks of the Potomac from Alexandria all the way to George Washington's home, Mount Vernon.

Rock Creek Park. A miraculously preserved bit of wilderness in the middle of Washington, Rock Creek Park has 15 miles of trails, a bicycle path, a bridle path, picnic groves, playgrounds, and a boulder-strewn rolling stream, from which it gets its name (the creek is not safe for swimming). Starting at P Street on the edge of Georgetown, Rock Creek Park runs all the way to Montgomery County, Maryland. The most popular run in the park is a trail along the creek extending from Georgetown to the National Zoo (about a 4-mile loop). In summer, there is considerable shade, and there are water fountains at an exercise station along the way. The roadway is closed to traffic on weekends. On Sunday mornings, the **Fleet Feet Sports Shop** (tel. 202/387–3888) in Adams-Morgan near the National Zoo, sponsors 5-mile runs in Rock Creek Park.

The Chesapeake & Ohio Canal. Now maintained by the National Park Service, the Chesapeake & Ohio Canal National Historical Park is a favorite spot with both runners and cyclists. A packed-down-dirt-and-gravel trail leads from Georgetown through wooded areas along the Potomac and northward into Maryland. The most popular loop is from a point just north of Key Bridge in Georgetown to Fletcher's Boat House (approximately 4 miles round-trip).

Information and Organizations For information on group runs and weekend races, check the calendar in the "Weekend" sections in the Friday *Washington Post* and Thursday *Washington Times*. For general information about running and races in the area, call the **Gatorade/Road Runners Club of America Hotline** (tel. 703/683–7722). For a list of running clubs in the Washington area, contact the **Road Runners Club of America,** 629 S. Washington St., Alexandria, VA 22314, tel. 703/836–0558.

Swimming There are no beaches in the Washington area. If you want to swim during your visit, it's best to stay at a hotel that has a pool. A few years ago it was possible to gain entry to some hotel pools for a small fee, but that practice has by and large been discontinued. Health-club pools, too, are open only to members, though the downtown YMCA has a pool and welcomes members of out-of-town Ys—for a fee. The only alternative consists of public pools. The District of Columbia maintains eight indoor pools, 20 large outdoor pools, and another 15 outdoor pools, which are smaller but still fun for children. For more information and a list of public facilities, contact the **Aquatic Department** of the **DC Department of Recreation** (1230 Taylor St. NW, 20011, tel. 202/576–6436).

Tennis Tennis being the sport of the rich, famous, and powerful, it comes as no surprise that it's extremely popular in Washington. The District of Columbia maintains 144 outdoor courts. Some of these courts are located in rather seedy parts of town, however, so it is best to check on the neighborhood in question before heading out. Free permits, required at all public courts, are issued by the Department of Recreation. Send a self-addressed, stamped envelope for a permit and a list of all city-run courts. You can also call for information on specific courts (Department of Recreation, 3149 16th St. NW, 20010, tel. 202/673–7646).

The best courts in the area are at two locations: **Hains Point** (East Potomac Park, tel. 202/554–5962) has outdoor courts as well as courts under a bubble for wintertime play. Fees run from $15 to $24 an hour depending on the time and season. The **Washington Tennis Center** (16th and Kennedy Sts. NW, tel. 202/722–5949) has clay and hard courts. Fees range from $15 to $24 an hour, depending on the time. Both locations will take court reservations up to one week in advance.

Spectator Sports

Tickets for all USAir Arena, Patriot Center, and Baltimore Arena events can be purchased through **TicketMaster** (tel. 202/432–7328 in D.C., tel. 410/481–7328 in Baltimore, or tel. 800/551–7328 in other areas).

Baseball Because the District doesn't have its own professional baseball team, resident baseball fans go to Baltimore to root for the **Orioles.** Their beautiful new ballpark, Oriole Park at Camden Yards (333 W. Camden St., Baltimore, MD, tel. 202/432–7328 for tickets), seats 48,000, with tickets ranging from $4.75 for general admission seats to $13 for lower box seats. You can buy tickets to O's games—and also find out about bus and train packages to the stadium in Baltimore—at the **Orioles Baseball Store** (914 17th St. NW, tel. 202/296–2473) in downtown Washington.

If you prefer your baseball à la *Bull Durham,* head south of the Beltway to the County Stadium Complex in Woodbridge, Virginia, where you can watch the **Prince William Cannons** (tel. 703/590–2311 or 703/690–3622), the Class A affiliate of the New York Yankees. Tickets range from $3 to $5.50. Or travel north up I-270 in Maryland to either the Oriole Class A **Frederick Keys** (tel. 301/662–0013) or the Toronto Blue Jay Class A **Hagerstown Suns** (tel. 301/791–6266). Tickets range from $2 to $6, and children under 14 wearing Little League uniforms get in free. The **Bowie Baysox** (tel. 800/956–4004), the Orioles' Class AA farm team, are hoping to have a new stadium open by the 1994 season in suburban Prince Georges County, Maryland.

Basketball The **Washington Bullets'** home games are held at the USAir Arena in Landover, Maryland, just outside the Beltway. Their schedule runs from September to April. For tickets, call TicketMaster, tel. 202/432–7328 or 800/551–7328; call 301/NBA–DUNK for detailed schedule information. Tickets range from $10 to $100.

Among the Division I **college basketball** teams in the area, former NCAA national champion Georgetown University's Hoyas are the best known. Their home games are played at

American Express offers Travelers Cheques built for two.

American Express® Cheques *for Two*. The first Travelers Cheques that allow either of you to use them because both of you have signed them. And only one of you needs to be present to purchase them.

Cheques *for Two* are accepted anywhere regular American Express Travelers Cheques are, which is just about everywhere. So stop by your bank, AAA* or any American Express Travel Service Office and ask for Cheques *for Two*.

Travelers Cheques

the USAir Arena (tel. 301/350–3400). Other Division I schools include the University of Maryland (tel. 301/314–7070), George Mason University (tel. 703/993–3000), George Washington University (tel. 202/994–3865), American University (tel. 202/885–3267), the U.S. Naval Academy (tel. 410/268–6226), and Howard University (tel. 202/806–7198).

Football Washington is a football-crazy town—never, *never* say anything bad about the **Redskins**. Unfortunately, unless you're a close relative of the team's owner you can pretty much forget about getting tickets to a home game. Since 1966, all Redskins games at the 55,750-seat Robert F. Kennedy Stadium on the eastern edge of Capitol Hill have been sold out to season-ticket holders. Tickets are occasionally advertised in the classified section of the *Post*, but expect to pay considerably more than face value. You might have better luck trying to get tickets to one of the Skins' preseason games in August. After much negotiation, the city reached an agreement with team owner Jack Kent Cooke in 1993 to construct a new stadium next to RFK. If (and it's a *very* big "if") the 78,600-seat stadium is completed in time for the 1994 season it may at last be easier to get Redskins tickets.

The area **colleges** offer an excellent alternative for frustrated football fans. Teams from the University of Maryland (tel. 301/314–7070), the U.S. Naval Academy (tel. 410/268–6226) in Annapolis, and Howard University (tel. 202/806–7198) all play a full schedule of college football.

Horse Racing Maryland has a long-standing affection for the ponies. You can watch and wager on thoroughbreds at **Laurel Race Course** (Rte. 198 and Race Track Rd., Laurel, MD, tel. 301/725–0400) during a season that runs January to mid-March, June through August, and October through December. On the third Saturday in May the Preakness Stakes is run at Baltimore's **Pimlico Race Course** (Hayward and Winner aves., Baltimore, MD, tel. 410/542–9400). The course has additional thoroughbreds racing from the end of March through June, and August through the beginning of October. Race days at both Laurel and Pimlico are Tuesdays and Thursdays through Sunday. You'll find harness racing just outside the Beltway at **Rosecroft Raceway** (6336 Rosecroft Dr., Fort Washington, MD, tel. 301/567–4000). Race days are usually Wednesdays through Sundays in a season that runs from February to mid-December.

Ice Hockey The **Washington Capitals'** season runs from October through April. In recent years the team has come close to greatness, but it has always choked at playoff time. Washingtonians love the Capitals, nonetheless. Home games are played at the USAir Arena. Tickets range from $12 to $32. Call 301/350–3400 or TicketMaster at 202/432–7328 or 800/551–7328.

The Outdoors

Washington is a green and leafy city, with some neighborhoods a full 10 degrees cooler than the rest of town on hot summer days. Of course some of the capital's best parks are monuments, meaning much of Washington's parkland is dotted with inscribed slabs of stone. Washington does have a few wild streaks, though: Rock Creek Park, the 1,800-acre swath of green that snakes through the city (*see* Jogging in Sports, *above*), is home to native woodland, meadows, and all manner of fauna, from deer to shrews. The area along the C & O Canal west of Georgetown is an explosion of wildflowers, complete with songbirds and the occasional beaver colony. Theodore Roosevelt Island, an 88-acre nature preserve in the Potomac across from the Kennedy Center, features 2½ miles of trails through marshland, swampland, and upland forests.

Parks and Woodlands

Audubon Naturalist Society. A self-guided nature trail winds its way through this estate and around the local Audubon Society's suburban Maryland headquarters (in a mansion known as Woodend, designed in the 1920s by Jefferson Memorial architect John Russell Pope). You're never very far from the trill of birdsong here as the Audubon Society has turned the 40-acre grounds into something of a nature preserve, forbidding the use of toxic chemicals and leaving some areas in a wild, natural state. The bookstore stocks titles on conservation, ecology, and birding, as well as birdfeeders and birdhouses. *8940 Jones Mill Rd., Chevy Chase, MD, tel. 301/652–9188. Admission free. Grounds open daily sunrise–sunset. Bookstore open Tues.–Fri. 10–6, Sat. 9–5.*

Chesapeake & Ohio Canal National Historical Park. Started in 1828, the C & O Canal was designed to link a growing capital with an expanding America. It stretched 184 miles to the west, with canal boats carrying loads of coal, timber, and wheat. Today, the canal is a long, skinny park, with one end in Georgetown and the other in Cumberland, Maryland. Canoers paddle the canal's "watered" sections while hikers and bikers use the 12-foot-wide towpath that runs alongside it. In warmer months you can hop a mule-drawn canal boat for a brief trip on the canal. The Great Falls Tavern Visitors Center in Maryland serves as a museum and headquarters for the rangers who manage the C & O Canal. You can walk over a series of bridges to Olmsted Island in the middle of the Potomac for a spectacular view of the falls. Great Falls also offers mule-drawn boat rides. (*See also* Tour 6 in Chapter 3.) *Georgetown: 1055 Thomas Jefferson St. NW, tel. 202/472–4376. Great Falls: Terminus of MacArthur Blvd., Potomac, MD, tel. 301/299–2026. Admission to Great Falls weekends mid-Mar.–Memorial Day* *and daily June–Labor Day: $4 per vehicle. Great Falls open daily 8–sunset. Closed Thanksgiving and Dec. 25.*

East Potomac Park. This 328-acre tongue of land hangs down from the Tidal Basin between the Washington Channel to the east and the Potomac River to the west. Facilities include playgrounds, picnic tables, tennis courts, swimming pools, a driving range, two 9-hole golf courses, and an 18-hole golf course. The park's miniature golf course, built during the "midget golf" craze of the '20s, is the oldest in the area; its art deco–ish architecture is a welcome contrast to the artificial, theme-park design of most subsequent miniature golf courses. Double-blossoming cherry trees line Ohio Drive and bloom about two weeks after the single-blossoming variety that attracts throngs to the Tidal Basin each spring. *The Awakening,* a huge, fantastical sculpture of a man emerging from the ground, sits on Hains Point, at the tip of the park. Plans are in the making to build a "peace garden" here that will feature plantings resembling a giant olive branch. *Approach park via Maine Ave. SW, heading west; or from Ohio Dr., heading south. Follow signs carefully. Ohio Dr. closed to traffic weekends and holidays 3 PM–6 AM. Metro stops, Smithsonian and L'Enfant Plaza.*

Fort Washington Park. Built to protect the city from enemies sailing up the Potomac, this 1808 fort was burned by the British during the War of 1812. Rebuilt, it served as an Army post until 1945. The National Park Service maintains it now and holds historical programs there every weekend. *From the Capital Beltway (Rte. 95) take the Indian Head Hwy. exit (Rte. 210) and drive 4½ mi south; look for sign on right. Tel. 301/763–4600. Entrance fee April–Labor Day and weekends in Oct.: $4 per vehicle. Park open daily 8–sunset. Visitor center open daily 10–4:30. Fort open daily 9–5. Closed Dec. 25 and Jan. 1.*

Glen Echo Park. This park was once the site of the Chautauqua Assembly, built in 1891 to promote liberal and practical education among the masses. It served a stint as an amusement park and is now run by the National Park Service, which offers space to a variety of artists, who conduct classes year-round. Monthly exhibits of artists' work are shown in a stone tower left over from the Chautauqua period. An antique carousel is open in the summer, and there are big-band and square dancing in the Spanish ballroom. On weekends, Adventure Theater presents shows for children. (*See also* Tour 1 in Chapter 10, Excursions.) *7300 MacArthur Blvd., Glen Echo, MD, tel. 301/492–6282. Call for information on events, tours, performances, and carousel hours.*

Glover-Archbold Park. Groves of beeches, elms, and oaks dot stretches of grassland at this 183-acre park, part of the Rock Creek system. A 3.6-mile nature trail runs the length of Glover-Archbold, a gift to the city in 1924. *Garfield St. and New Mexico Ave. NW.*

Great Falls Park. The waters of the Potomac River cascade dramatically over a steep, jagged gorge, creating the spectacle that gives this 800-acre Virginia park its name. Climbers scale the rock faces leading down to the water while experienced kayakers shoot the rapids. You can watch both from the park's observation deck. The more athletic can follow blazed trails through the park, some of which offer views of the river. A visitor center offers information on the park and on the ruins from two previous endeavors: George Washington's unsuccessful Potowmack Canal, designed to skirt unnavigable portions of the river, and Matildaville, a town founded by Henry "Light-Horse Harry" Lee. Across the rapids is the C & O Canal National Historical Park (*see above*). Note: Although the area is ideal for hiking, picnicking, climbing, and fishing, the rocks and the river are extremely dangerous here. The Park Service urges caution. (*See also* Tour 1 in Chapter 10.) *9200 Old Dominion Dr., Great Falls, VA, tel. 703/285-2966. Admission weekends mid-Mar.–Memorial Day and daily June–Labor Day: $4 per vehicle. Open daily 8–sunset. Closed Thanksgiving and Dec. 25.*

Huntley Meadows. This 1,200-acre Alexandria, Virginia, refuge has a reputation as a birder's delight. More than 200 species of fowl—from ospreys to owls, egrets to ibis—can be spotted here. Much of the park is wetlands, making it a favorite of aquatic species. Fur can be found as well as feathers: A boardwalk circles through a marsh, putting visitors in sight of beaver lodges, and 3 miles of trails wend through the park, making it likely you'll spot deer, muskrats, and river otters. *3701 Lockheed Blvd., Alexandria, VA, tel. 703/768-2525. Admission free. Park open daily dawn–dusk. Visitor center open Mar.–Nov., Mon. and Wed.–Fri. 9–5, weekends noon–5; Dec.–Feb., weekends noon–5.*

Rock Creek Park. The 1,800 acres of park on either side of Rock Creek have provided a cool oasis for Washington residents since Congress set them aside in 1890. There's a lot to enjoy here. Thirty picnic areas are scattered throughout the park. Bicycle routes and hiking and equestrian trails wend through the groves of dogwoods, beeches, oaks, and cedar. Rangers at the **Nature Center and Planetarium** (south of Military Rd. at 5000 Glover Rd. NW, tel. 202/426-6829; open daily 9–5, closed federal holidays and Sun. preceding a Mon. holiday) will acquaint you with the park and inform you of scheduled activities. Guided nature walks leave from the center weekends at 3, and there are blazed trailheads for exploring at your own pace. A highlight of the park is **Pierce Mill,** a restored 19th-century gristmill powered by the falling water of Rock Creek. National Park Service employees grind grain into flour and sell it to visitors (Rock Creek Park at Tilden St. and Beach Dr., tel. 202/426-6908; open Wed.–Sun. 8–4:30; Metro stop, Van Ness/UDC). Other park features include **Fort Reno, Fort Bayard,**

and **Fort DeRussy,** remnants of the original ring of forts that guarded Washington during the Civil War, and the **Rock Creek Golf Course,** an 18-hole public course. *Between 16th St. and Connecticut Ave. NW, tel. 202/426–6829 for park activities, 202/882–7332 for golf course. Park open daylight hours only; hours for individual sites vary.*

Theodore Roosevelt Island. This 88-acre island wilderness-preserve in the Potomac River is a living tribute to the conservation-minded 26th president. It features 2½ miles of nature trails through marshland, swampland, and upland forest. Cattails, arrowarum, pickerelweed, willow, ash, maple, and oak all grow on the island, providing a habitat for frogs, raccoons, birds, squirrels, and the occasional red or gray fox. There is also a 17-foot bronze statue of Roosevelt, executed by Paul Manship. *A pedestrian bridge connects the island to a parking lot on the Virginia shore and is accessible from the northbound lanes of the George Washington Memorial Pkwy. From downtown, take Constitution Ave. west across the Theodore Roosevelt Bridge to GW Memorial Pkwy. north and follow signs. Tel. 703/285–2598. Admission free. Island open 8–dusk.*

Gardens

The Bishop's Garden. This compact, traditional English-style church garden is on the grounds of the Washington Cathedral. Boxwoods, ivy, tea roses, yew trees, and an assortment of arches, bas-reliefs, and stonework from European ruins provide a restful counterpoint to the nearby cathedral's Gothic towers. *Wisconsin and Massachusetts Aves. NW, tel. 202/537–6200. Admission free. Metro stop, Woodley Park/Zoo.*

Brookside Gardens. There's always something in bloom at this rolling 50-acre display garden in suburban Maryland. Outdoors, formal seasonal displays of bulbs, annuals, and perennials and a sprawling azalea garden flourish. Inside, the two conservatories house—depending on the time of year—Easter lilies, tropicals, Japanese chrysanthemums, or poinsettia trees. *1500 Glenallan Ave., Wheaton, MD, tel. 301/949–8230, TDD 301/929–6509. Admission free. Grounds open daily 9–sunset; conservatories open weekdays 10–5, weekends and holidays 10:30–4. Closed Dec. 25.*

Constitution Gardens (*see* Tour 2 in Chapter 3). The area south of Constitution Avenue between 17th and 23rd streets NW features paths winding through groves of trees, a lake, a memorial to signers of the Declaration of Independence, and the sobering Vietnam Veterans Memorial. *Metro stop, Foggy Bottom.*

Dumbarton Oaks (*see* Tour 6 in Chapter 3). These 10 acres of formal gardens, in a variety of styles, are some of the loveliest in the city.

Kahlil Gibran Memorial Garden. Dedicated in 1991, this tiny urban park combining Western and Arabian symbols is perfect for quiet contemplation. Limestone benches engraved with sayings from Gibran curve around a fountain and a bust of the Lebanese-born poet. *3100 block of Massachusetts Ave. NW.*

Hillwood Museum. The grounds of Marjorie Merriweather Post's Georgian-style Hillwood House feature a French-style parterre, a rose garden, a Japanese garden, paths that wind through azaleas and rhododendrons, and a greenhouse in which 5,000 orchids bloom. Tours of the Hillwood Museum are often booked up months in advance, but reservations are not needed for the garden. *4155 Linnean Ave. NW, tel. 202/686–5807. Admission: $2. Open Tues.–Sat. 11–3. Metro stop, Van Ness/ UDC.*

Kenilworth Aquatic Gardens. Exotic water lilies, lotuses, hyacinths, and other water-loving plants thrive in this 12-acre sanctuary of quiet pools and marshy flats. In a pool near the visitor center bloom East Indian lotus plants grown from 350-year-old seeds recovered from a dry Manchurian lake-bed. The gardens are home to a variety of wetland animals, including turtles, frogs, muskrats, and some 40 species of birds. Early morning may be the best time to visit, when day-bloomers are just opening and night-bloomers have yet to close. July may be the best month to visit, as nearly everything is in bloom. *Kenilworth Ave. and Douglas St. NE, tel. 202/426–6905. Admission free. Gardens and visitor center open daily 8–4. Garden walks held on summer weekends at 9, 11, and 1.*

Lafayette Square (*see* Tour 3 in Chapter 3). The White House faces this park and its five statues honoring heroes of the American Revolution and the War of 1812. *Metro stop, McPherson Square.*

Meridian Hill Park. Landscape architect Horace Peaslee created this often-overlooked park after a 1917 study of the parks of Europe. It contains elements of France (a long, straight mall bordered with plants), Italy (terraces and wall fountains), and Switzerland (a lower-level reflecting pool based on one in Zurich). It's also known as Malcolm X Park. Drug activity makes it unwise to visit this park alone, even in daylight hours. Steer clear after dark. *16th and Euclid Sts. NW, tel. 202/426–6851.*

National Arboretum. During the azalea season, from the middle of April to the end of May, this 444-acre oasis is a blaze of color. In the summer, clematis, ferns, peonies, rhododendrons, and roses bloom. Paths and roadways make the arboretum an ideal place to visit for either a relaxing stroll or a scenic drive. Also popular are the National Bonsai Collection and National Herb Garden. *3501 New York Ave. NE, tel. 202/475–4815. Admission free. Open week-*

days 8–5, weekends and holidays 10–5. Bonsai Collection open daily 10–3. Closed Dec. 25.

Pershing Park (*see* Tour 3 in Chapter 3). Inscribed granite slabs in this downtown park recount battles of World War I. There's ice skating here in winter. *Metro stop, Federal Triangle.*

United States Botanic Gardens (*see* Tour 4 in Chapter 3). This conservatory houses all manner of plants, from cacti to orchids. *Metro stop, Federal Center SW.*

West Potomac Park (*see* Tour 2 in Chapter 3). This park between the Potomac and the Tidal Basin is best known for its flowering cherry trees. *Metro stop, Smithsonian.*

Zoos

National Aquarium (*see* Tour 5 in Chapter 3). Housed in the Department of Commerce Building and featuring tropical and freshwater fish, this is the nation's oldest public aquarium. *Metro stop, Federal Triangle.*

National Zoological Park (*see* Tour 9 in Chapter 3). One of the foremost zoos in the world, the 160-acre zoo is known for its giant panda, Hsing-Hsing, and ambitious Amazonia ecosystem. Many animals are shown in naturalistic settings. *Metro: Cleveland Park and Woodley Park/Zoo.*

Cemeteries

No jogging is allowed, no picknicking, and you have to be careful where you step. Still, cemeteries have an appeal unlike any other park. There's the history of those buried there and the art of the tombstones and memorials that mark their graves. Washington has its share of politicians' graves, but more fascinating are the surprises you'll discover in its cemeteries.

Arlington National Cemetery (*see* Tour 11 in Chapter 3). Once the estate of Robert E. Lee and his family, Arlington's 612 acres are a veritable Who's Who of the American military and politics. Buried here are John F. Kennedy and his brother Robert, war hero and movie star Audie Murphy, boxer Joe Louis, actor Lee Marvin, writer Dashiell Hammett, and 200,000 other veterans. *Metro: Arlington Cemetery.*

Congressional Cemetery (1801 E St. SE, tel. 202/543–0539) dates back to 1807 and was the first national cemetery created by the government. Notables buried here include William Thornton, architect of the U.S. Capitol; John Philip Sousa, composer of the Marine Corps march; Civil War photographer Mathew Brady; and FBI director J. Edgar Hoover. There are also 76 members of Congress, many of them buried under ponderous markers. A brochure for a self-guided walking tour is available at the office.

Glenwood Cemetery (2219 Lincoln Rd. NE, tel. 202/667–1016), not far from Catholic University, has its share of notable residents, including the artists Constantino Brumidi, responsible for much of the U.S. Capitol's beauty, and Emanuel Leutze, the painter of *Washington Crossing the Delaware.* More striking are the tombstones of two more obscure citizens. Benjamin Greenup was the first fireman killed on duty in Washington, and he's honored with an obelisk carved with his death scene. Teresina Vasco, a child said to have died at age 2 after playing with matches, is immortalized sitting in her favorite rocking chair.

Oak Hill Cemetery (*see* Tour 6 in Chapter 3), set on terraces stepping down to Rock Creek, may be the most beautiful in Washington. Among those buried here are John H. Payne, who penned "Home Sweet Home," William Corcoran, founder of the Corcoran Gallery of Art, and Edwin M. Stanton, Lincoln's secretary of war.

Rock Creek Cemetery (Rock Creek Church Rd. and Webster St. NW, tel. 202/829–0585), the city's oldest cemetery, is administered by the city's oldest church, St. Paul's Episcopal, which built its first building in 1775 (though all that remains of that one are its brick walls). There are many beautiful and imposing monuments in the cemetery, but the best known and most moving is the one honoring Marion Hooper "Clover" Adams. The wife of historian Henry Adams committed suicide in 1885, and sculptor Augustus Saint-Gaudens created the enigmatic figure of a seated, shroud-draped figure. Saint-Gaudens called it *The Peace of God That Passeth Understanding*, though it's best known by a more descriptive nickname: "Grief."

Organizations

Hikes and nature walks are listed in the *Washington Post*'s Friday "Weekend" section. Outings are sponsored by the following organizations:

Audubon Naturalist Society (8940 Jones Mill Rd., Chevy Chase, MD 20815, tel. 301/652–9188, ext. 3006) offers wildlife identification walks, environmental education programs, and—in the spring—a weekly Saturday "bird walk" at its suburban Maryland headquarters. Birders interested in new local avian sightings will want to call the Audubon Society's Voice of the Naturalist tape (tel. 301/652–1088).

Potomac-Appalachian Trail Club (118 Park St. SE, Vienna, VA 22180, tel. 703/242–0965) sponsors hikes—usually free—on trails from Pennsylvania to Virginia, including the C & O Canal and the Appalachian Trail.

Sierra Club (tel. 202/547–2326 and 202/547–5551) offers regional outings for a nominal fee of about $1.

7 Dining

By Deborah Papier

*Updated by
Jeanne Cooper*

Although particular restaurants may falter or fall, in general, Washington's restaurants are getting better and better. (And sometimes, cheaper and cheaper: The sluggish economy of the early '90s has meant more reasonably priced fare and fixed-price specials in many of the city's top dining rooms.) In the past few years Italian restaurants have come to rival French establishments, which for a long time set the standard in fine dining. There has also been an explosion of the kind of cooking usually called New American, which has energized and raised the standards of healthy eating in this health-conscious town.

Despite the dearth of ethnic neighborhoods in Washington and the corresponding lack of the kinds of restaurant districts found in many cities, you *can* find almost any type of food here, from Nepalese to Salvadoran to Ethiopian. In the city's one officially recognized ethnic enclave, **Chinatown** (centered on G and H streets NW between 6th and 8th, with its own Metrorail station at Gallery Place), innovations such as Mongolian barbecue and hotpot are starting to enliven the menus of the area's plentiful but unexceptional traditional Chinese restaurants. (First-rate Thai restaurants, however, are common throughout the city.)

Aside from Chinatown, there are eight areas of the city where restaurants are concentrated:

Most of the deluxe restaurants are on or near **K Street NW,** also the location of many of the city's blue-chip law firms. These are the restaurants that feed and feed off of expense-account diners and provide the most elegant atmosphere, most attentive service, and often the best food. In 1992 and early '93, the area's recession led to some reshuffling among some of the best-known New American eateries: Twenty-One Federal closed and was looking for a new home while McPherson Grill closed and was scheduled to reopen as Georgia Brown's, featuring Southern fare. And across from the latter on McPherson Square, Michelin two-star chef Gerard Pangaud opened Gerard's Place in the former Jacques restaurant. The exorbitant prices have either come down or at least not gone up; President Clinton's edicts on government ethics have led to $20 lunch "specials" aimed at lobbyists.

In the old downtown district, remodeling and new construction slowed in the early '90s. Those restaurants that opened during the building boom, however, continue to thrive, especially if they're located along redeveloped **Pennsylvania Avenue.** Visitors with children can take advantage of the many sandwich shops geared to office workers but will find far fewer choices evenings and weekends.

The other area of town long known as a restaurant district is **Georgetown,** whose central intersection is Wisconsin Avenue and M Street. Georgetown contains some of the city's priciest houses as well as some of its cheesiest businesses, and its restaurants are similarly diverse, with white-table-cloth dining places next door to hole-in-the-wall joints. Keep an eye out, also, for restaurants in the adjacent **West End.** This area, bounded roughly by Rock Creek Park to the west, N Street to the north, 20th Street to the east, and K Street to the south, is increasingly bridging the gap between Georgetown and downtown restaurant zones.

A youthful culinary competitor to Georgetown is **Adams-Morgan.** Eighteenth Street NW extending south from Columbia Road is wall-to-wall restaurants, with new ones opening so fast it's almost impossible to track them. Although the area has retained some of its Hispanic identity, the new eating establishments tend to be either Italian, New American, Ethiopian, or Caribbean. The nearest Metrorail stop—Woodley Park/Zoo—is a 10- to 20-minute walk, and parking can be impossible, so it's better to take a cab here at night. **Woodley Park,** however, has its own line-up of popular ethnic restaurants right by the Metro.

South from Adams-Morgan and north from K Street is **Dupont Circle,** around which a number of restaurants are clustered. Some of the city's best Italian places can be found here, as can a variety of cafés, most boasting outdoor seating. Espresso bars, nurtured here before popping up all over Washington in 1992, are a good source for breakfast and light or late fare. Those on 17th Street NW are especially popular with young adults.

Capitol Hill has a number of bar/eateries that cater to congressional types in need of fortification after a day spent running the country. The dining possibilities on Capitol Hill are boosted by Union Station, which contains some very good restaurants and a large food court with fast food ranging from barbecue to sushi.

Outside the city limits are some thriving restaurant districts. Downtown **Bethesda, Maryland,** offers a wealth of possibilities; some even think that Georgetown is losing business to Bethesda's bistros. Virginia has its Georgetown equivalent, in **Old Town Alexandria,** as well as some of the area's best Asian restaurants. Wilson Boulevard in **Arlington** features many popular Vietnamese establishments and branches of other DC restaurants. The Bethesda, King Street, and Clarendon Metro stations make these gourmet "ghettos" accessible to visitors.

Highly recommended restaurants are indicated by a star ★.

Category	Cost*
Very Expensive	over $35
Expensive	$25–$35

Washington Dining

Primi Piatti, **27**
Red Sage, **45**
The River Club, **8**
Sala Thai, **23**
Sam and Harry's, **31**
Sarinah Satay
House, **6**
Sea Catch, **12**
701 Pennsylvania
Avenue, **48**
Sfuzzi, **52**

Skewers, **39**
Tabard Inn, **35**
Taberna del
Alabardero, **28**
Two Quail, **51**
Unkai, **15**
Vincenzo, **20**
The Willard, **44**
Zorba's Cafe, **18**

| Moderate | $15–$25 |
| Inexpensive | under $15 |

*average cost of a 3-course dinner, per person, excluding drinks, service, and (9%) sales tax

Adams-Morgan/Woodley Park

Caribbean **Café Atlántico.** One of the liveliest spots in Adams-Morgan,
★ Café Atlántico serves Caribbean specialties in a casual atmosphere. Appetizers include conch or cod fritters, shrimp and potato croquettes, and yucca fritters, all beautifully fried. Pork loin, jerk chicken, a vegetarian plate, and lamb curry are among the main courses. Service is friendly and helpful. *1819 Columbia Rd. NW (5½ blocks from Woodley Park/Zoo Metro stop), tel. 202/575–2233. No reservations. Dress: casual. AE, DC, MC, V. Closed lunch. Moderate.*
The Grill from Ipanema. Although its young crowd rivals Café Atlántico's, the equally vibrant Grill focuses more on Brazilian cuisine, from spicy seafood stews to grilled steak and other hearty meat dishes. There's even grouper "à Carmen Miranda," wrapped in phyllo with a tropical sauce. Appetizers include clams baked with hot peppers and cilantro and fried alligator. The traditional *feijoada*, a stew of black beans, pork, and smoked meat, is served Wednesdays and Saturdays. *1858 Columbia Rd. NW (5 blocks from Woodley Park/Zoo Metro stop), tel. 202/986–0757. Reservations only for before 7:30. Dress: casual. AE, DC, MC, V. Closed lunch Mon.–Fri. Moderate.*
Fish, Wings & Tings. This Caribbean café (or *mini kafe*, according to the menu) is the idiosyncratic creation of the husband-and-wife Jamaican chef and Panamanian manager. Their tiny dining room almost always has a line waiting to get in. The menu includes stewed oxtail and curry goat, but most people come here for the curry-ginger chicken wings, or the jerk (spicy barbecued) thighs. *2418 18th St. NW (6 blocks from Woodley Park/Zoo Metro stop), tel. 202/234–0322. No reservations. No no-smoking area. Dress: casual. AE. Closed Sun. Inexpensive.*

Ethiopian **Fasika's.** Overlooked by some American diners in favor of Meskerem, Fasika's nevertheless attracts plenty of Ethiopian expatriates and Washingtonians with its version of Adams-Morgan's most ubiquitous cuisine. There is no silverware here; instead, the food is scooped up with *injera*, a spongy flat bread that also does duty as the platter on which the meal is presented. The country's main dish is the *watt*, or stew, which may be made with chicken, lamb, beef, or shrimp in a spicy sauce; mild versions are called *alicha*. Several vegetarian watts and alichas are also available. Prices are nearly one-third lower from 5 to 7 PM. Ethiopian musicians entertain Thursday through Sunday nights. *2447 18th St. NW (6 blocks from Woodley Park/Zoo Metro stop),*

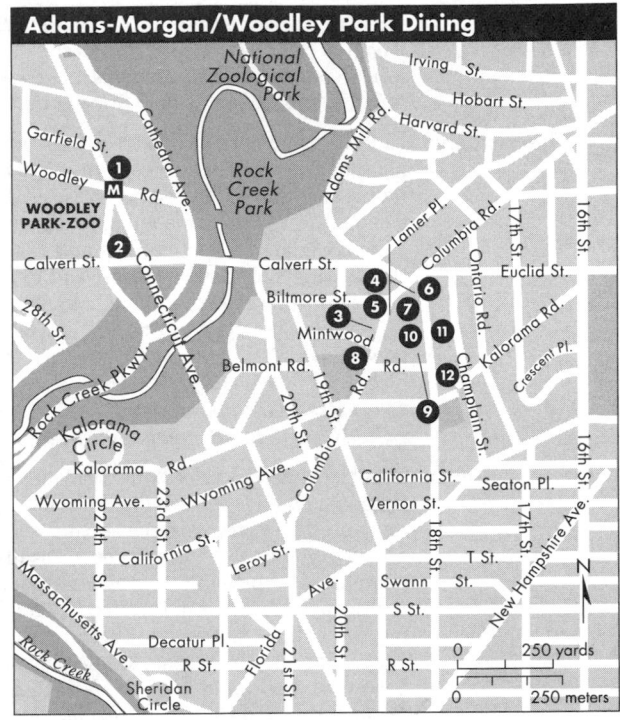

Adams-Morgan/Woodley Park Dining

tel. 202/797–7673. *Reservations advised. Dress: casual but neat. AE, DC, MC, V. Closed lunch. Inexpensive.*

★ **Meskerem.** Meskerem is distinctive for its bright, appealingly decorated dining room. Another attractive feature: Like Fasika's, it has a balcony where you can eat Ethiopian-style—seated on the floor on leather cushions, with large woven baskets for tables. The specialties here are *fitfit* dishes, in which the injera is served in pieces already soaked in the watt stews; *kitfo*, a buttery raw beef dish like steak tartare that can also be served very rare; and the green chile-spiked potato salad. Meat and vegetarian combination platters are also available. *2434 18th St. NW (6 blocks from Woodley Park/Zoo Metro stop), tel. 202/462–4100. Reservations advised. Dress: casual but neat. AE, DC, MC, V. Closed lunch Mon.–Thurs. Inexpensive.*

French **La Fourchette.** Located on a block in Adams-Morgan where new restaurants are opening almost weekly and closing just as fast, La Fourchette has stayed in business since 1975 by offering good bistro food at reasonable prices. Most of the menu consists of daily specials and an early-bird fixed-price menu, but you can pretty much count on finding bouillabaisse and rabbit on the list. The most popular entrées on the regular menu are the hearty veal and lamb shanks. La Fourchette also looks the way a bistro should, with an exposed brick wall, tin ceiling, bentwood chairs, and quasi-post-Impressionist murals. *2429 18th St. NW (6 blocks from Woodley Park/Zoo Metro stop), tel. 202/332–3077. Reservations advised for groups. Dress: casual but neat. AE, DC, MC, V. Closed Sun. lunch. Moderate.*

International **Cities.** The owners of this trendy restaurant ask us to imagine that the concrete and chain-link decor represents a different city every four months or so as the menu changes. In the past few years this culinary odyssey has taken diners from Bangkok to Mexico City and Los Angeles. Wherever the destination, pasta, pizzas, and grilled dishes are standard fare. The crowd is young and noisy, the food and service not as consistent as one would wish, but Cities is still a good place for a light, informal meal. *2424 18th St. NW (6 blocks from Woodley Park/Zoo Metro stop), tel. 202/328–7194. Reservations advised. Dress: casual but neat. AE, DC, MC, V. Closed lunch Mon.–Sat. Moderate.*

Italian **i Matti.** Owned by chef Roberto Donna of the highly praised Galileo, i Matti is a much less formal but just as popular restaurant. The stark modern setting and the crowds of well-dressed young people somehow encapsulate Adams-Morgan chic. It's possible to order anything from a pizza to a multicourse meal from the large menu. The breads, including the grilled *bruschetta* (bread with olive oil and garlic) variations and the pizzas, are delicious. Osso buco is a good bet in winter. *2436 18th St. NW (6 blocks from Woodley Park/Zoo Metro stop), tel. 202/462–8844. Reservations advised. Dress: casual. AE, DC, MC, V. Moderate.*

New American **New Heights.** With its precise geometrical design softened by pastel colors, New Heights is one of Washington's most attractive restaurants. (Robert De Niro booked it for a private lunch during Clinton's inauguration week.) The menu varies seasonally but always includes a vegetarian entrée, such as Thai-style ravioli. Salmon, a frequent offering, might be sautéed and served with pecan rice and crawfish cream. The restaurant is a good choice for Sunday brunch. *2317 Calvert St. NW (1 block from Woodley Park/Zoo Metro stop), tel. 202/234–4110. Reservations advised. Dress: casual but neat. AE, DC, MC, V. Closed lunch. Expensive.*

Southwestern/ Tex-Mex **Peyote Café.** Located downstairs from Roxanne Restaurant, this Southwestern pub takes cheeky liberties with its decor and food, and wins with both. Twinkling lights, tables with bar stools, and a swinging jukebox attract a young crowd of primarily students and singles. The eclectic menu aims to please everyone: Meat eaters can choose from such dishes as *carne asada* (ribeye steak), grilled salmon, "gringo-killer" fried chicken, and "sweat hot fire" shrimp, and vegetarians look for the cactus sign on the menu that indicates meatless dishes. *2319 18th St. NW (7 blocks from Woodley Park/Zoo Metro stop), tel. 202/462–8330. No reservations. Dress: casual. AE, MC, V. Closed weekday lunch. Inexpensive.*

Thai **Star of Siam.** This three-restaurant chain doesn't offer the hottest or most elaborately presented Thai cuisine, but its dishes are among the most reliable in the city. Spicy-food lovers can try the squid salad or boneless roast duck appetizers and an entree such as beet curry with coconut milk, eggplant, potato, and peanut. Vegetarians should skip the blander rice and egg noodle plates and opt for *pad pik pak*, a stir-fry of mixed vegetables with hot pepper. Soups are fragrant and on the tangy side. *2446 18th St. NW (upstairs, 6 blocks from Woodley Park/Zoo Metro stop), tel. 202/986–4133; also 1136 19th St. NW (2 blocks from Dupont Circle Metro stop), tel. 202/785–2839; and 1735 N Lynn St. in Arlington, VA (at the Rosslyn Metro), tel. 703/524–1208. Reservations advised on weekends. Dress: casual. AE, MC, V. Closed Sun. lunch. Moderate.*

Vietnamese **Saigon Gourmet.** Service is brisk and friendly at this popular, French-influenced dining room. The upscale neighborhood patrons return for the ultracrisp *cha-gio* (spring rolls), the savory *pho*-style (beef broth) and seafood soups, and the delicately seasoned and richly sauced entrées. Shrimp Saigon mixes prawns and pork in a peppery marinade, and another Saigon dish—grilled pork with rice crepes—is a Vietnamese variation on Chinese moo shu. Bananas flambé are an entertaining way to end a meal, as the waiter appears to pour flames from one plate to the other. *2635 Connecticut Ave. NW (across from Woodley Park/Zoo Metro stop), tel. 202/265–1360. Reservations advised. No no-smoking area. Dress: casual. AE, DC, MC, V. Moderate.*

Capitol Hill

American **America.** A Washington outpost of owner Michael Weinstein's America in New York, Union Station's America is installed in the west front, with a two-story section in the center and a seasonal outdoor café. The high ceilings of the renovated station amplify the din of this lively bar and restaurant. The menu is enormous, with nearly four square feet of regular offerings ranging from Kansas City steaks and Minnesota scrambled eggs to New Orleans muffaletta sandwiches, New Mexico–style pasta, Jersey pork chops, and San Diego fish tacos. The kitchen has its successes and failures—a good general rule is "the simpler the better." Desserts are good, and service is pleasant though chaotic. *Union Station, 50 Massachusetts Ave. NE (Union Station Metro stop), tel. 202/682–9555. Reservations advised. Dress: casual but neat. AE, DC, MC, V. 2-hr parking validated in Union Station lot. Expensive.*

The Monocle. Separated in both location and ambience from the younger, more bustling Capitol Hill scene, the Monocle is still probably the best place for spotting senators at lunch and dinner; management keeps members of Congress informed on when it's time to vote. The cooking, American cuisine with a Continental touch, is adequate if unexciting, but it's the old-style Capitol Hill atmosphere, not the food, that's the real draw here. Seafood is a specialty; try the crab cakes, and take advantage of the fresh fish specials. The fireplaces and political portraits in this former pair of town houses add to the aura of cozy tradition. *107 D St. NE (1½ blocks from Union Station Metro stop), tel. 202/546–4488. Reservations advised. Jacket and tie advised. AE, DC, MC, V. Closed Sat. lunch and Sun. Valet parking weekends. Expensive.*

Two Quail. A welcome respite from the men's club atmosphere of traditional Capitol Hill eateries, this cute, floral-patterned tearoom is tops among women for both romantic and power dining. The smallish menu has both rich fare— apricot-stuffed pork chop, chicken stuffed with cornbread and pecans, or filet mignon—and lighter, seafood pastas and meal-sized salads. Service can be leisurely. *320 Massachusetts Ave. NE (2½ blocks from Union Station Metro stop), tel. 202/543–8030. Reservations advised. Dress: casual but neat. AE, DC, MC, V. Closed weekend lunch. Moderate.*

French **La Brasserie.** La Brasserie is one of Capitol Hill's most pleasant and most satisfying restaurants. The dining rooms are on two floors of adjoining town houses, with outdoor dining in season. Chef Gaby Aubouin's basically French menu changes daily, but the four-course, fixed-price meals are excellent values and a good indication of the cuisine's character. The crème brûlée, served cold or hot with fruit, is superb. For breakfast, this small spot is charming. *239 Massachusetts Ave. NE (2 blocks from Union Station Metro stop), tel. 202/546–9154. Reservations advised. Dress: casual but neat. AE, DC, MC, V. Expensive.*

★ **La Colline.** Chef Robert Gréault has worked to make La Colline into one of the city's best French restaurants and the best of any type on Capitol Hill. The menu, which changes daily, places an emphasis on seafood, with offerings ranging from simple grilled preparations to fricasśes and gratins with imaginative sauces. The nonseafood menu usually offers duck with an orange or cassis sauce and veal with chanterelles. The dessert selection is plentiful, as is the wine list. Capitol Hill power brokers also favor La Colline, with its in-house bakery, for breakfast. *400 N. Capitol St. (3 blocks from Union Station Metro stop), tel. 202/737–0400. Reservations advised. Jacket and tie advised. AE, DC, MC, V. Closed weekend lunch. Free parking in underground lot. Expensive.*

Italian **Sfuzzi.** Its prime location in the northeast corner of Union Station, Capitol view upstairs, and trompe l'oeil classical-Italian interior attract a young, noisy crowd of Hill staffers. Although more elaborate American-Italian concoctions are available, the best items on the menu are the pizzas, which may be ordered as an appetizer to be shared or as a main course. The crust is crisp, yeasty, and flavorful, and the toppings immaculately fresh and varied. *Union Station, 50 Massachusetts Ave. NE (Union Station Metro stop), tel. 202/842–4141. Reservations advised. Dress: casual but neat. AE, DC, MC, V. Parking validated in Union Station garage. Expensive.*

Downtown

American   **The Palm.** Food trends come and go, but the Palm pays no attention; it offers the same hearty food it always has— gargantuan steaks and lobsters, several kinds of potatoes, New York cheesecake. The staff's been packing them in since the mid-'70s with this kind of fare, and they're not about to let the calorie- and cholesterol-counters spoil the party. The look of the restaurant is basement basic—acoustic ceiling tiles, wooden fans—and the businesslike air is matched by the clientele. The Palm also offers a bargain lunch menu that includes shrimp, veal, and chicken salad. *1225 19th St. NW (2 blocks from Dupont Circle Metro stop), tel. 202/293–9091. Reservations advised. Dress: casual but neat. AE, DC, MC, V. Closed Sat. lunch and Sun. Very Expensive.*

Prime Rib. Despite its name, the Prime Rib is no longer really a steakhouse. In response to the increasing popularity of seafood, it now devotes half its menu to fish and shellfish, some of it shipped express from Florida. The most popular of the seafood dishes is the imperial crab, made only of jumbo lump-crabmeat; you can also order it stuffed in a two-pound lobster. The aged beef from Chicago includes a steak au poivre in addition to New York strip, porterhouse, filet mignon, and the restaurant's namesake. Also served are simple preparations of veal, pork, lamb, and chicken. The black walls, leather chairs, and leopardskin print rugs give this attractive restaurant a timeless sophistication. *2020 K St. NW (2½ blocks from Farragut West Metro stop), tel. 202/466–8811. Reservations advised. Jacket and tie required. AE, DC, MC, V. Closed Sat. lunch and Sun. Very Expensive.*

Sam and Harry's. The surroundings are understated and genteel, the bar is a popular downtown gathering place, and the dining room is packed at lunch and dinner. While the miniature crab cakes are a good way to begin, the main attractions are the porterhouse steak, the prime rib, and the signature strip steak. For those who've sworn off beef, Sam and Harry's also has daily fish specials. Desserts are lackluster, but who needs them after all that meat. *1200 19th St. NW (2 blocks from Dupont Circle Metro stop), tel. 202/296–4333. Reservations advised. Jacket and tie advised. AE, DC, MC, V. Closed Sat. lunch and Sun. Very Expensive.*

Duke Zeibert's. At lunch, this 450-seat restaurant is filled with regulars such as Larry King who come to talk sports with Duke and eat heartily from a menu that essentially hasn't changed in 40 years—boiled beef and chicken in a pot, deli sandwiches, and specials, such as corned beef and cabbage. At dinner, only the front room is used, and the restaurant becomes a different place, with couples and families replacing the deal-makers. In the evening the signature chicken and beef in a pot are still available, but the menu leans toward broiled items, such as lamb chops and sirloin, not to mention two dishes for which the restaurant is famous—prime rib and crab cakes. *1050 Connecticut Ave. NW (on the mezzanine of the Washington Sq. Bldg. at Farragut North Metro stop), tel. 202/466–3730. Reservations required. Jacket and tie advised. AE, DC, MC, V. Closed Sun. lunch. Closed Sun. in July and Aug. Validated parking at Washington Sq. lot. Expensive.*

The Peasant. The Atlanta-based Peasant Corporation, which also owns the Pleasant Peasant in Mazza Gallerie at the Friendship Heights Metro stop, made its downtown location traditional and clubby, with dark-wood paneling and crisp white tablecloths. Its proximity to Capitol Hill makes it a popular spot for lobbying lunches. The daily menu, which is presented on individual chalkboards, is in the New American melting pot style and likely to include pasta selections, grilled fish, and steaks. The signature desserts are enormous and rich, but if you want to try one, go easy on the complimentary cheesebread provided with your meal. *801 Pennsylvania Ave. NW (½ block from Archives Metro stop), tel. 202/638–2140. Reservations advised. Dress: casual but neat. AE, DC, MC, V. Valet parking at dinner. Closed weekend lunch. Expensive.*

Old Ebbitt Grill. This reincarnation of Washington's longest-lived restaurant is obviously doing something right—it does more business than almost any other eating place in town. People flock here to drink at the several bars, which seem to go on for miles, and to enjoy carefully prepared bar food that includes buffalo chicken wings, hamburgers, and Reuben sandwiches. But this is not just a place for casual nibbling; the Old Ebbitt offers serious diners homemade pastas and a list of daily specials, with the emphasis on fish dishes and steak. Despite the crowds, the restaurant never feels cramped, thanks to its well-spaced, comfortable booths. Service can be slow at lunch. *675 15th St. NW (2 blocks from Metro Center Metro stop), tel. 202/347–4800. Reservations advised. Dress: casual but neat. AE, MC, V. Moderate.*

E.E. Wolensky's. The entrance through the historic Pennsylvania Avenue facade belies the sprawling basement-level restaurant. Although the street-level bar is smoky and singles-minded, the dining room courts students, families, and Foggy Bottom/Kennedy Center visitors with a wide-ranging menu. Turkey chili, Mexican pizza, and grilled tuna share space with burgers, pasta, and strip steak. Quality and service are inconsistent; Sunday brunch, low prices, and location are the draws. *2000 Pennsylvania Ave. NW (2 blocks from Foggy Bottom Metro stop), tel. 202/463–0050. Dress: casual. AE, MC, V. Inexpensive.*

Hard Rock Cafe. If you can stand the loud music—and the tourist-season line to get in—you'll find respectable American fare at one of the few downtown restaurants open daily for lunch *and* dinner. A veggie Reuben and a veggie burger are two alternatives to the heartier offerings, such as the pulled-pork "pig sandwich," predictable burgers, and a Texas T-bone steak. Desserts include shakes, sundaes, and a banana split. *999 E St. NW (3 blocks from Metro Center Metro stop), tel. 202/737–ROCK. No reservations. Dress: casual. AE, DC, MC, V. Inexpensive.*

Asian **Cafe Asia.** One of the rare pan-Asian restaurants with few weak spots, Cafe Asia presents Japanese, Chinese, Thai, Singaporean, Indonesian, and Vietnamese variations on succulent themes. Highlights include grilled shrimp paste on sugarcane, moist *satays* (skewered meats), and spicy bluefish in banana leaves. Vegetarians can choose from several tofu dishes and salads. The decor is Spartan and the staff small, but the low prices and multiple cuisines make waits worthwhile. At dinnertime the patrons are more the young Dupont Circle crowd than suited downtowners. *1134 19th St. NW (2 blocks from Dupont Circle Metro stop), tel. 202/659–2696. Dress: casual. AE, MC, V. Inexpensive.*

French **Jean-Louis at the Watergate Hotel.** A showcase for the cook-
★ ing of Jean-Louis Palladin, who was the youngest chef in France ever to be recognized with two stars by the Michelin raters, this small restaurant is often cited as one of the best in the United States. The contemporary French fare is based on regional American ingredients—crawfish from Louisiana, wild mushrooms from Oregon, game from Texas—combined in innovative ways. There are two limited choice, fixed-price dinners: one with five courses for $85 per person, the other with six courses (the additional course is a foie-gras dish), for $95. There is also a pretheater menu of four courses for $43, designed for but not limited to those attending the nearby Kennedy Center. In general, the first course is a soup or terrine; corn soup with oysters and lobster quenelles is a signature offering. Next comes a shellfish preparation, perhaps a potato stuffed with lobster mousseline; then a fish course, such as snapper with braised cabbage; and last, a meat dish, perhaps rack of lamb with artichoke ragout. The wine cellar is said to be the largest on the East Coast. *2650 Virginia Ave. NW (downstairs in the Watergate Hotel, which can be entered from Virginia or New Hampshire Aves., 3 blocks from Foggy Bottom Metro stop), tel. 202/298–4488. Reservations required. Jacket and tie required. AE, DC, MC, V. Closed lunch, Sun. and Aug. Validated parking. Very Expensive.*
★ **Le Lion D'Or.** Other French restaurants may flirt with fads, but this one sticks to the classics—or at any rate the neoclassics—and does them so well that its popularity remains undiminished year after year. This is the sort of food that makes the French posture of cultural superiority almost defensible: lobster soufflé, crepes with oysters and

caviar, ravioli with foie gras, salmon with crayfish, and roast pigeon with mushrooms. The long list of daily specials can get rather confusing unless you take notes while the waiter recites them. But don't forget to place an order for a dessert soufflé. *1150 Connecticut Ave. NW (entrance on 18th St. NW, 1 block from Farragut North Metro stop), tel. 202/296–7972. Reservations advised. Jacket and tie required. AE, DC, MC, V. Closed Sat. lunch and Sun. Free parking in lot next door at dinner. Very Expensive.*

Maison Blanche. No matter whether Democrats or Republicans are in power, Maison Blanche is the restaurant elected by the city's power brokers and those who enjoy gawking at them. It owes its bipartisan popularity in large part to its location near the White House and executive office buildings but also to its Old World elegance, the friendliness of the family that runs it, and its large repertory of classic and modern French dishes. The menu, which changes four times a year, is supplemented by a large number of daily specials, primarily fish. Maison Blanche goes to great lengths to obtain Dover sole, which it serves simply grilled in butter. This is perhaps the restaurant's most popular dish, but also exceptional are the rack of lamb and the pasta dishes, such as shrimp sautéed with tomatoes and garlic, served over angel hair pasta. The pastry chef has a proper reverence for chocolate, and the wine list is extensive, with California wines well represented. *1725 F St. NW (4 blocks from Farragut West Metro stop), tel. 202/842–0070. Reservations advised. Jacket and tie advised. AE, DC, MC, V. Closed Sat. lunch and Sun. Free valet parking at dinner. Very Expensive.*

The Place on K. In 1991, Jean-Michel Farret closed the popular but pricey Jean-Pierre restaurant at this location and reopened as the more moderately priced but still elegant Place on K. Chef Guy Gateau emphasizes country French cooking with urbane touches. Dishes are generally hearty—a lunch entrée of grilled chicken breast, for instance, might come sandwiched between savory potato pancakes. Dinner fare is even heavier—filet mignon and coq au vin—with well-chosen accompaniments, such as crisp vegetables. Desserts are exquisite, ranging from delicate pastries to house-made ice creams. The interior's soft hues encourage romantic dining. *1835 K St. NW (1½ blocks from Farragut North Metro stop), tel. 202/466–2022. Reservations advised. Jacket and tie advised. AE, DC, MC, V. Closed Sat. lunch and Sun. Expensive.*

Indian
★ **The Bombay Club.** Located just a block from the White House, the Bombay Club tries to re-create for tired Executive Office bureaucrats, power lawyers, and journalists the kind of solace they might have found in a private club had they been 19th-century British colonialists in India rather than late-20th-century Washingtonians. It's a beautiful restaurant. The bar, which serves hot hors d'oeuvres at cocktail hour, is furnished with rattan chairs and paneled

with dark wood. The dining room, with potted palms and a bright blue ceiling above white plaster moldings, is elegant and decorous. The menu includes unusual seafood specialties, such as lobster Malabar and a large number of vegetarian dishes, but the real standouts are the breads and the seafood appetizers. *815 Connecticut Ave. NW (1 block from Farragut West Metro stop), tel. 202/659-3727. Reservations advised. Jacket and tie advised. AE, DC, MC, V. Closed Sat. lunch and Sun. dinner. Moderate.*

International **701 Pennsylvania Avenue.** This sleek restaurant features an eclectic cuisine drawn from Italy, France, Asia, and the Americas. You might start your meal with a butternut squash bisque with smoked duck, progress to a Moroccan-style chicken and couscous dish, and finish with an Italian almond-and-cherry tart. The restaurant's Caviar Lounge offers choices ranging from Beluga to Louisiana "Choupiquet Royale" and 18 types of vodka, and the tapas bar serves up sherry and 18 of Spain's "little dishes." The fixed-price pretheater dinner is popular; diners include Shakespeare Theatre patrons and well-dressed political power brokers. *701 Pennsylvania Ave. NW (at Archives Metro stop), tel. 202/393-0701. Reservations advised. Dress: casual but neat. AE, DC, MC, V. Closed weekend lunch. Valet parking at dinner. Expensive.*

Madeo. Each month the adventurous chef here offers a different three-course fixed-price dinner ($18.95) to tempt large appetites. Recent entree choices have included salmon and spinach napoleon, angel hair pasta with lobster and scallops, and a French-cut pork chop with date and Calvados compote. Be prepared for hefty portions of desserts, such as bread pudding and cannoli. The long, narrow shape of this pretty room is mitigated by an airy atrium ceiling. *1113 23rd St. NW (3 blocks from Foggy Bottom Metro stop), tel. 202/457-0057. Reservations advised. Dress: casual but neat. AE, DC, MC, V. Parking $1.50 in lot next door. Moderate.*

Italian **Bice.** Washington's Bice, like its other American locations, has an elegant interior—wood, brass, warm lighting, and art deco details—suggested by the original in Milan. The large menu, which changes twice daily, features Milanese and Northern Italian specialities, such as risotto verdi with mascarpone cheese and spinach, and a classic breaded veal cutlet alla Milanese. Mineral water here costs $5 a bottle; the only bargain is the free basket of focaccia and fresh breads. Service is geared to the high-profile customer. *601 Pennsylvania Ave. NW (1 block from Archives Metro stop), tel. 202/638-2423. Reservations advised. Jacket and tie advised. AE, DC, MC, V. Closed weekend lunch. Very Expensive.*

★ **Galileo.** Chef Roberto Donna's more formal companion to i Matti (*see above*), this spacious, popular restaurant boasts homemade everything, from breadsticks to mozzarella. And it all tastes terrific. The menu changes daily, but there are always risotto; a long list of grilled fish; a game bird, such as quail, guinea hen, or woodcock; and one or two beef or veal dishes. Preparations are generally simple. For example, the veal chop may be served with mushroom-and-rosemary sauce, the beef with black-olive sauce and polenta. *1110 21st St. NW (3½ blocks from Foggy Bottom Metro stop), tel 202/293–7191. Reservations advised. Jacket and tie advised. AE, DC, MC, V. Closed weekend lunch. Valet parking at dinner (except Sun.). Very Expensive.*

★ **i Ricchi.** Priced for expense accounts, i Ricchi remains a favorite of critics and crowds for its earthy Tuscan cuisine. There are two menus, one for spring and summer, one for fall and winter. The spring list includes such offerings as rolled pork and rabbit roasted in wine and fresh herbs, and skewered shrimp; winter brings grilled lamb chops, thick soups, and sautéed beef filet. But whatever the calendar says, it always feels like spring in this airy dining room, which is decorated with terra-cotta tiles, cream-colored archways, and floral frescoes. *1220 19th St. NW (2 blocks from Dupont Circle Metro stop), tel. 202/835–0459. Reservations advised. Jacket and tie advised. AE, DC, MC, V. Closed Sat. lunch and Sun. Expensive.*

Notte Luna. This glitzy, power-lunch spot features a dramatic black-and-neon dining room, an open kitchen with wood-burning pizza oven, and informal, ambitious cuisine. The menu offers the Italian-restaurant staples of pasta, pizza, and veal dishes, but with unexpected twists. You can order your cracker-thin pizza topped with gravlax or lamb sausage or your pasta with grilled salmon. All meals start with crisp bread, cheese spread, and olives. Desserts, such as berries served in a cookie-dough basket, are always a treat. *809 15th St. NW (1 block from McPherson Square Metro stop), tel. 202/408–9500. Reservations advised. Dress: casual but neat. AE, DC, MC, V. Closed weekend lunch. Valet parking at dinner (except Sun.). Moderate.*

Primi Piatti. A meal here is like a taxi ride in Rome at rush hour—the crowds and the noise are overwhelming, but you'll never forget the trip. The restaurant makes a point of serving dishes that are both authentically Italian, and light and healthful. There's a wood-burning grill, on which several kinds of fish are cooked each day—tuna with fresh mint sauce is one preparation—as well as lamb and veal chops. Meat is also done to a succulent turn on the rotisserie. Pastas are made in house and are quite good, as are the pizzas. The wine list is unusually descriptive. *2013 I St. NW (2 blocks from Farragut West and Foggy Bottom Metro stops), tel. 202/223–3600; Fairfax Square, VA tel. 703/893–0300. Reservations advised. Jacket and tie advised. AE, DC, MC, V. Closed weekend lunch. Moderate.*

Moroccan **Marrakesh.** This is one of Washington's happy surprises: a bit of Morocco located in a part of the city better known for auto-supply shops. The menu is a fixed-price ($22) feast shared by everyone at your table and eaten without silverware. The first course is a platter of three salads; the second, *b'stella*—a chicken version of Morocco's traditional pigeon pie. For the first main course, you choose among several chicken preparations; the second main course consists of beef or lamb. These are followed by vegetable couscous, fresh fruit, mint tea, and pastries. Belly dancers put on a nightly show. Alcoholic drinks can really drive up the tab here. *617 New York Ave. NW (½ block from Mount Vernon Square Metro stop), tel. 202/393–9393. Reservations required. Jacket and tie advised. No credit cards (checks accepted). Closed lunch. Valet parking. Moderate.*

New American **The Willard.** An exact replica of the 1904 dining room of the
★ historic Willard Hotel, this restaurant exudes turn-of-the-century splendor. The food, however, is strictly contemporary and might include seafood medley with wilted spinach and angel hair pasta; rack of Delaware lamb coated with mustard and fresh herbs; and veal steak with Belgian endive and basil cream sauce. The unusual wine list includes regional American varieties drawn from the vineyards of Virginia and the Pacific Northwest as well as California; an extensive selection of cognacs is presented on a rolling cart. As one might expect, such luxury does not come cheap, but this is one place where a meal really is an occasion. *1401 Pennsylvania Ave. NW (2 blocks from Metro Center Metro stop), tel. 202/637–7440. Reservations required. Jacket and tie required. AE, DC, MC, V. Free valet parking at dinner. Very Expensive.*

★ **Occidental Grill.** In the stately Willard Hotel complex, this popular restaurant used to be two separate establishments: the formal Occidental upstairs and the clubby Occidental Grill downstairs. But in keeping with the economizing sensibility of today's city, the two were merged in late 1991. Now both levels offer innovative and artful dishes, attentive service, and lots of photos of politicians and other power brokers past and present. The menu changes frequently, but you can count on poultry, fish, and steak as grilled options (tuna might be served with a pepper sauce or marlin with bananas, rum, and a mango relish), plus salads and sandwiches. *1475 Pennsylvania Ave. NW (2 blocks from Metro Center Metro Stop), tel. 202/783–1475. Reservations advised. Dress: casual but neat. AE, DC, MC, V. Expensive.*

Southwestern/ **Red Sage.** Within lassoing distance of the White House, this
Tex-Mex upscale rancher's delight has pulled in George Bush and
★ now Bill Clinton–team players since its opening in 1992. Millions were spent on the decor, which includes simulated lightning in thunderclouds, a barbed-wire-and-lizard theme, and a pseudo-adobe rabbit warren of dining rooms. Upstairs is the chili bar, where thrifty trendsetters can enjoy the comparatively inexpensive sandwiches and appetizers. Downstairs, chef Mark Miller's Berkeley/Santa Fe background surfaces in elaborate, artful presentations, such as grilled duck breast with habanero pepper and fig

sausage, spicy lamb chops with wild-mushroom tamale, and even a vegetarian plate with pumpkin-pecan flan. Chilis are everywhere, but the entrées include lighter options now. That's good, because you'll want to save room for homey desserts, such as plum cobbler with cinnamon ice cream. An in-house market sells baked goods and savories. *605 14th St. NW (1 block from Metro Center Metro stop), tel. 202/638–4444. Reservations advised. Dress: casual but neat. AE, DC, MC, V. Closed Sun. lunch. Expensive.*

Spanish **Taberna del Alabardero.** Spanish is spoken here—a regal Castilian that matches the formal dining room and high-class service. You can start with tapas appetizers ranging from a hefty gazpacho to fried calamari and venture to authentic paella, seafood casseroles, and elegant Spanish "country" dishes. The plush, Old World decor and handsome bar create a romantic atmosphere. The clientele is similarly well-heeled and cosmopolitan. *1776 I St. NW (entrance on 18th Street, ½ block from Farragut West Metro stop), tel. 202/429–2200. Reservations advised. Jacket and tie advised. AE, DC, MC, V. Closed Sat. lunch and Sun. Expensive.*

Dupont Circle

Greek **Zorba's Cafe.** A family of four can eat heartily—and tastily—for under $25 at this popular Greek eatery. Two inside levels and outdoor seating in season accommodate fans of Zorba's grilled meat and homey vegetable dishes. The half-chicken marinated in oregano is a winner, but be sure to check out the specials. Vegetarians and light eaters will find much to choose from. Pizza, subs, and sandwiches are available for non-Greek palates. Service is from a counter but moves quickly. The grill is open until 11 PM daily (10 PM Sundays). *1612 20th St. NW (½ block from Q St. exit of Dupont Circle Metro Stop), tel. 202/387–8555. No reservations. Dress: casual. No credit cards. Inexpensive.*

Italian **Vincenzo.** Vincenzo has relaxed somewhat since its early
★ days, when it was so determined to be authentically Italian that it refused to serve butter with the bread. Butter is now available (on request), and the once exclusively seafood menu has been supplemented with a few meat dishes— game in autumn, pork in winter, lamb in spring. But it is still a restaurant for purists who appreciate its commitment to finding the best fish it can and serving it as simply as possible. The fixed-price dinner ($29) includes an appetizer, first course, main dish, side dish, and dessert; lunch is à la carte. Along with its enlarged menu, Vincenzo has expanded its dining space, adding a glassed-in courtyard to an already light and airy space. *1606 20th St. NW (½ block from Q St. exit of Dupont Circle Metro stop), tel. 202/667–0047. Reservations advised. Dress: casual but neat. AE, DC, MC, V. Closed Sat. lunch and Sun. Very Expensive.*

★ **Obelisk.** One of the most exciting restaurants in Washington, Obelisk serves eclectic Italian cuisine, with a small, fixed-price menu ($30–$35) that includes both traditional dishes and chef Peter Pastan's imaginative innovations. The list, which changes daily, usually offers one meat, one fish, and one poultry entrée. The meat is likely to be lamb, with garlic and sage or perhaps anchovies; fish might be a pompano stuffed with bay leaves; a typical poultry selection is the hardly typical pigeon with chanterelles. In winter there is lasagna, but what lasagna—layered with wild mushrooms or with artichokes and sweetbreads. The minimally decorated dining room is tiny, with tables so closely spaced that even whispers can be overheard. *2029 P St. NW (3 blocks from Dupont Circle Metro stop), tel. 202/872–1180. Reservations advised. No no-smoking area. Dress: casual but neat. MC, V. Dinner only. Closed Sun. and last 2 weeks of Aug. Expensive.*

Pizzeria Paradiso. Sharing a kitchen with elite Obelisk, this petite pizzeria sticks to crowd-pleasing basics: pizzas, *panini* (sandwiches), a few salads, and desserts. Although the standard pizza is satisfying, you can enliven things by ordering it with fresh buffalo mozzarella or unusual toppings such as potatoes, capers, and mussels. The sandwiches are assembled with homemade focaccia; the gelato is also a house specialty. The trompe l'oeil ceiling adds space and light to a simple interior. *2029 P St. NW (3 blocks from Dupont Circle Metro stop), tel. 202/223–1245. No reservations. No no-smoking area. Dress: casual. MC, V. Inexpensive.*

Middle Eastern **Bacchus.** Lebanese rather than Greek, Bacchus attracts an older crowd more akin to downtown than Dupont Circle patrons. In the Lebanese tradition, appetizers far outnumber entrées; it is possible to put together a feast just from the list of hot and cold first courses, which include hummus and baba ghannouj, as well as more exotic concoctions of ground beef, eggplant, and yogurt. Among the main courses, *ouzi* (lamb with spiced rice, mushrooms, almonds, and pine kernels), *kafta* (grilled logs of ground beef), and *shish taouk* (grilled chunks of marinated chicken) are outstanding. Service is solicitous but disorganized for such a small room. *1827 Jefferson St. NW (2 blocks from Dupont Circle Metro stop), tel. 202/785–0734; 7945 Norfolk Ave., Bethesda, MD, tel. 301/657–1722. Reservations advised. No no-smoking area. Dress: casual but neat. AE, MC, V. Closed Sat. lunch and Sun. Moderate.*

Skewers. As the name implies, the focus is on kebabs, served with almond-flaked rice or pasta. The lamb with eggplant and the chicken with roasted pepper are the most popular, but filet mignon and shrimp are equally tasty. The vegetable kebabs and the array of appetizers, such as hummus with *foole* (warm baked beans), make this ideal for vegetarians. Minikebabs are available, served either with pita bread or in a salad. If the restaurant is too crowded, you can enjoy the lively coffeehouse style and cheap California eats downstairs at Café Luna (tel. 202/387–4005). *1633 P St. NW (3 blocks from Dupont Circle Metro stop), tel. 202/387–7400. Reservations advised weekends. Dress: casual. AE, DC, MC, V. Moderate.*

New American **Nora.** Although it bills itself as an "organic restaurant," Nora is no collective-run juice bar. The food is sophisticated and attractive, like the quilt-decorated dining room. Starters have included spicy sweet-potato soup and smoked trout, and the obligatory radicchio salad has been enlivened with spicy pecans and bosc pear. Entrées such as fish or lamb liver may be grilled, with a vegetarian plate to offset hearty items such as veal marengo or leg of lamb. Desserts are listed with recommended wines and brandies, such as apple-pecan pie and caramel coffee ice cream with calvados. *2132 Florida Ave. NW (3 blocks from Q St. exit of Dupont Circle Metro stop), tel. 202/462–5143. Reservations advised. Dress: casual but neat. MC, V. Expensive.*

Tabard Inn. With its artfully artless decor and quasi-health-food menu, the Tabard is an idiosyncratic restaurant that has a devoted clientele of baby-boomers with '60s values and '80s incomes. The lounge looks like a garage sale waiting to happen, and the two dining rooms are likewise somewhat shabby. But the courtyard may be Washington's prettiest outdoor eatery, and the Tabard's New American cuisine, although it doesn't always quite come off, is fresh and interesting. The Tabard raises much of its produce, without pesticides, on its own farm; meat is additive free. Most of the menu changes daily; complicated preparations of fish are a specialty. Breakfast and brunch here are a treat. *1739 N St. NW (3 blocks from Dupont Circle Metro stop), tel. 202/833–2668. Reservations advised. Dress: casual. MC, V. Expensive.*

South American/ **Lauriol Plaza.** Located in upper Dupont Circle, halfway to
Spanish Adams-Morgan, this charming corner enclave flirted briefly with Tex-Mex before popular demand restored Spanish dishes to prominence. Tortilla chips and other Mexican/Latin American standards are still available, but sangria and rustic entrées like tongue are specialties. The simply decorated dining room, with white tablecloths and white walls enlivened by gilt-framed paintings, can get noisy; the terrace is preferable in good weather. *1801 18th St. NW, tel. 202/387–0035. No reservations. Dress: casual. AE, DC, MC, V. Moderate.*

Thai **Sala Thai.** This is not the sort of Thai restaurant where you go for the burn; Sala Thai will make the food as spicy as you wish, but the chef is interested in flavor, not fire. Among the subtly seasoned offerings are *panang goong* (shrimp in curry-peanut sauce), chicken sautéed with ginger and pineapple, and flounder with a choice of four sauces. Mirrored walls and soft lights soften the ambience of this small downstairs dining room. *2016 P St. NW (3 blocks from Dupont*

Circle Metro stop), tel. 202/872–1144. Reservations accepted. No no-smoking area. Dress: casual but neat. AE, DC, MC, V. Closed Sun. lunch. Moderate.

Georgetown/West End

Afghani **Bamiyan.** Although the area's best Afghani restaurants are in suburban Virginia, Bamiyan is the oldest in the area and so enjoys a loyal following, even though it does look like a motel that has seen better days. Kebabs—of chicken, beef, or lamb—are succulent. More adventurous souls should try the *quabili palow* (lamb with saffron rice, carrots, and raisins) or the *aushak* (dumplings with scallions, meat sauce, and yogurt). For a side vegetable, order the sautéed pumpkin in season; it's sweet but not cloying. Vegetarians may order any of the side dishes as main courses. *3320 M St. NW, tel. 202/338–1896. Reservations accepted. Dress: casual. AE, MC, V. Closed lunch. Moderate.*

American **Morton's of Chicago.** This national steakhouse chain claims to serve the country's best beef, and it's certainly not the vinyl-boothed dining room that keeps it busy. In the classic steakhouse tradition, Morton's emphasizes quantity as well as quality. The New York strip and porterhouse steaks, two of the most popular offerings, are well over a pound each. For diners with even larger appetites (or those sharing), there's a 3-pound porterhouse. Morton's also includes lamb, veal, chicken, lobster, and grilled fish on its menu—which for some reason is not printed but instead recited by a waiter who displays the raw ingredients on a cart. *3251 Prospect St., tel. 202/342–6258; 8075 Leesburg Pike, Vienna, VA, tel. 703/883–0800. Reservations advised. Jacket and tie advised. AE, DC, MC, V. Closed lunch. Valet parking. Very Expensive.*

American Café. In 1980 someone had the bright idea of opening a Georgetown restaurant that would serve fresh, healthy food—but not health food—at affordable prices in a casual environment. And so the American Café empire was born. Sandwiches, such as the namesake roast beef on a humongous croissant, are still the mainstay of the café, with salads and nibbles rounding off the regular menu. But the list of specials, which changes every two weeks, offers intriguing possibilities: a fresh fish, a seafood pie, a chicken dish, and barbecued ribs. Weekend brunches offer temptations such as strawberry-banana-nut waffles and stuffed French toast. Service can be slow, but families and downtown diners on a budget find the American Cafés a lifesaver. *1211 Wisconsin Ave. NW, tel. 202/944–9464. Also at 227 Massachusetts Ave. NE, tel. 202/547–8500; 1331 Pennsylvania Ave. NW, tel 202/626–0770; 1701 Pennsylvania Ave. NW, tel. 202/833–3434; the Shops at National Place, tel. 202/393–6400; Union Station, tel. 202/682–0937;1200 19th St. NW, tel. 202/223–2121; 5252 Wisconsin Ave. NW, tel. 202/363–5400; and suburban locations. Reservations*

accepted only for large parties. Dress: casual. AE, DC,
MC, V. Inexpensive.

Argentinian **Las Pampas.** Grilled fresh fish and a smattering of Tex-Mex
staples now supplement the traditional Argentinian menu,
which reflects that country's love of beef and its Continental heritage. The beef, which is fresh, not aged, is cooked
over a special grill that simulates charcoal heat; the result is
a firm-textured steak with a crusty surface and a juicy interior. The familiar New York strip and filet mignon are
available from the grill, but the preferred choice is the
churrasco, a special Argentinian cut. The wine list includes
a preponderance of Argentinian vintages. Upstairs, a colorful Southwestern cantina comes alive weekend nights, although the diners in general are a conservative,
international lot. *3291 M St. NW, tel. 202/333–5151. Reservations advised. No no-smoking area. Dress: casual but
neat. AE, DC, MC, V. Closed Sat. lunch. Moderate.*

Barbecue **Old Glory.** Always teeming with visiting Texans, Georgetown students, and closet Elvis fans, the flag-waving Old
Glory sticks to barbecue basics: sandwiches and platters of
pulled and sliced pork, beef brisket, smoked and pulled
chicken, ribs, and sausage. The open pit will also roast vegetables, but they're an unusual choice here. Side dishes are
likely to be succotash, hopping John (black-eyed peas and
rice), or Silver Queen corn on the cob in season. Desserts
are also Southern influenced: tin roof sundae, coconut-cherry cobbler and fresh fruit pies. *3139 M St. NW, tel. 202/337–
3406. Reservations accepted for large groups. Dress: casual. AE, DC, MC, V. Moderate.*

French **Bistro Français.** This French country restaurant is a favorite among the city's chefs. What do the professionals order
when they want to eat someone else's cooking? The minute
steak maître d'hôtel, a sirloin with herb butter, accompanied by french fries. Among amateur eaters, the big draw is
the rotisserie chicken. Though the bistro excels at such simple fare, it also does well with the more complicated dishes
it offers on the extensive list of daily specials, such as suprême of salmon with broccoli mousse and beurre blanc.
The restaurant is divided into two parts—the café side and
the more formal dining room; the café menu includes sandwiches and omelets in addition to the entrées. The bistro
also offers $13 fixed-price lunches and $15 early and late-night dinner specials and stays open until 2:45 AM Sunday–
Thursday, 3:45 AM Friday and Saturday. *3128 M St. NW, tel.
202/338–3830. Reservations advised. Dress: casual but
neat. AE, DC, MC, V. Moderate.*

La Chaumière. A longtime favorite of Washingtonians
seeking an escape from the hurly-burly of Georgetown, La
Chaumière has the rustic charm of a French country inn,
particularly during the winter, when its central stone fireplace warms the room. The food is country French, with an
emphasis on seafood—crab meat in a crêpe, mussels, and

scampi are on the regular menu, and there is usually a grilled fish special and a seafood brochette. The restaurant also has a devoted following for its meat dishes, which include such hard-to-find entrées as blood sausage and calf's brain. Many local diners plan their meals around La Chaumière's rotating specials, particularly the couscous on Wednesday and the cassoulet on Thursday. *2813 M St. NW, tel. 202/338–1784. Reservations required.No no-smoking area. Jacket and tie advised. AE, DC, MC, V. Closed Sat. lunch. and Sun. 2-hr validated parking at dinner at Four Seasons Hotel lot. Expensive.*

Le Caprice. With only nine tables (and a sidewalk café in season), this classic French restaurant can be hard to get into. Those who do enter will find exceptional fixed-price bargains ($12.50 lunch, $18.50 and $29.50 dinners) featuring intricate creations such as salmon napoleon, smoked liver pâté with figs and Gruyère salad, velvety soups, and wild game entrées with savory stuffings. Alsatian specialties such as sausages and duck confit with turnips in white wine augment the Parisian-influenced menu. The wine list contains rare and older vintages. *2348 Wisconsin Ave. NW, tel. 202/337–3394. Reservations advised. No no-smoking area. Jacket and tie advised. AE, DC, MC, V. Closed weekend lunch and Mon. Expensive.*

Indian **Aditi.** At first glance this two-story dining room seems to be too elegant for a moderately priced Indian restaurant. The dim interior features burgundy carpets and chairs and pale mint-colored walls with brass sconces. There's a small first floor, with a dramatic staircase leading to a larger room with windows that overlook the busy street. But the decor is not the only draw: Tandoor and curry dishes, although not aggressively spiced, are otherwise expertly prepared. The rice *biryani* entrées are good for lighter appetites, and $4.95 will get you a delicious bread sampler. *3299 M St. NW, tel. 202/625–6825.Dress: casual but neat. AE, DC, MC, V. Closed Mon. lunch. Moderate.*

Madurai. Although the dining room (just above Zed's restaurant) is plain and worn, the extensive menu and well-prepared dishes at this all-vegetarian Indian establishment make up for the ambience. Seasonings range from mild to piquant, with hot spices largely contained in side condiments. The mushroom, eggplant, and exotic lotus root curries are specialties. Students and other cost-conscious diners stake out the restaurant's Sunday buffet (noon to 4 and 5 to 10 PM), which offers all-you-can-eat curries, basmati rice and Indian breads for $6.95. Service is pleasant but languid. *3318 M St. NW, tel. 202/333–0997. Reservations accepted. Dress: casual. AE, MC, V. Inexpensive.*

Indonesian **Sarinah Satay House.** All you can see of this delightful restaurant from busy Wisconsin Avenue is its wooden sign above a green door. Open it, follow the stairs down and up again, and you're in a lush, enclosed garden with real trees growing through the ceiling. Carved monkeys, parrots, and puppets add to the setting, where batik-clad waiters offer serenely unrushed service. The food is exquisite. Potato croquettes and the traditional *loempia* and *resoles* (crisp and soft spring rolls) come with a tangy, chili-spiked peanut dipping sauce, while the perfectly grilled chicken *satay* is accompanied by a smoky-sweet peanut dip. A bargain is the combination *nasi rames:* chicken in coconut sauce, beef skewers, and spicy green beans with rice ($7.95). Vegetarians may order well-seasoned noodle, rice, and vegetable dishes. Cool your palate afterward with an *es teler*, a shaved-ice dessert with exotic fruits. *1338 Wisconsin Ave. NW, tel. 202/337–2955. Reservations advised. Dress: casual but neat. AE, DC, MC, V. Closed Sun. lunch and Mon. Moderate.*

Japanese Unkai. The suburbs are the place to find Japanese bargains; the high prices in town mean you may as well treat yourself to the best. The Japanese-run ANA Hotel naturally hosts one of the most authentic and exquisite restaurants. Tea-ceremony rituals gave rise to the artful *kaiseki* meals served in a *tatami* (rice mat) room such as those re-created here—they begin at $50 per person. The main dining room with its *teppanyaki* grill offers more reasonably priced fare, from a $6.50 business lunch including soup and salad to sushi and sashimi raw-fish samplers ($22 to $24). Exotic ice creams such as red bean, ginger, and green tea round off the thoroughly Japanese experience. *1250 24th St. NW (4½ blocks from Foggy Bottom/GWU Metro stop), tel. 202/466–2299. Reservations advised. Dress: casual but neat (jacket and tie advised for tatami room). AE, DC, MC, V. Closed Sun. Expensive.*

New American The River Club. Until someone invents a time machine, there is no better way to experience the Jazz Age than by taking a trip to the River Club, an art deco extravaganza in an out-of-the-way part of Georgetown. Decorated in ebony, silver, neon, and marble, the River Club is in fact a club, with a disc jockey who plays '30s and '40s music for the two dance floors. After several chef changes, the menu, which changes seasonally, is no longer limited to Asian-American creations. There might also be veal stuffed with wild mushrooms, swordfish with mint pesto, and grilled chicken stuffed with goat cheese. You can also stick with caviar, champagne, or "tasting" portions. *3223 K St. NW, tel. 202/333–8118. Reservations advised. Jacket and tie required. AE, DC, MC, V. Closed lunch and Sun. Valet parking available. Expensive.*

Seafood Sea Catch. Despite the proximity of Chesapeake Bay, Washington isn't known for casual seafood restaurants or crab houses the way nearby Baltimore is. At this formal establishment, hidden in a courtyard overlooking the C & O Canal from busy M Street, the standards at least match the high prices. A gleaming raw bar offers huge shrimp, farm-raised clams and oysters, and American caviar with black-bean blinis. The jumbo crab cakes have little filler, but the scallops are plump, just cooked, and lightly dressed. The entrées come ungarnished; a side order of potatoes, mushrooms with pecans, or sautéed spinach can be shared. The staff is likely to bring you a complimentary aperitif if you have to wait for your lobster or other cooked-to-order entrée. *1054 31st St. NW, tel. 202/337–8855. Reservations advised. Jacket and tie advised. AE, DC, MC, V. Closed Sun. Free valet parking adjacent to courtyard entrance off 31st St. Expensive.*

8 Lodging

By Jan Ziegler
Updated by
Jeanne Cooper

Although the nation's capital rode a hotel boom in the 1980s, the emphasis these days is on renovation rather than new construction. Still, visitors who plan to spend the night, a week, or a month in DC will find a large variety of accommodations from which to choose. Hostelries include grand hotels with glorious histories, quiet Victorian inns, the hotel and motel chains common to every American city, and small independently operated hotels that offer little more than good location, a smile, and a comfortable, clean place to lay your head.

Because Washington is an international city, nearly all hotel staffs are multilingual. All hotels in the Expensive and Very Expensive categories have concierges; some in the Moderate group do, too. All of the hotels here are air-conditioned. All the large hotels and many of the smaller ones offer meeting facilities and special features for business travelers, ranging from state-of-the-art teleconferencing equipment to modest conference rooms with outside catering. Unlike those in many cities, nearly all of the finer hotels have superb restaurants; the traditionally high inhouse prices are almost completely justified.

Not all the city's hotels are included here; there are simply too many to list. Most of the major chains have hotels at desirable locations throughout town. For a complete listing of hotels in the area, contact the Washington D.C. Convention and Visitors' Association (1212 New York Ave. NW, Washington, DC 20005, tel. 202/789–7000). **Capitol Reservations** books rooms at over 70 better hotels in good locations at rates 20%–40% off; call 202/842–4187 or 800/VISIT–DC from 9 to 6 weekdays.

A word about reservations: They are crucial. Hotels are often full of conventioneers, politicians in transit, or families and school groups in search of cherry blossoms and monuments. If you're interested in visiting Washington at a calmer time—and if you can stand tropical weather—come in July or August, during the congressional recess. You may not spot many VIPs, but hotels will have more rooms to offer, and you'll be able to relax (August, however, is the busiest season for the Washington International Youth Hostel, so budget travelers should seek alternatives at this time).

The hotel reviews here are grouped according to price categories. Keep in mind that rates are variable and can be significantly lower depending on season and whether they are part of a group, corporate, or weekend package. Also, some of the older hotels have a few smaller rooms that rent for prices in a lower category. It's always worth a call to check for special rates.

Unless otherwise noted below, hotels charge extra for parking. Rates range from $5 to $15 a night, depending on how close to downtown you are. An 11% room tax and a $1.50 per night occupancy tax will be added to your bill.

Highly recommended lodgings are indicated by a star ★.

Category	Cost*
Very Expensive	over $190
Expensive	$145–$190
Moderate	$100–$145
Inexpensive	under $100

All prices are for a standard double room, excluding 11% room tax and $1.50 per night occupancy tax.

Bed-and-Breakfasts To find reasonably priced accommodations in small guest houses and private homes, contact either of the following bed-and-breakfast services: **Bed 'n' Breakfast Ltd. of Washington, D.C.** (Box 12011, Washington, DC 20005, tel. 202/328–3510) or **Bed and Breakfast League, Ltd.**, (3639 Van Ness St. NW, Washington, DC 20008, tel. 202/363–7767).

Home Exchange This is obviously an inexpensive solution to the lodging problem, because house-swapping means living rent-free. You find a house, apartment, or other vacation property to exchange for your own by becoming a member of a home-exchange organization, which then sends you its annual directories listing available exchanges and includes your own listing in at least one of them. Arrangements for the actual exchange are made by the two parties to it, not by the organization. Principal clearinghouses include **Intervac U.S./International Home Exchange** (Box 590504, San Francisco, CA 94159, tel. 415/435–3497), the oldest, with thousands of foreign and domestic homes for exchange in its three annual directories; membership is $62, or $72 if you want to receive the directories but remain unlisted. The **Vacation Exchange Club** (Box 650, Key West, FL 33041, tel. 800/638–3841), also with thousands of foreign and domestic listings, publishes four annual directories plus updates; the $50 membership includes your listing in one book. **Loan-a-Home** (2 Park La., Apt. 6E, Mount Vernon, NY 10552, tel. 914/664–7640) specializes in long-term exchanges; there is no charge to list your home, but the directories cost $35 or $45 depending on the number you receive.

Apartment and Villa Rentals If you want a home base that's roomy enough for a family and comes with cooking facilities, a furnished rental may be the solution. It's generally costwise, too, although not always—some rentals are luxury properties (economical only when your party is large). Home-exchange directories do list rentals—often second homes owned by prospective house swappers—and there are services that can not only look for a house or apartment for you (even a castle if that's your fancy) but also handle the paperwork. Some send an illustrated catalogue and others send photographs of specific properties, sometimes at a charge; up-front registration fees may apply.

Among the companies are **Interhome Inc.** (124 Little Falls Rd., Fairfield, NJ 07004, tel. 201/882–6864); **Overseas Connection** (31 North Harbor Dr., Sag Harbor, NY 11963, tel. 516/725–9308); and **Rent a Home International** (7200 34th Ave. NW, Seattle, WA 98117, tel. 206/789–9377 or 800/488–7368). **Hideaways International** (15 Goldsmith St., Box 1270, Littleton, MA 01460, tel. 508/486–8955 or 800/843–4433) functions as a travel club. Membership ($79 yearly per person or family at the same address) includes two annual guides plus quarterly newsletters; rentals are arranged directly between members, not by the club staff.

Capitol Hill

Very Expensive **Hyatt Regency on Capitol Hill.** One of the chain's more spartan entries in Washington, this hotel has the typical Hyatt garden atrium but with high-tech edges. Close to Union Station and the Mall, this is a mecca for families and for businesspeople with dealings on the Hill. In 1991, the Hyatt Regency completed a $14 million renovation of all guest rooms. Suites on the south side have a view of the Capitol dome, which is just a few blocks away. Sunday brunch at the Park Promenade restaurant is popular. *400 New Jersey Ave. NW, 20001, tel. 202/737–1234 or 800/233–1234. 803 rooms, 31 suites. Facilities: 24-hr room service; 3 restaurants; 2 bars; health club with weight equipment, steam room, sauna, pool; parking. AE, DC, MC, V.*

Washington Court. Formerly the Sheraton Grand, this luxury hotel is one of the few hostelries in DC where it is possible to make a truly grand entrance. Guests descend three terraced tiers of polished steps into an atrium surmounted by a skylight. It shares its view of the Capitol with the Hyatt and others on the same street. *525 New Jersey Ave. NW, 20001, tel. 202/628–2100 or 800/321–3010. 250 rooms, 15 suites. Facilities: room service 6:30 AM–11 PM; bar; restaurant; health club with Nautilus, free weights, treadmills, rowing machines, stationary bicycles; valet parking. AE, DC, MC, V.*

Expensive **Phoenix Park Hotel.** Just steps from Union Station and only four blocks from the Capitol, this high-rise hotel has an Irish club theme and is the home of the Dubliner, one of Washington's best bars. Leather, wood paneling, and leaded glass abound in the bar's re-creation of the decor favored by the 18th-century Irish gentry; guest rooms are bright, traditionally furnished, and quiet. Penthouse suites have fireplaces. The Powerscourt Restaurant is named after an Irish castle and imports chefs from the Emerald Isle annually to enhance its already popular Celtic-Continental fare. The hotel is expanding services for hearing-impaired guests, such as Gallaudet University visitors. *520 North Capitol St. NW, 20001, tel. 202/638–6900 or 800/824–5419.*

Washington Lodging

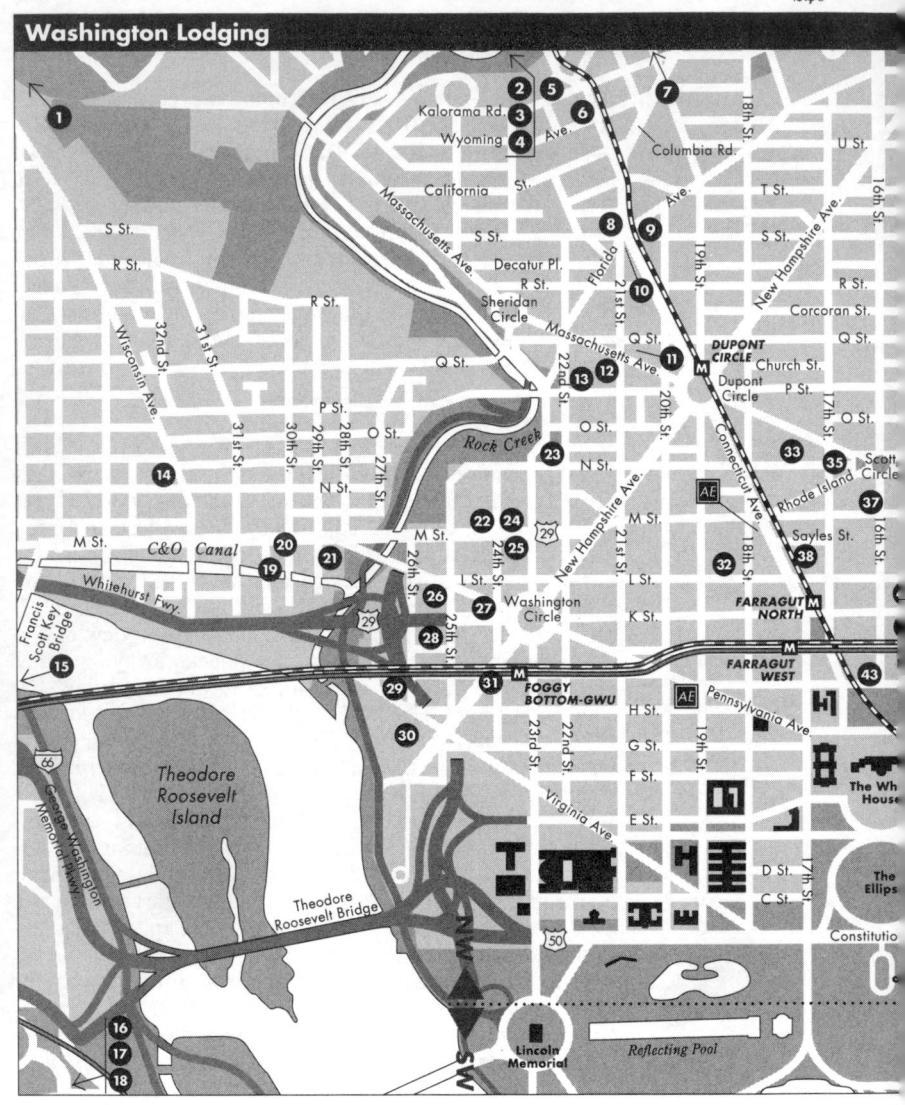

ANA Hotel, **22**
Bellevue Hotel, **55**
Capital Hilton, **41**
Capitol Hill Suites, **59**
Crystal City Marriott, **16**
Days Inn Connecticut Avenue, **2**

Embassy Row Hotel, **11**
Embassy Suites, **23**
Four Seasons Hotel, **1**
Georgetown Dutch Inn, **19**
Georgetown Inn, **14**
Grand Hotel, **25**
Grand Hyatt, **48**
Guest Quarters, **26, 31**
Hay-Adams Hotel, **43**
Henley Park Hotel, **46**

Holiday Inn Central, **34**
Holiday Inn Crowne Plaza at Metro Center, **49**
Holiday Inn Governor's House, **35**
Hotel Anthony, **32**
Hotel Tabard Inn, **33**

Hotel Washington, **50**
Hotel Windsor Park, **5**
Howard Johnson Kennedy Center, **29**
Hyatt Regency Bethesda, **1**
Hyatt Regency on Capitol Hill, **57**
Jefferson Hotel, **37**
J.W. Marriott, **52**
Kalorama Guest House, **7**
Key Bridge Marriott, **15**

Latham Hotel, **20**	Omni Shoreham Hotel, **4**
Loew's L'Enfant Plaza, **58**	Park Hyatt, **24**
The Madison Hotel, **40**	Phoenix Park Hotel, **54**
Mayflower, **38**	Pullman Highland Hotel, **10**
Morrison House, **17**	Quality Hotel Capitol Hill, **56**
Morrison-Clark Inn Hotel, **44**	Quality Hotel Central, **8**
Normandy Inn, **6**	Quality Hotel Silver Spring, **36**
Omni Georgetown, **13**	

Renaissance Hotel-Techworld, **47**	Washington Court, **53**
The Ritz-Carlton, **12**	The Washington Hilton and Towers, **9**
Ritz-Carlton, Pentagon City, **18**	Washington International AYH-Hostel, **45**
River Inn, **28**	Washington Vista Hotel, **39**
Sheraton Carlton Hotel, **42**	Watergate Hotel, **30**
Sheraton Washington Hotel, **3**	The Willard Inter-Continental, **51**
	Wyndham Bristol Hotel, **27**

84 rooms, 6 suites. Facilities: 2 restaurants, complimentary newspaper, valet parking. AE, DC, MC, V.

Moderate **Bellevue Hotel.** This charming and comfortable hotel has been in business for 65 years. The public rooms on the main floor have balconies and are modeled after great halls in manor houses of yore. Accommodations here are standard modest-hotel fare, but the staff is friendly. The location is convenient, near Union Station and major Metrorail stations and within six blocks of the Supreme Court and the Smithsonian museums. *15 E St. NW, 20001, tel. 202/638–0900 or 800/327–6667. 138 rooms, 2 suites. Facilities: restaurant, bar, library, free overnight parking. AE, DC, MC, V.*

Capitol Hill Suites. Tucked away on a quiet street behind the Madison Building of the Library of Congress, this former apartment building has been converted into an all-suite hotel. Its proximity to the House office buildings means that it is often filled with visiting lobbyists when Congress is in session, and its location makes it an ideal spot to get a feel for both residential and official Washington. A complete refurbishment was completed in 1990; all rooms have kitchens and are attractively furnished in Queen Anne style with a blue-and-rose color scheme. *200 C St. SE, 20003, tel. 202/543–6000. 152 suites. Facilities: in-room kitchens, access to health club, valet parking. AE, DC, MC, V.*

Quality Hotel Capitol Hill. A good value for the budget-minded traveler (some rooms are as low as $59), this hotel shares the block with the Hyatt and offers the same views and convenient location. A complete renovation of the hotel, including all guest rooms, was completed in 1990. *415 New Jersey Ave. NW, 20001, tel. 202/638–1616 or 800/ 228–5151. 341 rooms, 5 suites. Facilities: room service 6:30 AM–11 PM, restaurant, outdoor rooftop pool, free parking. AE, DC, MC, V.*

Downtown

Very Expensive **Capital Hilton.** There are three advantages here: location, location, and location. The busy Capital Hilton is not only just up the street from official Washington, including the White House and many monuments, but also smack in the middle of the K Street business corridor. Built in 1943 as a Statler Hotel, the building underwent a $55 million renovation in 1990 that enlarged rooms by a third. Now the theme is neo–art deco, with torchères, winding staircases, and columns finished with milled cherrywood. Rooms are sleekly furnished in shades of emerald green and salmon. The Towers section on the top four floors offers VIP accommodations. The Twigs restaurant has better food and service than the on-site Trader Vic's; still, the ticky-tacky tropical theme room is a tradition with some businesspeople. *1001 16th St. NW, 20036, tel. 202/393–1000 or 800/445–8667. 515* *rooms, 34 suites. Facilities: 24-hr room service; 2 restaurants; valet parking; barber and beauty salon; health club with treadmills, Nautilus equipment, steam room, sauna, tanning bed. AE, DC, MC, V.*

Grand Hyatt. Imagine a 1930s movie-musical set. Studio-built walls of a Mediterranean hillside village rise around a courtyard; a gazebo and curved lounge and dining areas surround a blue lagoon fed by waterfalls. On a small island in the lagoon is a man in black tie playing Cole Porter tunes on a white grand piano. The Hyatt has created just such a fanciful interior in this bustling new high-rise hotel that successfully compensates for the relative drabness of the neighborhood. Opened in June 1987, the Grand is across the street from the Washington Convention Center and just steps away from downtown shopping and theaters. Quiet, contemporary rooms are reached by glass-walled elevators; some suites have whirlpools or saunas. Conference suites are popular with businesspeople who may need to meet clients in their rooms. The Zephyr Deli is a popular lunch spot; the Grand Cafe features country breakfasts on weekends. Via Pacifica, the latest addition, offers Asian-American fare. *1000 H St. NW, 20001, tel. 202/582–1234 or 800/228–9000. 847 rooms, 61 suites. Facilities: 24-hr room service, 3 restaurants, bar, multilingual staff, health club, valet parking. AE, DC, MC, V.*

★ **Hay-Adams Hotel.** Built in 1927, the Hay-Adams sits upon the site of houses owned by John Hay and Henry Adams, social and political paragons in turn-of-the-century Washington. Italian Renaissance in design, the hotel looks like a mansion in disguise. Seventeenth-century Medici tapestries grace two lobby walls, and the John Hay Room restaurant seems to belong to an English Tudor residence. The guest rooms are the most brightly colored in the city, decorated in 23 different English-country-house schemes. Rooms on the south side have a picture-postcard view of the White House. Some rooms have kitchenettes, but the guests here are unlikely to cook for themselves. The hotel's afternoon tea is renowned, and the Adams Room is a popular spot for power breakfasts. The staff is dignified and friendly. *1 Lafayette Sq. NW, 20006, tel. 202/638–6600 or 800/424–5054. 123 rooms, 20 suites. Facilities: 24-hr room service, 3 restaurants, bar, valet parking. AE, DC, MC, V.*

★ **Jefferson Hotel.** Incoming and outgoing administration officials have stayed at the Jefferson since it opened. The undistinguished exterior of this 1923 building is deceiving; past the tiny foyer the atmosphere is classically elegant and smacks of the 18th and early 19th centuries. Rooms are furnished with antiques and reproductions as well as original art. Double-glass windows ensure quiet on a busy intersection. The restaurant features the widely praised New American cooking of chef Will Greenwood. The staff of this small hotel remembers guests' names and greets them by name; laundry is hand ironed and delivered in wicker baskets. *1200 16th St. NW, 20036, tel. 202/347–2200 or 800/*

*368–5966. 68 rooms, 32 suites. Facilities: 24-hr room ser-
vice, restaurant, bar, access to health club, multilingual
staff, valet parking. AE, DC, MC, V.*

J.W. Marriott. Opened in 1984, this large, glossy hotel is in
a prime location on Pennsylvania Avenue, close to the
White House and next door to the National Theatre. Rooms
are furnished in quiet colors. The best views are on the
Pennsylvania Avenue side. On other sides, you may end up
looking across a courtyard at the blank windows of another
section of the complex. Guests have indoor access to the National Press Building and the shops and restaurants of National Place. The signature dessert at the French/Oriental
Celadon restaurant is Painter's Palette, made of chocolate
topped with fruit sorbets. *1331 Pennsylvania Ave. NW,
20004, tel. 202/393–2000 or 800/228–9290. 732 rooms, 41
suites. Facilities: 24-hr room service, 4 restaurants, bar,
health club with Universal weights and stationary bikes,
indoor pool, valet parking. AE, DC, MC, V.*

The Madison Hotel. Elegance and fine service are the hall-
marks of the Madison, where guests may be visiting heads
of state or interview subjects of the *Washington Post,*
whose office is across the street. Deceivingly contemporary
on the outside, the 14-story Madison was built to house not
only guests from around the world but a world-class collection of antiques, Oriental rugs, and fine art. Even the front
lobby is graced by a rare antique Chinese altar table. The
guest rooms are also furnished with antiques and reproductions, and the Madison's suites are among the most opulent
and unhotellike in Washington. Renovated in 1992, the
rooms and suites are decorated in peach or blue tones and
Oriental touches. A fitness center was scheduled to open in
1993. The elegant Montpelier restaurant will give many
reasons to use it. *15th and M Sts. NW, 20005, tel. 202/862–
1600 or 800/424–8577. 318 rooms, 35 suites. Facilities: 24-
hr room service, 2 restaurants, bar, access to health club
with pool, valet parking. AE, DC, MC, V.*

Mayflower. The Mayflower was opened in 1925 for Calvin
Coolidge's inauguration and continues to be a central part
of Washington life. The renovated ornate lobby gleams
with gilded trim and electrified candelabra. Renovated in
1992, the rooms feature custom-designed furniture, warmly colored fabrics, full marble bathrooms, and indirect
lighting. Seventy-four suites have the original but non-
working fireplaces. A Japanese-style breakfast is offered,
afternoon tea is popular, and the Nicholas restaurant offers
sophisticated New American cuisine. The Mayflower is
steps from the K Street business corridor, the White
House, and Dupont Circle. *1127 Connecticut Ave. NW,
20036, tel. 202/347–3000 or 800/468–3571. 659 rooms, 82
suites. Facilities: 24-hr room service; 2 restaurants; bar;
fitness center with stationary bicycles, stair climbers, exercise machines, sauna; shops; access to National Capital
YMCA; parking at nearby garage. AE, DC, MC, V.*

Renaissance Hotel–Techworld. This 15-story hotel opened

in 1989 as part of Washington's World Technology Trade
Center, just across from the Washington Convention Center. A completely equipped convention hotel, even including a "secure" auditorium for top-secret meetings, the
Renaissance is primed for business travelers. The hotel's
spacious rooms are decorated in teal and cinnamon, with
mahogany furniture and floral upholstery. The Renaissance Club Tower, a hotel within a hotel served by private
elevators and a full-time concierge, pampers business travelers. The lobby's Chinese rock garden and fountain remind
guests of their proximity to Washington's Chinatown, and
the Techworld complex brings more than 50 shops, including a bank, florist, car-rental agency, and travel agency,
close to the hotel. The on-site Floreale restaurant features
seasonal menus of Continental fare. *999 9th St. NW, 20001,
tel. 202/898–9000 or 800/228–9898. 779 rooms, 21 suites.
Facilities: 24-hr room service; 2 restaurants; bar; valet
parking; health club with indoor pool, sauna, steam room,
whirlpool, weights, aerobics studio. AE, DC, MC, V.*
Sheraton Carlton Hotel. Entering the Sheraton Carlton is
like stepping into an updated Italian Renaissance mansion:
Gilt, carved wood, stone, plaster, and 19th-century details
abound. This hotel is in a bustling business sector, yet the
rooms are quiet and service is cordial and dignified. Built in
1926, the hotel underwent a $20 million face-lift, which be-
gan in 1988, in the course of which all rooms were completely refurbished and renovated. The rooms are decorated in
pastel colors and are furnished with antiques and reproductions. The ornate Allegro dining room serves Italian cuisine. *923 16th St. NW, 20006, tel. 202/638–2626 or 800/325–
3535. 184 rooms, 13 suites. Facilities: 24-hr room service,
personal safes in rooms, 3 telephones and 2 telephone lines
in each room, restaurant, bar, exercise room, exercise
equipment delivered to room, valet parking. AE, DC, MC,
V.*
★ **The Willard Inter-Continental.** "This hotel, in fact, may be
much more justly called the center of Washington and the
Union than either the Capitol, the White House, or the
State Department," Nathaniel Hawthorne wrote while
covering the Civil War. Indeed, the Willard, whose present
building dates from 1901, welcomed every American president from Franklin Pierce in 1853 to Dwight Eisenhower in
the 1950s. But the huge building fell on hard times and
closed in 1968. When renovation began in 1984, grass was
growing in the rooms and a tree had sprouted in one of the
restaurants. The new Willard is a faithful renovation, pre-
senting an opulent, beaux arts feast to the eye. Rooms are
furnished with mahogany Queen Anne reproductions; all
have a minibar. The sixth floor, which was designed with
the help of the Secret Service and the State Department,
has lodged numerous heads of state. One of the restaurants
here, the Willard Room, has won nationwide acclaim, and
the "Willard Collection" of shops includes Chanel and other
designer boutiques. *1401 Pennsylvania Ave. NW, 20004,*

tel. 202/628–9100 or 800/327–0200. 290 rooms, 50 suites (8 rooms designed for the handicapped). Facilities: 24-hr room service, 3 restaurants, 2 bars, valet parking. AE, DC, MC, V.

Expensive **Henley Park Hotel.** Constructed as an apartment building
★ in 1918 and converted to a small hotel in 1983, the Henley
Park offers a bit of Britain in the still dodgy neighborhood
near the Washington Convention Center. Though the architecture is Tudor style, the decor is Edwardian; a cozy sitting room with working fireplace could well have been
transplanted from an English country house. Afternoon tea
here is renowned, and the Coeur de Lion serves traditional
Continental meals. Guest rooms are warmly furnished with
chintz and Oriental porcelain lamps. The hotel is in an iffy
area that's only a short ride on public transportation to the
major sites, but it's best to take a cab if you're returning after dark. *926 Massachusetts Ave. NW, 20001, tel. 202/638–
5200 or 800/222–8474. 78 rooms, 18 suites. Facilities: 24-hr
room service, restaurant, bar, access to health club, valet
parking. AE, DC, MC, V.*

Holiday Inn Crowne Plaza at Metro Center. "Holiday Inn"
has come to be synonymous with standard American motel
decor, but this one belies all preconceptions, from the enormous mauve marble registration desk to the artwork
throughout the hotel especially commissioned from
Washington artists. The hotel's restaurant and bar—Metro
Center Grille and Bar—is a handsome two-level facility
decorated in mahogany, oak, brass, and marble. The New
American cuisine of executive chef Melissa Balinger has
made the restaurant a popular downtown lunch and dinner
spot for locals as well as guests. The larger-than-average
rooms, decorated in mauve and soft blue, are more comfortable than luxurious. Each has a desk and two easy chairs.
Two executive floors offer a complimentary Continental
breakfast, a courtesy bar, and a private lounge. *775 12th St.
NW, 20005, tel. 202/737–2200 or 800/465–4329. 453 rooms,
12 suites. Facilities: 24-hr room service; valet parking; restaurant; bar; health club with whirlpool, sauna, Lifecycles, StairMaster, rowing machines, Universal weights,
aerobics, indoor pool. AE, DC, MC, V.*

Washington Vista Hotel. This 14-story member of the Hilton International family is a few blocks from the White
House, the Washington Convention Center, and the K
Street business corridor. Designed to look like an urban
town square, the Vista features a garden-courtyard lobby
that is flooded by light from a 130-foot window facing M
Street. Guest rooms and restaurants are located in the surrounding towerlike structures. Opened in 1983, the hotel
has hosted Elizabeth Taylor, Kirk Douglas, and countless
business travelers from the United States and abroad; it
gained undeserved notoriety as the site of then-Mayor Marion Barry's arrest in 1990. Rooms are contemporary in design and decorated in earth tones, burgundy, and green.

The Presidential Suite and six other suites were designed by Hubert de Givenchy; these have whirlpools, French silk and cotton-blend wall coverings, and original artwork from France. *1400 M St. NW, 20005, tel. 202/429–1700 or 800/ 847–8232. 386 rooms, 14 suites. Facilities: 24-hr room service, 2 restaurants, 2 bars, health club with sauna, multilingual staff, baby-sitting service, valet parking. AE, DC, MC, V.*

Moderate **Holiday Inn Governor's House.** This hotel, often confused with the Central Holiday Inn down the road, is closer to the White House and Dupont Circle. All guest rooms were refurbished in the spring of 1990. The staff is friendly. Herb's Restaurant draws a lively professional and arty crowd. Families can take advantage of the rooms with kitchenettes. *1615 Rhode Island Ave. NW, 20036, tel. 202/296– 2100 or 800/821–4367. 152 rooms, 8 suites; 24 rooms have kitchenettes. Facilities: room service 7 AM–midnight, restaurant, bar, outdoor pool, access to health club, parking. AE, DC, MC, V.*

Hotel Anthony. This small hotel with courteous staff offers the basics in the midst of the K and L streets business district, close to the White House. Some rooms have a full kitchen, some a wet bar; king, queen, or extra-long double beds are available. *1823 L St. NW, 20036, tel. 202/223–4320 or 800/424–2970. 99 rooms. Facilities: room service 7 AM– 10 PM, restaurant, access to health club, parking. AE, DC, MC, V.*

★ **Hotel Washington.** Since its opening in 1918, this hostelry has been known as the hotel with a view. Washingtonians bring visitors to the outdoor rooftop bar for cocktails and a view of the White House grounds and the Washington Monument. The oldest continuously operating hostelry in the city and now a national landmark, the Hotel Washington sprang from the drawing boards of John Carrère and Thomas Hastings, who designed the New York Public Library. Renovated in 1987, the hotel has retained its Edwardian character. The guest rooms, some of which look directly onto the White House grounds, are furnished with antique reproductions; the windows are festooned with swags, heavy drapes, and lace underdrapes. Antique beiges predominate. Suite 506 is where Elvis Presley stayed on his trips to DC. Rates border on the expensive. *515 15th St. NW, 20004, tel. 202/638–5900. 344 rooms, 17 suites. Facilities: room service 7 AM–11 PM, restaurant, outdoor café, lounge, fitness center. AE, DC, MC, V.*

★ **Morrison-Clark Inn Hotel.** Victorian with an airy, modern twist, this unusual historic inn was created by merging two 1864 town houses. Appended to one of the houses is a 1917 Chinese Chippendale porch; Oriental touches echo throughout the public rooms, which also boast marble fireplaces and 14-foot-high mirrors with original gilding. Antique-filled rooms—some with bay windows, fireplaces, or access to a porch—have different personalities; one called the "deer and bunny room" because of its decorative trim, harbors a bedspread once owned by the mistress of a fin-de-siècle mayor of New York. A new addition contains 40 rooms in the neoclassical style. Country rooms are plainly furnished with pine, wicker, and rattan. The restaurant, with its New American–Southern cuisine has been roundly praised; a complimentary Continental breakfast is served. Take a cab to the hotel after dark. *Massachusetts Ave. and 11th St. NW, 20001, tel. 202/898–1200 or 800/332–7898. 54 rooms. Facilities: room service during meal periods, restaurant, valet parking. AE, DC, MC, V.*

Inexpensive **Holiday Inn Central.** After an eight-month renovation, this Holiday Inn overlooking Scott Circle reopened in June 1991 with a fresh approach to elegance on a budget. The rooms, a mix of parlor suites and deluxe rooms, are generally spacious. There are two nonsmoking floors. Teal predominates in the bright, attractive lobby, which hosts a bar and the Avenue Café and Lounge. The rooftop pool is open in summer. The McPherson Square Metro is four blocks away, although a cab is advised at night. *1501 Rhode Island Ave. NW, 20005, tel. 202/483–2000 or 800/465–4329. 183 rooms, 30 suites. Facilities: room service, restaurant, bar, exercise room, game room, rooftop pool, laundry, valet, gift shop, underground parking. AE, DC, MC, V.*

Washington International AYH-Hostel. This well-kept hostel offers clean dormitory rooms with 250 bunk beds and a kitchen, laundry room, and living room. Single men and women are in separate rooms; families are given their own room if the hostel is not full. Although blankets and pillows are provided, you must rent sheets for a nominal charge ($2 in 1993) or bring your own. The hostel also sponsors tours, movies, and other programs. Registration is from 7 AM until 2 AM, but exercise caution in this downtown neighborhood if you arrive here at night. The price for American Youth Hostels members is $15 ($18 for nonmembers); the maximum stay is six days, with extensions at the manager's discretion. Naturally, youthful European travelers predominate. *1009 11th St. NW, 20001, tel. 202/737–2333 (message in English, French, German, Spanish, and Japanese). 250 beds. Facilities: kitchen, laundry, travel store, lockers/baggage storage. MC, V.*

Dupont Circle

Very Expensive **Pullman Highland Hotel.** After having undergone a $6-million renovation, the 1906 Highland Hotel is now being managed by the French Pullman hotel group, the group's first venture in the United States. The hotel is small, 145 rooms, and the management is striving for the ambience of a small European luxury hotel. Decorated in warm peach tones with traditional furniture, the rooms are among the largest in any Washington hotel. All rooms have separate work spaces and three telephones. The Trocadero Café, an upscale American bistro, serves breakfast, lunch, and dinner; Sunday brunch is popular with locals. A fully equipped business center with translation service is available, and conference facilities accommodate up to 150 people. *1914 Connecticut Ave. NW, tel. 202/797–2000 or 800/424–2464. 108 rooms, 37 suites. Facilities: 24-hr room service, restaurant, bar, multilingual concierge, laundry and dry cleaning, massage, hair styling, access to health club and pool, valet parking. AE, DC, MC, V.*

★ **The Ritz-Carlton.** One of the nicest things to do at the Ritz on a winter day (aside from stay there) is to have a drink or afternoon tea in front of the fire in the warm, woody Fairfax Bar. Exclusive and intimate, the hotel has an English hunt-club theme. European furnishings abound and an extensive collection of 18th- and 19th-century English art, heavy on horses and dogs, graces the walls. This is the home of the pricey Jockey Club restaurant, where crowned heads of Washington like to have lunch (it was one of Nancy Reagan's favorite spots). Lee Iacocca, Carol Burnett, and Eddie Murphy have stayed here. The hotel was undergoing a complete renovation in 1993, with a reduced number of rooms available. *2100 Massachusetts Ave. NW, 20008, tel. 202/293–2100 or 800/241–3333. 215 rooms, 17 suites. Facilities: 24-hr room service, restaurant, access to health club. AE, DC, MC, V.*

Expensive **Embassy Row Hotel.** Located near Dupont Circle in a neighborhood of grand houses now used mostly as embassies, museums, and galleries, this hotel is equally convenient for business and vacation trips to Washington. The spacious rooms are decorated in neutral colors and light woods with accents of rich crimson and forest green. The bar is perhaps the coziest in Washington, and the cooking of chef Jim Papovich at Lucie, the hotel's elegant restaurant, has made it a favorite of locals and tourists alike. The roof deck and pool offer a fine view of the city. *2015 Massachusetts Ave. NW, 20036, tel. 202/265–1600 or 800/424–2400. 168 rooms, 28 suites. Facilities: 24-hr room service, restaurant, bar, rooftop pool, access to health club, valet parking. AE, DC, MC, V.*

Omni Georgetown. Although this hotel is not actually in Georgetown, it's close enough, in a convenient location on P Street near Dupont Circle. Its most striking feature is the size of the guest rooms, among the largest of any hotel in the city. Each room has a king- or two queen-size beds, a sofa and chairs, a large writing desk, a minibar, three telephones, and bathrooms equipped with hair dryer. The second-floor outdoor swimming pool, open only in summer, has a lovely setting—a brick courtyard enclosed by the walls of the hotel and the backs of a row of century-old town houses to the east. The Omni's Rock Creek Café, several steps down from busy P Street, attracts hip Dupont Circle residents as well as hotel guests. *2121 P St. NW, 20037, tel. 202/293–3100 or 800/843–6664. 238 rooms, 56 suites. Facilities:*

*room service 6:30 AM–11 PM, restaurant, bar, outdoor pool,
exercise room, sauna, business center, valet parking. AE,
DC, MC, V.*

★ **The Washington Hilton and Towers.** One of the city's busiest
convention hotels, this is as much an event as a place to
stay. At any moment, you could run into a leading actor, a
cabinet official, six busloads of teenagers from Utah, 500
visiting heart surgeons, or Supreme Court Justice Sandra
Day O'Connor, who is among the notables who have played
tennis here. The light-filled but compact guest rooms have
marble bathrooms. In back of the hotel is a miniresort with
a café. The hotel is a short walk from the shops and restaurants of Dupont Circle, Embassy Row, the National Zoo,
and the Adams-Morgan neighborhood. *1919 Connecticut
Ave. NW, 20009, tel. 202/483–3000 or 800/445–8667. 1,062
rooms, 88 suites. Facilities: 24-hr room service, 3 restaurants (1 seasonal), 2 bars, 3 lighted tennis courts, outdoor
pool, whirlpool, health club, pro shop, flower shop. AE,
DC, MC, V.*

Moderate **Quality Hotel Central.** A Holiday Inn until 1988, this high
★ rise just up the street from Dupont Circle is one of the city's
best values for travelers on a budget. Travelers who can't
find rooms at the Washington Hilton stay here, as do families and businesspeople. Rooms are clean, quiet, and decorated with light colors and blond wood. Rooms on the
western and southern sides have good views. *1900 Connecticut Ave. NW, 20009, tel. 202/332–9300 or 800/842–4211.
147 rooms. Facilities: room service 7 AM–9:30 PM, restaurant, outdoor pool, access to health club, free parking. AE,
DC, MC, V.*

Inexpensive **Hotel Tabard Inn.** Three Victorian town houses were linked
in the 1920s to form an inn, and the establishment is still
welcoming guests. Named after the hostelry of Chaucer's
Canterbury Tales, the hotel is furnished throughout with
broken-in Victorian and American Empire antiques. Dim
lighting and a genteel shabbiness strike some as off-put-
ting, others as charming. Rooms have phone but no TV, and
service can be uneven. There is no room service, but the
Tabard Inn Restaurant serves breakfast, lunch, and dinner. Located on a quiet street, the hotel is a quick walk to
Dupont Circle and the K Street business district. Reserve
early and be aware that most rooms with private bath are in
the Moderate price range. *1739 N St. NW, 20036, tel. 202/
785–1277. 40 rooms, 25 with private bath. Facilities: restaurant. MC, V.*

Georgetown

Very Expensive **Four Seasons Hotel.** A polished staff is at your service the
★ moment you approach the doors of this contemporary hotel
conveniently situated between Georgetown and Foggy
Bottom. The Four Seasons is a gathering place for
Washington's elite. Rooms, all of which have a minibar, are

traditionally furnished in light colors. The quieter rooms face the courtyard; others have a view of the C & O Canal. The restaurant, Aux Beaux Champs, serves classic and French nouvelle cuisine and is highly esteemed by locals. Afternoon tea is served in the Garden Terrace Lounge. The Four Seasons is also home to the private nightclub Desiree, which is open to hotel guests and perhaps the poshest health club of any hotel in America. Guests may choose between watching movies on a VCR or listening to French lessons on a Walkman as they burn calories on their exercise bikes. *2800 Pennsylvania Ave., NW, 20007, tel. 202/342–0444 or 800/332–3442. 160 rooms, 36 suites. Facilities: 24-hr room service, 2 restaurants, bar, nightclub, health club with pool, multilingual staff, valet parking. AE, DC, MC, V.*

Expensive **Latham Hotel.** A small, colonial-style hotel in the midst of one of the city's liveliest neighborhoods, the former Georgetown Marbury changed management in 1991, along with its name. Extensive renovation has banished the underground rooms and dark hallways. The remaining rooms have a sleek, updated look that contrasts with the redbrick, neocolonial exterior. Some rooms have minibars inside European-style armoires, while others have been remodeled for disabled travelers. Nine carriage suites offer two-level accommodations on the M Street side (courtyard views overlook the C & O Canal). The hotel is popular with Europeans, sports figures, and devotees of Georgetown. Chef Michel Richard of the trendy L.A.-based restaurant Citrus opened the much-anticipated Citronelle here in early 1993. *3000 M St. NW, 20007, tel. 202/726–5000 or 800/447–9559. 134 rooms, 9 suites. Facilities: room service 6:30 AM–11 PM, restaurant, bar, seasonal outdoor pool, access to health club, valet parking. AE, DC, MC, V.*

Moderate **Georgetown Dutch Inn.** Tucked away on a side street in Georgetown, this modest hotel has a homey ambience and a few clients who stay for months at a time. The small lobby is decorated with 18th-century touches; rooms have family-room-style furnishings. All have a sofabed in the living room and a walk-in kitchen. Some bedrooms lack windows. Nine suites are built on two levels, with the bedrooms upstairs. Continental breakfast is complimentary and served in the lobby. *1075 Thomas Jefferson St. NW, 20007, tel. 202/337–0900. Facilities: room service during peak meal hours only, access to health club, overnight valet service, free underground parking. AE, DC, MC, V.*

Georgetown Inn. With an atmosphere like a gentleman's sporting club of 80 years ago, the inn re-creates the intimacy and quiet of a small European hotel. The architecture is redbrick and 18th century in flavor, appropriate to the hotel's setting. Recent renovation has brought a fresh look to interiors. The Georgetown Bar & Grill, where everyone from shorts-clad tourists to businesspeople can feel comfortable, has been brightened. Traditionally furnished rooms, in teal and mauve color schemes, are unhotellike, with attractive wood furniture and gold-framed paintings. All rooms have two telephones and terrycloth robes. A hearty European-style breakfast with meats and cheeses is included in the room rate. *1310 Wisconsin Ave. NW, 20007, tel. 202/333–8900 or 800/424–2979. 95 rooms, 8 suites. Facilities: room service 6:30 AM–11 PM, restaurant, bar, access to exercise classes, valet parking. AE, DC, MC, V.*

Southwest

Very Expensive **Loew's L'Enfant Plaza.** Loew's is an oasis of velvet and chintz in L'Enfant Plaza—a concrete, fortresslike collection of office buildings with underground shops and its own Metrorail stop. Travelers with government business stay here, too, in proximity to several agency headquarters and just down the street from Capitol Hill. Each room has a fully stocked liquor cabinet and a refrigerator. All rooms were refurbished in fall 1992. Service is friendly, and Cafe Pierre serves an international menu at lunch and dinner. *480 L'Enfant Plaza SW, 20024, tel. 202/484–1000 or 800/223–0888. 348 rooms, 22 suites. Facilities: room service 6 AM–midnight, VCRs, 3 phones with 2 lines, TV and radio in bathrooms, 3 restaurants, 2 bars, year-round rooftop pool, health club, parking. AE, DC, MC, V.*

Northwest/Upper Connecticut Avenue

Very Expensive **Omni Shoreham Hotel.** You're in good company when you
★ check in at this grand, 1930s art deco–Renaissance hotel. The Beatles stayed here on their first U.S. tour, and John Kennedy courted Jackie in the Blue Room cabaret, where Judy Garland, Marlene Dietrich, and Maurice Chevalier once appeared (it's now a meeting room). Resembling an old-time resort, this hotel overlooks Rock Creek Park and its jogging and bike paths and is close to the Adams-Morgan neighborhood, Dupont Circle, and the National Zoo. In back is the pool, where you can look out to a sweeping lawn and woods beyond. The rooms are large and light filled. Some have fireplaces; half overlook the park. They are, however, beginning to show their age. Comedienne Joan Cushing frequently holds forth in the Marquee Lounge, which offers a weekend matinee cabaret for children. *2500 Calvert St. NW, 20008, tel. 202/234–0700 or 800/834–6664. 720 rooms, 50 suites. Facilities: room service 6 AM–11 PM, restaurant, bar, snack counter, cabaret, outdoor pool, 3 lighted tennis courts, shuffleboard court, horseshoe pits, half-size basketball court, fitness center, shops, art gallery, parking. AE, DC, MC, V.*

Sheraton Washington Hotel. A veritable city on a hill, this is Washington's largest hotel. It consists of an "old town"—a 1920s redbrick structure that used to be an apartment building—and the modern sprawl of the new, convention-ready, main complex. The 250 rooms and the public areas of the 10-story old section were renovated in 1988; they are furnished traditionally in soft colors and have large closets. Rooms in the newer section are contemporary, with chrome and glass touches. Most rooms have a good view. The courtyard is graced by a modernistic fountain; the hotel also has an airy atrium and plush, sunken-seating areas galore. Pastry chef Wolfgang Friedrich has a carry-out shop on the premises (calorie-watchers beware). The hotel is close to the National Zoo and just a few yards from the Woodley Park Metro station. *2660 Woodley Rd. NW, 20008, tel. 202/ 328-2000 or 800/325-3535. 1,381 rooms, 124 suites. Facilities: 24-hr room service, 4 restaurants, bar, health club with Universal weights and stationary bikes, 2 outdoor pools, baby-sitting service, parking. AE, DC, MC, V.*

Inexpensive   **Days Inn Connecticut Avenue.** An alternative for those who prefer to stay away from the downtown hustle and bustle, this Days Inn is on a wide avenue in a more residential area. The nearby Van Ness Metrorail stop provides quick transportation to the National Zoo (two stops away). The University of the District of Columbia is next door. Rooms have standard hotel furnishings and may be small. A complimentary Continental breakfast is provided in the lower lobby. There are several cafés nearby. *4400 Connecticut Ave. NW, 20008, tel. 202/244-5600. 150 rooms, 5 suites. Facilities: parking; room service from nearby Espresso Café is available. AE, DC, MC, V.*

Hotel Windsor Park. Directly across from the Chinese Embassy, in the residential Kalorama neighborhood, the Windsor Park offers small, immaculate rooms, decorated simply with modern furnishings and a blue and rose color scheme. Each room has a small refrigerator. The hotel is close to Dupont Circle, the National Zoo, and major convention hotels. *2116 Kalorama Rd. NW, 20008, tel. 202/483-7700 or 800/247-3064. 39 rooms, 5 suites. AE, DC, MC, V.*

★ **Kalorama Guest House.** Really great-grandma's house in disguise, this inn consists of four turn-of-the-century town houses: three on a quiet street in the Adams-Morgan neighborhood and one in residential Woodley Park. The Kalorama's comfortable atmosphere is created by dark wood on the walls; hand-me-down antique oak furniture; traditional, slightly worn upholstery; brass or antique wooden bedsteads; and calico curtains at the windows. Magazine illustrations, sheet music, and family photos from the 1890s and early 1900s decorate the walls. The coffeepot is always on, the staff is knowledgeable and friendly, and guests have the run of each house, its front parlor, and the areas where complimentary breakfast is served. Rooms range from large to tiny; none has phone or TV. The inn in Adams-Morgan is steps from one of Washington's most interesting neighborhoods. The Woodley Park inn is near the National Zoo and the Metro. The Kalorama is a good value for budget-minded travelers in search of atmosphere. *1854 Mintwood Place NW, 20009, tel. 202/667-6369; 2700 Cathe-*

dral Ave. NW, 20008, tel. 202/328–0860. 50 rooms (30 with private bath), 5 suites. AE, DC, MC, V.

★ **Normandy Inn.** A small, European-style hotel on a quiet street in the exclusive embassy area of Connecticut Avenue, the Normandy is near restaurants, the National Zoo, and some of the most expensive residential real estate in Washington. The rooms are standard and functional, but comfortable. A complimentary Continental breakfast is served. In addition, there is a wine and cheese reception for guests every Tuesday evening. *2118 Wyoming Ave. NW, 20008, tel. 202/483–1350 or 800/424–3729. 65 rooms, 10 suites. Facilities: room service 7–10 AM, underground parking. AE, MC, V.*

West End/Foggy Bottom

Very Expensive **ANA Hotel.** A Westin hotel before it was purchased by the
★ Japanese ANA company in 1990, this establishment is a stylish combination of the contemporary and the traditional. Built in 1985 and renovated in 1991, the ANA offers bright, airy, traditionally furnished rooms decorated in greens, blues, and burnished oranges. Each room is supplied with terry-cloth bathrobes and a minibar. About a third of the rooms have a view of the central courtyard. The hotel's informal restaurant, the Bistro, has the flavor of 19th-century Paris and contains an antique mahogany bar. The state-of-the-art health club includes rowing machines, a cross-country ski simulator, treadmills, Nautilus equipment, and a lap pool. *2401 M St. NW, 20037, tel. 202/429–2400 or 800/228–3000. 408 rooms, 7 suites. Facilities: 24-hr room service, 2 restaurants, bar, café, beauty salon, valet parking. AE, DC, MC, V.*

Grand Hotel. Probably the least known of Washington's luxury hotels, this hotel occupies its prime corner in the West End with an old-world assurance that has made it a favorite of international visitors. Its rooms, although not enormous, are impressive for their comfort and their anticipation of guests' needs. Decorated in light colors that give an impression of airiness and space, each room has an executive-size desk equipped with a two-line telephone. Each bathroom has floor-to-ceiling marble walls, a sunken tub, separate shower, television speaker, and extension telephone. Eight of the hotel's suites have working wood-burning fireplaces. The staff is well trained, and the emphasis on efficient, friendly, and discreet service is apparent in every department. *2350 M St. NW, 20037, tel. 202/429–0100 or 800/848–0016. 237 rooms, 26 suites. Facilities: 24-hr room service, 3 restaurants, bar, exercise room, outdoor heated pool, valet parking, laundry and dry-cleaning service. AE, DC, MC, V.*

Park Hyatt. A notable collection of modern art adorns this West End hotel, built in 1986. The interior of its main level is built of stone and polished marble, and guests walk on carpeting so thick it almost bounces. Bronzes, chinoiserie, and a fortune teller at tea in the recently renovated main-floor lounge are a few of the Old World touches that offset the spareness of the hotel's design. The rooms are a blend of traditional and contemporary elements and contain reproductions of Chinese antiques from Washington museum collections. The staff has a "never say no" policy, and cars left overnight are washed. *1201 24th St. NW, 20037, tel. 202/789–1234 or 800/228–9000. 92 rooms, 132 suites. Facilities: 24-hr room service; restaurant; outdoor café (in season); bar; health club with indoor pool, whirlpool, Nautilus equipment; beauty salon, valet parking. AE, DC, MC, V.*

★ **Watergate Hotel.** The internationally famous Watergate, its distinctive sawtooth design a landmark along the Potomac, completed a $14 million renovation in 1988 and is now offering guests a taste of old-English gentility. Scenic murals and a portrait of Queen Elizabeth contribute to the effect. The rooms here are among the largest in Washington. All have live plants or fresh flowers, many have balconies, and most have striking river views. The Jean-Louis restaurant has one of the few two-star Michelin chefs in the United States. The hotel is accustomed to serving the world's elite, but it also welcomes vacationing families and couples on getaway weekends. Part of the exclusive Watergate apartment and commercial complex, the hotel is next door to the Kennedy Center and a short walk from Georgetown. *2650 Virginia Ave. NW, 20037, tel. 202/965–2300 or 800/424–2736. 77 rooms, 160 suites. Facilities: 24-hr room service; 2 restaurants; bar; health club with weights, stationary bikes, steam room, sauna, indoor pool; complimentary limousine service to Capitol Hill or downtown weekdays, valet parking. AE, DC, MC, V.*

Expensive **Embassy Suites.** The hodgepodge of decorative details and cinderblock construction suggest the hanging gardens of Babylon reconstructed in a suburban shopping mall. In the atrium, waterfalls gush, tall palms loom, and plants drip over balconies. Classical columns are mixed with plaster lions and huge Asian temple lights. Ducks swim in the lagoon, to the delight of children and many grown-ups. Businesspeople flock to the hotel during the week, but it is also ideal for families. Each suite, furnished in neo–art deco, has two remote-control TVs, as well as a microwave, coffee maker, and queen-size sofabed. Complimentary cocktails and cooked-to-order breakfast are served in the atrium. The Italian restaurant, Panevino, has received favorable reviews. Situated in a fairly quiet enclave in the West End, Embassy Suites is within walking distance of Georgetown, the Kennedy Center, and Dupont Circle. *1250 22nd St. NW, 20037, tel. 202/857–3388 or 800/362–2779. 318 suites. Facilities: room service 11–11; restaurant; health club with weight-lifting equipment, treadmills, indoor pool, sauna; parking. AE, DC, MC, V.*

Wyndham Bristol Hotel. This hotel doesn't offer much in the way of views, but the location is excellent: Located midway between the White House and Georgetown, the Wyndham is a favorite place for movie and theater people because the Kennedy Center is just a few blocks away. The rooms here are quiet, although the building is bordered on two sides by major thoroughfares. The hotel looks as if it belongs to someone who collects Chinese porcelain: A whole cabinet-full greets guests on arrival in the small, quiet lobby. The rest of the hotel, created in 1984 from an apartment building, is English in decor; each room has a butler's table. *2430 Pennsylvania Ave. NW, 20037, tel. 202/955–6400, 800/822–4200, or 800/631–4200 in Canada. 218 rooms, 22 suites. Facilities: room service 7:30 AM–10:30 PM, 2 restaurants (with seasonal outdoor café), bar, access to health club, valet parking. AE, DC, MC, V.*

Moderate **Guest Quarters.** All of the units in these two all-suite hotels in Foggy Bottom, now under separate management, have a fully equipped walk-in kitchen, minibar, dishwasher, and sofa sleeper. The staff is small and so are the lobbies, but the rooms, decorated in a combination of traditional and contemporary decor, are well furnished and comfortable. The two-bedroom suites have a table that seats eight, which is good for family dinners as well as business conferences. The New Hampshire Avenue location has an outdoor rooftop pool (a great spot for viewing fireworks on July 4th). Both hotels are close to the Kennedy Center, Georgetown, and George Washington University. *801 New Hampshire Ave. NW, 20037, tel. 202/785–2000 or 800/424–2900; 2500 Pennsylvania Ave. NW, tel. 202/333–8060 or 800/424–2900. Together, 224 suites. Facilities: room service, access to health club, pool (New Hampshire Ave.), library. AE, DC, MC, V.*

River Inn. A member of the highly rated Potomac Hotel Group, which also operates the similar St. James and One Washington Circle hotels nearby, this small, all-suite hotel is steps from Georgetown, George Washington University, and the Kennedy Center. On the premises is the cozy River Inn restaurant, which is especially nice for breakfast. The best views are from the 14 Potomac Suites, each of which has a full walk-in kitchen. The lobby is sleek and contemporary, but the room furnishings are homey and modest. This is a popular spot with parents of George Washington University students. *924 25th St. NW, 20037, tel. 202/337–7600 or 800/424–2741. 127 suites. Facilities: room service 6:30 AM–11 PM, restaurant, use of outdoor pool at 1 Washington Circle and health club at the Watergate. AE, DC, MC, V.*

Inexpensive **Howard Johnson Kennedy Center.** This eight-story lodge offers HoJo reliability in a location close to the Kennedy Center, the Watergate complex, and Georgetown. Rooms are large and comfortable, and each has a refrigerator. *2601 Virginia Ave. NW, 20037, tel. 202/965–2700 or 800/654–2000. 192 rooms. Facilities: restaurant, rooftop pool, free parking for cars and low-clearance vans. AE, DC, MC, V.*

Suburban Maryland

Expensive **Hyatt Regency Bethesda.** The atrium lobby, with glass elevators and ferns, is reminiscent of other Hyatt Regencies. So are the attentive service and the comfortable—if unremarkable—rooms, decorated in peach or hunter green with modern furnishings and light wood accents. The hotel's sunlit, airy restaurant is a pleasant place for breakfast before setting out on the Metrorail red line to see the sights of downtown Washington, about 15 minutes away. The adjacent Metro plaza has a small ice rink, open in winter, and an indoor food court. *1 Bethesda Metro Center, Bethesda, MD 20814, tel. 301/657-1234 or 800/233-1234. 368 rooms, 13 suites. Facilities: room service, 2 restaurants, bar, exercise room, indoor pool, sauna, valet parking. AE, DC, MC, V.*

Moderate **Quality Hotel Silver Spring.** Formerly the Sheraton Inn, this conveniently located hotel is about three blocks from the Silver Spring Metro station and close to the shops and restaurants in downtown Silver Spring, including the glossy new, discount-oriented City Place complex. The lobby, with its small front desk, marble floors, and many places to sit, is comfortable and intimate. A major renovation of all sleeping rooms—in gray and soft pink—and the lobby was completed in 1990. *8727 Colesville Rd., Silver Spring, MD 20910, tel. 301/589-5200 or 800/228-5151. 228 rooms, 28 suites. Facilities: room service, 2 restaurants, bar, exercise room with sauna, indoor pool, free parking. AE, DC, MC, V.*

Suburban Virginia

Very Expensive **Morrison House.** The architecture and furnishings of the
★ Morrison House in Old Town Alexandria are so faithful to the style of the Federal period (1790–1820) that it is often thought to be a renovation of a historic building rather than a new building built in 1985. Owner Robert Morrison consulted with experts from the Smithsonian in furnishing the hotel, and the parquet floors, crystal chandeliers and sconces, and period furnishings re-create the atmosphere of a grand American house of 200 years ago. The guest rooms are an elegant blend of early American charm and modern conveniences, including four-poster beds and armoires, but also remote control television sets and Italian marble bathrooms equipped with hair dryer and telephone. The Grill at Morrison House, under the direction of executive chef Charles Hill, serves innovative New American cuisine in a handsome club room atmosphere, with a pianist every day but Sunday accompanying. *116 S. Alfred St., Alexandria, VA 22314, tel. 703/838-8000 or 800/367-0800. 42 rooms, 2 suites. Facilities: 24-hr room service, restaurant, access to health club, multilingual staff, valet parking. AE, DC, MC, V.*

★ **Ritz-Carlton, Pentagon City.** The Washington area's newest luxury hotel, the Ritz-Carlton, Pentagon City, opened its doors for guests in May 1990. The 18-story hotel is located in Arlington, just across from the Pentagon, but its location at the Pentagon City Metro stop makes it more convenient to downtown Washington than many closer hotels. The decor of the new hotel looks to the Virginia horse country for its inspiration, and a $2 million collection of art and antiques, mostly from the 18th and 19th centuries, may be seen in the hotel's public spaces. Rooms, many with views of the monuments across the river, are among the most luxurious in Washington; each standard room, decorated in rose or blue, has an overstuffed chair with ottoman, Chippendale-style furniture, and silk bed coverings. To use the hotel's fully equipped fitness center, all you need to bring is your sneakers—a full line of workout clothing, including swimsuits, is provided. *1250 S. Hayes St., Arlington, VA 22202, tel. 703/415-5000 or 800/241-3333. 304 rooms, 40 suites. Facilities: 24-hr room service; concierge; restaurant; lounge; health club with indoor pool, whirlpool, sauna, rowing and cycling machines, complete Universal system; valet parking. AE, DC, MC, V.*

Expensive **Crystal City Marriott.** This business hotel is located close to National Airport and the Pentagon, in a thicket of office and apartment buildings. It's a good bet for families because the Metrorail yellow line can take you to the sights of the Mall in a matter of minutes. The lobby, with its lush plantings and thick carpets, is more luxurious than the rooms, which, although renovated in 1989 in an attractive seafoam green and mauve color scheme, are plain. The atrium restaurant is light filled and pleasant. *1999 Jefferson Davies Hwy., Arlington, VA 22202, tel. 703/413-5500 or 800/228-9290. 331 rooms, 9 suites. Facilities: room service; restaurant; 2 bars; business center; health club with pool, free weights, whirlpool, sauna; parking. AE, DC, MC, V.*

Key Bridge Marriott. Situated just across the Potomac from Georgetown, the Key Bridge Marriott in Arlington provides a room away from it all. The hotel is a short walk across the Key Bridge to Georgetown and sits near the Rosslyn Metro station, which provides easy access to Washington's major sites. The rooms were redecorated in 1988 in contemporary decor; many of them have a view of Washington, as does the rooftop restaurant. You can swim from the indoor to the outdoor pool via an underwater connection; when it gets cold, the portal is closed, and guests can stay wet in the interior section. Air traffic from Washington National can be noisy at times. *1401 Lee Hwy., Arlington, VA 22209, tel. 703/524-6400 or 800/228-9290. 568 rooms, 20 suites. Facilities: 24-hr room service; 2 restaurants; 2 bars; health club with Universal weights, stationary bikes, indoor-outdoor pool; valet service; beauty salon; shops; parking. AE, DC, MC, V.*

9 The Arts and Nightlife

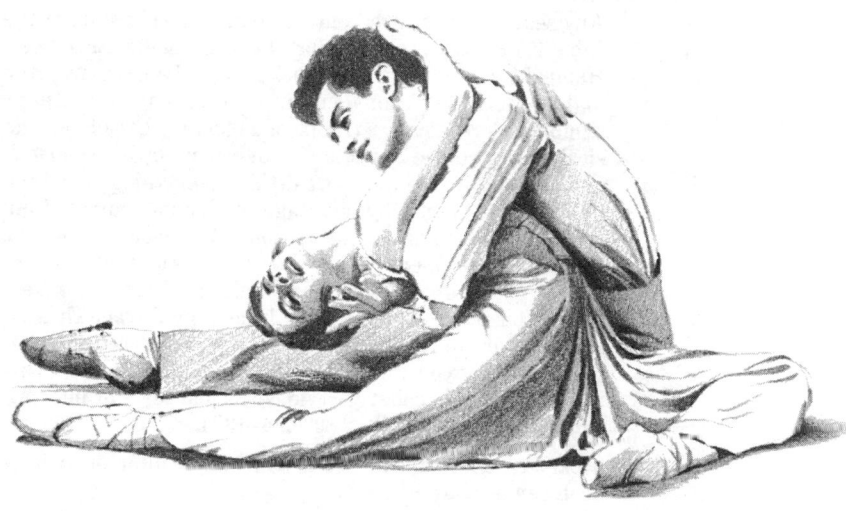

The Arts

By John F. Kelly   Washingtonians no longer balance a chip on their shoulder when it comes time to discuss sophisticated entertainment. In the past 20 years this cultural backwater has been transformed into a cultural capital. The Kennedy Center is a world-class venue, home of the National Symphony Orchestra and host to Broadway shows, ballet, modern dance, opera, and more. Several art galleries present highly regarded chamber music series. The service bands from the area's numerous military bases ensure an endless supply of martial music of the John Philip Sousa variety as well as rousing renditions of more contemporary tunes. At the other end of the spectrum, Washington was the birthplace of hardcore, a socially aware form of punk rock music that has influenced young bands throughout the country. Go-go—infectious, rhythmic music that mixes elements of rap, rhythm and blues, and funk—was touted as the next big thing to come out of the capital city but seems to have confined itself largely to Washington.

Friday's *Washington Post* "Weekend" section is the best guide to events for the weekend and the coming week. The *Post*'s daily "Guide to the Lively Arts" also outlines cultural events in the city. The *Washington Times* "Weekend" section comes out on Thursday. The free weekly *City Paper* hits the streets on Thursday and covers the entertainment scene well. You might also consult the "City Lights" section in the monthly *Washingtonian* magazine.

Any search for cultured entertainment should start at the **John F. Kennedy Center for the Performing Arts** (New Hampshire Ave. and Rock Creek Pkwy. NW). On any given night America's national cultural center may be hosting a symphony orchestra, a troupe of dancers, a Broadway musical, *and* a comedic whodunit. In other words, America's national cultural center has a little of everything. The Kennedy Center is actually five stages under one roof: the **Concert Hall,** home park of the National Symphony Orchestra; the 2,200-seat **Opera House,** the setting for ballet, modern dance, grand opera, and large-scale musicals; the **Eisenhower Theater,** usually used for drama; the **Terrace Theater,** a Philip Johnson–designed space that showcases chamber groups and experimental works; and the **Theater Lab,** which is home to cabaret-style performances. For information, call 202/467–4600 or 800/444–1324.

Tickets   Tickets to most events are available by calling or visiting each venue's box office.

TicketPlace sells half-price, day-of-performance tickets for selected shows; a "menu board" lists available performances. Only cash is accepted for same-day tickets; cash and credit cards may be used for full-price, advance tickets. *L St. between 15th and 16th Sts. NW., tel. 202/TICKETS.*

*Open Tues–Fri. noon–4, Sat. 11–5. Tickets for Sun. and
Mon. performances sold on Sat.*

Protix (tel. 703/218–6500) takes reservations for events at
Wolf Trap and elsewhere in the city. It also has outlets in
selected Woodward & Lothrop stores.

TicketMaster (tel. 202/432–7328 or 800/551–7328) takes
phone charges for events at most venues around the city.
You can purchase TicketMaster tickets in person at all
Hecht Company department stores. No refunds, exchanges, or cancellations.

Theater

**Commercial
Theaters and
Companies**

Arena Stage (6th St. and Maine Ave. SW, tel. 202/488–
3300). The city's most respected resident company (established 1950), the Arena was the first theater outside New
York to win a Tony award. It presents a wide-ranging season in its three theaters: the theater-in-the-round Arena,
the proscenium Kreeger, and the cabaret-style Old Vat
Room. The ambitious New Voices series in the Old Vat allows audiences to see plays in development at reduced
prices.

Ford's Theatre (511 10th St. NW, tel. 202/347–4833). Looking much the way it did when President Lincoln was shot at
a performance of *Our American Cousin*, Ford's is host
mainly to musicals, many with family appeal. Dickens's
Christmas Carol is presented each winter.

National Theatre (1321 E St. NW, tel. 202/628–6161). Destroyed by fire and rebuilt four times, the National Theatre
has operated in the same location since 1835. It presents
pre- and post-Broadway shows.

Shakespeare Theatre (450 7th St. NW, tel. 202/393–2700).
Four plays—three by the Bard and another classic from his
era—are presented each year by the acclaimed Shakespeare Theatre troupe. In 1992 it moved from its former
home in the Folger Library to a new, state-of-the-art, 447-
seat space.

Warner Theatre (13th and E Sts. NW, tel. 202/783–4000).
One of Washington's grand theaters, the 1924 building received a complete face-lift in 1992. The renovated space now
hosts road shows, dance recitals, and the occasional pop
music act.

**Small Theaters
and
Companies**

Washington's small theaters and companies long labored in
obscurity. They are spread out over the District, often performing in churches and other less-than-ideal settings.
Fans of independent theater have been encouraged recently by the development of what many regard as the District's
own off-Broadway: a five-block section of 14th Street NW
that in the past few years has become home for almost a half
dozen alternative stages. (Note: Take a cab here after
dark.) Other fledgling theaters are located near Dupont
Circle.

Gala Hispanic Theatre (1625 Park Rd. NW, tel. 202/234–7174). Established in 1976, this company produces Spanish classics as well as contemporary and modern Latin American plays in both Spanish and English.

Olney Theatre (2001 Rte. 108, Olney, MD, tel. 301/924–3400). Musicals, comedies, and summer stock are presented in this converted barn, an hour from downtown in the Maryland countryside.

Source Theatre (1835 14th St. NW, tel. 202/462–1073). The 107-seat Source Theatre presents established plays with a sharp satirical edge and modern interpretations of classics. Each July and August, Source hosts the Washington Theater Festival, a celebration of new plays, many by local playwrights.

Studio Theatre (1333 P St. NW, tel. 202/332–3300). An eclectic season of classic and offbeat plays are presented in this 200-seat theater.

Washington Stage Guild (924 G St. NW, tel. 202/529–2084). Founded in 1985 and performing in historic Carroll Hall, Washington Stage Guild tackles the classics as well as more contemporary fare.

Woolly Mammoth (1401 Church St. NW, tel. 202/393–3939). Unusual, imaginatively produced shows have earned this company good reviews and favorable comparisons to Chicago's Steppenwolf.

Music

Orchestra **The National Symphony Orchestra** (tel. 202/416–8100). The season at the Kennedy Center extends from September to June. During the summer, the NSO performs at Wolf Trap and presents concerts on the West Terrace of the Capitol on Memorial Day and Labor Day weekends and on July 4th. One of the cheapest ways to hear—if not necessarily see—the NSO perform in the Kennedy Center Concert Hall is to get a $7.50 "obstructed view" ticket.

Concert Halls **USAir Arena** (1 Harry S Truman Dr., Landover, MD, tel. 301/350–3400 or 202/432–7328). The home stadium for the Washington Capitals hockey and Washington Bullets basketball teams is also the area's top venue for big-name pop, rock, and rap acts. The Cap Centre, as it's known, seats 20,000.

DAR Constitution Hall (18th and C Sts. NW, tel. 202/638–2661). Constitution Hall was the home of the National Symphony Orchestra before the Kennedy Center was built. It still hosts visiting performers, from jazz to pop to rap.

John F. Kennedy Center for the Performing Arts (New Hampshire Ave. and Rock Creek Pkwy. NW). (*See above.*)

Lisner Auditorium (21st and H Sts. NW, tel. 202/994–6800). This 1,500-seat theater on the campus of George Washington University is the setting for pop, classical, and choral music acts.

George Mason University (Rte. 123 and Braddock Rd.,

Fairfax, VA). The GMU campus in suburban Virginia is home to the ambitious Center for the Arts, a glittering complex that opened in 1990 and hosts a full range of performing arts events, from music to ballet to drama. There is a 1,900-seat concert hall, the 500-seat proscenium Harris Theatre, and the intimate 200-seat Black Box Theatre (tel. 703/993–8888 for center events). Also on campus is the 9,500-seat Patriot Center, site of pop acts and sporting events (tel. 703/993–3033 for recorded calendar, 703/993–3000 or 202/432–7328 for ticket information).

Merriweather Post Pavilion (tel. 301/982–1800 or 301/596–0660 off-season). An hour north of Washington, in Columbia, Maryland, Merriweather Post is an outdoor pavilion with some covered seating. It plays host in warmer months to big-name pop acts.

National Gallery of Art (6th St. and Constitution Ave. NW, tel. 202/842–6941 or 202/842–6698). Free concerts by the National Gallery Orchestra, conducted by George Manos, as well as performances by outside recitalists and ensembles, are held in the venerable West Building's West Garden Court on Sunday evenings from October to June. Most performances highlight classical music, though April's American Music Festival often features jazz. Admission is free, on a first-come basis.

Smithsonian Institution (tel. 202/357–2700). An amazing assortment of music—both free and ticketed—is presented by the Smithsonian. Some highlights: American jazz, musical theater, and popular standards are performed in the National Museum of American History's Palm Court. In the third-floor Hall of Musical Instruments, musicians periodically perform on historic instruments from the museum's collection. The Smithsonian's Resident Associate Program (tel. 202/357–3030) offers everything from a cappella groups to Cajun zydeco bands, many of which perform in the National Museum of Natural History's Baird Auditorium. In warm weather performances are held in the courtyard between the National Portrait Gallery and the National Museum of American Art.

Wolf Trap Farm Park (1551 Trap Rd., Vienna, VA, tel. 703/255–1860). Just off the Dulles Toll Road, about a half-hour from downtown, Wolf Trap is a national park dedicated to the performing arts. On its grounds is the **Filene Center** (tel. 703/255–1868), an outdoor theater that is the scene of pop, jazz, opera, ballet, and dance performances each June through September. The rest of the year, the intimate, indoor **Barns at Wolf Trap** (tel. 703/938–2404) hosts folk, jazz, rock, chamber music, and other acts. On summer performance nights, Metro operates a $3 round-trip shuttle bus between the West Falls Church Metro station and the Filene Center. The bus leaves 20 minutes after the show, or no later than 11 PM, whether the show is over or not.

Choral Music **Choral Arts Society** (tel. 202/244–3669). Founded in 1965, this 180-voice choir performs a varied selection of classical pieces at the Kennedy Center from September to April. Three Christmas sing-alongs are scheduled each December.

Choral and church groups frequently perform in the impressive settings of the **Washington Cathedral** (tel. 202/537–6200) and the **National Shrine of the Immaculate Conception** (tel. 202/526–8300).

Chamber Music **Corcoran Gallery of Art** (17th St. and New York Ave. NW, tel. 202/638–3211). Hungary's Takacs String Quartet and the Cleveland Quartet, playing on matched sets of Amati and Stradivarius string instruments owned by the gallery, are among the groups that appear in the Corcoran's Musical Evening Series October–May, with some summer offerings. Concerts are followed by a reception with the artists. **Folger Shakespeare Library** (201 East Capitol St. SE, tel. 202/544–7077). The Folger Shakespeare Library's internationally acclaimed resident chamber music ensemble regularly presents a selection of instrumental and vocal pieces from the medieval, Renaissance, and Baroque periods, during a season that runs from October to May.
National Academy of Sciences (2101 Constitution Ave. NW, tel. 202/334–2436). Free performances by such groups as the Juilliard String Quartet and the Beaux Arts Trio are given October through May in the academy's acoustically nearly perfect 670-seat auditorium. In 1994, the academy will also host programs normally held in the Library of Congress Jefferson Building while that space undergoes renovation.
Phillips Collection (1600–1612 21st St. NW, tel. 202/387–2151). The long, paneled music room of gallery founder Duncan Phillips's home is the setting for Sunday afternoon recitals from September through May. Chamber groups from around the world perform; May is devoted to performing artists from the Washington area. Arrive early for the 5 PM concerts.

Performance Series **Armed Forces Concert Series.** From June to August, service bands from all four branches of the military perform nightly, Sunday through Friday evenings, on the East Terrace of the Capitol and at the Sylvan Theater on the Washington Monument grounds. The traditional band concerts include marches, patriotic numbers, and some classical music. The bands often perform at other locations throughout the year. *For information: Air Force, tel. 202/767–5658; Army, tel. 703/696–3718; Navy, tel. 202/433–2525; Marines, tel. 202/433–4011.*
Carter Barron Amphitheater (16th St. and Colorado Ave. NW, tel. 202/426–6837 or 202/619–7222 off-season). On Saturday and Sunday nights from mid-June to August this lovely, 4,250-seat outdoor theater in Rock Creek Park plays host to pop, jazz, gospel, and rhythm and blues artists, such as Chick Corea, Nancy Wilson, and Tito Puente. The National Symphony Orchestra also performs, and for two

weeks in June the Shakespeare Theatre presents a free play by the Bard.

District Curators (tel. 202/783–0360). An independent, non-profit organization, District Curators presents adventurous contemporary performers from around the world. Past artists have included Laurie Anderson, Philip Glass, the World Saxophone Quartet, and the Japanese dance troupe Sankai Juku.

Fort Dupont Summer Theater (Minnesota Ave. and F St. SE, tel. 202/426–7723 or 202/619–7222). The National Park Service presents national and international jazz artists at 8:30 on Friday and Saturday evenings from mid-June to August at this outdoor theater. Past performers at the free concerts have included Wynton Marsalis, Betty Carter, and Ramsey Lewis.

Sylvan Theater (Washington Monument grounds, tel. 202/ 619–7225 or 202/619–7222). Service bands from the four branches of the military perform at this outdoor theater from mid-June to August every evening except Wednesday and Saturday. On Wednesday there's dancing to big-band and swing music.

Washington Performing Arts Society (tel. 202/833–9800). An independent nonprofit organization, WPAS books high-quality classical music, ballet, modern dance, and some drama into halls around the city. Most of the shows—ranging from the Harlem Boys Choir to the Vienna Philharmonic—are held at the Kennedy Center. The **Parade of the Arts** series features shows with family appeal.

Opera

Mount Vernon College (2100 Foxhall Rd. NW, tel. 202/625–4655). The college's intimate Hand Chapel is the setting for rarely produced chamber operas each fall and spring.

Opera Theater of Northern Virginia (tel. 703/549–5039). The three operas in this company's season are sung in English and produced at an Arlington, Virginia, community theater. Each December the company presents a one-act opera especially for young audiences.

Summer Opera Theater Company (Hartke Theater, Catholic University, tel. 202/526–1669). This independent professional company mounts two fully staged productions each July and August.

Washington Opera (tel. 202/416–7800 or 800/87–OPERA). Seven operas—presented in their original languages with English supertitles—are performed each season (November–March) in the Kennedy Center's Opera House and Eisenhower Theater. Performances are often sold out to subscribers, but returned tickets can be purchased an hour before curtain time. Standing room tickets go on sale at the Kennedy Center box office each Saturday at 10 AM for the following week's performances.

Dance

Dance Place (3225 8th St. NE, tel. 202/269–1600). This studio theater, which presented its first performance in 1980, hosts a wide assortment of modern and ethnic dance every weekend.

Joy of Motion (1643 Connecticut Ave. NW, tel. 202/387–0911). A dance studio by day, Joy of Motion is the home of several area troupes, including Michelle Ava and Company (modern dance), the Dupont Alley Dance Company (jazz), and TAPestry (you guessed it—tap).

Mount Vernon College (2100 Foxhall Rd. NW, tel. 202/625–4655). An emerging center for dance in Washington, this women's liberal arts college presents eight dance companies a year—three in the fall, five in the spring. Past participants in the dance series have included the troupes of Robert Small, Nancy Meehan, and Gus Solomons, Jr.

Smithsonian Resident Associate Program (tel. 202/357–3030). National and international dance groups often perform at various Smithsonian museums.

The Washington Ballet (tel. 202/362–3606). In October, February, and May this company presents classical and contemporary ballets from the works of such choreographers as George Balanchine, Marius Pepita, and Choo-San Goh, mainly at the Kennedy Center. Each December the Washington Ballet presents *The Nutcracker*.

Film

Washington has a wealth of first-run movie theaters, in the city and in nearby suburbs:

The AMC Union Station 9 (Union Station, tel. 202/842–3757) on Capitol Hill features nine screens and validated, 3-hour parking at an adjacent parking lot. Closer to downtown are **Cineplex Odeon's West End 1–4** (23rd and L Sts. NW, tel. 202/293–3152) and **West End 5, 6, 7** (23rd and M Sts. NW, tel. 202/452–9020). The art deco **Cineplex Odeon Uptown** (3426 Connecticut Ave. NW, tel. 202/966–5400) boasts a single huge screen, Dolby sound, and a wonderful balcony. Other first-run movie theaters are clustered near Dupont Circle, in Georgetown, and around upper Wisconsin Avenue.

If you find movie-theater seats a little too confining or the choice of soft drinks a little too soft, there are two locations in the suburbs where films are shown in a dinner-theater-like setting of tables and chairs and where waiters and waitresses move through the audience taking orders for pizza, hot dogs, nachos, and beer and delivering it to your table (you must be 21 or over or with a parent to attend): the **Bethesda Theatre Cafe** (7719 Wisconsin Ave., Bethesda, MD, tel. 301/656–3337) and the **Arlington Cinema 'N' Drafthouse** (2903 Columbia Pike, Arlington, VA, tel. 703/486–2345).

Several Washington theaters screen revivals and foreign, independent, and avant-garde films.

The American Film Institute (Kennedy Center, tel. 202/785–4600, 4601). More than 700 different movies—including contemporary and classic foreign and American films—are shown each year at the American Film Institute's theater in the Kennedy Center. Filmmakers and actors are often present to discuss their work.

The Biograph (2819 M St. NW, tel. 202/333–2696). Washington's home for alternative cinema, the Biograph presents a mixture of first-run and repertory domestic and foreign films that have in common "their position out of the mainstream."

Filmfest DC, an annual citywide festival of international cinema, takes place in late April and early May. For information, write Box 21396, Washington, DC 20009, or call 202/727–2396.

The Hirshhorn Museum (tel. 202/357–2700), **National Gallery of Art East Building** (tel. 202/737–4215), and **National Archives** (tel. 202/501–5000). These museums on the Mall often show historical, unusual, or experimental films.

The Key (1222 Wisconsin Ave. NW, tel. 202/333–5100). This four-screen theater specializes in foreign films and presents an annual animation festival.

Mary Pickford Theater (Jefferson Bldg. of the Library of Congress, 1st St. and Independence Ave. SE, tel. 202/707–5677). This 64-seat theater shows classic films for free.

National Geographic Society (17th and M Sts. NW, tel. 202/857–7588). Educational films with a scientific, geographic, or anthropological focus are shown here weekly.

Nightlife

Washington's nightlife scene has contracted a bit in the last few years; locals have seen some favorite spots close their doors for good. But the city still boasts a range of choices. Its bars and nightclubs cater to a wide spectrum of customers, from proper political appointees to blue-collar regulars in from the suburbs. Many night spots are clustered in a few key areas, simplifying things for the visitor who enjoys bar-hopping. Georgetown, in northwest Washington, leads the pack with an explosion of bars, nightclubs, and restaurants on M Street east and west of Wisconsin Avenue and on Wisconsin Avenue north of M Street. A half dozen Capitol Hill bars can be found on a stretch of Pennsylvania Avenue between 2nd and 4th streets SE. There is another high-density nightlife area around the intersection of 19th and M streets NW. Located near the city's lawyer- and lobbyist-filled downtown, this neighborhood is especially active during happy hour.

As for music, Washington audiences are catholic in their tastes and so are Washington's music promoters. That means you can hear funk at a rock club, blues at a jazz club, and calypso at a reggae club. And it means big-name acts often perform at venues that also book Broadway shows and other nonmusical forms of entertainment. The music listings below are an attempt to impose order on this chaos. Your best bet is to consult Friday's "Weekend" section in the *Washington Post* and the free, weekly *City Paper*. It's also a good idea to call clubs ahead of time to find out who's on that night and what sort of music will be played.

Bars and Lounges

Brickskeller. A beer lover's mecca, this is the place to go when you want something more exotic than a Bud Lite. More than 500 brands of beer are for sale—from Central American lagers to U.S. microbrewed ales. Bartenders oblige beer-can collectors by opening the containers from the bottom. *1523 22nd St. NW, tel. 202/293–1885. Open Mon.–Fri. 11:30 AM–2 AM, Sat. 6 PM–3 AM, Sun. 6 PM–2 AM. AE, D, DC, MC, V.*

Capitol City Brewing Company. Capitalizing on the microbrewery trend so popular elsewhere, Capitol City is the first brewery to operate in Washington since Prohibition. A gleaming copper bar dominates the airy room, with metal steps leading up to where the brews are actually made. Capitol City makes everything from a bitter to a bock, though not all types are available at all times. As at a restaurant with a constantly changing menu, consult the brewmaster's chalkboard to see what's on tap. *1100 New York Ave. NW, tel. 202/628–2222. Open weekdays 7 AM–2 AM; Sat. 11 AM–2 AM, Sun. 11 AM–midnight. AE, DC, MC, V.*

Champions. Walls covered with jerseys, pucks, bats, and balls, and the evening's big game on the big-screen TV, leave little doubt that this popular Georgetown establishment is a sports lover's bar. Ballpark-style food enhances the mood. *1206 Wisconsin Ave. NW, tel. 202/965–4005. Open Mon.–Thurs. 5 PM–2 AM, Fri. 5 PM–3 AM, Sat. 11:30 AM–3 AM, Sun. 11:30 AM–2 AM. One-drink minimum Fri. and Sat. after 10 PM. AE, MC, V.*

The Dubliner. Snug, paneled rooms; thick, tasty Guinness; and nightly live entertainment are the main attractions at Washington's premier Irish pub. You don't have to be Irish to enjoy it, as scores of staffers from nearby Capitol Hill attest. *520 North Capitol St. NW, tel. 202/737–3773. Open Mon.–Thurs. 11 AM–2 AM, Fri. 11 AM–3 AM, Sat. 7 AM–3 AM, Sun. 7 AM–2 AM. AE, DC, MC, V.*

Durty Nelly's. Outside, it's an unassuming restaurant/bar crowded by the office blocks taking over downtown Bethesda in suburban Maryland. Inside is a massive horseshoe-shaped bar, around which weekend-greeting office workers and victory-celebrating softball players swarm. Most nights bands play rock and roll, old and new. *4714 Montgomery La., Bethesda, MD, tel. 301/652–1444. Open Mon.–*

Thurs. 11:30 AM–1 AM, Fri. 11:30 AM–2 AM, Sat. 7 PM–2 AM, Sun. 7 PM–1 AM. AE, D, MC, V.

15 Mins. A college-age clientele ventures downtown to enjoy the funky decorations, tiny dance floor, progressive music, and black lights that bathe this room in an eerie, purplish glow. Blues bands, local new music bands, and obscure alternative music heroes such as Eugene Chadbourne and Marc Ribot play at the club or in the adjacent Rothschild's Cafeteria. The name? It's how much fame Andy Warhol said we'd each have in the future. *1030 15th St. NW, tel. 202/408–1855. Open Mon.–Thurs. 5 PM–2 AM, Fri. 5 PM–3 AM, Sat. 8 PM–3 AM. Cover charge. AE, MC, V.*

The Fishmarket. There's something different in just about every room of this multilevel, multiroom space in Old Town Alexandria, from piano bar crooner to ragtime piano shouter to guitar strummer. The operative word here is boisterous. If you like your beer in massive quantities, be sure to order the largest size: It comes in a glass big enough to wash your face in. *105 King St., Alexandria, VA, tel. 703/ 836–5676. Open Mon.–Sat. 11:15 AM–1 AM, Sun. 11:15– midnight. AE, MC, V.*

Food for Thought. Lots of Birkenstock sandals, natural fibers, and activist conversation give this Dupont Circle lounge and restaurant (vegetarian and organic meat) a '60s coffeehouse feel. Nightly folk music completes the picture. *1738 Connecticut Ave. NW, tel. 202/797–1095. Open Mon.– Thurs. 11:30 AM–12:30 AM, Fri. 11:30 AM–1:30 AM, Sat. noon–1:30 AM, Sun. 5 PM–12:30 AM. AE, DC, MC, V.*

Hard Rock Cafe. There's something sweetly ironic about its location in the shadow of the J. Edgar Hoover FBI Building. One assumes Hoover would not have been amused by the raucous atmosphere, pumping rock music, and grand piano–shaped bar (he may have liked the barbecue sandwiches, though). Ask your waiter for the guide that shows where all the Hard Rock memorabilia—from Chuck Berry's guitar to a platinum record awarded to the Village People—are hung. *999 E St. NW, tel. 202/737–7625. Open daily 11 AM–2 AM. AE, CB, D, DC, MC, V.*

Hawk 'n' Dove. A friendly neighborhood bar in a neighborhood coincidentally dominated by the Capitol building. Regulars include political types, lobbyists, and well-behaved Marines (from a nearby barracks). *329 Pennsylvania Ave. SE, tel. 202/543–3300. Open Sun.–Thurs. 10 AM–2 AM, Fri.–Sat. 10 AM–3 AM. AE, CB, D, DC, MC, V.*

Sign of the Whale. The best hamburger in town is available at the bar in this well-known post-Preppie/neo-Yuppie haven. *1825 M St. NW, tel. 202/785–1110. Open daily 11:30 AM–2 AM. AE, D, DC, MC, V.*

Yacht Club. Enormously popular with well-dressed, middle-aged singles, this suburban Maryland lounge was one of the first in the area to introduce billiard tables, a notion several other local night spots have been quick to adopt. *8111 Woodmont Ave., Bethesda, MD, tel. 301/654–2396.*

Jacket and tie required. Open Tues.–Thurs. 5 PM–1 AM, Fri. 5 PM–2 AM, Sat. 8 PM–2 AM. AE, D, DC, MC, V.

Cabarets

Chelsea's. The musical political satire of the Capitol Steps, a group of current and former Hill staffers, is presented on Friday and Saturday. (The troupe's name comes from a purported trysting spot of politician John Jenrette and wife, Rita, not the current First Daughter.) *1055 Thomas Jefferson St. NW, tel. 202/298–8222 (Chelsea's) or 703/683–8330 (the Capitol Steps). Shows Sat. and occasionally Fri. at 7:30 PM. Ticket charge. Reservations required. AE, MC, V.*
Gross National Product. After years of spoofing Republican administrations with such shows as *The Phantom of the White House* and *Man without a Contra*, this irreverent comedy troupe is aiming its barbs at the Democrats. Its inaugural show was dubbed *Clintoons*. GNP, which the *Washington Post* has compared to the original cast of "Saturday Night Live," performs at the Bayou in Georgetown. *3135 K St. NW, tel. 202/333–2897 (Bayou) or 202/783–7212 (GNP). Show Sat. 7:30 PM. Ticket charge. Reservations suggested. MC, V.*
Marquee Lounge. This cabaret in the Omni Shoreham Hotel is where Mark Russell was ensconced for many years. Today funnywoman Joan Cushing assumes the character of quintessential Washington insider "Mrs. Foggy-bottom" and, with a small cast, pokes fun at well-known political figures in satirical skit and song. Other entertainers include home-grown diva Julia Nixon, belting out R&B and jazz on Friday and Saturday nights, and Now This, a musical-comedy improv troupe acting out audience suggestions every other Monday night. *2500 Calvert St. NW, tel. 202/745–1023. Joan Cushing: shows Thurs.–Sat. 8 PM. Julia Nixon: Fri. and Sat. 10:30 PM. Now This: 2nd and 4th Mon. 8 PM. Ticket charge. Reservations required. AE, D, DC, MC, V.*

Comedy Clubs

In the past few years the number of comedy groups in Washington that welcome, indeed rely on, the zany suggestions of audience members has mushroomed. These improvisation groups pop up at various venues, performing in the laughs-at-any-cost style of Chicago's Second City troupe. They aren't all successful, though, and many burst on the scene, then burst themselves. Among those with some stability are **ComedySportz** (Fri. and Sat. at the Little Cafe, 2039 Wilson Blvd., Arlington, VA, tel. 703/471–5212) and **Skits-O-Phrenic** (Sat. at Square One Theatre, Wisconsin Ave. and Q St. NW, tel. 202/829–0529).

Comedy Cafe. Local and national comics appear at this club in the heart of downtown. Wednesday is open-mike night; Thursday is local talent; on Friday and Saturday, name comedians headline. *1520 K St. NW, tel. 202/638–JOKE. Shows Thurs. 8:30 PM, Fri. 8:30 and 10:30 PM, Sat. 7, 9, and 11 PM. Cover charge. AE, D, DC, MC, V.*

Comedy Connection. This suburban Maryland club hosts comics six nights a week. Black comedians, such as Franklin Ajaye, Sherman Hemsley, and Jimmie Walker, call the Connection home when in town. *6000 Greenbelt Rd., Greenbelt, MD, tel. 301/345–0563. Shows Wed.–Thurs. 9 PM, Fri.–Sat. 8 and 10:30 PM, Sun. 9 PM. Cover charge. Reservations advised. AE, DC, MC, V.*

Garvin's Comedy Clubs. Garvin's is one of the oldest names in comedy in Washington and pioneered the practice of organizing comedy nights in suburban hotels. *Tel. 202/298–7200 for information and reservations for all locations, including Savoy Suites Hotel, 2505 Wisconsin Ave. NW (shows Tues.–Thurs. 8:30 PM, Fri. and Sat. 8:30 and 10:30 PM); Westpark Hotel, 8401 Westpark Dr., Tysons Corner, VA; Ramada Inn Seminary Plaza, I–395 and Seminary Rd., Alexandria, VA (show times vary). Cover charge and drink minimum. Reservations required. MC, V.*

Headliners. This comfortable club in a suburban Virginia hotel books local and regional acts on weekdays and national talent on the weekends. *Radisson Plaza Hotel, I–395 and Seminary Rd., Alexandria, VA, tel. 703/379–4242. Shows Fri. and Sat. 8:30 and 10:30 PM. Cover charge. Reservations required. AE, D, DC, MC, V.*

The Improv. A new heavyweight on the Washington comedy scene, the Improv is descended from the club that sparked the stand-up boomlet in New York City and across the country. Name headliners are common. *1140 Connecticut Ave. NW, tel. 202/296–7008. Sun.–Thurs. 8:30, Fri. and Sat. 8:30 and 10:30. Cover charge and two-item (not necessarily drinks) minimum. AE, MC, V.*

Acoustic/Folk/Country

Perhaps surprisingly, Washington has a very active local folk scene. For information on different folk events—from contra (a form of folk) dancing to story-telling to open sings—call the recorded information line of the **Folklore Society of Greater Washington** (tel. 703/281–2228).

Afterwords. This place could just as easily be called Beforewords or Duringwords, shoehorned as it is in a bookshop near Dupont Circle. Folkish acts entertain browsing bohemian bookworms as well as patrons seated at a cozy instore café. *1517 Connecticut Ave. NW, tel. 202/387–1462. Open Mon.–Thurs. 7:30 AM–1 AM and Fri. 7:30 AM–Mon. 1 AM. AE, MC, V.*

Birchmere. The best place in the area to hear acoustic folk and bluegrass acts is in an unpretentious suburban strip shopping center. Favorite sons the Seldom Scene are Thursday-night regulars. Audiences come to listen, and the management politely insists on no distracting chatter.

3901 Mt. Vernon Ave., Alexandria, VA, tel. 703/549–5919.
Open Tues.–Sat. 7 PM–11:30 PM. MC, V.
Country Junction. A suburban Maryland hotel lounge is the
scene of country dance lessons followed by country and
swing dancing to recorded music. *11410 Rockville Pike,*
Rockville, MD, tel. 301/231–5761. Open daily 7 PM–1 AM.
Cover charge Fri.–Sat. AE, D, MC, V.
Zed Restaurant. Can cowboy hats and boots exist in the
same city as Brooks Brothers suits? A visit to Zed proves
that they can. Each evening, bands in this suburban Virgin-
ia night spot play hits from Nashville and other points south
and west. Two-stepping is encouraged. *6151 Richmond*
Hwy., Alexandria, VA, tel. 703/768–5558. Open daily 11
AM–2 AM. Dress: casual but neat. MC, V.

Dance Clubs

Washington's dance clubs have taken a hint from their New
York counterparts, transforming themselves nearly every
night into different incarnations. Club owners rent their
spaces to entrepreneurs who tailor the music and ambience
to a certain type of crowd. Thus, a club might offer heavy
"industrial" music on a Wednesday, host a largely gay clientele on a Thursday, and thump to the sounds of '70s disco on
a Friday. It's best to call ahead or consult the often intriguing ads in the free weekly *City Paper*.

Chelsea's. Should a dance like the lambada ever again bubble up from South America, you'll find it at this elegant
Georgetown club near the C & O Canal. Hot Latin acts perform Thursday through Saturday; for a change of pace, it's
Persian music on Wednesday and Sunday. *1055 Thomas*
Jefferson St. NW, tel. 202/298–8222. Open Wed., Thurs.,
and Sun. 10 PM–2 AM, Fri.–Sat. 10 PM–4 AM. Cover charge
Fri. and Sat. AE, MC, V.
Dancers. The name describes this suburban Maryland
club's clientele. They're attracted to the 1,200-square-foot
dance floor and the club's no-smoking, no-alcohol policy.
Generally it's rhythm-and-blues bands on Thursdays,
swing dancing on Fridays, and Latin sounds on Saturdays.
Good old (vintage '70s) disco finds its way into the mix, too.
Dance lessons are usually offered early in the evening. *4609*
Willow La., Bethesda, MD, tel. 301/656–0595. Open
Thurs.–Sat. 8 PM–12:30 AM. Cover charge. No credit cards.
Fifth Column. A trendy, well-dressed crowd waits in line to
dance to the latest releases from London and Europe on
three floors of this converted bank. Avant-garde art installations change every six months. *915 F St. NW, tel. 202/*
393–3632. Open Mon. 9 PM–2 AM, Tues.–Thurs. 10 PM–2 AM,
Fri. and Sat. 10 PM–3 AM. Cover charge. AE, MC, V.
Kilimanjaro. Deep in ethnically diverse Adams-Morgan,
the Kilimanjaro specializes in "international" music from
the Caribbean and Africa. Every Thursday there's a local
reggae band, and international artists often perform on

Sunday. *1724 California St. NW, tel. 202/328–3838. Open Wed.–Thurs. 5 PM–2 AM, Fri. 5 PM–4:30 AM, Sat. 8 PM–4 AM, Sun. 6 PM–2 AM. Cover charge. D, MC, V.*

The Ritz. This downtown nightclub sits in the shadow of the J. Edgar Hoover FBI Building. The club, which is popular with the black professional crowd, features five separate rooms of music, with DJs spinning everything, from Top 40 and reggae in "Club Matisse" to house music in the upstairs "Freezone." There's live jazz every Tuesday, Friday, and Saturday. *919 E St. NW, tel. 202/638–2582. Open Thurs.– Fri. 5 PM–3 AM, Sat. 9 PM–3 AM, Sun. 9 PM–2 AM. Cover charge. Jacket and tie required. AE.*

The Roxy. Wednesday and Friday nights at this downtown club shake to the jackhammer beat of "industrial" dance music. High-energy reggae bands play on Thursdays and Saturdays. *1214 18th St. NW, tel. 202/296–9292. Open Wed.–Sat. 8:30 PM–2 AM. Cover charge. AE, MC, V.*

Tracks. A gay club with a large contingent of straight regulars, this warehouse-district disco has one of the largest dance floors in town and stays open late. *1111 1st St. SE, tel. 202/488–3320. Open Tues. 9 PM–2 AM, Wed.–Thurs. 9 PM–4 AM, Fri.–Sat. 9 PM–6 AM, Sun. 9 PM–4 AM. Cover charge. AE, MC, V.*

Zei. The latest entry in Washington's competition to be as hip as the Big Apple, Zei (pronounced "zee") says it wants to attract "young, upscale politically aware women and men." To that end a former electric power substation has been transformed into a New York–style dance club, with a wall of television sets peering down on the proceedings and the relentless thump of Euro-Pop dance music filling the air. *1415 Zei Alley NW (14th St. between H and I Sts. NW), tel. 202/842–2445. Open Wed. and Thurs. 9 PM–2 AM, Fri. and Sat. 9 PM–3 AM. Fashionable clothing, no sneakers. Cover charge. AE, D, DC, MC, V.*

Jazz Clubs

Blues Alley. The restaurant turns out Creole cooking, while cooking on stage are such nationally known performers as Charlie Byrd and Ramsey Lewis. You can come for just the show, but those who come for a meal get better seats. *Rear 1073 Wisconsin Ave. NW, tel. 202/337–4141. Open Sun.– Thurs. 6 PM–midnight, Fri. and Sat. 6 PM–2 AM. Shows at 8 and 10, plus a midnight show Fri. and Sat. Cover charge and $7 food/drink minimum. AE, DC, MC, V.*

Cafe Lautrec. The Toulouse-Lautrec decor, French food, and Gallic atmosphere are almost enough to convince you you're on the Left Bank of the Seine rather than the right bank of the Potomac. Cool cats play cool jazz nightly with tap-dancing fixture Johne Forges hoofing atop tables most Fridays and Saturdays. *2431 18th St. NW, tel. 202/265– 6436. Open Sun.–Thurs. 5 PM–2 AM, Fri.–Sat. 5 PM–3 AM. $6 minimum Thurs.–Sun. AE, DC, MC, V.*

One Step Down. Low-ceilinged, intimate, and boasting the best jazz jukebox in town, this small club books talented local artists and the occasional national act. The venue of choice for many New York jazz masters, the place is frayed and smoky, the way a jazz club should be. Live music is presented Thursday–Monday. *2517 Pennsylvania Ave. NW, tel. 202/331–8863. Open Mon.–Thurs. 11 AM–2 AM, Fri. 11 AM–3 AM, Sat. noon–3 AM, Sun. noon–2 AM. Cover charge and minimum. AE, DC, MC, V.*

Takoma Station Tavern. In the shadow of the Metro stop that lends its name, this club hosts local favorites such as Marshall Keys and Keith Killgo, with the occasional nationally known artist stopping by to jam. The jazz happy hours starting at 6:30 Thursday through Saturday pack the joint. There's reggae on Sundays. *6914 4th St. NW, tel. 202/829–1999. Open Sun.–Thurs. 4 PM–2 AM, Fri. and Sat. 4 PM–3 AM. Dress: casual but neat. AE, D, DC, MC, V.*

219 Basin Street Lounge. Across the Potomac in Old Town Alexandria above the 219 Restaurant, jazz combos perform Thursday through Saturday in an attractive Victorian-style bar. Musicians from local service bands often stop by to jam. *219 King St., Alexandria, VA, tel. 703/549–1141. Open Sun. 10 AM–10 PM, Mon.–Thurs. 11 AM–10:30 PM, Fri. 11 AM–11 PM, Sat. 8 AM–11 PM. Cover charge. AE, D, DC, MC, V.*

Rock, Pop, and Rhythm and Blues Clubs

The Bayou. Located in Georgetown, underneath the Whitehurst Freeway, the Bayou is a Washington fixture that showcases national acts on weeknights and local talent on weekends. Bands cover rock in all its permutations: pop rock, hard rock, soft rock, new rock, and classic rock. Tickets are available at the door or through TicketMaster. Occasional no-alcohol, all-ages shows allow those under 18 a chance to dance. *3135 K St. NW, tel. 202/333–2897. Open daily 8 PM–2 AM. Cover charge. No credit cards.*

Grog and Tankard. A college-age crowd downs cheap pitchers of beer while listening to exuberant local bands in this small, comfortably disheveled night spot. *2408 Wisconsin Ave. NW, tel. 202/333–3114. Open daily 6 PM–2 AM. Cover charge after 8 PM. AE, MC, V.*

9:30 Club. This trendy club in the center of Washington's old downtown books an eclectic mix of local, national, and international artists, most of whom play what used to be known as "new wave" music. The regulars dress to be seen, but visitors won't feel out of place. Get tickets at the door or through TicketMaster. *930 F St. NW, tel. 202/393–0930. Hours vary according to shows but generally open Tues. 7:30 PM–2 AM, Wed.–Thurs. 4 PM–2 AM, Fri. 4 PM–3 AM, Sat. 9 PM–3 AM. Cover charge. No credit cards.*

Tornado Alley. Owner Mark Gretschel is a great booster of "roots" music, such as blues, Cajun, zydeco, and anything else that swirls in like the eponymous wind from America's heartland. This suburban Maryland club resembling a high school gym hosts such national cult favorites as Filé, Wayne Toups and Zydecajun, Danny Gatton, and "Gatemouth" Brown, as well as local heroes, such as Stratocaster master Tom Principato and ex-Commander Cody guitarist Bill Kirchen. *11319 Elkin St., Wheaton, MD, tel. 301/929–0795. Hours vary according to shows but generally open Tues.– Thurs. 5 PM–1 AM, Fri. and Sat. 5 PM–2 AM, Sun. 5 PM–1 AM. Cover charge. D, MC, V.*

10 Excursions

Tour 1: The C & O Canal and Great Falls

By Michael Dolan
Updated by
John F. Kelly

In the 18th and early 19th centuries, the Potomac river was the main transport route between Cumberland, Maryland, one of the most important ports on the nation's frontier, and the seaports of the Chesapeake Bay. Tobacco, grain, whiskey, furs, iron ore, timber, and other commodities were sent down the Potomac from Cumberland to the ports of Georgetown and Alexandria, which served as major distribution points for both domestic and international markets.

Although it served as a vital link with the country's western territories, the Potomac did have some drawbacks as a commercial waterway: Rapids and waterfalls along the 190 miles between Cumberland and Washington made it impossible for traders to navigate the entire distance by boat. Just a few miles upstream from Washington, the Potomac cascaded through two such barriers—the breathtakingly beautiful Great Falls and the less dramatic but no less impassable Little Falls.

To help traders move goods between the eastern markets and the western frontier more efficiently, 18th-century engineers proposed that a canal with a series of elevator locks be built parallel to the river. The first such canal was built at the urging of George Washington, who actually helped found a company just for this purpose. In 1802, after 17 years of work, his firm opened the Patowmack Canal on the Virginia side of the river.

In 1828 Washington's canal was replaced by the **Chesapeake & Ohio Canal,** which had been dug along the opposite shore. The C & O stretched from the heart of Washington to Cumberland. Starting near what is now the intersection of 17th Street and Constitution Avenue NW (the public rest room there was originally a lockhouse), the C & O moved barges through 75 locks.

Ironically, the C & O Canal began operation the same day as the Baltimore & Ohio Railroad, the concern that eventually put the canal out of business. The C & O route to the west nevertheless did prove to be a viable alternative for traders interested in moving goods through the Washington area and to the lower Chesapeake. During the mid-19th century, the canal boats carried as many as a million tons of merchandise a year. The C & O Canal stopped turning a profit in 1890 but remained in business until 1924, when a disastrous storm left it in ruins. Ownership then shifted to the B & O Railroad, which sold the canal to the federal government in 1938 for $2 million. In 1939 the canal became part of the National Capital Parks System.

In the 1950s a proposal to build a highway over the canal near Washington was defeated by residents of the Palisades, a neighborhood that overlooks the waterway. Since 1971 the canal has been a national park, providing Washingtonians and visitors with a window into the past and a marvelous place to pursue recreational activities.

The twin parks of **Great Falls**—on either side of the river 13 miles northwest of Georgetown—are also now part of the National Park system. The 800-acre park on the Virginia side is a favorite place for outings for local residents and is easily accessible by tourists. The steep, jagged falls roar into a narrow gorge, providing one of the most spectacular scenic attractions in the East.

Escorted Tours

A tour of the visitors center and museum at **Great Falls Park** (tel. 703/285–2966) in Virginia takes 30 minutes. Staff members conduct special tours and walks year-round. Visitors are encouraged to take self-guided tours along well-marked trails, including one that follows the route of the old Patowmack Canal.

On the Maryland side, the old **Great Falls Tavern** (tel. 301/299–2026) serves as a museum and headquarters for the rangers who manage the C & O Canal. During warm weather, replicas of mule-drawn boats carry visitors along this stretch of the canal; similar trips also begin in Georgetown. History books and canal guides are on sale at both parks as well as at many bookstores in the District.

Getting Around

By Car To reach the Virginia side of Great Falls Park, take the scenic and winding Route 193 (Exit 13 off Route 495, the Capitol Beltway) to Route 738, and follow the signs. It takes about 25 minutes to drive to the park from the Beltway. You can get to the Maryland side of the park by following MacArthur Boulevard from Georgetown or by taking Exit 41 off the Beltway, following the signs to Carderock.

By Foot, Canoe, or Bicycle The C & O Canal Park and its towpath are favorite destinations for joggers, bikers, and canoeists. The towpath has only a slight grade, which makes for a leisurely ride or hike. Most recreational bikers consider the 13 miles from Georgetown to Great Falls an easy ride; there's only one short stretch of rocky ground near Great Falls where bikers need to carry their cycle. You can also take a bike path that parallels MacArthur Boulevard for much of the distance to the Maryland side of the park. Storm damage has left parts of the canal dry, but many segments remain intact and navigable by canoe. You can rent canoes or bicycles at **Fletcher's Boat House,** just upriver from Georgetown (*see* Exploring, *below*). In winter the canal sometimes freezes solid enough to allow for ice skating; during particularly hard freezes it's possible to skate great distances along the canal, occasionally interrupting your stride for short clambers around the locks.

Exploring

Numbers in the margin correspond to points of interest on the C & O Canal and Great Falls map.

This tour moves from Georgetown northwest along the Potomac to Great Falls Park. The canal itself is worth a day's stroll or ride.

❶ The towpath along the canal in **Georgetown** passes traces of that area's industrial past, such as the Godey Lime Kilns near the mouth of Rock Creek, as well as the fronts of numerous houses dating to 1810. From mid-April through mid-October mule-drawn barges leave for 90-minute trips from the Foundry Mall on Thomas Jefferson Street NW, half a block south of M Street. No reservations are required for the public trips. *For information, tel. 202/472–4376. For group reservations and rates, tel. 202/653–5844. Cost: $5 adults, $3.50 senior citizens and children under 13.*

❷ **Fletcher's Boat House** (4940 Canal Rd. NW, tel. 202/244–0461) rents canoes and bicycles and sells fishing tackle and DC fishing licenses. Fishermen often congregate here to try their luck with shad, perch, catfish, striped bass, and other freshwater species. In the spring Fletcher's opens at 5:30 AM and stops renting equipment at 5 PM. Summer hours are 7 AM–7:30 PM. During the coldest months of the year Fletcher's shuts down.

❸ **Chain Bridge**—named for the chains that held up the original structure—links the District with Virginia. The bridge was built to enable cattlemen to bring Virginia herds to the slaughterhouses located along the Potomac on the Maryland side. During the Civil War the bridge was guarded by Union troops stationed at earthen fortifications located along what is now Potomac Avenue NW. The Virginia side of the river in the area around Chain Bridge is known for its good fishing and narrow, treacherous channel.

Glen Echo is a charming village of Victorian houses that was founded in 1891 when brothers Edwin and Edward Baltzley fell under the spell of the Chautauqua movement, an organization that promoted liberal and practical education among the masses. The brothers sold land and houses to further their dream, but the Glen Echo Chautauqua lsted only one season. Their compound served a stint as an amusement park and is now run by the National Park Ser-
❹ vice as an arts and cultural center. **Glen Echo Park** (7300 MacArthur Blvd., tel. 301/492–6282) is noted not only for its whimsical architecture, including a stone tower left from the Chautauqua period, but also for its splendid 1921

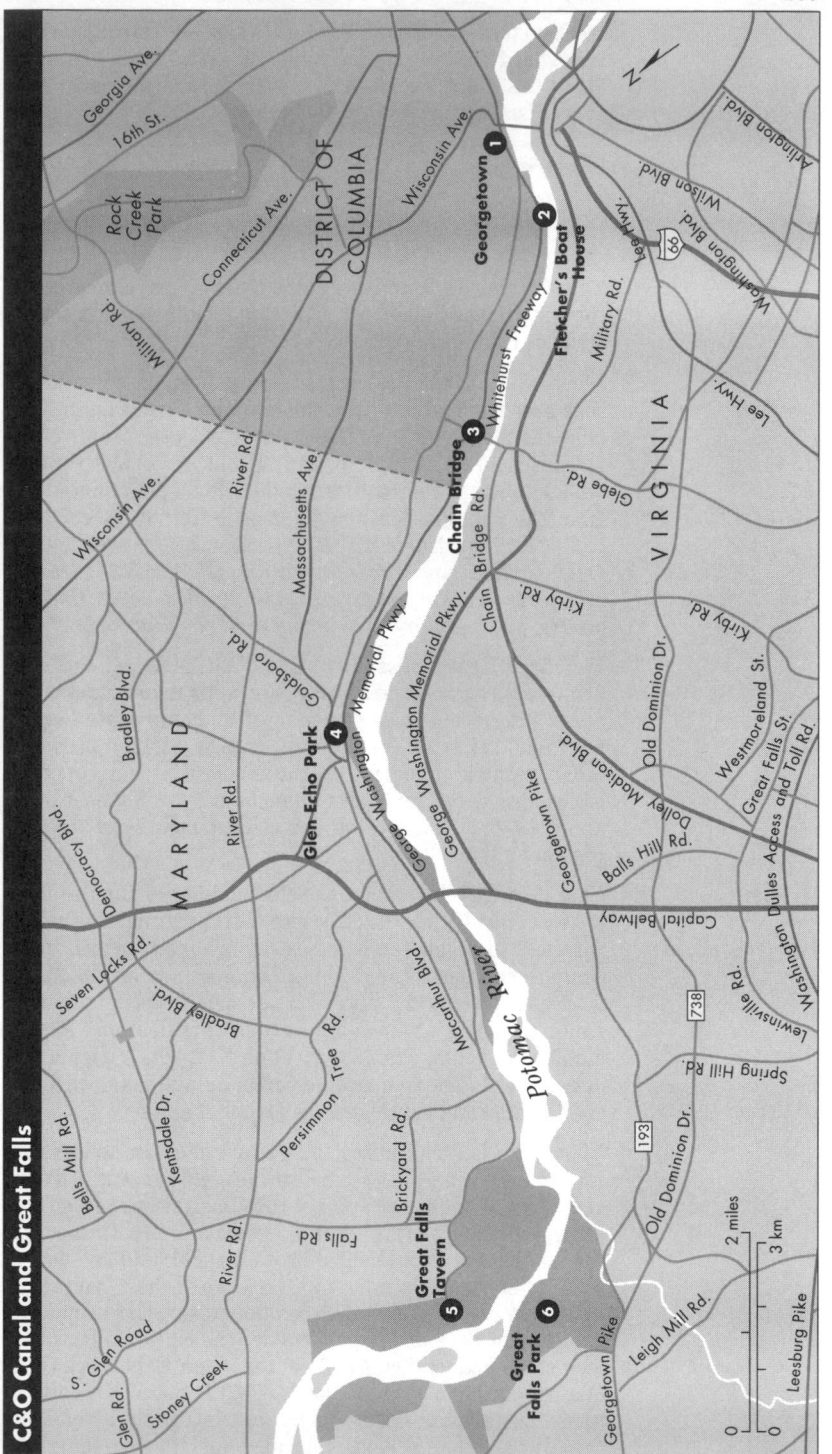

C&O Canal and Great Falls

Dentzel carousel. From late spring to early fall you can buy a cheap trip into the past, complete with music from a real calliope. The park is also the site of frequent folk festivals, and dances are held in the ornate Spanish Ballroom. For scheduling information, check the "Weekend" section in Friday's *Washington Post* or the free weekly *City Paper*.

The nearby **Clara Barton House,** one of the most striking Victorian structures in Glen Echo, has been preserved as a monument to the founder of the American Red Cross. Barton moved here toward the end of her life, using the place for a while to store Red Cross supplies and as the organization's headquarters. Today the building is furnished with original period artifacts. *5801 Oxford Rd., Glen Echo, MD, tel. 301/492-6245. Admission free. Open daily 10-5; guided tours hourly on the ½ hour.*

⑤ Great Falls Tavern, on the Maryland side of Great Falls Park, features displays of canal history and a platform from which to view the falls. Better yet, walk over the Olmsted Bridges out to a small island in the middle of the river for a spectacular view of the falls. On the canal walls are "rope burns" caused by decade upon decade of friction from barge lines. Half a mile west a flood marker shows how high the Potomac can go—after a hurricane in 1972 the river crested far above the ground where visitors stand. Canal barge trips start here between April and October. The tavern ceased being a hostelry long ago, so if you're hungry head for the snack bar a few paces north of the tavern. *Park, tel. 301/299-2026. Admission: $4 per vehicle weekends mid-Mar.–Memorial Day and daily June–Labor Day, $1 per person without vehicle, good for 7 days for MD and VA sides of the park. Open daily sunrise–sunset. Tavern and museum, tel. 301/299-3613. Open daily 9-5.*

⑥ The Virginia side of **Great Falls Park,** which is not accessible from the Maryland side of the park, offers the best views of the Potomac, as well as trails leading past the old Patowmack Canal and among the boulders and forests lining the edge of the falls. Horseback riding is permitted—maps are available at the visitors center—but you can't rent horses in the park. Swimming and wading are prohibited, but there are fine opportunities for fishing (a Virginia, Maryland, or DC license is required for anglers 16 and older), rock climbing (climbers must register at the visitors center beforehand), and white-water kayaking (*below* the falls only, and only by experienced boaters). From peaks beside the river and from several man-made platforms you can watch helmeted kayakers and climbers test their skills against the river and the rocks. As is true all along this stretch of the river, the currents are deadly. Despite frequent signs and warnings, each year some visitors dare the water and lose. It's best to keep away from even the most benign-looking ripple. *Tel. 703/285-2966. Admission: $4 per vehicle weekends mid-Mar.–Memorial Day and daily*

June–Labor Day, $1 per person without vehicle, good for 7 days for MD and VA sides of the park. Open daily 7 AM until dark. Closed Dec. 25.

Tour 2: Annapolis

Although it has long since been overtaken by Baltimore as the major Chesapeake port, **Annapolis** is still a popular destination for oystermen and yachtsmen, and on warm sunny days the City Dock is thronged with billowing sails set strikingly against a background of redbrick waterfront buildings, mostly shops and restaurants. Annapolis's enduring nautical reputation derives largely from the presence of the United States Naval Academy, whose handsomely uniformed midshipmen grace the city streets in their summer whites and winter navy-blues (the *real* navy blue, which is practically black). October Sailboat and Powerboat shows attract national attention, keeping local hotels and restaurants full even after the summer tourist season has ended.

In 1649 a group of Puritan settlers relocated from Virginia to a spot at the mouth of the Severn River; the community that they called Providence is now an upscale residential area. Lord Baltimore—who held the Royal charter to settle Maryland—named the area around the new town Anne Arundel County, after his wife; in 1684 Anne Arundel Town was established, across from Providence, on the south side of the Severn. Ten years later, Anne Arundel Town became the capital of Maryland and was renamed Annapolis—for Princess Anne, who later became queen. Annapolis received its city charter in 1708.

Annapolis—not the better-known Baltimore—is the state capital. One of the country's largest assemblages of 18th-century architecture (including 50 pre-Revolutionary buildings) recalls the city's days as a major port, particularly for the export of tobacco. In fact, in 1774 local patriots matched their Boston counterparts (who had thrown their famous tea party the previous year) by burning the *Peggy Sue*, a ship loaded with taxed tea. A decade later, in 1783 and 1784, Annapolis served as the nation's first peacetime capital. Annapolis's waterfront orientation makes it possible for visitors to do the city justice in a single well-planned day.

Escorted Tours

"Acoustiguide" walking tours of the city's historic district, prepared by the **Historic Annapolis Foundation** (tel. 410/267–8149) and narrated by Walter Cronkite, are available at the **Maritime Museum** (*see below*). The rental is $7 adults, $3.50 children 6–18. Guides from **Three Centuries Tours** (tel. 410/263–5401) wear colonial dress and take visitors to the State House, St. John's College, and the Naval Academy. The fee is $6 adults, $3 children 6–18, under 6 free.

Cruises offered by **Chesapeake Marine Tours, Inc.** (tel. 410/268–7600 or 301/261–2719 in Washington, DC) depart from the city dock in good weather. Tours range from 40 minutes to 7½ hours, extending as far as St. Michael's, a preserved 18th-century fishing village and a yachting mecca on the eastern shore of the bay. Prices range from $5 to $33.

Getting Around

There is no regular train or bus service from Washington to Annapolis. The drive from Washington (east on U.S. Route 50, to the Rowe Boulevard exit) normally takes 35–45 minutes, but if you travel between 3:30 and 6:30 PM you could be stuck in traffic for as long as two hours.

Parking spots on Annapolis's historic downtown streets are rare, but there's a free lot at the Navy–Marine Corps Stadium (to the right of Rowe Boulevard as you enter town from Route 50), from which a shuttle heads to downtown for 35¢ (75¢ at rush hour).

Exploring

Numbers in the margin correspond to points of interest on the Annapolis map.

1 Start your tour at the redbrick **Information Booth** operated by the **Annapolis–Anne Arundel County Conference and Visitors Bureau,** where you can pick up maps and brochures. The booth is on the city dock, adjacent to the harbor master's office (tel. 410/268–8687; open Apr.–Oct., daily 10–4). Outside, both motor- and sail-craft dozens of feet long moor at the edges of Dock Street and Market Place. A variety of shops, restaurants, and bars populate the dock area.

Time Out The **reconstructed Market House** pavilion—originally a collection of mid-19th-century market stalls in the center of Market Square—now sells baked goods, fast food, and fish (prepared or to cook at home). The building offers no seating, but you've got the entire dock on which to set up your picnic.

2 On Main Street by the dock, the **Maritime Museum** occupies a warehouse that stored supplies for the Revolutionary Army during the War of Independence, when the city was a vital link in the supply chain. Exhibits pertain to the history of maritime commerce in Annapolis and include artifacts of Colonial-era trade and a diorama of the city's waterfront in the 18th century. *77 Main St., tel. 410/268–5576. Admission free. Open daily 9–5. Closed Thanksgiving, Dec. 24, and Dec. 25.*

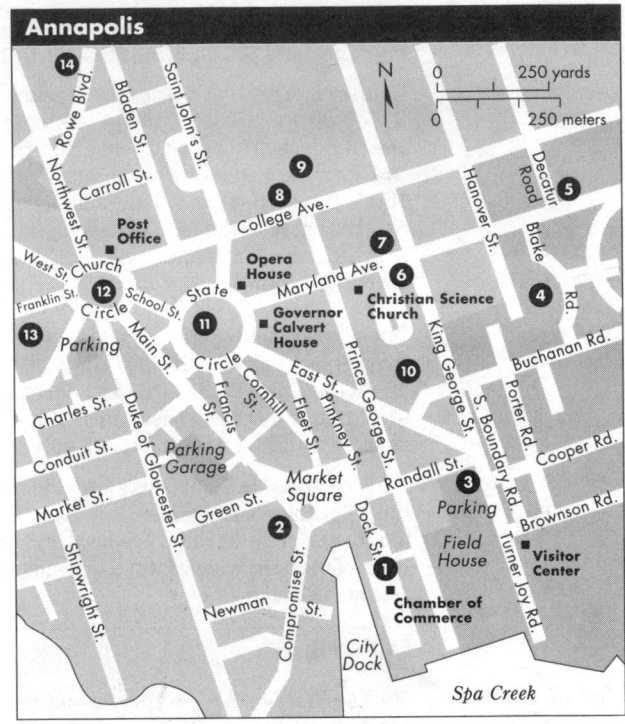

Cross the square and follow Randall Street a few blocks to reach the **United States Naval Academy.** By the gate at King George Street you'll find Ricketts Hall, where you can join a guided tour or pick up information for your own excursion. The academy, established in 1845 on the site of a U.S. Army fort, occupies 329 scenic riverside acres, earning the dubious title of "country club on the Severn" from its West Point rivals. In the center of campus the bronze-domed, interdenominational **U.S. Naval Chapel** contains the crypt of the Revolutionary War hero John Paul Jones, who, in an engagement with a British ship, uttered the famous declaration, "I have not yet begun to fight!" The **museum in Preble Hall** tells the story of the U.S. Navy, with displays of miniature ships and flags from the original vessels. Periodic full-dress parades and (in warmer months) daily noontime musters of the midshipmen take place at various spots around campus, but the most remarkable sight may be the sample student quarters open to the public—they're quite a bit neater than the typical college dorm! *Tel. 410/267–3363 or 410/263–6933. Visitor center open daily 9–4. Admission free. Cost of tour: $3 adults, $1 children 6th grade and below. 1-hr tours depart June–Aug., every ½ hr, Mon.–Sat. 9:30–4, Sun. 11–4; Mar.–May and Sept.–Nov., hourly, Mon.–Sat. 10–3, Sun. 11–3. Closed Thanksgiving and from Christmas to New Year's Day.*

Leave the Academy via Maryland Avenue and you will pass
⑥ the three-story redbrick **Hammond-Harwood House.** The
house is the only verifiable full-scale example of the work of
William Buckland, the most prominent Colonial architect at
the time of his death, in 1774—the year in which the house
was completed. Buckland was famous for his interior woodwork, which may also be seen in the Chase-Lloyd House
across the street and in George Mason's Gunston Hall in
Lorton, Virginia. Exquisite moldings, cornices, and other
carvings appear throughout, including garlands of roses
above the front doorway. These were meant to be part of
the manorial wedding present from Matthias Hammond, a
lawyer and revolutionary, to his fiancée, who jilted him before the project was finished. Hammond never married,
and he died in 1784. The Harwoods took over the house toward the turn of the century. Today the house is furnished
with 18th-century pieces, and the garden is tended with regard to period authenticity. *19 Maryland Ave., tel. 410/
269–1714. Open Mon.–Sat. 10–4, Sun. noon–4. Admission: $4 adults, $3 children 6–18, under 6 free. Closed
Thanksgiving, Christmas, and New Year's. Call for group
rates.*

Across the street is the gracefully massive facade—sheer
except for a center third beneath a pediment—of the
⑦ **Chase-Lloyd House.** In 1774 the tobacco planter and revolutionary Edward Lloyd IV completed work begun five years
earlier by Samuel Chase, a Supreme Court justice and future signer of the Declaration of Independence. The first
floor is open to the public and contains more of Buckland's
handiwork, including a parlor mantelpiece with tobacco
leaves carved into the marble. The house is furnished with a
mixture of 18th-, 19th-, and 20th-century pieces. The staircase parts dramatically around a Palladian window (an
arched, triple window whose center segment is taller than
its flanks). For more than 100 years the house has served as
a home for elderly Episcopalian women. *22 Maryland Ave.,
tel. 410/263–2723. Admission: $2. Open Mar.–Dec.,
Thurs.–Sat. 2–4.; Jan. and Feb., Thurs.–Sat. 2–4.*

A left on King George Street will take you to College Ave-
⑧ nue and **St. John's College,** which graduated Francis Scott
Key, lyricist of *The Star Spangled Banner.* The college has
been best known since 1937, however, for its Great Books
curriculum—a four-year program of required courses, including math, science, music, languages, and the works of
great authors from Homer to Freud. Climb the gradual
slope of the long, brick-paved path to the impressive golden
⑨ cupola of **McDowell Hall,** the third-oldest academic building
in the country, just as St. John's is the third-oldest college
in the country (after Harvard and William and Mary).
Founded as King William's School in 1696, the school was
chartered under its current name in 1784. The enormous
tulip poplar called the **Liberty Tree,** on the lawn fronted
by College Avenue, is possibly 600 years old. In its shade

colonists and Indians made treaties in the 17th century, revolutionaries rallied in the 18th century, Union troops encamped in the 19th century, and commencement takes place every spring. The **Elizabeth Myers Mitchell Art Gallery** (tel. 410/626–2556; open Tues.–Sun., noon–5, Fri. noon–5 and 7–8 PM), located on the east side of Mellon Hall, presents a variety of exhibits and special programs related to the fine arts. Down King George Street toward the water is the **Carroll-Barrister House,** now the college admissions office. The house was built in 1722 at Main and Conduit streets and was moved onto campus in 1957. Charles Carroll—not the signer of the Declaration, but his cousin—who helped draft Maryland's Declaration of Rights, was born here. *Tel. 410/263–2371. Free tours available by appointment.*

Head right on King George Street and make another right on College Avenue. A left on Prince George Street brings you to the **William Paca House and Garden**—the house built in 1765 and the garden originally finished in 1772 and gradually restored in this century. These compose the estate of William Paca, a signer of the Declaration of Independence and governor of Maryland from 1782 to 1785. Inside, the main floor (furnished with 18th-century antiques) retains its original Prussian-blue and soft-gray color scheme. The second floor contains a mixture of 18th- and 19th-century pieces. The adjacent 2-acre garden provides a longer perspective on the back of the house, plus worthwhile sights of its own: a Chinese Chippendale bridge, a pond, a wilderness area, and formal arrangements. *House: 186 Prince George St., tel. 410/263–5553. Admission: house and garden, $6 adults, $3 children 6–18, under 6 free; house only: $4 adults, $2.50 children 6–18; garden only: $3 adults, $1.50 children 6–18. A combination admission is offered for the Paca House and Garden and the Hammond-Harwood House (see above) at $9 adults. House and garden open Jan.–Feb., Fri.–Sat. 10–4, Sun. noon–4; Mar.–Dec., Mon.–Sat. 10–4, Sun. noon–4. Closed Thanksgiving, Dec. 24, and Dec. 25.*

Return on Prince George Street to Maryland Avenue and turn left. Completed in 1780, the domed **Maryland State House** is the oldest state capitol in continuous legislative use and the only one that has ever hosted the U.S. Congress. During 1783 and 1784 when Congress convened here, it accepted the resignation of General George Washington as commander in chief of the Continental Army, and it ratified the Treaty of Paris with the king, concluding the War of Independence. Both of these matters were determined in the Old Senate Chamber, filled with intricate woodwork (featuring the ubiquitous tobacco motif) that is also attributed to Buckland (*see above*). Also decorating this room is Charles Willson Peale's painting *Washington at the Battle of Yorktown,* considered to be the masterpiece of the Revolutionary War period's finest portrait artist. The state Senate and House now hold their sessions in two other chambers in the building. Also on the grounds is the oldest public building in Maryland, the minuscule redbrick **Treasury,** built in 1735. *State Circle, tel. 410/974–3400. Admission free. Open weekdays 9–5, weekends 10–4. Half-hr tours daily at 11 and 3. Closed Thanksgiving, Dec. 25, and New Year's Day.*

School Street leads you to the center of Church Circle, where you'll see the Episcopal **St. Anne's Church**—the third church of that name on that spot. The first, built in 1704, was torn down in 1775. The second, built in 1792, burned down in 1858; however, parts of the walls survived and were incorporated into the present structure, which was built in 1859. The parish was founded in 1692, and King William III donated the communion silver. The churchyard contains the grave of the last Colonial governor, Sir Robert Eden. *Church Circle, tel. 410/267–9333. Admission free. Open daily 7:30–6.*

Time Out **Ram's Head Tavern,** at 33 West Street, serves award-winning chili, sandwiches, and salads, as well as bottled beer from more than two dozen countries.

One block down Franklin Street brings you to the ivy-covered redbrick former church that houses the **Banneker-Douglass Museum of Afro-American Life.** Changing exhibits, lectures, films, and literature are brought together here to give a picture of the African-American experience in Maryland. *84 Franklin St., tel. 410/974–2894. Admission charged. Open Tues.–Fri. 10–3, Sat. noon–4.*

Return to Church Circle and follow Northwest Street to Rowe Boulevard. A 10-minute walk on Rowe Boulevard brings you to the 6-acre **Helen Avalynne Tawes Garden.** This botanical garden, across from the Navy–Marine Corps Stadium parking lot, next to the Tawes State Office Building Complex, is planted with flora representative of different regions of the state. Western Maryland's mountain forests and the marshland along the Chesapeake are evoked by rhododendrons and reeds, respectively; the ponds host various fish, fowl, and amphibians. Naturally, the state flower, the black-eyed Susan, is well represented. *580 Taylor Ave., tel. 410/974–3717. Admission free. Open daily dawn–dusk. Call for information on weekday guided tours.*

Tour 3:
Mount Vernon,
Woodlawn,
and Gunston Hall

Long before the capital city was planned, the shores of the
Potomac had been divided into plantations by wealthy traders and gentleman farmers. Even though most traces of the
Colonial era were obliterated as the capital grew in the 19th
century, several splendid examples of plantation architecture remain on the Virginia side of the Potomac just 15
miles or so south of the District. The three mansions described in this section can easily be visited in a single day:
Mount Vernon, one of the most popular sites in the area,
was the home of George Washington; **Woodlawn,** the estate
of Washington's granddaughter; and **Gunston Hall,** the
home of George Mason—patriot and author of the document on which the Bill of Rights was based. Spread out on
hillsides overlooking the river, these estates offer a look
into a way of life long gone.

Escorted Tours

Tourmobile offers trips to and from Mount Vernon. Tours
depart from April through October, daily at 10 AM, noon,
and 2 PM from Arlington Cemetery and the Washington Monument. Reservations must be made in person one hour before
departure. *Tel. 202/554–5100. Cost: $16.50 adults, $8 children 3–11. 2-day combo tickets good for Mount Vernon and
several sites in Washington: $25.50 adults, $12.50 children.*

Gray Line Tours runs half-day trips to Mount Vernon and
Old Town Alexandria. Buses depart daily at 8:30 AM from
Union Station. *Tel. 301/386–8300. Cost: $20 adults, $10 chil-
dren 3–11; 15% discount for AARP members. No tours on
Thanksgiving, Dec. 25, or Jan. 1.*

Getting Around

By Car To get to Mount Vernon from the Capitol Beltway (Route
495), take exit 1 onto the George Washington Memorial
Parkway, and follow the signs. From downtown Washington, cross into Arlington on either the Key Bridge or Memorial Bridge, and drive south on the George Washington
Memorial Parkway toward National Airport. Proceed past
the airport and through Alexandria straight to Mount Vernon. The trip from Washington takes about a half-hour.

To reach Woodlawn and Gunston Hall from Mount Vernon,
continue south on the George Washington Parkway to
Route 1. The entrance to Woodlawn is straight across from

the exit; to reach Gunston Hall, turn left and follow the signs.

By Subway and Bus You can get to Mount Vernon from the District by using the Metro and bus service. From downtown, take the yellow line train to Huntington ($1.50–$2.05, depending on the time of day). Then catch a Fairfax County Connector Bus, the No. 101/Ft. Hunt, to Mt. Vernon (50¢). The No. 101 leaves Huntington once an hour and operates Monday–Saturday 6:30 AM–9:15 PM, Sunday 9:30 AM–6 PM. Returning to Huntington from Mt. Vernon, the bus will be labeled the No. 101/Huntington.(Call 703/339–7200 for specific schedule information.)

By Boat An especially pleasant way to travel down the Potomac is to cruise on the *Spirit of Washington,* which makes the trip from Washington to the plantation twice daily from mid-June through early September and once daily from mid-September through October and late March through early June. (Boats leave from Pier 4, 6th and Water Sts. SW, tel. 202/554–8000.)

By Bicycle An asphalt bicycle path leads from the Virginia side of Memorial Bridge (adjacent to the Lincoln Memorial), past National Airport, and through Alexandria all the way to Mount Vernon. The trail is steep in places, but a biker in moderately good condition can make the 23-mile trip in less than two hours. Bicycles can be rented at several locations in Washington (*see* Bicycling in Chapter 6).

Exploring

Numbers in the margin correspond to points of interest on the Mount Vernon, Woodlawn, and Gunston Hall map.

Mount Vernon
❶ **Mount Vernon** and the surrounding lands had been in the Washington family for nearly 90 years by the time George inherited it all in 1761. Before taking over command of the Continental Army, Washington was a yeoman farmer, directing the management of the 8,000-acre plantation, of which more than 3,000 acres were under cultivation. He also oversaw the transformation of the main house from an ordinary farm dwelling into what was for the time a grand mansion. His improvements resulted in a dwelling more suited to his status as Founding Father.

The main house, with its red roof, is elegant though understated. The exterior is made of yellow pine painted and coated with layers of sand—"rusticated," in the language of the day—to resemble white-stone blocks.

The inside of the building is more ornate, especially the formal receiving room with its molded ceiling decorated with agricultural motifs. Throughout the house you'll find other, smaller symbols of the owner's eminence, such as a key to the main portal of the Bastille, presented to Washington by the Marquis de Lafayette; Washington's presidential chair;

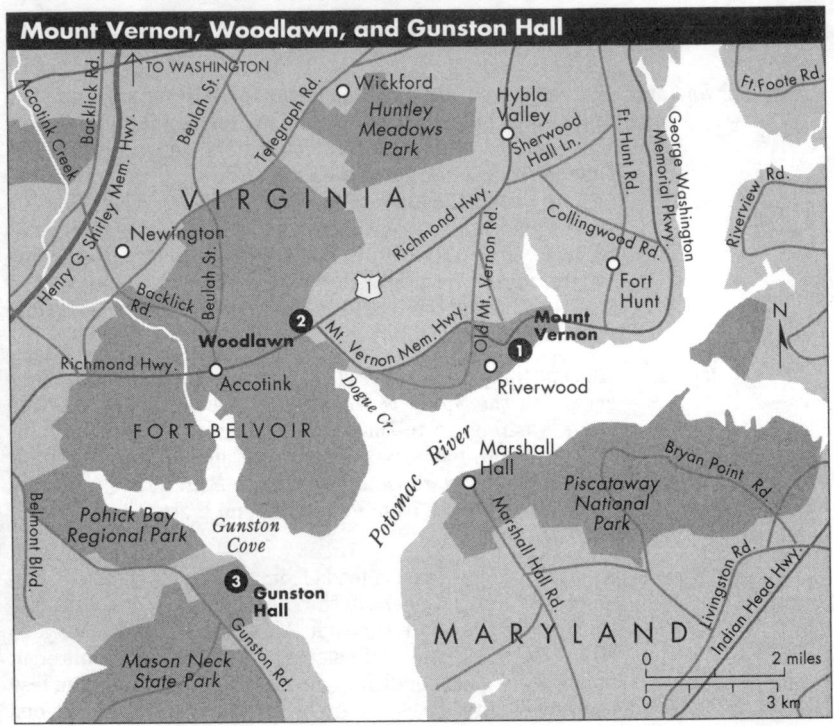

and a case of traveling wine bottles. Small groups of visitors are ushered from room to room, each of which is staffed by a guide who describes the furnishings and answers questions.

The real (often overlooked) treasure of Mount Vernon is the view from around back: Beneath a 90-foot portico (George Washington's contribution to the language of architecture) the home's dramatic riverside porch looks out on an expanse of lawn that slopes down to the Potomac. In springtime the view of the river (a mile wide at the point at which it passes the plantation) is framed by the blossoms of wild plum and dogwood. Ships of the U.S. and foreign navies always salute when passing the house.

Tours of the sprawling grounds are self-guided. Visitors are free to visit the plantation workshops, the kitchen, the carriage house, the gardens, reconstructions of the slave quarters, and, down the hill toward the boat landing, the tomb of George and Martha Washington. Among the souvenirs sold at the plantation are stripling boxwoods that began life as clippings from bushes planted in 1798, the year before Washington died. *Tel. 703/780–2000. General admission: $7 adults, $6 senior citizens 62 and older, $3 children 6–11 accompanied by adult. Regular group admission (minimum 20 paid admissions): $6.50 adults; $5.50 senior citizens, $3 children. One professional tour escort and 1*

*bus driver admitted free with each group. Youth and stu-
dent group admission (minimum 12 paid admissions): $3
grades pre-K–12, $3 chaperons (1 per 10 students; addi-
tional chaperons $6.50). A limited number of wheelchairs
is available at the main gate. Open Mar., daily 9–5; Apr.–
Aug., daily 8–5; Sept.–Oct., daily 9–5; Nov.–Feb., daily
9–4. The tour of the house and grounds takes about 2 hrs.*

Woodlawn   Three miles south of Mount Vernon on Route 1, **Woodlawn**
②   Plantation occupies a piece of ground that was originally
part of the Mount Vernon estate; even today you can see the
red roof of Washington's home from Woodlawn. The house
at Woodlawn was built for Washington's step-granddaugh-
ter, Nellie Custis, who married his favorite nephew, Lawrence Lewis. (Lewis had come to Mount Vernon from
Fredericksburg to help the general manage his five farms.)

The Lewises' home, completed in 1805, is noteworthy from
an architectural standpoint. It was designed by William
Thornton, who drew up the original plans for the Capitol.
Like Mount Vernon, the Woodlawn house is made wholly of
native materials, including the clay for its bricks and the
yellow pine used throughout the interior.

In the tradition of Southern riverfront mansions, Woodlawn has a central hallway that provides a cool refuge during the summer. At one corner of the passage is a bust of
George Washington, set on a pedestal so that the crown of
the head is at 6'2"—Washington's actual height. Elsewhere
is a music room with a ceiling two feet higher than any other
in the building, built that way to improve the acoustics for
the harp and clavichord recitals that the Lewises and their
children enjoyed.

After Woodlawn passed out of the Lewis family's hands it
was owned by a Quaker community, which established
there a meetinghouse and the first integrated school in Virginia. Subsequent owners included the playwright Paul
Kester and Senator and Mrs. Oscar Underwood of Ala-
bama. The property was acquired by the National Trust for
Historic Preservation in 1957.

Also on the grounds of Woodlawn is the **Pope-Leighey
House,** designed by Frank Lloyd Wright and built in 1940.
The structure originally stood in nearby Falls Church, Virginia; it was rescued from the path of a highway and moved
to the Woodlawn grounds in 1964. Wright's modernist design in cypress, brick, and glass offers a peculiar counter
point to the Georgian stylings of Woodlawn. It is not to
every taste, but it *is* an architectural education. *Woodlawn,
3 mi straight down the GW Pkwy. from Mount Vernon, tel.
703/780–4000. Admission: $5 adults, $3.50 students and
senior citizens, children under 5 free. Open Jan.–early
Feb., weekends 9:30–4:30; mid-Feb.–Dec., daily 9:30–4:30.
Tours every ½ hour. Last tour at 4 PM. Pope-Leighey House
admission: $4 adults, $2.75 students and senior citizens.*

Open Mar.–Dec., daily 9:30–4; Jan.–Feb., weekends only 9:30–4. Tours every ½ hour. Last tour at 4. An $8 combination ticket ($6 senior citizens) covers admission to both Woodlawn and Pope-Leighey House. Closed Thanksgiving, Christmas, and New Year's Day.

Gunston Hall
3

Unlike Mount Vernon, **Gunston Hall,** 15 miles away in Lorton, is rarely crowded with visitors. This was the home of a lesser-known George: George Mason—gentleman farmer, captain of the Fairfax militia, and author of the Virginia Declaration of Rights. Mason was one of the framers of the Constitution but refused to sign the final document because it did not prohibit slavery, adequately restrain the powers of the federal government, or include a bill of rights.

Completed in 1759, Gunston Hall is built of native brick, black walnut, and yellow pine. The architectural style of the time demanded absolute balance in all structures. Hence the "robber" window on a second-floor storage room and the fake door set into one side of the center hallway. The house's interior, with its carved woodwork in styles from Chinese to Gothic, has been meticulously restored, with paints made from the original recipes and with carefully carved replacements for the intricate mahogany medallions in the moldings.

The formal gardens are famous for their boxwoods, some of which were planted in the 1760s and have now grown to be 12 and 14 feet high. In Mason's day boxwood was used as a garden border because its acrid smell repelled deer.

To reach Gunston Hall, turn south on Route 1 from Woodlawn and follow the highway 7 miles, then turn left and follow the signs. The tour takes 45 minutes to an hour. *Tel. 703/550–9220. Admission: $5 adults, $4 senior citizens, $1.50 grades 1–12, under 6 free. Open daily 9:30–5. Last tour at 4:30. Closed Thanksgiving, Christmas, and New Year's Day.*

Tour 4:
Fredericksburg, Virginia

Situated on land once favored by Indian tribes as fishing and hunting ground, this compact city near the falls of the Rappahannock River figured prominently at crucial points in the nation's history, particularly during the Revolutionary and Civil wars. Just 50 miles south of Washington on I-95, Fredericksburg is today a popular day-trip destination for history buffs. The town's 40-block **National Historic District** contains more than 350 original 18th- and 19th-century buildings, including Mary Washington's home, James Monroe's law office, the Rising Sun Tavern, and Kenmore, the magnificent 1752 plantation home of George Washington's sister. The town is a favorite with antiques collectors, who enjoy cruising the dealers' shops along Caroline Street.

Although its site was visited by explorer Captain John Smith as early as 1608, the town of Fredericksburg wasn't founded until 1728. Established as a frontier port to serve nearby tobacco farmers and iron miners, Fredericksburg took its name from England's crown prince at the time, and the streets still bear names of members of his family: George, Caroline, Sophia, Princess Anne, Hanover, William, and Amelia.

George Washington knew Fredericksburg well, having grown up just across the Rappahannock on Ferry Farm. He lived there from age 6 to 16, and the legends about chopping down a cherry tree and throwing a coin across the Rappahannock—later mythologized as the Potomac—go back to this period of his life. In later years Washington often returned to visit his mother at the home he bought for her on Charles Street.

Fredericksburg prospered in the decades after independence, benefiting from its location midway along the 100-mile path between Washington and Richmond, an important intersection of railroad lines and waterways. When the Civil War broke out in 1861, Fredericksburg became the linchpin of the Confederate defense of Richmond and, as such, the inevitable target of Union assaults. In December 1862, Union forces attacked Fredericksburg in what was to be the first of four major battles fought in and around the town. In the battle of Sunken Road, Confederate defenders sheltered by a stone wall at the base of Marye's Heights mowed down Union soldiers by the thousands as they charged across the fields on foot and on horseback.

By war's end, the fighting in Fredericksburg and in battles at nearby Chancellorsville, the Wilderness, and Spotsylvania Court House had claimed more than 100,000 dead or wounded. Fredericksburg's cemeteries hold the remains of 17,000 soldiers from both sides. Despite heavy bombardment and house-to-house fighting, however, much of the city remained intact, and the historic district today contains many fine examples from the period.

A walking tour through the town proper takes three to four hours; battlefield tours each can take that long. The short hop across the Rappahannock to Chatham Manor is well worth it, if for no other reason than that the site offers a splendid view of all of Fredericksburg.

Tours

Stop at the **Fredericksburg Visitors Center** (706 Caroline St., tel. 703/373–1776 or 800/678–4748) for information on these tours.

The Fredericksburg Department of Tourism offers a booklet that includes a short history of Fredericksburg and a self-guided tour covering 29 sites.

Fredericksburg Guide Service arranges group tours of the city as well as of battlefields and other historic sites in the area. Advance reservations are required. Contact Tour Coordinator.

Getting Around

By Car To get to Fredericksburg from the District, take I-95 south to Route 3, turn left, and follow the signs. The drive takes about 60 minutes one way, except during rush hour.

By Train **Amtrak** trains bound for Fredericksburg depart six times daily from Washington's Union Station and take about an hour (tel. 202/484–7540 or 800/872–7245). The Fredericksburg railroad station is near the historic district (Caroline St. and Lafayette Blvd). A round-trip ticket from Washington costs $17.

By Bus **Greyhound-Trailways** (tel. 301/565–2662) departs several times a day from Washington to Fredericksburg. A round-trip ticket is $10.75 if purchased 21 days in advance; $16.90 if purchased seven days in advance; and $21 if purchased the same day. Buses stop at a station on alternate Route 1, about 2 miles from the center of town; cabs are available there.

Exploring

Numbers in the margin correspond to points of interest on the Fredericksburg map.

❶ The **Fredericksburg Visitors Center** offers booklets and pamphlets on local history, information on restaurants and lodging, and a slide show that orients visitors to the city. You can get parking passes here, good for a whole day in what would normally be two-hour zones. Also available are money-saving Hospitality Passes to city attractions. A pass to seven sites costs $16 for adults, $6 for those 6–18; the costs of any four sites are $11.50 and $4, respectively. The center is in a structure that was built in 1824 as a residence and confectionary; during the Civil War it was used to hold prisoners of war. *706 Caroline St., tel. 703/373–1776 or 800/ 678–4748. Open daily 9–5, extended summer hours. Closed Thanksgiving, Christmas, and New Year's Day.*

❷ At the **Fredericksburg Battlefield Visitor Center** you can learn about Fredericksburg's role in the Civil War by attending the succinct, informative slide show and then moving on to displays of soldiers' art and battlefield relics. The center offers taperecorded tour cassettes ($2.75) and maps showing how to reach hiking trails at the nearby Wilderness, Chancellorsville, and Spotsylvania Court House bat-

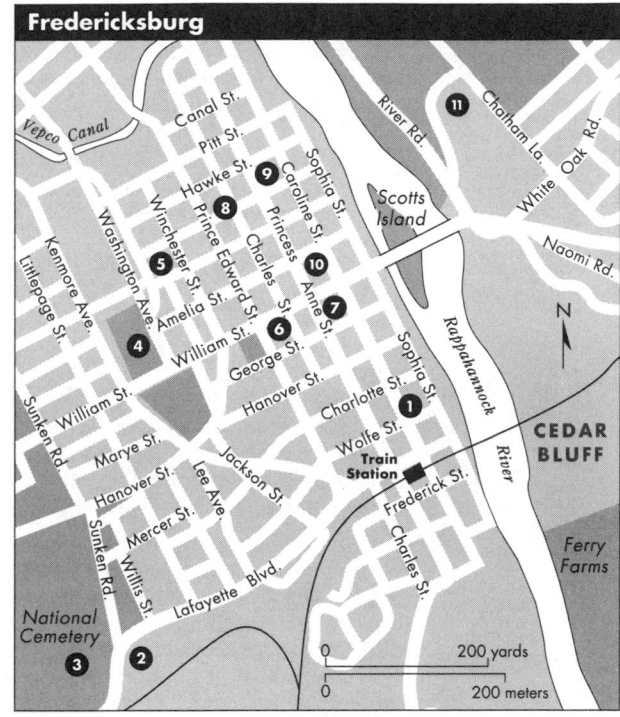

Fredericksburg

tlefields (all within 15 miles of Fredericksburg). Just outside the center is Sunken Road, where from December 11 to
13, 1862, General Robert E. Lee led his troops to a bloody
but resounding victory over Union forces attacking across
the Rappahannock; 18,000 men from both sides died in the
clash. Much of the stone wall that hid Lee's sharpshooters
has been rebuilt, but 100 yards from the visitors center part
of the original wall looks out on the statue *The Angel of
Marye's Heights,* by Felix de Weldon. This memorial honors Sergeant Richard Kirkland, a South Carolinian who
risked his life to bring water to wounded foes; he later died
at the Battle of Chickamauga. *Lafayette Blvd. at Sunken
Rd., tel. 703/373–6122. Open daily 9–5, extended summer
hours. Closed Christmas and New Year's Day.*

❸ The **National Cemetery** is the final resting place of 15,000
Union casualties, most of whom were never identified. *Lafayette Blvd. at Sunken Rd., tel. 703/373–6122. Open daily
sunrise–sunset.*

❹ The **Confederate Cemetery** contains the remains of more
than 2,000 soldiers (most of them unknown) as well as the
graves of generals Dabney Maury, Seth Barton, Carter
Stevenson, Daniel Ruggles, Henry Sibley, and Abner
Perrin. *Entrance at 1100 Washington Ave., near the corner
of Washington Ave. and Amelia St., no phone. Open dawn–
dusk.*

5 **Kenmore** was the home of Fielding Lewis, a patriot, plantation owner, and brother-in-law of George Washington.
(Lewis sacrificed much of his fortune to operate a gun factory that supplied the American forces during the Revolution.) Kenmore's plain exterior belies the lavish interior;
these have been called some of the most beautiful rooms in
America. The plaster moldings in the ceilings are outstanding and even more ornate than Mount Vernon's. Of equal elegance are the furnishings, which include a large standing
clock that belonged to Mary Washington. Across the street
are fine examples of Victorian architecture and a monument to Mary Washington, as well as the entrance to the
Confederate cemetery. After the 60-minute tour visitors to
Kenmore are served tea and gingerbread made according to
a Washington family recipe. *1201 Washington Ave., tel. 703/
373–3381. Admission: $5 adults, $2.50 students 6–18, 20%
discount to groups of 10 or more, $10 "family ticket." Open
Mar.–Nov., daily 9–5; Dec.–Feb., daily 10–4. Closed
Thanksgiving, Dec. 24, 25, 31, and Jan. 1.*

6 The **James Monroe Museum and Memorial Library** is the
tiny one-story building where the man who was to be the
fifth president of the United States practiced law from 1787
to 1789. In this building are many of Monroe's possessions,
collected and preserved by his family until this century, including a mahogany dispatch-box used during the negotiation of the Louisiana Purchase and the desk on which
Monroe signed the doctrine named for him. *908 Charles St.,
tel. 703/899–4559. Admission: $3 adults, $1 children 6–18,
$2.40 group adult, 80¢ group student. Open Mar.–Nov.,
daily 9–5; Dec.–Feb., daily, 10–4. Closed Thanksgiving,
Dec. 24, 25, 31, and Jan. 1.*

7 A block away is the **Fredericksburg Area Museum and Cultural Center.** Housed in an 1816 building once used as a market and town hall, the museum's six permanent exhibit
galleries tell the story of the area from prehistoric times,
through the Revolutionary and Civil wars, to the present.
Displays include dinosaur prints from a nearby quarry, Native American artifacts, an 18th-century plantation account book with an inventory of slaves, and Confederate
memorabilia. *907 Princess Anne St., tel. 703/371–3037. Admission: $3 adults, $1 children 6–18. Open Mar.–Nov.,
Mon.–Sat. 9–5, Sun. 1–5; Dec.–Feb., Mon.–Sat. 9–4, Sun.
1–4. Closed Thanksgiving, Dec. 24, 25, 31, and Jan. 1.*

Time Out Stop for a gourmet sandwich or a slice of quiche at the **Made
in Virginia Store Deli** (101 William St., tel. 703/371–2233).
Do not skip the rich desserts.

8 On Charles Street is the modest white **home of Mary Washington.** George purchased it for her in 1772, and she spent
the last 17 years of her life there, tending the charming garden, where her boxwood still flourishes and where many a
bride and groom now exchange their vows. Displays in-

clude many of Mrs. Washington's personal effects, as well as period furniture and a boxwood garden that includes plants she herself started. *1200 Charles St., tel. 703/373–1569. Admission: $3 adults, $1 students, $2.50 group adult, 75¢ group student. Open Mar.–Nov., daily 9–5; Dec.–Feb., daily 10–4. Closed Thanksgiving, Dec. 24, 25, 31, and Jan. 1.*

In 1760 George Washington's brother Charles built as his ❾ home what became the **Rising Sun Tavern,** a watering hole for such pre-Revolutionary patriots as the Lee brothers, Patrick Henry, Washington, and Jefferson. A "wench" in period costume leads the tour without stepping out of character. From her perspective you watch the activity—day and night, upstairs and down—at this busy institution. In the taproom you are served spiced tea. *1306 Caroline St., tel. 703/371–1494. Admission: $3 adults, $1 students, $2.50 group adult, 75¢ group student. Open Mar.–Nov., daily 9–5; Dec.–Feb., daily 10–4. Closed Thanksgiving, Dec. 24, 25, and Jan. 1.*

❿ The **Hugh Mercer Apothecary Shop** offers a close-up view of 18th- and 19th-century medicine. It was established in 1771 by Dr. Mercer, a Scotsman who served as a brigadier general of the Revolutionary Army (he was killed at the Battle of Princeton). General George S. Patton of World War II fame was one of Mercer's great-great-great grandsons. Dr. Mercer might have been more careful than most other Colonial physicians, yet his methods will make you cringe. A costumed hostess will explicitly describe amputations and cataract operations. You will also hear about therapeutic bleeding and see the gruesome devices used in Colonial dentistry. *1020 Caroline St. at Amelia St., tel. 703/373–3362. Admission: $3 adults, $1 students 6–18, $2.50 group adult, 75¢ group student. Open Mar.–Nov., daily 9–5; Dec.–Feb., daily 10–4. Closed Thanksgiving, Dec. 24, 25, 31, and Jan. 1.*

⓫ **Chatham Manor** is a fine example of Georgian architecture, built between 1768 and 1771 by William Fitzhugh on a site overlooking the Rappahannock and the town of Fredericksburg. Fitzhugh, a noted plantation owner, frequently hosted such luminaries of his day as George Washington and Thomas Jefferson. During the Civil War, Union forces commandeered the house and converted it into a headquarters and hospital. President Abraham Lincoln visited to confer with his generals; Clara Barton and the poet Walt Whitman tended the wounded. After the war the house and gardens were restored by private owners and eventually donated to the National Park Service. Concerts often are held here during the summer. *Chatham La., Stafford County (take William St. across the bridge and follow signs approx. ½ mi). Tel. 703/373–4461. Admission free. Open daily 9–5 (extended summer hours); closed Dec. 25 and Jan. 1.*

Index

Personal Itinerary

Departure *Date*

Time

Transportation

Arrival *Date* *Time*

Departure *Date* *Time*

Transportation

Accommodations

Arrival *Date* *Time*

Departure *Date* *Time*

Transportation

Accommodations

Arrival *Date* *Time*

Departure *Date* *Time*

Transportation

Accommodations

Personal Itinerary

Arrival   *Date*   *Time*

Departure   *Date*   *Time*

Transportation

Accommodations

Arrival   *Date*   *Time*

Departure   *Date*   *Time*

Transportation

Accommodations

Arrival   *Date*   *Time*

Departure   *Date*   *Time*

Transportation

Accommodations

Arrival   *Date*   *Time*

Departure   *Date*   *Time*

Transportation

Accommodations

Personal Itinerary

Arrival *Date*   *Time*

Departure *Date*   *Time*

Transportation

Accommodations

Arrival *Date*   *Time*

Departure *Date*   *Time*

Transportation

Accommodations

Arrival *Date*   *Time*

Departure *Date*   *Time*

Transportation

Accommodations

Arrival *Date*   *Time*

Departure *Date*   *Time*

Transportation

Accommodations

Addresses

Name	*Name*
Address	*Address*
Telephone	*Telephone*
Name	*Name*
Address	*Address*
Telephone	*Telephone*
Name	*Name*
Address	*Address*
Telephone	*Telephone*
Name	*Name*
Address	*Address*
Telephone	*Telephone*
Name	*Name*
Address	*Address*
Telephone	*Telephone*
Name	*Name*
Address	*Address*
Telephone	*Telephone*
Name	*Name*
Address	*Address*
Telephone	*Telephone*
Name	*Name*
Address	*Address*
Telephone	*Telephone*

Fodor's Travel Guides

Available at bookstores everywhere, or call 1–800–533–6478, 24 hours a day.

U.S. Guides

Alaska

Arizona

Boston

California

Cape Cod, Martha's Vineyard, Nantucket

The Carolinas & the Georgia Coast

Chicago

Colorado

Florida

Hawaii

Las Vegas, Reno, Tahoe

Los Angeles

Maine, Vermont, New Hampshire

Maui

Miami & the Keys

New England

New Orleans

New York City

Pacific North Coast

Philadelphia & the Pennsylvania Dutch Country

The Rockies

San Diego

San Francisco

Santa Fe, Taos, Albuquerque

Seattle & Vancouver

The South

The U.S. & British Virgin Islands

The Upper Great Lakes Region

USA

Vacations in New York State

Vacations on the Jersey Shore

Virginia & Maryland

Waikiki

Walt Disney World and the Orlando Area

Washington, D.C.

Foreign Guides

Acapulco, Ixtapa, Zihuatanejo

Australia & New Zealand

Austria

The Bahamas

Baja & Mexico's Pacific Coast Resorts

Barbados

Berlin

Bermuda

Brazil

Brittany & Normandy

Budapest

Canada

Cancun, Cozumel, Yucatan Peninsula

Caribbean

China

Costa Rica, Belize, Guatemala

The Czech Republic & Slovakia

Eastern Europe

Egypt

Euro Disney

Europe

Europe's Great Cities

Florence & Tuscany

France

Germany

Great Britain

Greece

The Himalayan Countries

Hong Kong

India

Ireland

Israel

Italy

Japan

Kenya & Tanzania

Korea

London

Madrid & Barcelona

Mexico

Montreal & Quebec City

Morocco

Moscow & St. Petersburg

The Netherlands, Belgium & Luxembourg

New Zealand

Norway

Nova Scotia, Prince Edward Island & New Brunswick

Paris

Portugal

Provence & the Riviera

Rome

Russia & the Baltic Countries

Scandinavia

Scotland

Singapore

South America

Southeast Asia

Spain

Sweden

Switzerland

Thailand

Tokyo

Toronto

Turkey

Vienna & the Danube Valley

Yugoslavia

Special Series

Fodor's Affordables

Caribbean

Europe

Florida

France

Germany

Great Britain

London

Italy

Paris

Fodor's Bed & Breakfast and Country Inns Guides

Canada's Great Country Inns

California

Cottages, B&Bs and Country Inns of England and Wales

Mid-Atlantic Region

New England

The Pacific Northwest

The South

The Southwest

The Upper Great Lakes Region

The West Coast

The Berkeley Guides

California

Central America

Eastern Europe

France

Germany

Great Britain & Ireland

Mexico

Pacific Northwest & Alaska

San Francisco

Fodor's Exploring Guides

Australia

Britain

California

The Caribbean

Florida

France

Germany

Ireland

Italy

London

New York City

Paris

Rome

Singapore & Malaysia

Spain

Thailand

Fodor's Flashmaps

New York

Washington, D.C.

Fodor's Pocket Guides

Bahamas

Barbados

Jamaica

London

New York City

Paris

Puerto Rico

San Francisco

Washington, D.C.

Fodor's Sports

Cycling

Hiking

Running

Sailing

The Insider's Guide to the Best Canadian Skiing

Skiing in the USA & Canada

Fodor's Three-In-Ones (guidebook, language cassette, and phrase book)

France

Germany

Italy

Mexico

Spain

Fodor's Special-Interest Guides

Accessible USA

Cruises and Ports of Call

Euro Disney

Halliday's New England Food Explorer

Healthy Escapes

London Companion

Shadow Traffic's New York Shortcuts and Traffic Tips

Sunday in New York

Walt Disney World and the Orlando Area

Walt Disney World for Adults

Fodor's Touring Guides

Touring Europe

Touring USA: Eastern Edition

Fodor's Vacation Planners

Great American Vacations

National Parks of the East

National Parks of the West

The Wall Street Journal Guides to Business Travel

Europe

International Cities

Pacific Rim

USA & Canada

INTRODUCING

Fodor's
WORLDVIEW
TRAVEL UPDATE

AT LAST, YOUR OWN PERSONALIZED LIST OF WHAT'S GOING ON IN THE CITIES YOU'RE VISITING.

KEYED TO THE DAYS WHEN YOU'RE THERE, CUSTOMIZED FOR YOUR INTERESTS, AND SENT TO YOU BEFORE YOU LEAVE HOME.

EXCLUSIVE FOR PURCHASERS OF FODOR'S GUIDES...

Introducing a revolutionary way to get customized, time-sensitive travel information just before your trip.

Now you can obtain detailed information about what's going on in each city you'll be visiting <u>before</u> you leave home—up-to-the-minute, objective information about the events and activities that interest you most.

This is a special offer for purchasers of Fodor's guides – a customized Travel Update to fit your specific interests and your itinerary.

Travel Updates contain the kind of time-sensitive insider information you can get only from local contacts – or from city magazines and newspapers once you arrive. But now you can have the same information before you leave for your trip.

The choice is yours: current art exhibits, theater, music festivals and special concerts, sporting events, antiques and flower shows, shopping, fitness, and more.

The information comes from hundreds of correspondents and thousands of sources worldwide. Updated continuously, it's like having your own personal concierge or friend in the city.

You specify the cities and when you'll be there. We'll do the rest — personalizing the information for you the way no guidebook can.

It's the perfect extension to your Fodor's guide and the best way to make the most of your valuable travel time.

Your Itinerary:
Customized reports available for 160 destinations

to
99
Rege
The a
in this
domain o
tion as Joe
worthwhile.
the perforan
Tickets are usu
venue. Alternat
mances are cancel
given. For more info
Open-Air Theatre, Inn
NW1 4NP Open Air T
Tel: 935-5756. Ends: 9-11.
International Air Tattoo
Held biennially, the world'
military air display in
demostra-
tions, milit
bands

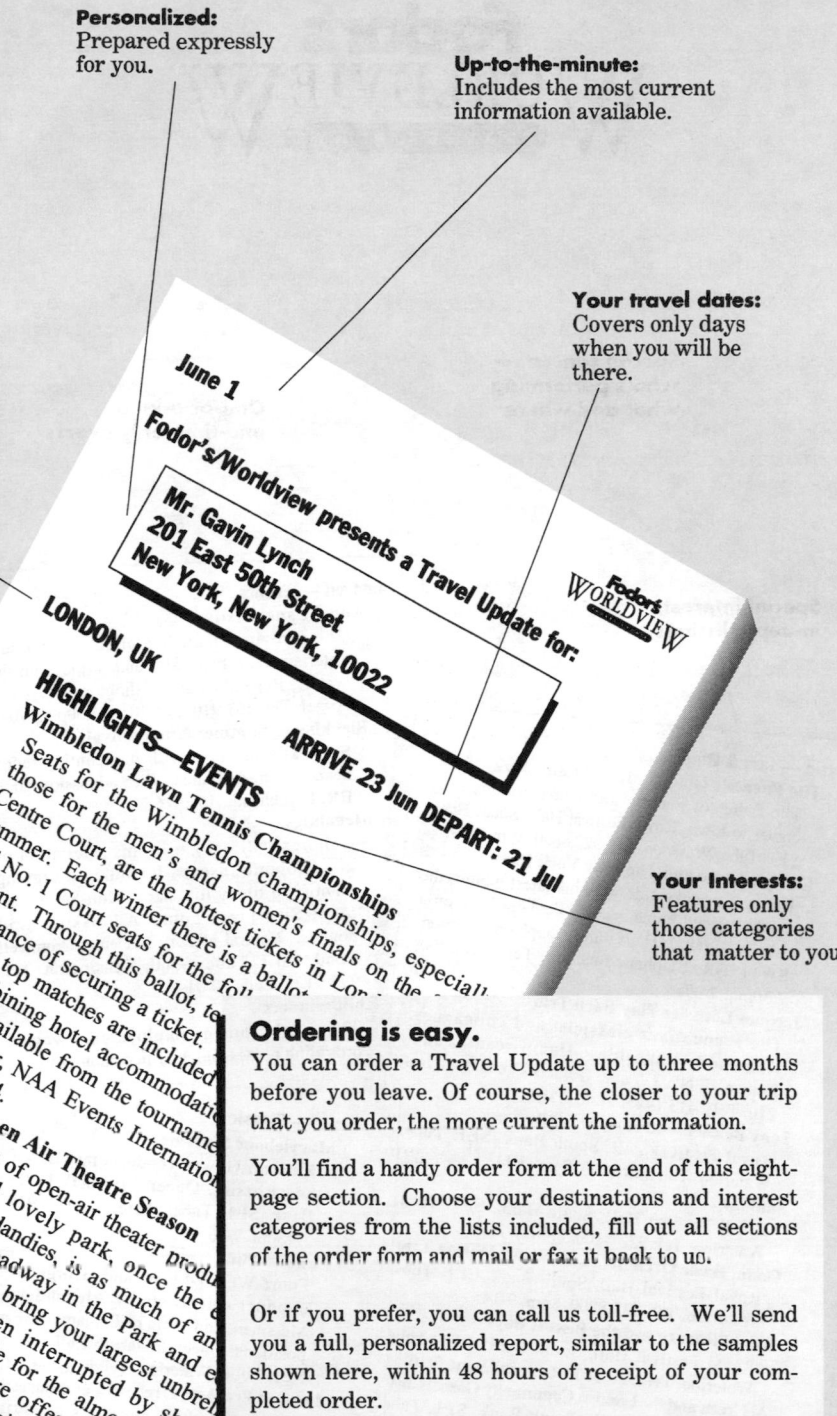

Personalized:
Prepared expressly
for you.

Up-to-the-minute:
Includes the most current
information available.

Your travel dates:
Covers only days
when you will be
there.

June 1

Fodor's/Worldview presents a Travel Update for:

Mr. Gavin Lynch
201 East 50th Street
New York, New York, 10022

Fodor's
WORLDVIEW

LONDON, UK

ARRIVE 23 Jun DEPART: 21 Jul

HIGHLIGHTS—EVENTS
Wimbledon Lawn Tennis Championships
Seats for the Wimbledon championships, especiall
those for the men's and women's finals on the
Centre Court, are the hottest tickets in Lon
summer. Each winter there is a ballo
nd No. 1 Court seats for the fol'
ment. Through this ballot, te
chance of securing a ticket.
for top matches are included
mbining hotel accommodati
available from the tournam
tor, NAA Events Internatio
'04.

Open Air Theatre Season
on of open-air theater produ
nd lovely park, once the
dandies, is as much of an
3roadway in the Park and e
to bring your largest unbre'
ften interrupted by showe
ble for the almost 1,200-seat
are offered when perfor-
rain, but refunds are not
contact Sheila Benjamin
Regent's Park, I
Regent's P

Your Interests:
Features only
those categories
that matter to you.

Ordering is easy.
You can order a Travel Update up to three months
before you leave. Of course, the closer to your trip
that you order, the more current the information.

You'll find a handy order form at the end of this eight-
page section. Choose your destinations and interest
categories from the lists included, fill out all sections
of the order form and mail or fax it back to us.

Or if you prefer, you can call us toll-free. We'll send
you a full, personalized report, similar to the samples
shown here, within 48 hours of receipt of your completed order.

**Special interest,
in-depth listings**

**Special concerts—
who's performing
what and where**

**One-of-a-kind,
one-time-only events**

Children — Events

Angel Canal Festival
The festivities include a children's funfair, entertainers, a boat rally and displays on the water. Regent's Canal. Islington. N1. Tube: Angel. Tel: 267 9100. 11:30am-5:30pm. 7/04.

Blackheath Summer Kite Festival
Stunt kite displays with parachuting teddy bears and trade stands. Free admission. SE3. BR: Blackheath. 10am. 6/27.

Megabugs
Children will delight in this infestation of giant robotic insects, including a praying mantic 60 times life size. Mon-Sat 10am-6pm; Sun 11am-6pm. Admission 4.50 pounds. Natural History Museum, Cromwell Road. SW7. Tube: South Kensington. Tel: 938 9123. Ends 10/01.

Childminders
This establishment employs only women, providing nurses and qualified nannies to

Music — Jazz & Blues

Tito Puente's Golden Men of Latin Jazz
The father of mambo and Cuban rumba king comes to town. Royal Festival Hall. South Bank. SE1. Tube: Waterloo. Tel: 928 8800. 8pm. 7/15.

Georgie Fame and The New York Band
Riding a popular tide with his latest album, the smoky-voiced Fame and his keyboard are on a tour yet again. The Grand. Clapham Junction. SW11. BR: Clapham Junction. Tel: 738 9000. 7:30pm. 7/07.

Jacques Loussier Play Bach Trio
The French jazz classicist and colleagues. Kenwood Lakeside. Hampstead Lane. Kenwood. NW3. Tube: Golders Green, then bus 210. Tel: 413 1443. 7pm. 7/10.

Tony Bennett and Ronnie Scott
Royal Festival Hall. South Bank. SE1. Tube: Waterloo. Tel: 928 8800. 8pm. 7/11.

Santana
Royal Festival Hall. South Bank. SE1. Tube: Waterloo. Tel: 928 8800. 8pm. 7/12.

Count Basie Orchestra and Nancy Wilson Trio
Royal Festival Hall. South Bank. SE1. Tube: Waterloo. Tel: 928 8800. 8pm. 7/14.

King Pleasure and the Biscuit Boys
Royal Festival Hall. South Bank. SE1. Tube: Waterloo. Tel: 928 8800. 6:30 and 9pm. 7/16.

Al Green and the London Community Gospel Choir
Royal Festival Hall. South Bank. SE1. Tube: Waterloo. Tel: 928 8800. 8pm. 7/13.

BB King and Linda Hopkins
Mother of the blues and successor to Bessie Smith, Hopkins meets up with "Blues Boy" King. Royal Festival Hall. South Bank. SE1. ... 928 8800. 6:30 and 9pm

Music — Classical

Marylebone Sinfonia
Kenneth Gowen conducts music by Puccini and Rossini. Queen Elizabeth Hall. South Bank. SE1. Tube: Waterloo. Tel: 928 8800. 7:45pm. 7/16.

London Philharmonic
Franz Welser-Moest and George Benjamin conduct selections by Alexander Goehr, Messiaen, and some of Benjamin's own compositions. Queen Elizabeth Hall. South Bank. SE1. Tube: Waterloo. Tel: 928 8800. 8pm.

London Pro Arte Orchestra and Forest Choir
Murray Stewart conducts selections by Rossini, Haydn and Jonathan Willcocks. Queen Elizabeth Hall. South Bank. SE1. Tube: Waterloo. Tel: 928 8800. 7:45pm. 7

Kensington Symphony Orchestra
Russell Keable conducts Dvorak's Dnieper Elizabeth Hall. South Bank. SE1.

Here's what you get . . .

Detailed information about what's going on — precisely when you'll be there.

Show openings
during your visit

Reviews by
local critics

Exhibitions & Shows—Antique & Flower

Westminster Antiques Fair
Over 50 stands with pre-1830 furniture and other Victorian and earlier items. Thu-Fri 11am-8pm; Sat-Sun 11am-6pm. Admission 4 pounds, children free. Old Royal Horticultural Hall. Vincent Square. SW1. Tel: 0444/48 25 14. 6-24 thru 6/27.

Royal Horticultural Society Flower Show
The show includes displays of carnations, summer fruit and vegetables. Tue 11am-7pm; Wed 10am-5pm. Admission Tue 4 pounds, Wed 2 pounds. Royal Horticultural Halls. Greycoat Street and Vincent Square. SW1. Tube: Victoria. 7/20 thru 7/21.

Hampton Court Palace International Flower Show
Major international garden and flower show taking place in conjunction with the British

Theater — Musical

Sunset Boulevard
In June, the four Andrew Lloyd Webber musicals which dominated London's stages in the 1980s (Cats, Starlight Express, Phantom of the Opera and Aspects of Love) are joined by the composer's latest work, a show rumored to have his best music to date. The 1950 Billy Wilder film about a helpless young writer who is drawn into the world of a possessive, aging silent screen star offers rich opportunities for Webber's evolving style. Soaring, aching melodies, lush technical effects and psychological thrills are all expected. Patti Lupone stars. Mon-Sat at 8pm; matinee Thu-Sat at 3pm. In-person sales only at the box office; credit card bookings, Tel: 344 0055. Admission 15-32.50 pounds. Adelphi Theatre. The Strand. WC2. Tube: Charing Cross. Tel: 836 7611. Starts: 6/21

Leonardo A Portrait of Love
A new musical about the great Renaissance artist and inventor comes in for a London premiere tested by a brief run at Oxford's Old Fire Station this autumn. The work explores the relationship between da Vinci and the woman

Alberquerque • Atlanta • Atlantic City •
Baltimore • Boston • Chicago • Cincinnati
Cleveland • Dallas/Ft.Worth • Denver • D
• Houston • Kansas City • Las Vegas • Los
Angeles • Memphis • Miami • Milwaukee •
New Orleans • New York City • Milwaukee
Springs • Philadelphia • Phoenix • Orlando •
Portland • Salt Lake • San Antonio • Pittsburg
San Franc   Seattle • St Louis • San Di
Oslo • Was   Tamp
Hawaii • Kauai • Maui • Abacos • Bimini
Bermu   Countryside • Hamilton • Anguilla
Antigua & B   Nevis • Torto
Gorda • Barbados • Dominica • Gren
cia • St. Vincent • Trinidad &Tobago •
ymans • Puerto Plata • Santo Doming
Aruba • Bonaire • Curacao • St. Ma
c City • Montreal • Ottawa • Toron
Vancouver • Guadeloupe • Martiniqu
helemy • St. Martin • Kingston • Ixta
o Bay • Negril • Ocho Rios • Ponce
n • Grand Turk • Providenciales • S
St. John • St. Thomas • Acapulco •
& Isla Mujeres • Cozumel • Guadal
a • Los Cabos • Manzinillo • Mazatl
City • Monterrey • Oaxaca • Puerto
do • Puerto Vallarta • Veracruz • Ix
dam • Athens • Barcelona

Fodor's WORLDVIEW TRAVEL UPDATE

Spectator Sports — Other Sports

Greyhound Racing: Wembley Stadium
This dog track offers good views of greyhound racing held on Mon, Wed and Fri. No credit cards. Stadium Way. Wembley. HA9. Tube: Wembley Park. Tel: 902 8833.

Benson & Hedges Cricket Cup Final
Lord's Cricket Ground. St. John's Wood Road. NW8. Tube: St. John's Wood. Tel: 289 1611. 11am. 7/10.

Business-Fax & Overnight Mail

Post Office, Trafalgar Square Branch
Offers a network of fax services, the Intelpost system, throughout the country and abroad. Mon-Sat 8am-8pm, Sun 9am-5pm. William IV Street. WC2. Tube: Charing Cross. Tel: 930 9580

Interest Categories

For <u>your</u> personalized Travel Update, choose the categories you're most interested in from this list. Every Travel Update automatically provides you with *Event Highlights* – the best of what's happening during the dates of your trip.

1.	**Business Services**	Fax & Overnight Mail, Computer Rentals, Photocopying, Secretarial , Messenger, Translation Services

Dining

2.	**All Day Dining**	Breakfast & Brunch, Cafes & Tea Rooms, Late-Night Dining
3.	**Local Cuisine**	In Every Price Range—from Budget Restaurants to the Special Splurge
4.	**European Cuisine**	Continental, French, Italian
5.	**Asian Cuisine**	Chinese, Far Eastern, Japanese, Indian
6.	**Americas Cuisine**	American, Mexican & Latin
7.	**Nightlife**	Bars, Dance Clubs, Comedy Clubs, Pubs & Beer Halls
8.	**Entertainment**	Theater—Drama, Musicals, Dance, Ticket Agencies
9.	**Music**	Classical, Traditional & Ethnic, Jazz & Blues, Pop, Rock
10.	**Children's Activities**	Events, Attractions
11.	**Tours**	Local Tours, Day Trips, Overnight Excursions, Cruises
12.	**Exhibitions, Festivals & Shows**	Antiques & Flower, History & Cultural, Art Exhibitions, Fairs & Craft Shows, Music & Art Festivals
13.	**Shopping**	Districts & Malls, Markets, Regional Specialities
14.	**Fitness**	Bicycling, Health Clubs, Hiking, Jogging
15.	**Recreational Sports**	Boating/Sailing, Fishing, Ice Skating, Skiing, Snorkeling/Scuba, Swimming
16.	**Spectator Sports**	Auto Racing, Baseball, Basketball, Football, Horse Racing, Ice Hockey, Soccer

Please note that interest category content will vary by season, destination, and length of stay.

Destinations

The Fodor's/Worldview Travel Update covers more than 160 destinations worldwide. Choose the destinations that match your itinerary from this list. (Choose bulleted destinations only.)

United States (Mainland)
- Albuquerque
- Atlanta
- Atlantic City
- Baltimore
- Boston
- Chicago
- Cincinnati
- Cleveland
- Dallas/Ft. Worth
- Denver
- Detroit
- Houston
- Kansas City
- Las Vegas
- Los Angeles
- Memphis
- Miami
- Milwaukee
- Minneapolis/ St. Paul
- New Orleans
- New York City
- Orlando
- Palm Springs
- Philadelphia
- Phoenix
- Pittsburgh
- Portland
- St. Louis
- Salt Lake City
- San Antonio
- San Diego
- San Francisco
- Seattle
- Tampa
- Washington, DC

Alaska
- Anchorage/Fairbanks/Juneau

Hawaii
- Honolulu
- Island of Hawaii
- Kauai
- Maui

Canada
- Quebec City
- Montreal
- Ottawa
- Toronto
- Vancouver

Bahamas
- Abacos
- Eleuthera/ Harbour Island
- Exumas
- Freeport
- Nassau & Paradise Island

Bermuda
- Bermuda Countryside
- Hamilton

British Leeward Islands
- Anguilla
- Antigua & Barbuda
- Montserrat
- St. Kitts & Nevis

British Virgin Islands
- Tortola & Virgin Gorda

British Windward Islands
- Barbados
- Dominica
- Grenada
- St. Lucia
- St. Vincent
- Trinidad & Tobago

Cayman Islands
- The Caymans

Dominican Republic
- Puerto Plata
- Santo Domingo

Dutch Leeward Islands
- Aruba
- Bonaire
- Curacao

Dutch Windward Islands
- St. Maarten

French West Indies
- Guadeloupe
- Martinique
- St. Barthelemy
- St. Martin

Jamaica
- Kingston
- Montego Bay
- Negril
- Ocho Rios

Puerto Rico
- Ponce
- San Juan

Turks & Caicos
- Grand Turk
- Providenciales

U.S. Virgin Islands
- St. Croix
- St. John
- St. Thomas

Mexico
- Acapulco
- Cancun & Isla Mujeres
- Cozumel
- Guadalajara
- Ixtapa & Zihuatanejo
- Los Cabos
- Manzanillo
- Mazatlan
- Mexico City
- Monterrey
- Oaxaca
- Puerto Escondido
- Puerto Vallarta
- Veracruz

Europe
- Amsterdam
- Athens
- Barcelona
- Berlin
- Brussels
- Budapest
- Copenhagen
- Dublin
- Edinburgh
- Florence
- Frankfurt
- French Riviera
- Geneva
- Glasgow
- Interlaken
- Istanbul
- Lausanne
- Lisbon
- London
- Madrid
- Milan
- Moscow
- Munich
- Oslo
- Paris
- Prague
- Provence
- Rome
- Salzburg
- St. Petersburg
- Stockholm
- Venice
- Vienna
- Zurich

Pacific Rim Australia & New Zealand
- Auckland
- Melbourne
- Sydney

China
- Beijing
- Guangzhou
- Shanghai

Japan
- Kyoto
- Nagoya
- Osaka
- Tokyo
- Yokohama

Other
- Bangkok
- Hong Kong & Macau
- Manila
- Seoul
- Singapore
- Taipei

Fodor's WORLDVIEW Order Form

THIS TRAVEL UPDATE IS FOR (Please print):

Name

Address

City	State	ZIP

Country	Tel # ( ) -

Title of this Fodor's guide:

Store and location where guide was purchased:

INDICATE YOUR DESTINATIONS/DATES: Write in below the destinations you want to order. Then fill in your arrival and departure dates for each destination.

			Month	Day		Month	Day
(Sample)	LONDON	From:	6 /	21	To:	6 /	30
1		From:	/		To:	/	
2		From:	/		To:	/	
3		From:	/		To:	/	

You can order up to three destinations per Travel Update. Only destinations listed on the previous page are applicable. Maximum amount of time covered by a Travel Update cannot exceed 30 days.

CHOOSE YOUR INTERESTS: Select up to eight categories from the list of interest categories shown on the previous page and circle the numbers below:

1   2   3   4   5   6   7   8   9   10   11   12   13   14   15   16

CHOOSE HOW YOU WANT YOUR TRAVEL UPDATE DELIVERED (Check one):

❑ Please mail my Travel Update to the address above **OR**

❑ Fax it to me at **Fax #** ( ) -

DELIVERY CHARGE (Check one)

	Within U.S. & Canada	Outside U.S. & Canada
First Class Mail	❑ $2.50	❑ $5.00
Fax	❑ $5.00	❑ $10.00
Priority Delivery	❑ $15.00	❑ $27.00

All orders will be sent within 48 hours of receipt of a completed order form.

ADD UP YOUR ORDER HERE. *SPECIAL OFFER FOR FODOR'S PURCHASERS ONLY!*

	Suggested Retail Price	Your Price	This Order
First destination ordered	$13.95	$ 7.95	$ 7.95
Second destination (if applicable)	$ 9.95	$ 4.95	+
Third destination (if applicable)	$ 9.95	$ 4.95	+
Plus delivery charge from above			+
		TOTAL:	$

METHOD OF PAYMENT (Check one):   ❑ AmEx   ❑ MC   ❑ Visa   ❑ Discover
                                      ❑ Personal Check   ❑ Money Order

Make check or money order payable to: Fodor's Worldview Travel Update

Credit Card #   **Expiration Date:**

Authorized Signature

SEND THIS COMPLETED FORM TO:
Fodor's Worldview Travel Update, 114 Sansome Street, Suite 700, San Francisco, CA 94104

OR CALL OR FAX US 24-HOURS A DAY
Telephone **1-800-799-9609** • Fax **1-800-799-9619** (From within the U.S. & Canada)
(Outside the U.S. & Canada: Telephone 415-616-9988 • Fax 415-616-9989)

(Please have this guide in front of you when you call so we can verify purchase.)

Offer valid until 12/31/94.